DELUXE JIM CROW

KAREN KRUSE THOMAS

Deluxe Jim Crow

CIVIL RIGHTS AND

AMERICAN HEALTH POLICY,

1935–1954

The University of Georgia Press Athens and London

Portions of the book have appeared, in somewhat different
form, in the *Journal of African American History*, the
Journal of Southern History, and the *Nursing History
Review*. Full credits are given on page xiii and constitute
an addendum to this copyright page.

Library of Congress Cataloging-in-Publication Data

Thomas, Karen Kruse.
Deluxe Jim Crow : civil rights and American health policy,
1935–1954 / Karen Kruse Thomas.
        p.   cm.
Includes bibliographical references.
ISBN-13: 978-0-8203-3016-7 (hardback)
ISBN-10: 0-8203-3016-7 (cloth)
ISBN-13: 978-0-8203-4044-9 (paperback)
1. Minorities—Medical care—United States—History—
20th century. 2. Discrimination in medical care—United
States—20th century. 3. Equality—Health aspects—United
States—20th century. 4. African Americans—Medical
care—United States—20th century. I. Title.
RA563.M56T46 2011
362.1089'00973—dc23   2011022468

British Library Cataloging-in-Publication Data available

FOR MY GRANDFATHER,

TOM FOREST DAVENPORT, M.D.

(1895–1995),

ATLANTA PEDIATRICIAN

FROM 1923 TO 1980

CONTENTS

TABLES

FIGURES

ACKNOWLEDGMENTS

Portions of the book have been previously published in somewhat different form as articles and appear with the permission of the following journals and their sponsors: "The Hill-Burton Act and Civil Rights: Expanding Hospital Care for Black Southerners, 1939–1960," *Journal of Southern History* 72.4 (2006): 823–70; "'Law unto Themselves': Black Women as Patients and Practitioners in North Carolina's Campaign to Reduce Maternal and Infant Mortality," *Nursing History Review* 12 (2004): 47–66 (reproduced with permission of Springer Publishing Company); and "Dr. Jim Crow: The University of North Carolina, the Regional Medical School for Negroes, and the Desegregation of Southern Medical Education, 1945–1960," *Journal of African American History* 88.3 (2003): 223–44 (by permission of ASALH). Support for research and writing came from the National Endowment for the Humanities, the Harry S. Truman Presidential Library, the Claude Pepper Library at Florida State University, the University of Alabama at Birmingham Archives, and the Southern Oral History Program at the University of North Carolina. I have benefited from the insightful comments of many fine scholars, including first and foremost my adviser at the University of North Carolina, Jim Leloudis, and the members of my dissertation committee, Jacquelyn Hall, Spencie Love, James C. Thomas, Keith Wailoo, and Joel Williamson. Clarence Mohr has provided invaluable encouragement and advice since my days as a Tulane undergrad, and Teresa Toulouse has been an inspiration to me and many other American studies students. For their scholarship and constructive criticism, my deep appreciation also goes to Gert Brieger, Colin Gordon, Elna Green, Margaret Humphreys, Bill Link, John Parascandola, Susan Reverby, Todd Savitt, and the anonymous grant and journal reviewers who have read my work along the way. Thank you to the able archivists and librarians at the University of North Carolina at Chapel Hill's Wilson Library, the state archives of Florida and North Carolina, the Harry S. Truman Presidential Library, the National Archives at College Park, the Moorland-Spingarn Research Center at Howard University, the University Archives at University of Pittsburgh, the Claude Pepper Library at Florida State University, the Smathers Library Special Collections at University of Florida, and the University of Alabama at Birmingham Archives. And finally, thank you to the members of my family for their support over the many years it took to write this book.

DELUXE JIM CROW

TIMELINE

1935   Social Security Act Titles V and VI target the South with federal health funding and shift oversight of public health programs to Washington.

1936   Thomas Parran is appointed U.S. surgeon general and focuses the efforts of the Public Health Service on the South and on fighting syphilis as the primary public health problem.

1938   The Roosevelt administration releases the *Report on the Economic Conditions of the South* and the Technical Committee on Medical Care's report on a national health program.

Congress passes La Follette–Bulwinkle Venereal Disease Control Act.

Southern Conference for Human Welfare founded in Birmingham, Alabama.

Claude Pepper and Lister Hill elected to the U.S. Senate.

In *Gaines v. Missouri*, the U.S. Supreme Court rules that the legality of segregation depends on *equal* facilities within the state. Southern states begin funding scholarships to send black medical students to Meharry Medical College.

1939   Dr. Louis Wright of the NAACP introduces the concept of racial parity into federal health legislation during the Wagner Health Bill hearings. Nearly all major national African American organizations testify in favor of national health reform, but the National Medical Association opposes a national health insurance provision as a threat to fee-for-service medicine and prioritizes ensuring that black physicians can treat their patients in federally funded facilities.

1940   Congress holds the first hearings on federal hospital construction legislation.

1943–44   Claude Pepper chairs the U.S. Senate Subcommittee on Wartime Health and Education to investigate "the educational and physical fitness of the civilian population as related to national defense."

1945   After Franklin D. Roosevelt's death, Harry S. Truman becomes the first president to fully support national health insurance and equal rights for African Americans.

1946   The Hill-Burton Hospital Survey and Construction Act is enacted with a racial parity clause and a need-based allocation formula favoring the South.

1947   Oscar R. Ewing is named head of the Federal Security Agency, where he becomes the first high-ranking federal official to take a public stand in favor of full integration.

The President's Commission on Civil Rights releases *To Secure These Rights*.

1948   Fourteen southern governors sign the Southern Regional Education Compact. The Regional Medical School Bill, championed by Claude Pepper, fails to win congressional approval by one vote.

Federal legislation establishes the National Institutes of Health, and Leonard Scheele replaces Thomas Parran as surgeon general, signaling a shift away from New Deal public health programs targeting the South and acute communicable diseases of poverty.

Edith Mae Irby enrolls at the University of Arkansas, becoming the first black student to attend medical school at a desegregated southern university.

1949   The Pepper Federal Aid to Medical Education Bill, with an antidiscrimination clause, is defeated.

1951   The Universities of Texas, Arkansas, North Carolina, and Louisville and the Medical College of Virginia have admitted at least one black medical student.

1954   The U.S. Supreme Court declares segregation inherently unequal and unconstitutional in *Brown v. Board of Education of Topeka*.

1955   Enrollment of black medical students in predominantly white schools peaks at 236 during the preintegration era.

1956   The University of Florida enrolls its first medical school class.

        In *Hawkins v. Florida*, the U.S. Supreme Court declares
        segregation in higher education unconstitutional.

1961   Since 1949, the Southern Regional Education Board has disbursed
        $2.5 million to aid approximately five hundred black medical
        students and an additional $1 million for black dental students to
        attend Meharry Medical College, representing its largest single
        source of income.

1963   The U.S. Supreme Court lets stand the federal appeals court's
        Simkins v. Cone decision, which declared unconstitutional Hill-
        Burton's "separate but equal" clause.

1964   The Civil Rights Act prohibits racial discrimination by any
        recipient of federal funds, promoting the full desegregation of
        southern health care, particularly after the passage of the Medicare
        amendments to Social Security the following year.

DELUXE JIM CROW

THE DEVIL'S BARGAIN

OF DELUXE JIM CROW

HEALTH REFORM

> Brand new segregated hospitals constitute a
> kind of *de luxe* Jim Crow which is supposed to
> be more palatable than the customary variety
> and therefore more acceptable. *De luxe* Jim
> Crow is just as objectionable as any other kind.
> It is merely a new line of defense against the
> slow, but irresistible advance of liberal change.
>
> "The Crushing Irony of De Luxe Jim Crow,"
> *Journal of the National Medical Association*, 1952

The phrase *deluxe Jim Crow* was first coined in the *Baltimore Afro-American* in 1927 to describe the first-class compartment for blacks on the Memphis Special, a train running through the heart of the segregated South. Thurgood Marshall later applied the phrase to the southern states' attempts to shore up segregation by improving black school facilities. For the purposes of this book, *deluxe Jim Crow* conveys the ethical complexity and ambiguity of segregation in health policy during the Franklin D. Roosevelt and Harry S. Truman administrations. In 1952, medical civil rights activist and Howard University anatomy professor W. Montague Cobb employed the term to decry the publicly funded proliferation of thousands of new hospital beds for blacks in segregated wards, floors, and wings across the South. He denied that any form of segregation, no matter how purportedly beneficial, could ever be considered equal, and he feared that this allegedly kinder, gentler strain might become impossible to eradicate, like an antibiotic-resistant bacteria. Cobb, Louis T. Wright, and other early integration-ists fought ferociously against the expansion of segregated health care, even at the cost of public and philanthropic aid to black health in the short term. Yet before the medical civil rights movement fixed on integration as the "magic bullet" that would eradicate racial health disparities as surely as penicillin conquered infectious disease, black leaders pursued a troubled alliance with southern liberalism that profoundly influenced early national health policy.[1]

The downfall of segregation commenced in 1938 with the U.S. Supreme Court's *Gaines v. Missouri* mandate that the constitutionality of segregation laws rested "wholly upon the equality of the privileges which the laws give to the separated groups within the State." For sixteen years before the *Brown v. Board of Education* school desegregation decision, *Gaines* fueled the legal challenge mounted by the National Association for the Advancement of Colored People (NAACP) to the idea of separate but equal facilities, a campaign intended to force southern states to spend millions to provide truly equal facilities for blacks or—since NAACP strategists were sure that states would not do so—to require full integration. But this strategy was less viable in health than in education, since both black leaders and southern liberals solidly backed federal legislation intended to raise southerners' health status to a par with northern whites, resulting in concrete gains for both races. Mounting pressure from the *Gaines* decision and other NAACP antidiscrimination lawsuits pushed southern state officials to initiate efforts to equalize public services and facilities for blacks just as wartime shortages of health personnel and high rates of draft rejections generated public and political support for federal and state health reform. Southern liberals in Washington leveraged the Roosevelt administration's *Report on the Economic Conditions of the South* and the country's mobilization for war to call for federal aid to uplift the South's economy, schools, and health care.[2]

The convergence of regional and racial equalization in health care prompted Carl V. Reynolds, North Carolina's state health officer, to proclaim in 1946, "The influential are determined to make available adequate medical, surgical, obstetrical and hospital care—certainly for the underprivileged citizens—regardless of race, creed or color." Louisiana novelist Walker Percy described Reynolds and other southern moderates as "aware both of the enormous difficulty of the problem [of segregation] and of the pressing need to do something about it." In the face of "social dangers which could make the cure worse than the disease"—that is, the destruction of the southern public school system in defiance of integration—the southern moderate's role was "not to press for a quick solution, but to humanize, to moderate, the solution which is surely coming." The language of regional uplift allowed southern liberals to aid blacks substantially while remaining silent on race, a strategy that later foundered under pressure from black integrationists and northern liberals in the Truman administration.[3]

Black reformers declared their own vision of the solution that was surely coming. The growing activism and political muscle of national black organizations, the NAACP foremost among them, was fueled by an unprecedented rise in black per capita income and the advent of a sizable black middle class in the South as well as the North. Even the most discriminatory federal programs, such as public housing, received enthusiastic support from these organizations because the New Deal offered black bureaucrats and lobbyists a golden chance to uplift the African American community. The congressional hearings on federal health legislation forged an essential link between New Deal liberalism and civil rights activism by providing a new and effective forum for promoting black equality. The testimony of black activists during the 1940s bespoke the utility of interracial consensus building but also revealed growing divisions within the medical civil rights movement. Should blacks continue to pursue equalization that would bring them immediate benefits, or should they fight for full integration in government health programs?[4]

The 1939 national health bill proposed by Senator Robert Wagner of New York and its successors, the Wagner-Murray-Dingell Bill and President Truman's national health program, represented the first plans for comprehensive national health reform, including provisions for universal health coverage. This book begins, however, with a survey of pre-1933 southern health conditions in the context of widening racial and regional health disparities and outlines the origins of federal and philanthropic efforts to address those inequities. The book then follows the evolution of deluxe Jim Crow policy in the health reform proposals and programs of the Roosevelt and Truman administrations, with sections on the formation of the policy's basic tenets in New Deal public health during the 1930s, its coming of age in national and state health reform between 1938 and 1945, and its postwar impact on hospital construction, medical education, and national health insurance. Even-numbered chapters focus on the debates over national health legislation in Washington and the southern states (defined here as per the U.S. Census Bureau's sixteen-state standard: Alabama, Arkansas, Delaware, Florida, Georgia, Kentucky, Louisiana, Maryland, Mississippi, North Carolina, Oklahoma, South Carolina, Tennessee, Texas, Virginia, and West Virginia). Except for chapter 1, odd-numbered chapters analyze the application of each policy issue in North Carolina, where deluxe Jim Crow reached its full-est potential among the state's nearly 1 million black residents. The conclusion compares the consequences of deluxe Jim Crow policy in the arenas of health and education.[5]

Southern historian Joel Williamson has designated the turn-of-the-twentieth-century South as the crucible of American race relations, but the midcentury South was the crucible of American health policy. During the deluxe Jim Crow era, health reform apologists from across the racial spectrum masterfully deployed statistics to highlight racial, regional, and rural-urban disparities and argued that they must be closed for the sake of white health, black civil rights, southern pride, economic productivity, and national defense. The resulting heterogeneous collection of federal programs strengthened the public portion of the two-tiered health-care system but left the private portion virtually unchanged. American health care was a glass that was either half empty, waiting to be filled with sparkling universal national health insurance, or half full of noxious, pink-tinted social medicine spiked with federal meddling in segregation.[6]

Scholars of both civil rights and national health reform have almost universally argued that the best policy approach to the problems of racism and health disparities was comprehensive federal legislation through measures such as the Wagner-Murray-Dingell national health bill of the 1940s and the Civil Rights Act of 1964. In line with what might be called the orthodoxy of integration that came to dominate the civil rights movement, these scholars have criticized the incremental measures that resulted from political compromise as piecemeal and ineffective and have dismissed as inherently racist the states' rights arguments that limited federal control and favored local autonomy. Yet "deluxe Jim Crow" was also a backhanded acknowledgment that compared to the gross inequality of funding and infrastructure in education and the whole southern public sphere, new hospital facilities for African Americans were indeed "deluxe." With the expert guidance of the U.S. Public Health Service and massive federal aid from New Deal and wartime health initiatives, especially the 1946 Hill-Burton Hospital Survey and Construction Act, southern states came closer to achieving racial parity in health care than in any other aspect of segregation-era public policy.

Deluxe Jim Crow was deluxe precisely because it was not limited to racial parity for blacks but encompassed a broader political philosophy of equalization unique to health under which both black and white southerners argued for a need-based calculus that would channel public resources to their medically disadvantaged constituencies. By the 1950s, deluxe Jim Crow policy had considerably weakened the legal basis for segregation, which ideally positioned the direct-action civil rights movement to deliver a series of rapid and devastating blows. The more targeted, pragmatic New and Fair Deal reforms were foundational to the sweeping Great Society milestones of the Civil Rights Act and Medicare/Medicaid, which together banned racial discrimination in all federally funded health programs and dramatically expanded health-care access for the poor, elderly, and disabled, including large numbers of minorities.[7]

part one

THE NATION'S

NUMBER

ONE HEALTH

PROBLEM,

1900–1938

chapter 1

THE ROOTS OF

DELUXE JIM CROW

I n all regions of the United States, white American policy makers have historically neglected the health of minorities yet have used their high rates of death and disease to justify legalized segregation, immigration restriction, and other overt forms of racial and ethnic discrimination. What are the historical origins of health disparities, how did they change during the course of the twentieth century, and what caused them to improve or worsen? When, why, and how did the federal government begin to address racial and regional disparities in health as a national problem?

Until at least the Progressive Era, the South was a bastion of antifederalism where state investment in public services was minimal or nonexistent. After the Civil War, Reconstruction had "reinforced blacks' identification with federal authority" and had the opposite effect on whites. Yet southern health was exceptional because public health and political leaders together pursued policies that not only sought to restrict federal oversight but also emphasized the national consequences of southern health problems and the need to apply federal resources to solve those problems. Two early examples of federally sponsored southern health facilities were the marine hospitals and the Government Free Bathhouse in Hot Springs, Arkansas. In the 1830s, the governors of Louisiana and Mississippi asked the northern states for aid in providing hospital care for the large transient population aboard riverboats and barges traveling the Mississippi River. This effort represented an extension of the first federal health program, the U.S. Marine Hospital Service, established in 1798 to provide medical care to sailors and merchant marines in ports along the Atlantic coast and later reorganized as the U.S. Public Health Service (PHS) in 1912. As settlement spread westward and the cotton trade made New Orleans a major port during the antebellum era, cities and towns in the Mississippi Valley petitioned Congress to establish additional interior marine hospitals, and in 1837 the Marine Hospital Service was extended to include Lake Erie and the Ohio and Mississippi Rivers. By 1945, nine of the twenty-seven marine hospitals operated by the PHS were located along the coastlines of the southeastern Atlantic seaboard, the Gulf Coast, and the lower Mississippi River Valley.[1]

Poor men and women came from miles around Hot Springs to seek healing in the steamy waters located on a public federal reservation under the authority of the Department of the Interior. One of the hot springs was believed specifically to cure venereal diseases, particularly when accompanied by heavy oral doses of mercury. In 1878, Congress appropriated funds to provide free bathing facilities for indigent patients. Over the next thirty years, federal funds supported new construction and expansion, including a free dispensary opened in 1898 on the second floor of the bathhouse and staffed by volunteer physicians. In 1902, racially segregated facilities replaced open pool bathing with individual recessed porcelain tubs and a variety of other amenities, foreshadowing the simultaneous emergence of racial and medical segregation in twentieth-century hospitals. By 1911, more than 220,000 baths were administered each year, and a medical director was appointed for the first time to improve the quality of care for indigent patients.[2]

During the Progressive Era, Jim Crow was only one of many proliferating forms of segregation designed to protect society from corruption and expressed in geographical, temporal, spatial, and architectural forms for a variety of purposes including but not limited to racial separation. The Government Free Bathhouse met the specific medical needs of poor venereal disease patients but signified their exclusion from other sources of care on racial, financial, and moral grounds. In 1921, surgeon general Hugh Cummings, National Parks Service director Stephen T. Mather, and Arkansas state health officer C. W. Garrison established a model venereal disease treatment clinic at Hot Springs, which became a major PHS training and research center. The bathhouse, however, did not survive the end of segregation and closed in 1956.[3]

The scope of public health broadened during the early twentieth century, but important regional variations persisted. The federal role in public health grew through measures such as the U.S. Death Registration Area (begun in

1900), the 1906 Pure Food and Drug Act, and the medical examination of arriving immigrants by PHS officers. During the 1910s, the PHS spearheaded the rural sanitation movement, helped establish county health departments, and initiated rural health education and prevention programs with the assistance of such organizations as the National Tuberculosis Association, the American Red Cross, and the federal Children's Bureau. At the state and local levels, southern public health departments were established later, had weaker authority and less funding, and were far slower to hire full-time, professionally trained staff than were health departments in the North. In Alabama and South Carolina, where the state medical societies functioned as the state boards of health, physicians had exclusive control over public health policy, whereas outside the South, more professional and ideological separation (and often conflict) existed between public health officials and organized medicine. In the urban North, as public health activities shifted from environmental sanitation to protecting individual health, physicians increasingly opposed such activities as a source of competition with private practice. In the South, the relatively undeveloped state of public health gave physicians both a rationale for requesting federal aid and more exclusive control over health reform than their northern counterparts possessed.[4]

RACE, BIOSTATISTICS, AND THE DEVELOPMENT OF PUBLIC HEALTH

Race as well as region was a factor in the growth of federal and state health programs and the medical profession's ascent to national political influence, since these phenomena played out in the context of the post-Reconstruction rapprochement between North and South, the rise of scientific racism, and the legalization of segregation and disfranchisement. The U.S. Supreme Court's 1896 *Plessy v. Ferguson* decision legitimized "separate but equal" as an adequate protection of black civil rights. For the next sixty years *Plessy* gave southern state and local governments carte blanche to segregate their black citizens as whites saw fit, with virtually no federal enforcement of the promise of equal. Such policies were based in part on white fears of communicable disease that were fueled by the new availability of morbidity and mortality figures for specific neighborhoods and the racial groups within them. In Baltimore, for example, the concentration of tuberculosis deaths within specific blocks of a black residential section caused public health authorities to label the area the "lung block" and use it in a campaign of "infectious fear" that depicted blacks as sources of contagious disease. Black tuberculosis patients were targeted first for surveillance by charities and the city health department and later for coercive institutionalization in Maryland's two all-black state facilities, Henryton Sanitorium and Crownsville Mental Hospital.[5]

When cities and towns began systematically to collect statistics to measure rates of birth, death, and disease, they exposed the appalling scope of morbidity and mortality among the turn-of-the-century urban poor, particularly racial and ethnic minorities. Existing stereotypes framed the way whites interpreted health statistics and understood diseases that struck disproportionate numbers of ethnic and racial minorities. At first, these ghastly numbers were cited as evidence of inborn racial differences that made health reform seem a futile attempt to interfere with "nature." The "Negro health problem" was a major concern for white organized medicine; for the Medical Society of the State of North Carolina, the problem persisted into the 1940s. In his 1941 presidential address, the society's Hubert Haywood blamed blacks for many of North Carolina's health problems and lamented that "modern civilization, human sympathy and charity have intervened in nature's plan"—the extinction of the black race via their increasing susceptibility to diseases such as tuberculosis and syphilis. But Haywood's main concern was the "adverse effect on the white race," since "the close proximity of the two races will increase the prevalence of these diseases in whites." To ward off catastrophe, he recommended "further extension of birth control information to this group which breeds from the bottom." Even though tuberculosis, not syphilis, was the most prevalent communicable disease among blacks, the characterization of blacks as "breeders" of disease fomented the stereotype of black hypersexuality, minimized the distinction between sexual and nonsexual transmission of disease, and served as a justification for providing birth control or sterilization to blacks in line with negative eugenics. According to medical historian David McBride, the belief that "blacks were one with the causative agents of infectious diseases" remained a common epidemiological paradigm in American medical thought at least until the outbreak of World War II.[6]

Not only did statistics feed racism, but racism also shaped the methods of collecting health data. In 1914, John Watkins, a U.S. congressman representing Shreveport, Louisiana, introduced a bill to require the U.S. Census Bureau to differentiate mortality statistics by race because he wanted to ameliorate the South's unfavorably high death rate, which he claimed was unfairly determined by the region's large black population. Although the bill did not pass, the Census Bureau began recording mortality by race, marking the first time that federal and southern officials attempted to measure racial health disparities, although such efforts sought to improve the reputation of white southerners rather than to address African American health problems. Improved reporting of death and disease rates by race and locality assisted health officials in controlling disease outbreaks, but poor blacks and immigrants were further stigmatized as potential disease vectors when epidemiologists recognized that maladies such as typhoid, hookworm, tuberculosis, and syphilis could be spread by healthy carriers who showed no outward symptoms of illness.[7]

Individual diseases further illuminate the varying degrees to which race influenced the gathering and interpretation of biostatistics. Although John D. Rockefeller's original reason for funding the Rockefeller Sanitary Commission for the Eradication of Hookworm Disease in 1909 was to win support among southern whites for his larger goal of improving black education, the hookworm campaign's success ironically had the opposite effect despite its leaders' attempts to avoid partiality. Wickliffe Rose, the commission's executive secretary, refused to record race in statistics and emphasized that education and treatment activities had been done "without any suggestion of race distinction." The commission's scientific director, Charles Wardell Stiles, urged whites to act in their own self-interest to "lend a helping hand to improve the sanitary surroundings of the negro." Yet Stiles and other researchers found that higher percentages of whites than of blacks were infected with hookworm disease, thereby feeding accusations in the popular press that blacks who carried and spread the parasite were responsible for the deaths of tens of thousands of innocent whites. The pattern of identifying racial and ethnic minorities as primarily healthy carriers who threatened whites rather than as fellow victims of disease persisted in public attitudes toward hookworm, as it had with typhoid fever, syphilis, tuberculosis, and other infectious bacterial illnesses. The conquest of hookworm was commonly portrayed as a racial victory for whites as well as a scientific victory for public health.[8]

Hookworm and pellagra, a nutritional disease caused by protein deficiency, were considered the twin scourges of the southern white cracker. But unlike hookworm, both pellagra and malaria disproportionately affected African Americans, who were not feared as healthy carriers, perhaps because neither pellagra nor malaria spreads directly from human to human as bacterial illnesses do. Both diseases were barometers of the South's declining economy and health status during the farm crisis of the 1920s, particularly in cotton-growing areas. To supplement their diets, farm families had always relied on subsistence gardens, but they were displaced by the exclusive planting of cash crops, resulting in widespread malnutrition and an increase in nutritional deficiencies such as rickets and pellagra. Access to meat, dairy, and fresh vegetables was further limited by the inadequate supplies and distribution of local food networks and debt-related pressures to sell livestock.

Within this scenario, women and children of both races were more vulnerable to the exigencies of poverty and malnutrition since adult males typically ate first at mealtimes and nutritional deficiency directly caused pellagra and facilitated malaria infection. At least half (and probably more as a consequence of underreporting in southern states) of pellagra victims were black, and more than two-thirds were female. Medical historian Harry Marks notes that "by comparison with discussions of tuberculosis and other infectious diseases," pellagra researchers' explanations of racial variances "were noticeably race neutral, placing little or no emphasis on African-Americans as reservoirs of pellagra." Edgar Sydenstricker and other epidemiologists imposed a northern industrial model of the family wage that blinded them to racial and gender differences among southern tenants and sharecroppers that influenced rates of pellagra.[9]

Malnutrition also lowered resistance to contagious diseases and increased the severity of parasitic conditions such as hookworm and malaria. Long after malaria had faded from the North, it remained problematic in the Atlantic and Gulf coastal areas from the Carolinas to Alabama and particularly acute in the Mississippi Delta cotton-growing regions. There, a nearly all-black workforce lived and labored in swampy, crowded conditions ideal for the propagation of malaria's insect vector, the *Anopheles quadrimaculatus* mosquito. The growing racial disparities in malaria were evidence of the plummeting economic status of black sharecroppers. Various studies conducted between 1912 and 1930 showed black infection rates ranging from 20 to 54 percent, while white rates were lower but nevertheless increased during the 1920s. Throughout the 1920s and 1930s, approximately ten times as many blacks as whites died of malaria, although the overall rates for both races declined during that period. Southern officials largely ignored malaria, viewing it as a primarily black problem, and simply denied the existence of pellagra, a stance facilitated by most southern states' failure to collect vital statistics.[10]

Local health officials were responsible for reporting statistics on mortality to the U.S. Census Bureau and on morbidity for reportable communicable diseases to the PHS, but compliance varied according to local and state codes and the levels of funding and personnel provided to enforce them. The first southern state was not admitted to the U.S. Census Death Registration Area until 1916, and no southern state joined the Birth Registration Area until 1921, since the Census Bureau required that at least 90 percent of births or deaths be accurately reported using a standardized certificate. Vital statistics for many southern states remained spotty, particularly for rural blacks, who had virtually no contact with physicians or public health officials. Biostatistics continued to rise in importance as a public health discipline, and statistical reporting became a central line of inquiry in the reports of the Committee on the Cost of Medical Care, a public-private coalition sponsored by the PHS and a variety of philanthropic foundations and private groups. The committee conducted the first broad study of health disparities during the late 1920s and early 1930s. Rural morbidity and mortality rates were probably higher than reported as a consequence of the dearth of doctors and public health personnel, challenging the belief that rural areas were healthier than urban ones. Until 1939, the U.S. Census Bureau recorded deaths by place of death, not by place of residence, which increased urban numbers and decreased rural rates, since rural patients usually sought care in urban hospitals. Race also skewed birth and death statistics. The PHS estimated that in 1940, the percentage of registered to actual births was 98 percent for Chinese and Japanese, 94 percent for whites, 82 percent for blacks, and 69 percent for American Indians.[11]

In 1937, Ruth Rice Puffer, a statistician for the Tennessee Department of Public Health, examined the margin of error in black death rates. She determined that urban black death rates were probably close to accurate but that rural rates, especially in the Deep South, had a higher margin of error. This higher margin resulted from the significant percentage of unregistered deaths and of deaths for which no cause was recorded because no physician was present, particularly in the case of infants. Although southern states had higher reported mortality rates than the North, regional and racial disparities might have been even greater because of southern underreporting, particularly among rural blacks. In 1933, twelve southern states classified an average of 8 percent of nonwhite deaths as resulting from ill-defined and unknown causes, with Missouri, Kentucky, Virginia, and Louisiana reporting the lowest percentages of deaths in this category. In Mississippi, the cause of death was unknown in one in five nonwhite deaths; in Alabama, that number was one in seven, with Tennessee, South Carolina, Georgia, and Arkansas also failing to classify causes for more than 10 percent of nonwhite deaths. Among the twelve southern states Puffer studied, the causes of 23 percent of nonwhite deaths under age one were unknown; the figure was 49 percent in Mississippi. As Puffer noted, "This large percentage of deaths from unknown causes invalidates any discussion of colored death rates from specific causes."[12]

Despite their abundant flaws, health statistics that quantified racial disparities could also be used as evidence to loosen scientific racism's hold on medical thought.[13] A prime opponent was the National Medical Association (NMA), founded in 1895 by an interracial group of physicians in the Washington, D.C., area who in the early 1870s had been excluded from membership in the American Medical Association (AMA) in deference to its all-white affiliate, the Medical Society of the District of Columbia. Like the NAACP, the NMA had been founded by both blacks and whites, most of whom were doctors associated with Howard University. The NMA was part of a small, diverse, progressive corps from a variety of professional backgrounds who challenged the racialization of disease, fought to open training programs to black professionals, and pushed to reverse the widespread neglect of health problems among minorities. During the Progressive and interwar decades, black women provided critical leadership in the lay health reform movement. By the 1930s, some prominent white southerners, notably Thomas Parran of the PHS, the Duke Endowment's Watson Smith Rankin, and medical economist Michael M. Davis, supported a stronger system of hospitals and health professionals to serve blacks but did not directly challenge segregation. All of these health reformers rejected "anatomic geneticism," or the belief that phenotypical differences signified the innate, discrete physical and biological qualities of various races, as an explanation for racial disparities in health and instead focused on environmental factors. These reformers believed that immunity and resistance to disease did not vary significantly across racial or ethnic groups and that scientific medicine could be applied universally to all human beings.[14]

PHILANTHROPIC CAMPAIGNS TO UPLIFT SOUTHERN HEALTH AND EDUCATION

Most of the parameters for deluxe Jim Crow health policy were determined during Progressive Era campaigns by philanthropies, voluntary organizations, and the PHS to uplift the health and educational status of black and rural southerners. The Commonwealth, Milbank, and Kellogg Foundations as well as the Phipps Institute and the Rockefeller Sanitary Commission were key players in rural health. Major sponsors of health and education initiatives among southerners of both races included the Rockefeller General Education Board (GEB), the Phelps-

Stokes Fund, the Slater Fund, and the Jeanes Fund, along with smaller private organizations and individuals. The Chicago-based Julius Rosenwald Fund made its name as the foremost benefactor of black health and education. Depending on their viewpoint, different observers saw Rosenwald, the Sears-Roebuck magnate, as an apostle of either Jim Crow or social justice. NMA president John A. Kenney exulted, "Every Negro in the United States of America should get down on his knees and thank God for Julius Rosenwald." His partnership with Booker T. Washington built more than five thousand schools for rural black children across the South with a combination of Rosenwald Fund money, contributions from local blacks and whites, and state funds.[15]

The GEB also worked to improve Negro education and develop competent southern state departments of education. In 1900, no southern state had a full-time superintendent of education, and "the office of state superintendent was usually under the hat of the gentleman who wore it. There were no Southern public-school systems in the sense in which a public-school system existed, whatever its defects, north of the Ohio River." In Virginia, the GEB paid the salary and traveling expenses of the first state agent for Negro education, and other southern states soon began to accept GEB aid to hire Negro agents. The GEB also used state agents to promote the development of high schools for rural whites, which were until then unknown. By 1922, the GEB had invested just over $3 million to promote southern schools, yielding two thousand new high schools (urban and rural, black and white) constructed for a total of $60 million. Southern school districts increased their annual tax-supported appropriations from $1.7 million in 1905 to $15 million by 1922.[16]

Southern educational and health reform drew on similar or identical methods, leadership, and organizations. Rosenwald and Rockefeller also played essential roles alongside the PHS in the campaigns to uplift rural and black health. In 1909, with the cooperation of the PHS and the expertise of its Hygenic Laboratory, Rockefeller committed $1 million to establish the Rockefeller Sanitary Commission, which tested rural citizens for hookworm, provided thymol to those who were infected, and built sanitary privies. By 1915, nearly a million southern children in six hundred counties had been examined, revealing a 39 percent rate of infection. In Alabama, hookworm was present in every county, with infection rates as high as 62 percent. The chief cause of infestation was the lack of sanitary toilet facilities in many areas: surveys revealed open dirt trenches in Louisiana and no rural privies in Arkansas. Despite resistance from the southern public and from members of the medical profession, who often regarded the Rockefeller agents and PHS officers as meddling outsiders or unwelcome competition, the hookworm campaign helped establish and strengthen public health departments across the South, providing a template for the work of the Rockefeller International Health Division. The joint campaign of the Rockefeller Sanitary Commission and the PHS to eradicate hookworm created a southern health nexus of philanthropy, academic medicine, and public health agencies that would shape the course of regional, national, and international public health throughout the twentieth century.[17]

If the Rockefeller Foundation was credited with vanquishing the "germ of laziness" among southern whites, Rosenwald stood out as the foremost benefactor of black health. Since the Rosenwald schools were handicapped by their students' high rates of sickness and death, the fund addressed black health problems with more than $1.6 million in grants between 1917 and 1940. After the fund's reorganization in 1928 with Edwin Embree as the new president, black health became Rosenwald's primary focus, and it began to induce southern governments to hire more black public health nurses, beginning with $12,000 awarded to county health units in North Carolina and Tennessee. Rosenwald also supported efforts to open public health department staffs and hospital residencies to black physicians, thereby prompting initiatives to upgrade hospital training programs for black health professionals as well as to improve the hospital facilities themselves.[18]

Even though the triumph of segregation and disfranchisement closed the formal political structure to blacks and white control tightened even further after World War I, blacks and their philanthropist allies "leverage[d] state policy by intertwining private with public resources to create and sustain state services." Rosenwald and Rockefeller funding enabled black parents to pressure states to expand educational opportunities for children and enabled black educators to penetrate and reform state educational bureaucracies. Rosenwald also sponsored and placed white "Negro Agents" within state departments of education. In both school and health programs, philanthropic support for southern uplift promoted the grassroots growth of a competent cadre of professionals who continued to lobby for increased state funding even after Rosenwald, the GEB, and the Sanitary Commission ended their active involvement.[19]

Rosenwald fulfilled his intention to stimulate greater social responsibility by public agencies, with the share of state funding in North Carolina rising from just under half of Rosenwald school construction costs during 1914–17 to more than 80 percent by the end of the campaign in 1928. In Alabama, the increase in state funding for black Rosenwald schools during the same period was even greater, from 16 percent to more than 60 percent. As the GEB and Rosenwald Fund had done in education, the PHS urged state and local governments to provide permanent tax support for public health as a condition of federal grants-in-aid, but the PHS initially had less success. Until World War II, southern governments remained largely unwilling to tax for public welfare initiatives, especially those benefiting politically and economically marginal blacks. But in the long run, the strategy of using federal matching grants to induce state and municipal governments to assume permanent responsibility for the health and education of all southerners would become a primary tenet of deluxe Jim Crow policy.[20]

In his seminal history of southern health care for blacks and millworkers, E. H. Beardsley calls the Rosenwald Fund "a godsend to black people in the South." The fund's programs found enthusiastic support within the NMA, whose president, M. O. Bousfield, was a consultant to the fund and later its associate director. The fund's southern focus dovetailed with the NMA leadership's strong connections with Tuskegee Institute in Alabama, Meharry Medical College in Nashville, and Howard University in Washington, D.C. But other historians have criticized white philanthropies, including Rosenwald, during this period as dominated by paternalism, capitalism, and biological reductionism rather than an awareness of the effects of social and economic environments on disease. Rosenwald's "extensive and visible programs in black social welfare and race relations," medical historian Vanessa Northington Gamble argues, made the fund "the primary target for condemnation by integrationists." In the early 1930s, Rosenwald was called a "semitic Santa Claus" who gave "alms, not opportunity." Such barbs came primarily from northern blacks who feared that new Rosenwald-funded hospitals for blacks might interfere with efforts to gain equal access to existing white-run hospitals.[21]

The debates over the motives and consequences of white philanthropic support for black southern uplift have crescendoed in the historical analyses of medical education. Here, the stakes were higher: study required significant preparation, time, and money, and medical schools were costly to build and operate but produced the precious doctors for the whole health system. Far fewer physicians, black or white, practiced in the South, where widespread poverty and rural isolation made doctoring a financially risky proposition. The South's dearth of medical schools and hospitals affected all physicians.[22]

The careers of Abraham Flexner and Louis T. Wright illustrate how racial and regional considerations powerfully shaped philanthropic attempts to modernize medical education, which in turn molded the meager ranks of the black medical profession. Historians of race and medicine have labeled Flexner a racist and Wright a visionary for his dogged pursuit of integration. In his 1910 report to the Carnegie Foundation, *Medical Education in the United States and Canada*, Flexner wrote that "the practice of the Negro doctor will be limited to his own race, which in its turn will be cared for better by good negro doctors than by poor white ones," a statement frequently cited as evidence of racism rather than as an observation of reality at the time. Historians charge that Flexner wanted black physicians to treat only black people and wanted black schools to focus on general practice and public health rather than surgery. Flexner thereby insulted blacks' ability and aspirations and was allegedly among the early twentieth-century white health reformers whose self-interest motivated them to improve black morbidity and mortality chiefly to protect whites. Undoubtedly, Flexner acted to raise the standards and reduce the number of American medical schools, particularly those for blacks. Whereas ten black medical schools existed in 1900, by 1923, only Howard and Meharry remained—the only two Flexner had deemed worthy of further development and support. These institutions were headed by whites until Numa P. G. Adams was appointed dean at Howard in 1929 and Harold West was appointed dean at Meharry in 1952.[23]

In the two decades after the report's publication, Flexner, more than any other individual, guided the development of black and southern medical education. Most controversially, he stated that the majority of black schools were "wasting small sums annually sending out undisciplined men, whose lack of real training is covered up by the imposing M.D. degree." The same could be said of many white medical schools, which deserved the epithet "diploma mills." Flexner visited 148 U.S. schools, judging two-thirds of them "utterly hopeless." Rising licensure standards and increasing operating costs for laboratories, libraries, and clinical sites were already driving scores of smaller proprietary schools out of business, a trend only accelerated by the Flexner Report and the philanthropic response to its recommendations.[24]

Flexner, the son of a merchant who had fallen on hard times after the Panic of 1873, grew up in Louisville, Kentucky, where he played street baseball with both black and white neighbors. He later recalled that for him and his six brothers and two sisters, Herbert Spencer, the father of Social Darwinism, and English scientist Thomas H. Huxley, "then at the height of their fame and influence, replaced . . . the Bible and the prayer book." Many of Flexner's contemporaries were unreconstructed southern sympathizers, and he counted a former Confederate colonel as one of his closest friends. But he credited Wallace Buttrick, chair of the GEB, with opening his eyes to the special educational problems southern blacks faced.[25]

Flexner's criticisms of black medical schools must be understood in the context of his equally gloomy appraisal of white southern schools and his sustained efforts to assist both types of institutions. Flexner's visit to the Southwestern Homeopathic Medical College in Louisville, for example, revealed an annual budget of eleven hundred dollars, one "wretchedly dirty" building, no laboratory facilities, and "no recent sign of dissecting being performed." At Atlanta's Georgia College of Eclectic Medicine and Surgery, the anatomy room was "indescribably foul," and pathology was taught with three microscopes and "a few dirty slides." Flexner saw Vanderbilt University's medical school as the only one in the South capable of reaching "the modern ideal." He judged Baltimore's Johns Hopkins as the southernmost of the leading northern schools, alongside Harvard, Yale, Columbia, Penn, and Chicago, although Harvard president Charles Eliot considered Hopkins "a small and weak university" in a "provincial community" with a medical school not on par with Harvard or Columbia. Even as late as 1942, when Virginius Dabney published his study of southern universities, *Below the Potomac*, the region's colleges and universities remained "woefully underfinanced, overburdened with political and religious intrusion, and seriously deficient in library holdings, Ph.D. programs, and research activities."[26]

Medical historian Todd L. Savitt cites Flexner's similarly biting comments about five of the seven black schools that he visited to object to the 1910 report's negative message that "black students, and by implication, current black practitioners who had graduated from these schools, did not receive an adequate medical education." They had not, judging by their high failure rates on state medical board licensing exams, and neither had most white southern physicians. In 1910, seventy-six of the U.S. medical schools from which fifty or more graduates sat for the exams had failure rates higher than 20 percent; seventy-four of those institutions were located in the South. Among the thirty-two states and the District of Columbia that had medical schools in 1910, the southern states and the border state of Missouri had the highest rates of failure on licensing exams, ranging from a 20 percent rate for District of Columbia students to 52 percent for Mississippians. One-quarter of examinees from the lowest-ranking eight southern states and the District failed, whereas only 9 percent of test takers failed in the four states with the strongest schools (Georgia, Louisiana, Virginia, and Texas). The low-ranking states produced three-quarters of the 2,052 examinees from southern schools, but their graduates failed at nine times the rate of those from the higher-ranked southern states, whose medical schools produced fewer total graduates but more well-prepared ones.[27]

Of the 183 examinees from the three top black schools, Howard, Meharry, and Leonard, just over three-quarters were tested out of state, compared to about half of all 1910 examinees. Since failure rates overall were twice as high (20 percent) for those who were examined outside the state where they had attended medical school, the many black physicians who migrated were at a disadvantage. In 1920, only 1 of the 31 Howard and Meharry graduates examined in the District of Columbia and Tennessee, respectively, failed the exam, whereas half of the 137 out-of-state examinees failed in those two localities. Although the national average failure rate on board exams had been reduced only slightly from 18 to 15 percent, all but two southern states, Arkansas and Florida, had reduced their failure rates to below 20 percent. Thus, for both black and white southern schools, fewer schools in the post-Flexner era meant fewer graduates but equal or greater numbers of board-licensed physicians.[28]

Flexner emerges as a tough but fair critic of American medical schools at a time when they warranted extensive rehabilitation, and his remarks about the inadequacies of all southern schools accurately reflect the region's lack of financial capital and the primitive state of its higher education system, of which medicine was the most expensive and complex component. Despite his low opinion of southern medical schools, he and Carnegie Foundation president Henry S. Pritchett recognized the limitations imposed by southern conditions and advocated tolerance of "greater unevenness" as a result of the underdevelopment of southern education. Flexner went head-to-head with Arthur Dean Bevan of the AMA Council on Medical Education, who criticized Flexner's advocacy of full-time teaching in medical schools. However, Bevan also began to exert increasing pressure on southern schools, including Howard and Meharry, to raise their standards and require one year of college science for admission. With Pritchett's support, Flexner wrote to the council in 1914 to protest the unrealistic attempt to enforce the AMA's new entrance requirements strictly and immediately when many poor southern communities still lacked adequate high schools and existing schools typically prepared graduates for vocations, not college study. Throughout the 1920s, Flexner and Pritchett continued to confront the Council on Medical Education on the issue of ensuring opportunity for southerners, particularly blacks, to study medicine. After the council downgraded Meharry to Class B status in 1914, Pritchett protested the "grave injustice done to negro schools," while Flexner exclaimed, "Meharry is as good an *A* school for the Negro race as half a dozen institutions or more rated *A* for whites." He charged that the council was already adapting its standards for white schools in recognition of local variations and urged that Howard and Meharry receive the same consideration.[29]

During the 1920s, Flexner undertook the restructuring of American medical education with the aid of $80 million from the GEB and an additional $550 million from the Rockefeller and Carnegie Foundations as well as other philanthropies and matching funds from the universities with which most medical schools were now affiliated. He pursued the goals he had first proposed in his Carnegie report: drastically reducing the number of medical schools (from 148 to 31), strategically placing them in large cities to serve surrounding regions, ensuring access to modern facilities with a sufficient number and diversity of patients for clinical teaching, and replacing the local clinicians on whom most medical schools relied for instruction with full-time, trained teachers and researchers. At Hopkins, Vanderbilt, and the University of Cincinnati (which trained significant numbers of southern doctors), Flexner negotiated large GEB grants in response to both the schools' receptiveness to transformative change and the quality of their existing programs and facilities. In the rest of the South, medical education was "trembling on the verge of extinction," but he still urged the GEB to fund specific measures to improve the schools, including the construction of laboratory facilities, the establishment of residency programs, and the creation of a $500,000 endowment for teaching and equipment at Howard, which Flexner declared "must not be permitted to disappear." Flexner thus played a critical role in generating support for medicine at Howard, Meharry, and the white southern schools.[30]

Flexner had reason to worry about the fates of Howard and Meharry, which together turned out one hundred graduates yearly. Cognizant of the severe obstacles that the two schools faced, Flexner made black medical education a priority personally and within the foundations he so strongly influenced. Howard's College of Medicine was established in 1868, later joined by colleges of dentistry in 1881 and pharmacy in 1882. As units of the federal Department of the Interior and later the Federal Security Agency, the Freedmen's Hospital and Howard received annual federal appropriations that partially supported construction, operation, maintenance, and endowment, but both institutions were controlled by private boards independent of the federal government.[31]

Like Tuskegee and many other black institutions, Howard opportunistically straddled the lines of public and private and received substantial philanthropic as well as government funding. In addition to grants to build Howard's endowment, Flexner also secured support for new construction on the school's aging medical campus. In 1930, after he had completed most of his work in medical education, he joined Howard's board of trustees, becoming chair in 1932. But after unsuccessfully attempting to resolve severe internal conflicts among the university's administration, faculty, and board, he resigned in frustration in 1935. Eleanor Roosevelt, another Howard trustee active in southern uplift, urged Congress in the 1940s to increase federal funding for the College of Medicine and Freedmen's Hospital.[32]

Only two medical schools, Howard and the Naval Medical School, also located in Washington, D.C., were federally supported. Since Howard's finances were relatively stable, Flexner focused the majority of his efforts on Meharry, a private medical and dental school affiliated with the Methodist Episcopal Church. Flexner assisted in soliciting gifts totaling more than $8 million from Julius Rosenwald, George Eastman, Edward Harkness, and the GEB, which came to regard Meharry as its "medical god-child." The grants, together with the installation of John J. Mullowney, a former missionary to China, as president in 1921, improved Meharry's facilities and the quality of its faculty sufficiently to restore the school to Class A status in 1923.[33]

Attracting trained teachers was an ongoing problem for both Howard and Meharry as a result of the severely restricted opportunities for postgraduate study available to blacks. In 1919, Flexner convinced Julius Rosenwald, with whom Flexner had built a close relationship, to fund a program for Howard and Meharry graduates to obtain one additional year of training at a top-ranked medical school and research experience at the Rockefeller Institute. But the Rosenwald Fellows program lasted only two years, produced just six fellows, and was discontinued because recipients showed no interest in practicing or doing public health work in the South, choosing instead to pursue more lucrative opportunities in the North. More black physicians benefited from a subsequent Rockefeller Foundation program that sent black medical graduates to Europe and later to U.S. institutions for specialized residency training. Flexner and his philanthropist allies at the Carnegie, Rockefeller, and Rosenwald Foundations hoped that southern graduates of Howard and Meharry as well as the region's white schools would return to serve the South's poor small-town and rural communities. In neither case, however, did the benefactors of southern medical schools have any way of enforcing their wishes, and even at Meharry, the school that enrolled the largest number of black southerners, most graduates practiced in cities, and many left the South. Every subsequent program designed to redistribute the physician supply to underserved rural areas and more recently from specialized practice to primary care has faced the same obstacles and achieved less than desired results.[34]

Flexner's actions helped to speed the closure of the smaller proprietary black medical schools, while Wright's prevented the creation of additional all-black hospitals. Both men prioritized training a smaller cadre of highly skilled physicians over turning out large numbers of mediocre physicians. Both saw no point in starting or sustaining inferior institutions that would produce inferior doctors who were, as Flexner argued, "in no position to make any contribution of value to the solution of the [Negro health] problem." Moreover, the Flexner Report did not necessarily mirror Flexner's personal convictions. It was a public document commissioned by and for white philanthropists, who sought to apply their dollars shrewdly where they would do the most good. Had Flexner, like many black educators, physicians, and hospital administrators, not appealed to white self-interest in improving the health status of blacks, both the southern white public and its political leaders would likely have been more resistant to "outside interference" in race relations during an age of often extreme antiblack sentiment. Helping black physicians to become highly trained urban specialists would have promoted equity within the medical profession but would have done little to relieve the widespread unmet medical need among the South's poorest populations. Flexner's hope that black schools would prepare many competent sanitarians rather than a handful of surgeons was well founded in the greatest practical and humanitarian needs of the South, where far more deaths and illness would be prevented by the application of public health methods than by the slice of a scalpel. To call Carnegie, Rockefeller, and the GEB racist for failing to fund the training of blacks as surgeons or specialists in 1910 is a somewhat presentist misreading of the evidence. Before World War II, only one-tenth of American physicians were surgeons and only one-quarter were full-time specialists, and neither group had yet achieved the prestige, earning power, or numerical strength that would accrue following the war.[35]

The pros and cons of the philanthropist-led campaigns to improve southern health care and education were part of a heated debate that centered on the tension between the "already" and the "not yet." Flexner achieved national and worldwide renown not only for his comprehensive reforms in medical education but also for his advocacy of a universal, rational modern university built on scientific inquiry and objectivity. W. E. B. Du Bois, however, questioned the value of such a university for blacks and argued that Negro higher education should be uniquely suited to black needs and experiences. In 1933, Du Bois criticized Flexner's attempts to apply his theories of education at Howard:

> As President of the Board of Trustees, [Flexner] said he was seeking to build not a Negro university, but a University. And by those words he brought again before our eyes the ideal of a great institution of learning which becomes a center of universal culture. With all good will toward them that say such words . . . there can be no college for Negroes which is not a Negro college and . . . while an American Negro university, just like a German or Swiss university may rightly aspire to a universal culture unhampered by limitations of race and culture, yet it must start on the earth where we sit and not in the skies whither we aspire. . . .
>
> . . . We are segregated; we are a caste. This is our given and at present unalterable fact. Our problem is how far and in what way can we consciously and scientifically guide our future so as to ensure our physical survival, our spiritual freedom and our social growth? Either we do this or we die. There is no alternative. . . .
>
> . . . Therefore let us not beat futile wings in impotent frenzy, but carefully plan and guide our segregated life, organize in industry and politics to protect it and expand it and above all to give it unhampered spiritual expression.

Du Bois concluded that whatever the outcome of the battle to end segregation, it would require "long centuries and not years. We live in years, swift-flying, transient years." Despite his public and very vocal campaign to erase the color line, by the early 1930s Du Bois had begun to advocate black separatism. He broke with the NAACP leadership over this issue and in 1934 resigned as editor of the organization's magazine, *The Crisis*. He now viewed integration much as Flexner viewed the reform of medical education, as a worthwhile but long-term goal. In the more immediate future, both men appreciated the need to enable fledgling institutions to develop their potential at their own pace, rather than setting unreachable goals that would crush the institutions before they had had a chance to get off the ground.[36]

Although Flexner was certainly no integrationist, his approach to improving the quality of the medical profession had a great deal in common with that of Wright, a fellow southerner. A prominent surgeon, clinical researcher, and fellow of the AMA and American College of Surgeons, Wright chaired the NAACP board of directors from 1931 to 1952, when he led a national campaign to integrate health care and medical education. Just as Flexner had wanted "to build not a Negro university, but a University," Wright declared to the 1938 National Health Conference, "There is no such thing as Negro health. . . . [T]he health of the American Negro is not a separate racial problem to be met by special segregated setups or dealt with on a dual standard basis, but is an American problem which should be adequately and equitably handled by the identical agencies and met with the identical methods that deal with the health of the remainder of the population." As a fourth-year student at Harvard Medical School, Wright had participated in protests against D. W. Griffith's 1915 film, *Birth of a Nation*, which glorified Ku Klux Klan violence against blacks during Reconstruction. After returning home to Atlanta to obtain his medical license, Wright insisted that a white clerk address him as "Dr. Wright" rather than by his first name, in accordance with Jim Crow etiquette. When the clerk asked if Wright had been "peddling any dope or abortions," the physician threatened, "I will choke you right here if you open your Goddamned mouth again!" Wright subsequently moved to New York, where his ties with the Democratic machine helped him become the first black police surgeon on the city's force and the first black chief surgeon of Harlem Hospital, a municipal facility that mainly admitted black patients. Wright's blunt and uncompromising style inspired Walter Francis White's 1924 novel, *The Fire in the Flint*, an allegory about what might have happened to Wright had he stayed in the South.[37]

Wright and the New York NAACP opened Harlem's staff to black physicians in 1921. During the late 1920s, Wright's dismissal of numerous black physicians that he deemed incompetent revealed intraracial tensions rooted in questions of both professional and racial identity. Peter Murray, who later served as president of the NMA, and other doctors charged Wright and his northern-trained allies with neglecting professional standards and patient care in the name of political expediency; conversely, Wright viewed the qualifications of Howard- and Meharry-trained southern doctors with suspicion and never joined the NMA, which he considered a Jim Crow organization. Wright also stridently opposed the Rosenwald Fund's 1930 proposal to survey black hospital facilities and needs in New York City because he suspected that the survey would result in the construction of a new all-black hospital. (Wright had also led the North Harlem Medical Society and the NAACP in rejecting the city's proposal to build a new all-black hospital in 1921.) Wright's view of black institutions as corrupted and compromised by their relationships with white philanthropy was shared by a growing number of integrationist blacks such as Ralph Ellison, whose 1952 novel, *Invisible Man*, questioned whether Tuskegee and other established black institutions were in fact promoting the best interests of the race.[38]

Black medical graduates immediately confronted the problem of finding suitable hospitals in which to pursue residency training and obtain admitting rights, since only fourteen hospitals nationwide were both accredited for teaching and accepted black interns. According to Gamble, white philanthropies provided essential funding for the black hospital movement and the improvement of a handful of black hospitals as well as promoted separate black wards in white hospitals, but she chides trustees and foundation officers for failing to promote integration or to insist that segregated facilities be made equal with those for whites. Officials of the Rosenwald Fund failed, for example, to fulfill their intention to ensure staff privileges for black physicians when the fund sponsored a black wing of the Knoxville, Tennessee, municipal hospital. For nine years after the hospital opened in 1933, white physicians barred blacks from the staff.[39]

During the interwar years, the Rosenwald Fund and the Duke Endowment remained the only major private supporters of programs to improve southern black health per se, although blacks did benefit from the slow expansion of rural health initiatives. The Duke Endowment provided one dollar per day per patient toward the operating expenses of approved black, white, and biracial hospitals in the Carolinas, with significant numbers of blacks benefiting from the 70 percent rise in patient-days of care during the 1920s. Like Rosenwald, the Duke Endowment imposed white supervision on black hospitals rather than allowing them to be administered by African American physicians. Yet Gamble labels Watson Smith Rankin, a Duke Endowment trustee and head of the Hospital Section, a racist who viewed black physicians as incompetent and incapable of managing Lincoln Hospital, a black-run institution in Durham, North Carolina, founded with support from American Tobacco Company millionaire Washington Duke. Gamble acknowledges, however, that Rankin's plan to improve Lincoln's quality of care had the support of the NMA, including Peter Murray and M. O. Bousfield.[40]

The accusation that Flexner limited opportunity for blacks to study medicine and constricted the supply of black doctors applies to Wright as well. Like Flexner, Rankin and Wright were concerned about the poor qualifications of black graduates of Howard and Meharry. But in New York, Wright had the option of retaining better-qualified black doctors educated, as he was, at predominantly white northern schools with long-established, well-funded programs; Durham, in contrast, had no such black talent. If anything, Rankin was more diplomatic and sensitive toward the black doctors at Lincoln than Wright was toward those at Harlem. Wright's efforts earned him the label "anti-Negro" from his detractors, who charged him with cronyism in light of his Tammany Hall connections. Unlike Wright, who simply fired the doctors he deemed incompetent, Rankin referred decisions of the advisory committee to Lincoln's trustees for approval and retained Lincoln's physicians on staff, under the supervision of well-trained local white physicians, with the opportunity for black doctors to take on more responsibility as they improved their skills. Both Rankin's and Wright's efforts achieved the desired results: Harlem Hospital and Lincoln Hospital dramatically improved the quality of patient care and staff professional standards, with a resulting decrease in mortality rates and a rise in income as more nonindigent patients chose to be admitted. Finally, despite the closure of several black schools and rising educational and professional standards, the number of black southern doctors remained steady at around two thousand from the 1920s through the 1940s. The doctor-to-population ratio decreased, however, since the region's black population increased from 9 million to 10 million between 1920 and 1940.[41]

Wright and Rankin's actions must also be viewed in the context of foundations' paternalistic stance not only toward blacks but also toward southern whites. On one occasion, an officer of the Rockefeller International Health Board expressed reservations about committing funds for southern public health "because we haven't the men to send to them to help them spend it wisely." Northern white philanthropies at times treated both black and southern white health professionals with condescension, in part because neither group was adequately trained. In not just health but all areas of social welfare, complicated power negotiations and playing to stereotypes too often characterized white philanthropies' interactions with southern blacks as well as southern whites. Ultimately, however, Flexner, Rankin, and Wright helped more than harmed the black medical profession by encouraging higher standards that would enable black doctors to approach their white counterparts' qualifications. Without the Flexner Report and the support of white philanthropy, the black proprietary schools might have lasted a bit longer, but Howard and Meharry might well have closed or remained far weaker. Wright's apparent intolerance for some of his southern black colleagues was largely generational and abated as the two schools tightened their admissions requirements and modernized their curricula and facilities.[42]

During this period, the PHS emerged as the most prosouthern and the most problack federal agency. Its powerful connections with the Rockefeller Foundation and Johns Hopkins, the Rosenwald Foundation and Tuskegee Institute, the Duke Endowment and Duke University, and other philanthropic and academic players in southern health had two major consequences. First, they influenced the PHS to build more effective and mutually respectful relationships with black and white organized medicine and southern health officials, whose cooperation was essential for achieving the goals of improving the health status of the nation's most medically underserved groups. Second, the federal-philanthropic-university coalition also ensured that a disproportionate number of public health leaders either hailed from the South or spent significant portions of their careers there, thereby placing the South at the center of federal public health initiatives just as southern Democrats began to exert a deciding influence over New Deal policy. The South produced more than its share of surgeons general of the United States, beginning with South Carolinian Rupert Blue's appointment in 1912. Of the thirteen U.S. surgeons general who served over the next ninety years, six were native southerners who helmed the PHS for forty-six years. The South emerged as a source of leadership as well as a target for PHS public health efforts.[43]

RACIAL, REGIONAL, AND RURAL-URBAN HEALTH DISPARITIES, 1900–1940

A comparison of the state of southern and American health during the first third of the twentieth century highlights the relationships among racial, regional, and rural-urban disparities. At the beginning of the twentieth century, Americans of all classes and races were intimately familiar with death and disease, but by the onset of the Great Depression, slower rates of improvement for rural, southern, and black health indicators had concentrated the burden of illness in the region least equipped to bear it. What had initially been the plagues of overcrowded northern ghettoes became identified with the South, where blacks fared worse than whites in the delayed transition from a rural, agrarian society to a more urban, industrial one. During the early twentieth century, black southerners not only experienced intense racial oppression but also displayed greater demographic similarity with white southerners than with nonsoutherners.

America's most medically underserved populations were heavily concentrated in the South, the home of 76.6 percent of African Americans and 54.1 percent of rural Americans in 1940 (fig. 1.1). Yet southern communities had the least financial and institutional resources to meet their needs. The southern health care and medical education systems remained in the embryonic stage, so disparities in

FIGURE 1.1
Medically Underserved Populations, 1940

30.2 million rural Americans
¼ of U.S. population
½ lived in South

36.5 million southerners
28% of U.S. population

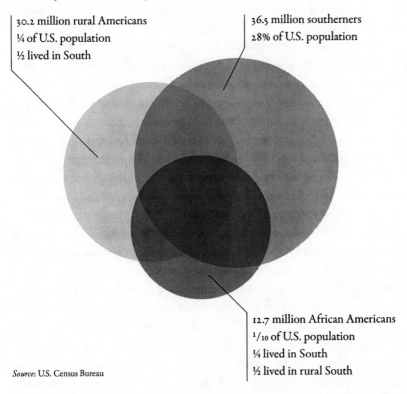

12.7 million African Americans
$^1/_{10}$ of U.S. population
¼ lived in South
½ lived in rural South

Source: U.S. Census Bureau

the per capita ratios of doctors and hospital beds were greater between the South and the rest of the country than between blacks and whites within the South. By 1920, public health departments in large northern cities provided services including vital statistics, sanitation, communicable disease control, maternal and child health, health education, and laboratory facilities. These services were not consistently available in most areas of the rural South until at least 1950. Existing public health departments in the region were typically grossly understaffed by personnel with little or no public health training, often on a part-time basis. By a number of socioeconomic and public health measures, southern blacks and whites were more similar than different and also more similar to each other than to their northern same-race counterparts.[44]

Before a joint congressional committee that was investigating the Tennessee Valley Authority in 1938, surgeon general Thomas Parran called the South "the

Nation's No. 1 health problem." He made the region his agency's public health laboratory for two related reasons: the South's economy and ecology fostered the types of communicable epidemic disease that responded most dramatically to public health methods, and its relatively underdeveloped private health system was less a source of competition than in the North, where fee-for-service hospital-based practice, well-established academic medical centers, organized medicine, and group payment plans flourished. During the Roosevelt and Truman administrations, the South's abysmal health status was starkly portrayed in a flurry of reports and articles that documented the nation's worst rates of morbidity, mortality, and wartime draft rejections. Compared to the rest of the nation, the South's population as a whole was poorer, younger, and more rural; had higher fertility rates and lower standards of living; had shorter life expectancies and higher rates of illiteracy; and was more isolated from a much smaller supply of doctors and hospital beds.[45]

Before 1920, the health disadvantages of the rural South had been outweighed by the conduciveness of urban conditions to communicable disease, since southern cities were slower to adopt public health and sanitation measures and public health spending per capita was extremely low. According to contemporary statistics, southern mortality was lowest for rural whites, who were virtually on par with white rural northerners. Reported rates of black rural and white urban mortality were in many cases within close range of each other, but black rural rates were underreported and likely were much higher. Health reformers believed that the most serious communicable disease threats—tuberculosis, typhoid, and venereal disease—were almost exclusively urban phenomena.[46]

Atlanta, the capital of the New South, provides a case in point. Atlanta's death rate in 1900 was 19.5 per thousand for blacks and 11.6 for whites. Tuberculosis and pneumonia deaths took a particularly heavy toll on black Atlantans, at a rate of 4.83 per thousand, 2.5 times the white rate. An astonishing 45 percent of black infants died before age one. Deplorable living conditions were largely responsible for the high rates of communicable disease and death: nearly half of Atlanta's black families lived in two- or four-room houses, and 20 percent of black homes were one-room alley houses that had originated as servants' quarters behind white homes and remained after business districts replaced residential areas. Residents obtained water from outside wells or street hydrants and shared outhouses with several other families. Black neighborhoods were often in hollows with the city's worst drainage, and standing pools of water and filth bred flies and mosquitoes. Atlanta's ten thousand surface privies were emptied only once every twelve days by the sanitary department, and many black neighbor-hoods had garbage collected less than monthly. In 1940, despite white business progressives' efforts to combat disease by extending sewer and water services to all Atlanta residents, 12 percent of Atlanta homes still lacked running water, 26 percent lacked indoor toilets, and 33 percent had no bathrooms.[47]

New Orleans was no better. In 1934, the social service department of the Flint-Goodrich Hospital and Tulane University conducted a study of 523 Negro households in a New Orleans neighborhood designated "probably the best for Negroes in the whole state." Investigators found most streets unpaved, "with such deep ruts that transit was impossible." New Orleans street department crews occasionally dumped refuse and tin cans to fill the ruts, sometimes in a layer three or four feet deep. Carleton Beals noted in the *Nation* that "although [the refuse] is supposed to have been put through incinerators, unburned garbage and dead animals are often uncovered." Black families rented one-room apartments in long, narrow tenements with three dozen units. A typical tenement had "four toilets in the front yard and running water in only six sinks in the lower gallery. There was no electric light or gas. Thirty-six such buildings in this district had been condemned. Only eight had actually been removed."[48]

The availability of health professionals and hospital beds also influenced racial and rural-urban health differentials. Many black doctors were unwilling to give up their civil rights to practice in the segregated South and, given the extreme difficulties of obtaining a medical education and setting up a practice, were unwilling to locate in rural communities that offered "little other than plenty of hard work and probably an early demise." In North Carolina, for example, fewer than one in ten black doctors served rural areas, where 70 percent of black residents lived in 1940. In 1945, black patients received medical care from some white physicians (who had separate waiting rooms or saw black patients one day of the week) as well as from the country's 8,000 black nurses, including 1,101 employed in public health. During the decade, the South had only 475 black public health nurses, 644 black dentists, and 2,018 black physicians, nearly all of them in cities.[49]

By around 1920, hospitals had become central to medical practice in the urban North. In the 1930s, American physicians still spent considerable time in their patients' homes, where four of ten doctor-patient contacts took place, as did half of doctor-attended births. But the era of the lone physician making house calls with his black bag lingered longer in rural and small-town America. In 1930, neither Mississippi nor the Carolinas had any maternity hospitals. Even in southern cities, home visits were still a major part of physician and nursing care through the 1950s. Despite the expansion of southern hospitals, automobiles remained central to medical practice, and physicians received higher gas ration cards during the war. Atlanta pediatrician Tom F. Davenport made as many as twenty-five house calls on Sundays and exhausted twenty cars while practicing between 1923 and 1980.[50]

Similarly, South Carolina public health nurse-midwife Maude Callen's missionary zeal pushed her to drive between three thousand and four thousand miles per month at her own expense. Black midwives practiced solely in homes, many of which could be reached only by trekking on foot down muddy, remote byways impassable by cars. Midwives attended approximately 80 percent of births to black southern women during the 1930s as well as a sizable number of white births. Yet the scattered populations of rural areas had to pay more for home medical and nursing care because professional services required greater time and travel expense. Patent medicines such as 666 and Hadacol were a frequent recourse of poor ailing southerners, promising cures for everything from malaria to "bad blood," to the great chagrin of many physicians. Constipation was a bane of many southerners, whose only option for relieving themselves was an often inconvenient outdoor privy. By the 1930s, hookworm infestation still plagued 11.2 percent of the southern population.[51]

DISPARITIES IN SOUTHERN HOSPITAL CARE

In the South, regionally distinctive factors of race, rurality, and methods of financing exacerbated the nationwide maldistribution of hospital beds. As the poorest region with a limited tax base and little credit or capital for construction, the South had approximately half as many hospital beds per capita as the rest of the country. All eight states with fewer than two beds per thousand population were southern. In addition, both hospitals and physicians were located primarily in urban areas with higher concentrations of patients and wealth, and much of the overwhelmingly rural South had neither hospitals nor good roads. Racial segregation further skewed access to hospital care for black patients, who suffered from higher rates of morbidity and mortality and were even poorer and more concentrated in rural areas than whites. Finally, the South's tradition of extremely conservative government spending, particularly on public welfare, resulted in proportionally fewer public hospital beds despite a larger proportion of citizens unable to pay for hospitalization. Especially true for the South was medical economist Michael M. Davis's observation that "in about 400 counties, the only local hospitals are proprietary institutions for paying patients only, and in many other places the voluntary nonprofit hospitals are too poorly financed to take more than 10 or 15 per cent of nonpaying patients." Proprietary facilities were also most likely to exclude black patients. Thus, the South had fewer beds overall; fewer government-owned beds to accommodate indigent patients; fewer large, efficient, modern facilities; and more small, obsolete hospitals.[52]

Rural hospital beds were paradoxically both scarce and underutilized, since they served the poorest populations, including disproportionate numbers of blacks, who could least afford hospital care. The majority of rural hospitals had fewer than twenty-five beds, and many were unregistered, proprietary facilities with fewer than ten beds. By 1940, the average net annual income of American farmers was $531 per capita, versus $1,273 for industrial workers. Only one-fifth of the nation's 6 million farms had gross incomes of more than $1,500, and one-third made less than $400 annually. The South's 3 million farms were the least mechanized and productive, with 80 percent grossing less than $1,000 yearly. The rural poor and unemployed were less likely to receive welfare services or free medical care, which was typically dispensed only in cities. The lack of electrification prevented the construction of hospitals in many rural areas.[53]

According to hospital architect Isadore Rosenfield, small, rural hospitals were "as a class inefficient, understaffed, the staff underpaid, ill-equipped to do the variety of things they are called upon to do, and living an economically uncertain existence.... There are exceptions, but as a class the small hospital leads a trying existence." The same was true of most southern and nearly all black hospitals. In rural areas with few resources and professional opportunities, poor schools, and a lower overall quality of life, hospitals struggled to recruit and retain adequate personnel, particularly trained physicians. The future of rural hospitals would remain in jeopardy as long as they were isolated from the mainstream of medical practice. Small rural hospitals were unlikely to become viable sources of care for medically underserved citizens unless they joined a coordinated system of hospitals and health centers that provided resources for both patients and professionals.[54]

Black hospitals shared many of the problems and characteristics of rural hospitals, and both were underutilized through the end of World War II. Yet existing scholarship on hospital segregation emphasizes the severe health consequences suffered by individuals who could not gain admittance to white-only facilities or overcrowded Jim Crow wards in biracial hospitals. Private black hospitals served a higher percentage of charity patients than did their white counterparts, resulting in perpetually strained budgets and an inability to modernize or even in many cases to make basic repairs. Poor facilities and equipment, in turn, compromised hospitals' ability to attract paying patients, although black hospitals were sometimes subsidized by city or county governments, especially where no black wards existed in local white hospitals. Such support proved critical, since small black hospitals had lower occupancy rates than larger white hospitals but depended on patient fees for a majority of their budgets.[55]

Throughout the United States, black patients were cared for primarily in all-black hospitals, whose number nationwide decreased from 202 in 1923 to 124 by 1944. Eighty-eight of these institutions were general hospitals, with 6,413 total beds; only 21 (including 12 in the South) were accredited by the American College of Surgeons, and only 16 were rated Grade A by the National Hospital Association and offered AMA-approved internships. In 1932, white-run hospitals that admitted blacks included 2,442 general and 568 special hospitals (not including mental institutions). The ratio of U.S. hospital beds per capita for whites was ten times the ratio for blacks; in the South, the racial discrepancy was smaller, but there were far fewer beds for both races. As Midian O. Bousfield noted in the *Journal of the National Medical Association*, the term *Negro hospital* was applied to institutions with varying racial combinations of ownership, administration, staff, and patients. Many hospitals serving black patients, such as the Negro unit of Atlanta's Grady Hospital, employed only white superintendents and physicians but hired black nurses. As Bousfield complained, even white northerners "found a hospital with all Negro nurses an acceptable institution, but to contemplate one with all Negro doctors, is anathema to them."[56]

In the South's sixteen states and the District of Columbia, 9.7 million African Americans were served by seventy-nine black hospitals, most of which were small, private, unaccredited, underequipped, and struggling to remain open. Black fraternal organizations ran facilities such as the modern, forty-two-bed Taborian Hospital constructed in Mound Bayou, Mississippi, in 1942 and the Mosaic State Templars' Hospital in Little Rock, Arkansas. Although occupancy rates were similar in black and white general hospitals, patient turnover (and thus revenue) was lower in black hospitals, with sixteen annual admissions per bed versus twenty in nonblack hospitals. In 1940, the AMA Council on Medical Education and Hospitals found that "Negroes do not utilize existing Negro hospitals to the same extent that the general population utilizes existing hospitals." This also held true for black beds in segregated biracial facilities. According to the Duke Endowment, occupancy rates in North Carolina's biracial general hospitals were much lower for black than for white beds, but large municipal hospitals that served black patients exclusively or in separate units had higher occupancy rates, reflecting the urban concentration of black health professionals and patients who could afford hospitalization as well as a higher level of tax-supported indigent care in larger cities.[57]

During the four decades before World War II, white-run southern hospitals evolved toward more inclusive and better-quality care for black patients. In 1910, 60 percent of southern hospitals reported admitting colored patients on some basis. Few private white hospitals admitted black patients at all, and government hospitals (North and South) that did not exclude blacks placed them in decrepit Jim Crow wards, often in the basement and usually with no separation by disease process, so that mothers of newborn infants might lay next to contagious cases. One of the earliest southern hospitals to provide care to blacks and whites in the same facility was Atlanta's Grady Hospital, which opened in 1892 with one operating room and one hundred beds split evenly between the two races. The facility honored New South proselyte Henry Grady's final wish of establishing a municipal charity hospital to serve the poor of both races. After Emory University acquired the Atlanta College of Medicine in 1915 and Grady became the teaching hospital for the Emory School of Medicine, the city built a new complex that featured separate buildings for each race connected by a tunnel under Butler Street. Each side had its own clinics, nurses' quarters, and emergency rooms, and Atlantans referred to the bifurcated facility, completed in 1918, as "the Gradies." Black physicians were barred from virtually all white-run U.S. hospitals, including Grady, the city's only facility caring for indigent black patients. Atlanta's three small private black hospitals provided only eighty-seven beds for paying patients of black doctors. In Birmingham, Alabama, and other communities, all available black beds were on charity wards in white-run hospitals that were not open to black physicians.[58]

After World War I, black patients began to enjoy improved access to care in southern public hospitals. In 1922, a young nurse, Irene Dixon, visited the new Louisville City Hospital and described it as "a four hundred bed hospital and well equipped (of course this includes colored patients too)." Her parenthetical observation marked the growing acceptance of black patients in municipal hospitals and the slow improvement in the quality of these facilities, often the result of pressure from black physicians and civic leaders. In the early 1930s, after persistent lobbying from black doctors, Knoxville, Tennessee, became the first southern city to build a public black hospital unit where black physicians could admit both private and public patients. Homer G. Phillips Hospital in St. Louis was the first truly modern, municipal, freestanding black hospital. At the laying of the hospital's cornerstone in 1933, Numa P. G. Adams, the first black dean of the Howard University College of Medicine, assessed the facility's significance in light of the limitations of most black hospitals: "I know the tragedies and disasters that must at times result from inadequate equipment, insufficient personnel, inaccessibility to necessary laboratory aids and the lack of a medical library when some important fact is needed and no one at hand has it. I wonder how many in this audience can appreciate what a blessing this hospital will be, and in how many important ways it will serve not only this community but also the whole country as well."[59]

In the long battle over who should determine hospital staff privileges, the civil rights of black physicians to utilize public facilities would for decades remain subordinate to the states' rights rationale of white government officials and hospital administrators. In 1940, more than one-fifth of all U.S. general hospitals still had racially exclusive admitting policies, and all but a handful of northern public hospitals excluded black physicians from their staffs. In 1943, New York's Sydenham Hospital became the nation's first voluntary hospital to embrace the full integration of its staff at all levels. In 1946, Sydenham's biracial board of trustees hired Jean Murray Smith as the first African American hospital administrator at a nonsegregated facility. In response to persistent lobbying by black physicians, other hospitals in New York and around the country subsequently adopted nondiscrimination policies in hiring and granting admitting rights.[60]

At the state level, there was little disparity in the supply of southern hospital beds for blacks and whites, reflecting the regionwide underdevelopment of the health-care system, which was at very close to ground zero in comparison to the urban Northeast. In the ten states and the District of Columbia where the overall supply of hospital beds was lowest, the ratio was less than one bed per thousand fewer for blacks than for the general population, and in only three (the District, Florida, and Louisiana) was the disparity between the black and general population ratios greater than one bed per thousand. Merely tracking the changes in aggregate hospital bed ratios can be extremely misleading, however, since they were also influenced by public-private ownership, segregation, provision for indigents, geographic distribution, and occupancy rates. The most important factor determining access to hospital facilities was the patient's ability to pay. Even health economists who wanted to improve the distribution of medical care emphasized the futility of building new rural facilities that farm families could not afford to use.[61]

THE TELESCOPING OF AMERICAN HEALTH DISPARITIES

A 1942 *Time* magazine article on "Negro Health" remarked on the irony that "the biggest health boost of any group in the U.S. population has been enjoyed in recent years by Negroes—and it still leaves Negroes far worse off than whites." The greatest racial differences in mortality resulted from tuberculosis, pellagra, malaria, syphilis, nephritis, influenza, pneumonia, and diseases of maternity and infancy. Tuberculosis, the leading cause of death for all Americans during the 1910s, killed blacks at twice the rate of whites in 1910; by 1940, the black rate was four times the white rate. By 1930, pellagra killed blacks at ten times the rate of whites. Why were racial disparities worsening even as overall black health was improving?[62]

American racial, regional, and rural-urban health disparities can be compared to a telescope whose sections represent various demographic combinations, such as rural black southerners or urban white northerners. The telescope was compact at the turn of the twentieth century, when morbidity and mortality rates were comparatively high among all groups. If the telescope were extended to its full length to indicate improving health status over the next four decades, the section representing the group with the least improvement would remain closest to the origin in 1900, and the group with the lowest rates by 1940 would be farthest out. The healthiest group in 1900 was rural whites, who largely avoided the deadly consequences of rapid urbanization and immigration that accompanied America's Industrial Revolution. The health of middle- and upper-class urban whites was protected even in cities by higher living standards and better access to medical care. African Americans, North and South, whether in cities or on farms, suffered the highest mortality rates.[63]

In the four decades before World War II, southerners and rural dwellers lost ground relative to white northerners. Between 1900 and 1940, the death rate declined 45 percent in cities but only 29 percent in rural areas. The average American life expectancy increased from forty-five to sixty, but the increase was eighteen years for city dwellers and only eleven years for rural residents. The health status of urban whites had advanced most as improved sanitation, modern public water and sewer systems, vaccinations, and better-quality, less crowded housing largely ameliorated the sources of big-city communicable diseases. Rural northerners trailed their urban counterparts only slightly, while rural westerners and southerners had begun to suffer more from diseases once associated exclusively with urban slums—typhoid fever, dysentery, typhus, trachoma, conjunctivitis, impetigo, tuberculosis, and pneumonia. Typhoid and diphtheria had been largely brought under control in most of the United States by 1920, and tuberculosis deaths had been reduced from 200 to 55 per 100,000 population since 1904. Yet these advances were slowest to reach the rural South, where preventable disease mortality rates stagnated or even increased and rates of vaccination remained low. By 1940, rural dwellers had lost the health advantages they enjoyed over urbanites in 1900. Rural deaths remained underreported by as much as 10 percent nationally and by even more in the South and West. The progress of black mortality and life expectancy is difficult to track accurately, since the states where most blacks lived did not join the U.S. Census death registry until the 1920s. During the 1930s, when figures are more accurate, the black mortality rate decreased 16 percent and the white rate declined by 4 percent, yet blacks could expect to live eleven years less than whites.[64]

By the late 1930s, epidemiologists had observed distinct regional patterns of increased incidence and virulence of tuberculosis and diphtheria. Martin Frobisher of the Johns Hopkins Department of Epidemiology argued that diphtheria was moving southward and that "the gravis type of diphtheria is definitely on the increase in Virginia and Alabama but not in the North." Frobisher, a former senior PHS bacteriologist, noted that "the increasing prevalence of virulent strains of the germ in the South seems significant in view of the decreasing prevalence or entire absence of these organisms in the North." In 1890, the urban tuberculosis rate had been 60 percent higher than the rural rate; by 1930, it was 5 percent *lower*. By 1935, the highest TB mortality rates were recorded in predominantly rural states: three in the Southwest with large Native American populations and seven in the South—Texas, Louisiana, Mississippi, Alabama, Tennessee, Kentucky, and Virginia. Southern state governments spent only one-fifth as much per tuberculosis death on TB control and hospitalization as did those in the Northeast, and the South devoted more of its TB spending to field services, which were less expensive than hospitalization.[65]

The PHS reported in 1941 that the vast majority of cases of reportable communicable diseases of poverty occurred among the southern population. With approximately one-third of the U.S. population, the South reported 96 percent of all U.S. cases of malaria, pellagra, and typhus fever, more than 80 percent of bacillary and amebic dysentery, 82 percent of influenza, and between 50 and

60 percent of diphtheria, septic sore throat, and typhoid. With increases in the percentage of rural deaths from infectious childhood diseases, conditions associated with maternity and infancy, and other preventable causes, these ailments came to be regarded as "rural diseases."[66]

A major cause of increased disease rates in the rural South was the sharp decline in living standards and the growing problem of overcrowding brought on by the severe agricultural crisis. Although rural areas had low population density overall, intensifying poverty had by 1940 caused "serious overcrowding" of more than 1.5 persons per room in 16 percent of dwellings on farms versus only 6 percent of those in cities. Only one in nine urban homes needed major repairs, compared to one in three rural farm homes, and the U.S. Department of Agriculture concluded in 1945 that 51 percent of tenant farmers' dwellings were "beyond repair." Moreover, many rural homes remained without adequate sources of clean water or sewage disposal. Even in North Carolina, where the hookworm campaign had originated and been most successful, more than one-tenth of children under age fifteen remained infested in 1940. America's rural families had been healthier in 1900 than they were by 1940, with southern and black farmers suffering most from the deterioration in rural living conditions.[67]

In 1948, Frederick Mott and Milton Roemer wrote in *Rural Health and Medical Care* that "rural America has become a casualty of the industrial revolution." This statement held most tragically true for the least urban racial groups, blacks and American Indians. Although the Great Migration of blacks to cities had already commenced, 92 percent of Native Americans still lived in rural areas, with three-fifths on farms. The industrialization of farming, particularly the introduction of the mechanical cotton picker and the shift to cash-crop agriculture, drove scores of southerners off the land and intensified the poverty of those who stayed. Yet the myth of the rosy-cheeked, clean-living country dweller persisted. Rural sociologists Homer Hitt and Alvin Bertrand observed in their 1947 report, *The Social Aspects of Hospital Planning in Louisiana*, "Notwithstanding the well-known scarcity of medical facilities and personnel in farm areas, Louisiana's rural people definitely live longer and enjoy better health than their urban fellows. In 1940 the death rate in rural areas of the state was 8.7 per 1000 as compared with 13.7 in urban territory." The residents of cities with populations between 2,500 and 10,000 recorded the highest mortality rates, while "the rural whites and Negroes are in the most favored position in all stages of life.... The student of mortality wonders how great this comparative advantage of rural areas would become, were the same opportunities for medical care already present in urban areas extended to rural people."[68]

Hitt and Bertrand's conclusions were likely based on less accurate reporting of black rural deaths, although death registration had improved in the decade since Puffer's study. Louisiana was, however, exceptional, since its public health and state charity hospital systems were among the South's most progressive. Moreover, the heavily black workforce on Louisiana's sugar and rice plantations (as well as in the rice fields of neighboring Arkansas and Texas) were better paid and enjoyed a moderately higher standard of living than those on cotton plantations. Better nutrition, window screens, and the ability to afford quinine and medical treatment significantly reduced the reservoir of malaria infection, despite the conduciveness of Louisiana's environmental conditions to breeding large numbers of anopheles mosquitoes. Therefore, although southern blacks generally died of malaria and pellagra at disproportionately high rates, the disparity was less pronounced in Louisiana.[69]

Hitt and Bertrand would probably have agreed with Johns Hopkins physician Howard Kelly's characterization of northern cities, where vice and disease were "bred in the pestilential hot house atmosphere of dark, dirty, ill-ventilated homes, which induces abnormal cravings in ill-conditioned bodies." But by the onset of the depression, that description more accurately fit the destitute rural environments of the South, as documented in the litany of journalistic and scholarly studies of southern poverty by such notables as James Agee and Walker Evans, Hortense Powdermaker, John Dollard, E. Franklin Frazier, W. E. B. Du Bois, Arthur Raper, Howard Odum, and Gunnar Myrdal. Fisk University president Charles S. Johnson's sociological study of black southern tenancy, *Shadow of the Plantation*, had originated as a profile of Macon County, Alabama, to guide the Rosenwald Foundation's syphilis control pilot program, which immediately preceded the Tuskegee Study of Untreated Syphilis in the Negro Male. Though sympathetic to the plight of poor southerners and egalitarian in their racial sentiments, these authors commented on the frequency of what Johnson termed "social disorganization": illegitimacy, incest, promiscuity, and overall breakdown of the traditional family structure as well as high rates of illiteracy, venereal disease, violent crime, substance abuse, and other illegal activities.[70]

Although racism further compounded the disadvantages of rural poverty and isolation for black southerners, their health ultimately suffered most in urban environments, which received 6.5 million black migrants from the rural South between 1920 and 1970. Urban blacks, who comprised 8 percent of southerners and 47 percent of African Americans in 1940, represented a disproportionate share of morbidity and mortality for these groups. The Great Migration to northern cities worsened mortality rates among urban blacks, at least initially. Deaths from tuberculosis increased during the 1920s, particularly among blacks in northern Illinois.[71]

Urbanization in both the North and the South was far more detrimental to black infants' health than to white infants despite the benefits of rural-to-urban migration such as higher income and proximity to health care. Economists William J. Collins and Melissa A. Thomasson have examined the influence of income, urbanization, women's education, physicians per capita, and southern versus nonsouthern residence on the racial gap in infant mortality rates between 1920 and 1970. They conclude that the differential rates of mortality for black and white infants resulted from increased rates of cigarette smoking and exposure to air pollution; increased costs of housing and health care exacerbated by racial discrimination; the concentration of blacks in crowded, unsanitary ghettos that promoted the spread of communicable disease; adjustment to a new disease environment; separation from extended family support networks; and employment in hazardous and debilitating industrial jobs.[72]

Maternal and infant health illustrates particularly well the telescoping of health disparities among black southerners as living conditions and access to health care improved more rapidly for whites and northerners. In New York City during the 1890s, children under age five accounted for 40 percent of deaths. In *Shame of the Cities*, Jacob Riis documented the abandonment of 170 live and 72 dead infants in the New York streets. Half a century later, rising incomes, expanded access to health care, and significant state and local funding for maternal and infant health had dramatically improved morbidity and mortality for white northern mothers and infants. By 1942, 87 percent of urban whites gave birth in hospitals with doctors in attendance, compared to 51 percent of rural whites and only 11 percent of rural nonwhites.[73]

Black women aged between fifteen and forty-four nationwide died more often from complications related to pregnancy and childbirth than from any other cause except tuberculosis. Of all African American infants born in 1940, 8.8 percent died before age one, comparable to the white rate twenty-five years earlier. America's black women were 2.5 times more likely to die in childbirth than were white women. The lethal combination of racism, poverty, and geographic isolation accounted for high morbidity and mortality among rural black women of childbearing age and their babies. Poor rural white and urban black women also suffered, but not to the same extremes, since these groups had at least limited access to obstetrical and pediatric care from health departments and either white country doctors or black physicians and hospitals in town.[74]

Sickness and death associated with maternity and infancy remained the single most pressing health issue for African American women, especially the 50 percent who lived in the rural South. In his 1938 study of rural Mississippi black children, Hildrus A. Poindexter concluded that "the worth while racial potentialities of Negro infants born and reared in rural southern environment are not sufficiently well developed at chronological maturity to make them either a local community asset or prepare them for respectable social adjustment elsewhere." Moreover, he predicted that "very few of the rural Negroes born and reared in the southern states become healthy adults." In the South in 1941, only one-third of all births took place in hospitals, compared to three-quarters of nonsouthern births, and midwives delivered 23 percent of southern babies but only 1.5 percent of nonsouthern babies. In 1938, toxemia killed women in southern states at rates from 50 to 150 percent higher than in the rest of the United States, largely as a consequence of lack of medical care. Hospital delivery was feasible mainly for urban whites, but even poor rural whites were far more likely than their black neighbors to give birth with physicians in attendance: only 4 percent of rural white deliveries were attended by midwives in 1942, compared to 65 percent of rural nonwhite births. Since most southern hospitals did not admit blacks and many rural counties had no hospitals at all, rural black mothers and infants benefited least from the medical advances available from trained professionals in modern hospitals.[75]

In summary, the telescoping of American health disparities between 1900 and 1940 left African Americans and rural southern whites in poverty and disease-promoting living conditions that resembled those of tenement-dwelling, impoverished northern immigrants at the turn of the century. As the health status of these populations lagged further behind the rest of the nation, health disparities would have major implications for the formation of early national health policy during the New Deal and World War II.

chapter 2

THE NEW DEAL

IN HEALTH

Although the U.S. Public Health Service (PHS) had begun to make inroads into the infectious diseases of poverty that beleaguered the South's growing urban population and its shifting rural areas, the farm crisis of the 1920s, the catastrophic Mississippi River flood of 1927, and the hardening of segregation amid post–World War I racial unrest worsened the plight of many of the region's most vulnerable residents. Cotton prices dropped from a high of forty cents per pound during the war to five cents per pound by the end of the 1920s, and both rural and black health initiatives stagnated in the areas hit hard and early. After visiting the cotton mill towns of Gaston County, North Carolina, in 1934, Martha Gelhorn, a field agent for the Federal Emergency Recovery Administration, expressed the fear that conditions for poor rural southerners had declined over the past generation: "The children are growing up in terrible surroundings; dirt, disease, overcrowding, undernourishment. Often their parents were farm people, who at least had air and enough food. This cannot be said for the children." According to local doctors, conditions were so dire that it seemed "as if the people were degenerating before your eyes: the children are worse mentally and physically than their parents." One black physician observed that the depression had caused "millions of whites [to experience] the mental and physical uncertainties which have characterized the existence of the Negro in this country for two generations." During the early 1930s, both private and public funding of health programs decreased, and personal income and spending for health services reached all-time lows. Racial and regional differences in American health care widened, but the crisis also promoted greater cooperation between private-practice physicians and public health professionals.[1]

INVITING BLACKS TO THE NEW DEAL TABLE

The National Urban League's *Opportunity* magazine upheld the PHS as one the few federal agencies that, even before 1933, "acknowledged the exclusion of the Negro from the normal stream of community and national life by employing Negro specialists to promote programs among Negroes to apprise the agency of the impact of social problems upon them." Once the New Deal began, the PHS's early focus on southern, rural, and black health was expanded by an interlocking directorate of New Deal officials, southern progressive activists and politicians, black intellectuals and reformers, and representatives of philanthropies interested in improving southern conditions.[2]

After Franklin Roosevelt's inauguration in 1933, three key officials of the Rosenwald Fund (president Edwin R. Embree, trustee Will Alexander, and director of research Charles S. Johnson) obtained FDR's enthusiastic approval for a plan to ensure that black southerners were included in federal programs. Based on previous experience with using "Negro specialists" in PHS and Rosenwald health projects, the fund provided salary support for an adviser on Negro affairs who would advocate on behalf of black interests within the administration. Secretary of the interior Harold Ickes, whose department oversaw Freedmen's Hospital and Howard University, was "the leading standard-bearer for social change in the early Roosevelt years, breaking the segregationist ice in the Interior Department and the Public Works Administration, which he also headed." In 1934, Clark Foreman, the young white grandson of the founder of the *Atlanta Constitution* who had worked under Alexander at the Commission on Interracial Cooperation and for Embree at the Rosenwald Fund, became the first federal racial adviser under Ickes. Foreman went on to serve as the lead editor of the *Report on the Economic Conditions of the South* and as president of the Southern Conference for Human Welfare.[3]

Twenty-six-year-old Robert C. Weaver, a black Harvard economics graduate, soon joined Foreman as a racial adviser in the Department of Interior and called attention to the ways residential segregation undermined public health. As the Roosevelt administration's premier adviser on Negro affairs, Weaver fought discrimination in housing, education, and employment and went on to become the first head of the Department of Housing and Urban Development under Lyndon Johnson. Other federal agencies soon appointed their own racial advisers, and the post became a fixture of New Deal social welfare programs. By 1943, blacks served in thirty senior federal posts and comprised 18 percent of all federal employees, and an internal Roosevelt administration memo reported that "in many important agencies, more than 50 per cent of the Negroes employed were in clerical, administrative and fiscal positions." Historian Karen Ferguson emphasizes the New Deal's departure from public policy's long-standing blindness to black needs, as evidenced in the incorporation of talented black professionals to administer programs that implicitly recognized blacks' rights to adequate income, housing, food, health care, and recreation, all of which provided an extraordinary boost to the civil rights movement.[4]

New disease-specific foundations also hired Negro advisers, including the National Foundation for Infantile Paralysis (NFIP), which Roosevelt founded in 1938 with his law partner, Basil O'Connor. At the same time that Roosevelt's presidency directed new attention to African American health disparities as well as child health and welfare, the number of polio victims was on the rise, with Roosevelt their most prominent representative. Although Roosevelt had founded the well-known NFIP polio rehabilitation center in Warm Springs, the facility abided by Georgia segregation law and accepted only white patients. Roosevelt was caught among conflicting loyalties to southern Democrats, whose support he was actively cultivating; black voters, who had helped offset his unpopularity with southern whites at the polls but objected to the exclusion of black polio patients; and the fledgling NFIP, which was trying to mount a national campaign to support polio treatment and research to find a cure. Although the neglect of black polio patients threatened to become a political embarrassment for Roosevelt and the NFIP, the organization stayed within the bounds of segregation and did not integrate Warm Springs until after World War II. In 1941, however, it joined with the Rosenwald Fund to establish a new treatment, research, and professional training facility for blacks at Tuskegee, Alabama, only eighty miles away. The polio center was based at the orthopedic surgery division of the John A. Andrew Memorial Hospital, which had pioneered in the treatment of black crippled children. *Opportunity* reported, "The beautiful, modern, scientifically equipped building that was thus made possible gave hope to many poor victims who previously had very little or none." The facility featured a gymnasium with massage facilities, whirlpool baths, electrotherapy machines, a large heated pool, and a special tank for the treatment of small children. In 1944, the NFIP hired Charles H. Bynum to head a new department of "Negro Activities," through which he increased fund-raising among African Americans and initiated the first March of Dimes posters to feature black children. He also pushed the NFIP leadership to promote more equitable and inclusive policies, including the replacement of racially separate local chapters with interracial fund drives. Therefore, in the NFIP as in federal health policy, Roosevelt pursued deluxe Jim Crow measures designed to answer blacks' growing demands to receive the benefits of modern medical treatment without disturbing the hornet's nest of segregation.[5]

One of the signature features of deluxe Jim Crow policy was its generation of unintended consequences, particularly the gradual undermining of segregation and empowerment of minorities as both recipients and shapers of federal health programs. Although the concept of a "Negro director" within state and local social welfare agencies in part reflected the ongoing exile of minorities from mainstream society, black bureaucrats "shaped federal activity to help bring some [blacks] from the social, economic, and political margins in ways never intended or dreamt of by white New Deal administrators." Deluxe Jim Crow health policy, like segregation as a whole, was a dynamic organism that was constantly being contested and reconfigured from every direction. Its central irony was that white policymakers, thinking they could give an inch toward equality to shore up and preserve segregation, unwittingly opened the way for black and white liberal reformers to take a mile toward integration.[6]

The first New Deal programs to have a major impact on southern black and rural health were the public works projects that dramatically improved sanitation and provided clean water in both urban and rural communities, directly and indirectly benefiting southerners of all races. In 1933, 86 percent of rural households lacked sanitary toilets, and only 3 percent had flush toilets. In just over five years, the Works Progress Administration (WPA) completed 11,200 miles of water mains, more than 20,000 miles of new or reconditioned sewer lines, and more than 1,100 new water and sewage treatment plants. In thirty-eight states and Puerto Rico, federal programs had constructed nearly 3 million sanitary privies by 1942, nearly two-thirds of these privies in the South. WPA sanitation projects drastically reduced the incidence of typhoid and dysentery in rural southern communities, which were also the primary beneficiaries of PHS and WPA malaria control programs. To curtail mosquito breeding, the WPA drained several million acres of swamp, and PHS officers sprayed mosquito-ridden areas with larvicides from airplanes and on foot. During World War II, the PHS used the powerful new pesticide DDT to control malaria around military bases, which were disproportionately located in the South.[7]

Despite severely limited access to hospitals and physicians, rates of death and disease among black and white southerners fell significantly during the second third of the twentieth century as a consequence of improvements in housing, sanitation, nutrition, and standards of living as well as rising income and levels of education. Deluxe Jim Crow health policy was most successful in building and expanding the South's health and sanitation infrastructure and less successful in promoting direct federal sponsorship of expanded health services, which carried a greater threat of federal intervention in both segregation and the health care market than did public works programs. But the New Deal still marked the beginning of a concerted federal effort to bridge racial and regional health disparities by improving and extending public health and medical care services.

In a 1938 report on the National Health Conference, surgeon general Thomas Parran stated, "At the present time, ... our proven ability to prevent disease exceeds greatly our proven ability to control other causes of poverty. . . . Medicine and public health, therefore, should lead economics, rather than follow it." The report concluded that "certainly one-third and perhaps one-half of the population is too poor to afford the full cost of adequate medical care." The unevenness and unpredictability of medical costs meant that fewer than 10 percent of the population could afford the full cost of care. Lower- and even middle-class people who became ill typically delayed treatment as long as possible (thereby reducing their chances of recovery and increasing the cost), relied on gifts or loans to meet the full costs, or defaulted on payment, which was particularly common for doctor and surgery bills. Catastrophic or long-term illness could easily drive families into bankruptcy. During the 1930s, health-care expenses became the leading cause of indebtedness. When the demand for free care overwhelmed private physicians and charities, they began to request financial help from welfare departments. As more doctors found themselves unable to collect fees, some softened in their attitudes toward government-sponsored health programs.[8]

The first New Deal medical care programs operated from 1933 to 1935 under the Federal Emergency Relief Agency (FERA), which served the unemployed and their families in 261 centers and 40 transient camps nationwide. It provided $1 million to the PHS for rural health in 1934, and, along with the WPA and Public Works Administration (PWA), FERA funded public health nursing and other services for city and state health departments. Medical clinics were an integral feature of services to transient individuals and families; the clinics were operated by local medical students in Memphis and by a full-time physician and staff in New Orleans. FERA also enabled transients to receive hospitalization and professional medical attention. The centers operated separate registration units for blacks, which often did not open until well after the white units were established. In Birmingham, local black leaders repeatedly petitioned FERA director Harry Hopkins for a bureau "staffed with Negro personnel." M. O. Bousfield reported, however, that "in the F.E.R.A. where fine relationships have been attained between Negro and white physicians, the Negro physician is invariably participating in the use of these funds." Negro units had been established in all southern cities by mid-1934, but blacks could generally expect only a short reprieve from homelessness and hunger, not the full complement of programs available at the white camps.[9]

In 1935, President Roosevelt announced that "the Federal Government must and shall quit this business of relief," and his administration shifted its emphasis from direct relief to work relief by discontinuing FERA and creating the WPA. The Social Security Act and the Farm Security Administration (FSA) birthed longer-lasting, more influential health programs that favored the South more heavily and treated blacks more fairly than had FERA. In the midst of both programs was sociologist Michael M. Davis, a native Virginian who had become an expert in health-care financing and played a key role during the late 1920s and early 1930s on the Committee on the Costs of Medical Care (CCMC). Davis was a confidant of Parran and widely known and respected in medical and public health circles across the country and political spectrum. He directed medical services for the Rosenwald Fund from 1928 to 1939 and was mindful that blacks represented 30 percent of Americans unable to pay for health services. Davis worked closely with Isadore S. Falk and Rufus Rorem on the CCMC to promote prepaid group insurance and later became a standard-bearer for the Wagner health plan and national health insurance. The CCMC's report, *Medical Care for the American People*, introduced radical solutions such as voluntary health insurance, group medical practice, and government aid for indigent care, but the committee's members failed to apply its recommendations as public policy or to convince the framers of the Social Security Act to include health insurance as an entitlement. The CCMC did, however, find a bully pulpit beginning in 1935 in the Resettlement Administration (RA) and its successor, the FSA, whose group plans to provide affordable health care to farm families complemented the PHS's existing rural health initiatives.[10]

Davis served as a consultant to the FSA during the 1930s; chair of the Committee on Medical Research in Economics during the 1940s; a member of the Federal Hospital Council, which advised the surgeon general on the administration of the Hill-Burton hospital construction program; and executive chair of the Committee for the Nation's Health during the Truman administration. In all these roles, he made remarkable progress in enlisting private and public support to extend medical care to rural southerners, with special attention to black needs. Davis was a towering figure in the world of health financing and public health reform, acting as a broker during often tense confrontations among representatives of private philanthropy, black organizations, organized medicine and health industry groups, federal agencies, and advocates of socialized medicine.[11]

The FSA was headed by Will Alexander, a Rosenwald Fund trustee, who worked closely with Davis to include health care in the rural rehabilitation program. The RA and FSA officers were up-front with Davis from the beginning about using the cooperative health associations as an "experimental opportunity" and a step toward broader national health care reform. The PHS assigned R. C. Williams, Frederick Mott, and Milton Roemer to the FSA: all were prominent in federal and public health reform circles, and all advocated national health insurance. Their research appeared regularly in public health and social welfare journals, including the *American Journal of Public Health*, *Survey Graphic*, *Public Health Reports*, the *Journal of Negro Education*, and the *Journal of the National Medical Association*. The strong preexisting connections from the southern and black health campaigns created an intimate fraternity of progressive medical policy experts and reformers with close ties to the PHS and private philanthropy, especially the Rosenwald Fund, Duke Endowment, Rockefeller International Health Division, and Commonwealth Fund.[12]

BLACK PHYSICIANS AND NEW DEAL PUBLIC HEALTH

Outside the FSA, PHS, and other racially moderate New Deal agencies, many white physicians, both within and outside the South, did not consider their black counterparts to be legitimate representatives of the medical profession. Black physician Lawrence Greely Brown raised this issue in a 1942 address to the New Jersey State Medical Society. To bar blacks from membership, white medical societies cited the "old-fashion, disorganized home practice" of black medics and accorded them "a status comparable to that of quacks, charlatans, and even laymen." W. A. Cleland, president of the National Medical Association, insisted that such attitudes were based on racial prejudice, not a fair judgment of black doctors' professional qualifications. "I admit that as a group we now occupy an inferior position which is not wholly of our making," he allowed, "but this does not indicate to me that we are inferior." Membership in a local affiliate was a prerequisite for national membership in the American Medical Association (AMA). African American physicians outside the South could meet this requirement, but other than Arkansas, none of the AMA's southern state affiliates, including the District of Columbia chapter, admitted black candidates. Barred from white medical societies, black medics founded their own, such as North Carolina's Old North State Medical Society, established in 1887 as the nation's first black state medical society.[13]

The AMA's laissez-faire policy on discrimination would remain virtually unchallenged until 1947, when the organization denied membership to Charles Drew, renowned for his work in developing blood plasma banking, because the District of Columbia Medical Society did not accept blacks. By 1956, Louisiana was the only southern state medical society that had not admitted black members, although some, such as Mississippi's, still did not grant blacks full voting membership and North Carolina barred black members from the society's social functions. Organized nursing integrated in 1951, and the American Dental Association banned racial discrimination by constituent societies in 1962. Not until 1968 did the AMA adopt an amendment banning racial discrimination in membership and barring delegates from state affiliates with discriminatory membership policies.[14]

Notwithstanding the racial divide in organized medicine, southern black physicians, like their white counterparts, were trained to focus their attention on individual patients rather than to consider the broader social context of disease. Black doctors were also members of an African American reform elite that worked for but not always with the black poor. Black physicians shared a caste position with their patients and the communities they served but were separated by class, education, and professional status. Physicians were prominent among the black leaders who transformed southern cities such as Atlanta in the 1930s: according to Ferguson, "Their project as self-defined race leaders thus was not only to agitate for civil rights or economic opportunity, but also to continue to 'lift' the majority of the black community to the perspective and behavior they considered necessary for inclusion and full citizenship. Therefore, while these leaders sought to democratize the South through mass action, theirs was not an egalitarian movement."[15]

During the New Deal, black doctors became more intensely involved in social and professional activism, and many criticized federal, state, and local health agencies for their failure to reduce death and disease substantially among blacks. The leadership of civil rights and health reform was often intertwined, as in the career of Boisey O. Barnes of Wilson, North Carolina, who combined private practice with public health work and efforts to promote racial uplift. Barnes, an obstetrician, was Wilson's only black specialist. As president of the Wilson Negro Civic Club, Barnes intervened on behalf of blacks assigned by the Unemployment Compensation Office to work on local strawberry farms. After the unemployment commissioner ruled in 1938 that "the moral, housing conditions and sanitation are no worse than the living condition [*sic*] from which [the workers] are sent," Barnes requested that the State Board of Public Welfare investigate the "general hygienic set up of the [farms'] water supply, sewage disposal, living and eating facilities." He expressed outrage at the poor sanitation, low wages, and low morale endured by the pickers. Many Wilson blacks "have refused to go and have lost their compensation not because they did not want to work but because of the terrible living conditions they had to encounter at the strawberry farms." In response to Barnes's request, William R. Johnson, the board's field agent on Negro work, investigated the strawberry farms in 1939. Johnson replied to the Civic Club that he had found conditions there "very much as stated by your committee" but added that nothing could be done for the current season. The commissioner of public welfare had suggested, however, that prior to the 1940 season, farm owners should be notified "that unless living conditions are improved with regards to housing and indiscriminate herding of workers counties will be urged to refuse to send pickers." The Department of Public Welfare files contain no evidence indicating whether the strawberry pickers' plight improved as the result of Barnes's and the Civic Club's actions.[16]

The situation in Wilson County was comparable to that of rural blacks across the South who attempted to better their living and working conditions through a combination of grassroots organizing and appeals to state and federal New Deal authorities. In Louisiana's sugarcane fields, for example, one thousand black members of the Louisiana Farmers' Union (LFU) registered their dissatisfaction with low wages, questionable weighing practices, the requirement that they spend their wages on overpriced goods at company stores, and the prohibition on growing their own food. LFU agent Peggy Dallet "refuted planters' contentions that the provision of free housing and medical care compensated for low pay, saying that in most cases accommodations were not fit for human habitation and sick people paid their own doctors' bills." At the late 1937 and early 1938 wage-setting hearings of the Sugar Section of the Agricultural Adjustment Administration (AAA), the testimony of LFU agents combined with a letter-writing campaign by LFU members to convince the U.S. Department of Agriculture to raise minimum compensation for sugar workers from sixty-five to seventy-five cents per ton, with safeguards to prohibit growers from using unjust means to reduce wages as well as requirements that producers provide laborers with customary benefits such as a "habitable house, a suitable garden plot with facilities for its cultivation, pasture for livestock, medical attention, and similar incidentals." These hard-won concessions remained in effect for the next four years, during which LFU members worked diligently to ensure that planters abided by the new rules: nearly four hundred wage claims were submitted to the AAA in August and September 1939, with AAA subsidies withheld from planters until the claims were settled. After wartime wage increases, compensation had nearly tripled by the 1949 season.[17]

Whether in the North Carolina strawberry fields or on the Louisiana sugarcane plantations, medical care was a primary need for all rural southern blacks. In addition to his social activism, Barnes combined private practice with public health work at infant, maternal, and venereal disease clinics for the Wilson County Health Department. Although weekly attendance at VD clinics had increased tenfold between 1932 and 1940, Barnes estimated that 60 percent of black residents of the city of Wilson remained infected with venereal disease. He lamented that "it is hard to convince the average Negro that he has a devastating disease and that therefore he needs treatment for two years" with arsenic and bismuth, which were used to cure syphilis before the advent of penicillin. Barnes's observation reflected the extreme difficulty of syphilis treatment for patients, who had to endure an extremely long series of often painful and potentially risky injections, and doctors, who could easily inflict damage on or even poison their patients without careful long-term observation and follow-up. Wilson's black doctors were more likely than white physicians to work at the health department, and among black physicians nationally, 24 percent worked in maternal and infant clinics and 38 percent were employed in tuberculosis clinics. Black doctors probably felt both a greater sense of responsibility for the predominantly black clientele of public health clinics and more financial pressure to work for the county than did whites with more lucrative private practices.[18]

Public health work offered black doctors a degree of security against the vicissitudes of private practice. Before the advent of broad-based government health care and welfare programs for the poor, most physicians of both races participated in an informal, community-based system of charity care. But African American physicians had less control within this system than their white counterparts. James Slade, an Edenton, North Carolina, pediatrician who began practicing in the late 1950s just as segregation was waning, explained some of the limitations he faced as a black practitioner:

> A lot of patients we took care of free. I started practicing before the days of Medicaid and Medicare. We never turned anyone away because of inability to pay. In fact, we didn't even ask them to pay until we had already treated them. A lot of them told us, "See you next week." In the larger cities, you might send them to the charity clinic. But in Chowan County, you're it. You may send them to another doctor, but that's not going to go over too good. Either you treat them, or they don't get treated. You didn't have the option of sending the patient to charity care unless you were willing to give it. Because there was nobody else to give it.... It's a lot more difficult for the black physician to turn away the poor people, particularly the blacks. If the black physician starts turning away his own people, he gets into all sorts of trouble. He's not going to attract a lot of non-blacks just because he turns away blacks, and he puts himself in a bad position with his own race, because people say, "Now he's a big shot, he won't even see us." Basically, he's taught not to reject his own.

As he struggled to attract pediatric patients early in his career, Slade agreed to supervise a children's clinic in neighboring Plymouth County. He estimated that 20 percent of his income came from the clinics he staffed for Chowan and surrounding counties. Although the compensation was much less than the rates Slade earned in private practice, public health provided a stable source of income.[19]

As the careers of Barnes and Slade indicate, increased government funding under New Deal programs helped to more closely link black and public health, and they shared several important characteristics. While the white private system of physicians and hospitals was largely separate from the public health system, black hospitals and training facilities for medical professionals were an integral part of black public health voluntarism. The white medical profession generally insisted on a strict separation between public health and fee-for-service practice, and many even opposed private health insurance. The poverty of most black patients made black doctors more willing to accept remuneration from third-party sources. Black physicians and their public health allies envisioned a comprehensive approach to health care that placed prevention, education, and treatment alongside one another. Black activists and public health professionals adhered to an environmentalist philosophy of disease that "emphasized the social neutrality of infectious microbes, maintaining that immediate living conditions, employment experiences, diet, and availability of health care were the primary determinants for the variation in disease rates among blacks and whites."[20]

The close interrelationship between minority and public health by no means precluded prejudice among public health professionals, but the *Journal of the National Medical Association* reflected a stronger public health emphasis than the *Journal of the American Medical Association*. The *American Journal of Public Health* featured articles by black and white authors on black health from the 1920s forward and announced the conferences of black organizations such as the National Urban League. The American Public Health Association elected several presidents with moderate racial views, including North Carolinians Watson Smith Rankin (1920) and John Ferrell (1933), Marylanders Thomas Parran (1937) and Abel Wolman (1939), and Lowell Reed (1950), a New Englander and dean of the Johns Hopkins School of Hygiene and Public Health. Scientific racism lost credibility as much as two decades sooner in public health than in medicine, and within universities such as Johns Hopkins and the University of North Carolina, schools of public health exhibited more racially liberal attitudes than did medical schools. Michael M. Davis reported in 1947 that "in both South and North, interracial cooperation in health work is increasing."[21]

In a 1943 *Opportunity* article, Pauline Redmond Coggs judged the New Deal's effectiveness in reaching blacks: "Inasmuch as Negroes necessarily constituted a good proportion of the group the New Deal set out to assist, the success of the New Deal program depended upon reaching and helping Negroes. For these reasons, therefore, the Negro was not a petitioner seeking special consideration, or a minority requiring token recognition, but the Achilles heel of the New Deal social and economic program." Southerners of all races were in fact the Achilles' heel of the New Deal, whose priorities were profoundly shaped by the concentration of blacks in the rural South as well as by the myriad other consequences of the region's history of cash-crop agriculture dependent on slavery and then debt peonage. In renouncing "special consideration," Coggs was joined by men and women across the racial and political spectrum, from Louisiana senator Allen Ellender to National Association for the Advancement of Colored People chair Louis Wright, who insisted that they were representing, in Florida senator Claude Pepper's phrase, "a South which will come to the bar of the Congress with clean hands asking justice," not favoritism. As Wright averred, "I am not a special pleader. I ask no special favors or consideration for Negroes." These leaders fomented a fundamental shift in public policy during the New Deal that made the southern poor of both races visible to health and social welfare agencies for the first time since Reconstruction. Previously regarded by white Republicans and Democrats alike as unredeemable, blacks now received consideration from federal officials as an important constituency worthy of economic and social rehabilitation.[22]

SOCIAL SECURITY'S IMPACT ON SOUTHERN HEALTH

Federal aid to hospital construction under the PWA, WPA, and wartime Lanham Act and to health services under the Social Security Act, the La Follette–Bulwinkle Venereal Disease Control Act, the FSA, and the Emergency Maternity and Infant Care (EMIC) program made significant inroads in expanding health care access among blacks as well as whites. The FSA cooperative health plans provided care to eighty-five thousand families in thirty-three states, while EMIC subsidized hospital births for one in six U.S. infants born in 1944. But Social Security had the greatest and most lasting impact on the provision and administration of public health services in the United States and particularly in the South.[23]

In 1937, FDR's newly appointed surgeon general, Thomas Parran, made a revolutionary statement: "We must accept as a major premise that citizens should have an equal opportunity for health as an inherent right with the right of liberty and the pursuit of happiness." More than any other single American of the twentieth century, Parran pursued the principle that health was a basic entitlement of citizenship and attempted to translate that idea into public policy, both in the United States and internationally. Parran was raised on a Maryland tobacco farm and spent his early career as a PHS officer on assignments across the rural South, where he gained experience with the region's people and their most serious health problems. As New York's state health commissioner from 1930 to 1936, Parran had served on Roosevelt's Science Advisory Board and helped propose Social Security's Titles V and VI, aiding maternal and child health and the establishment and support of state and local health departments, respectively. Using the precedents set by the Sheppard-Towner Act and the Rockefeller, Duke, and Rosenwald philanthropies in using matching grants to stimulate state and local communities to increase their support for public health programs, Title VI supported public health training programs and research and created federal matching grants to states using a need-based formula that accounted for population, financial constraints, and special health problems. With some variations, this formula would be incorporated into the 1938 La Follette–Bulwinkle Venereal Disease Control Act and the 1946 Hill-Burton Hospital Survey and Construction Act and would become standard in subsequent social welfare legislation.[24]

By 1935, southern public health departments had done little to address black needs, and states had often balked at providing the required matching funds for federal health programs. Parran noted that Title VI "put in the hands of our Public Health Service a large measure of control over state boards of health which has evidently been put to good use." The South's low per capita income and greater special health needs resulted in larger allotments, and the PHS placed the greatest emphasis on the primarily southern problems of hookworm control, typhus, trachoma, and psittacosis as well as on the nationwide issues of syphilis, cancer, mental hygiene, and rodent control. Within two years of the passage of the 1935 Social Security Act, state and local annual public health appropriations had increased by $8 million, and the number of full-time health units had doubled nationwide. Although the South benefited most from these developments, southern Democrats were among the most vocal opponents of the New Deal, even in North Carolina. Tar Heel congressmen enthusiastically supported federal efforts to increase farm prices, provide jobs, and improve health conditions but often used these programs to dispense patronage to established foes of Roosevelt without extending benefits to blacks.[25]

Social Security's public health and maternal and infant care titles offered nearly $15 million annually to states and provided the first large-scale resources for southern health programs. Despite overt resistance from conservatives suspicious of creeping federalism, the extreme conditions of the Great Depression helped to tip the balance of federal-state cooperation further toward Washington. Federal Social Security funds accounted for more than a third of public health spending in seven southeastern states (Alabama, Florida, Georgia, Mississippi, North Carolina, South Carolina, and Tennessee) in 1940–41 and helped spur state and local spending. Edward H. Beardsley credits the federal health programs of the

1930s and 1940s for "salvaging and securing the health of many thousands of the region's poor, white and black." Whites wanted to extend New Deal public health programs to southern blacks for a range of reasons, including protecting whites from communicable disease, promoting a healthy labor force, reducing the burden of the indigent sick, and religious or humanitarian compassion. Yet even with the influx of federal funding, the severe shortage of southern health personnel, particularly those with even minimal public health training, remained a major obstacle to delivering health services to the South's poor, widely scattered population.[26]

In the twenty years since the hookworm campaign, PHS officials had urged schools of public health to expand programs for training rank-and-file public health workers. In 1921, John A. Ferrell had concluded that U.S. schools of public health needed to produce three hundred graduates per year for the next twenty years to supply the estimated seven thousand full-time health officers required adequately to staff state and local health departments, and this calculation did not account for the disproportionate shortage of workers in the rural South, particularly among concentrated black populations. In 1930, the PHS began to cooperate with the Rosenwald Fund's Davis to recruit black public health personnel. Social Security dollars expanded these efforts by providing scholarships to train public health doctors, nurses, and sanitary engineers. A major objective of the public health title was to train a new corps of southern public health professionals who could bridge the chasm between the rural poor and modern, scientific medicine.[27]

Federal funding was particularly crucial to the dramatic expansion of public health nursing among black women. White health reformers believed that black doctors, dentists, and nurses could better treat members of their own race, and white practitioners were also often happy to concede black patients as a result of racial, class, and cultural prejudice; the difficulty of reaching black homes in remote rural areas; and many black patients' inability to pay for their care. In 1936, the Medical College of Virginia used Social Security funding to establish an accredited public health nursing program exclusively for black nurses. By the early 1940s, full-time health departments served two-thirds of counties in seven southeastern states from Florida to Tennessee. Paul Cornely's study of ninety-six of these counties found that by 1939, one-third employed black public health nurses, but black physicians worked in only ten, and black dentists in only eight.[28]

No southern state hired more blacks in public health than North Carolina: six dentists and nineteen physicians in part-time positions and forty-three full-time public health nurses—approximately one-tenth of the state's total. (Mississippi, by comparison, had only six black public health nurses.) Carl Reynolds, North Carolina's state health officer, explained to Parran in 1939, "We have tried to give negro nurses every consideration possible in new positions being created out of Social Security and other funds." Yet counties reserved the first two public health nursing positions for whites and hired black nurses only in areas with large, concentrated black populations. Although maintaining segregation of both patients and professionals made a separate black health corps necessary, public health programs offered black professionals unmatched opportunities to utilize their training, earn more than in most jobs available to blacks, and advance in government careers.[29]

Maternal and infant health demonstrates particularly well how federal aid transformed southern health policy to enable state and local governments to take substantial responsibility for black, rural, and indigent health. Southern state spending on maternal and child health quadrupled between 1930 and 1940. In North Carolina from 1936 to 1938, 13,500 expectant mothers and 22,000 infants, the vast majority of them black, attended maternal and infant clinics established with Social Security funds. More than 4,000 women were diagnosed with toxic conditions, 800 were sent to hospitals for delivery, and 20 percent of white and 30 percent of black babies were found to be malnourished. In 1940 in the eastern Black Belt, the Beaufort County health officer reported that clinics under his supervision had provided 90 percent of black expectant mothers with "the privilege and benefit of medical examination." In Alabama, maternity clinics cared for 28 percent of black expectant mothers in 1943 and were credited with halving the state's maternal mortality over the preceding three years. Virginia's public health care for women was remarkably integrated, and the University of Virginia's hospital was known for its contraceptive services for black and white women. North and South Carolina's county public health clinics also offered birth control to black and white women beginning in the late 1930s.[30]

Social Security funds also augmented state budgets for a variety of infant health services. Well-baby clinics served fifty-three thousand North Carolina children in 1940, with more than twice as many black patients as white. North Carolina provided free silver nitrate drops to physicians, midwives, and hospitals for prevention of blindness due to congenital gonorrhea (opthalmia neonatorum) in newborns, with the drops administered to 83 percent of the state's babies. About one-third of babies were immunized for diphtheria within two years of the program's inception in 1936: the board of health underwrote the cost of a variety of vaccines, including those for typhoid, pertussis, rabies, smallpox, scarlet fever, tetanus, and measles. Federal maternal and infant health programs were largely responsible for the South's marked decline in both infant and maternal mortality during the Roosevelt administration.[31]

In addition to training health professionals and targeting many of the South's leading causes of death and disease, the strengthening of public health efforts also helped to generate a flood of new data on health disparities that undergirded further calls for reform. By 1940, most states were keeping accurate records of vital statistics, including disease and death rates, and a wide range of universities, philanthropies, and state agencies surveyed the health needs of various populations, including those for whom little data had previously been available. The onset of World War II further drove the quantification and exposure of the South's serious health problems to answer the question posed by a special issue of the Southern Conference for Human Welfare's *Southern Patriot*: "How Sick Is the South?"[32]

How did organized medicine respond to the southern health crisis and the federal initiatives to address it? Dental societies were more prevention-oriented and favorably disposed toward government-sponsored efforts, but the AMA and its state and local affiliates frequently questioned or openly opposed New Deal health programs that threatened to cross the strict line between preventive and curative treatment as threats to fee-for-service medicine and physician autonomy. The AMA approved of Social Security Act grants to states but stipulated that public health and maternal and infant care programs "should not include the treatment of disease [unless it] cannot be successfully accomplished through the private practitioner." Davis warned that since medical societies were acting as agents of the government to administer New Deal programs that paid physicians to provide indigent care, "the price of public payment is public supervision."[33]

Although the AMA had initially warned state affiliates to boycott the FSA health plans, local medical societies agreed to participate. The AMA Committee on Legislative Activities did not give its formal approval until 1940, and the AMA Committee on Rural Health reported favorably on the FSA plans in 1942. The AMA eventually praised the FSA for consulting local physicians and allowing them significantly to influence the terms and administration of the plans. Such relatively smooth relations between the FSA and local medical societies were based on the preceding quarter century of cooperation between the PHS and southern state and local public health agencies, which had gone a long way toward neutralizing southerners' and physicians' antifederalism. Solidarity between the fields of medicine and public health reached its height during World War II, and the FSA's health reformers joined a wide-ranging group of New Dealers and national health insurance advocates in attempting to leverage both the expansion of specific wartime health programs and the passage of universal comprehensive federal insurance.[34]

THOMAS PARRAN'S CAMPAIGN
AGAINST VENEREAL DISEASE

One of the main fronts for cooperation between private physicians and public health officers was in controlling venereal disease, among the most costly classes of illness in both human and financial terms. Despite Paul Ehrlich's 1909 discovery of Salvarsan as a "magic bullet" for syphilis, treatment had many drawbacks. Arsenic and mercury, the most commonly used active ingredients in compounds to cure syphilis, both were highly toxic and could cause serious side effects or death. Standard treatment of syphilis was complicated and lengthy, with each course consisting of six weekly intravenous injections of arsphenamine and an overlapping course of twenty-four to thirty gluteal injections of soluble mercury over eight to ten weeks. If, after one month's rest, the patient's Wasserman test was positive, the entire course was repeated; if negative, the course of mercury was repeated and follow-up testing was done periodically for a year. Before the widespread use of intravenous drug therapy, inexperienced physicians often had trouble finding patients' veins. The many obstacles to successful treatment of venereal disease without harming the patient prompted one physician to exclaim, "Even the poor can scarcely be expected to submit with good grace to repeated barbarities offered in the name of medicine." As late as World War II, venereal disease specialist Walsh McDermott of Cornell still complained that there was "pathetically little information available today on the proper use of organic arsenicals in the treatment of syphilis."[35]

Well into the twentieth century, blacks suffered disproportionately from the complications of syphilis and gonorrhea, particularly in the South. By some estimates, syphilis reduced black life expectancy by 17 percent and was the third-leading cause of death among blacks nationwide in the early 1900s. It ranked among the most common topics of medical journal articles that compared the physiology and progress of disease in black and white patients. In the *Journal of Nervous and Mental Diseases*, Dr. Baldwin Lucke of the University of Pennsylvania maligned blacks as "a notoriously syphilis-soaked race." New Orleans physician C. Jeff Miller compared black and white female obstetrical patients over a ten-year period at Charity Hospital and reported that black women patients had twice the rate of pelvic infections as well as nine times the frequency of uterine fibroids as a consequence of high rates of gonorrhea. The prevalence of VD in blacks as well as the overall population may have been exaggerated by racist assumptions that most blacks were already infected as well as by the limitations of diagnostic methods, leading to the conflation of syphilis with other conditions. At North Carolina's state mental asylum for blacks, the white superintendent asserted that "the Negro does not have 'book insanity,'" and the only medicine available to patients was Salvarsan, the standard syphilis treatment.[36]

Another possible cause of alleged racial disparities in syphilis rates arose from the fact that whites generally received treatment from private physicians, while blacks went to public health VD clinics, which were more likely to report cases. Yet untreated syphilis among blacks also enlarged the reservoir of infection and caused its incidence to spiral. By World War II, black military inductees tested positive for syphilis at the phenomenal rate of 272 per thousand, compared to 48 per thousand whites. At that time, approximately three-quarters of African Americans still lived in the South and half in the rural South, making venereal diseases a prime example of the southernization of the infectious diseases of poverty during the interwar period. Racial, regional, and rural-urban disparities increased in rates of VD as well as other maladies that previously had been associated almost exclusively with northern immigrants living in squalid, crowded urban slums.[37]

What, then, was the best way to fight venereal disease, and where should efforts be focused? As with previous southern public health initiatives, the Rockefeller and Rosenwald philanthropies influenced the PHS campaign against venereal disease, which became the centerpiece of efforts to uplift southern health. John D. Rockefeller Jr. was instrumental in the 1911 founding the Bureau of Social Hygiene, which fought the evils of sexual immorality and venereal disease with rational scientific research and therapeutic methods rather than the hysterical propaganda typical of Progressive Era antivice campaigns. In its pragmatic, measured approach and its emphasis on medical expertise and the amassing of statistical data to ground its policy recommendations, the Bureau of Social Hygiene was a precursor of Parran's venereal disease campaign and deluxe Jim Crow health policy generally. When Parran took over the PHS Division of Venereal Diseases in 1926, he revived or established effective federal-state relationships, which would become a signature strength under his leadership. He also promoted scientific research, treatment demonstrations, and surveys, including PHS investigations that identified particularly high rates among southern blacks. In 1930, the PHS demonstrated its commitment to improving southern black health in two important ways: it took over responsibility for National Negro Health Week, established by Booker T. Washington at Tuskegee Institute in 1915, and with the help of the Rosenwald Fund mounted the first widespread antisyphilis effort among southern blacks.[38]

Davis was serving as Rosenwald's director of medical services when the PHS initiated its Study of Untreated Syphilis in the Negro Male at Tuskegee in 1932. Davis accompanied a white county health officer, a white senior PHS officer ("Dr. C."), and a black physician ("Dr. H.") through the Alabama countryside to explore local conditions. (Even writing in a relatively obscure publication years later, Davis did not name his companions for fear that their work might by hindered by news of their clandestine interracial cooperation.) Since a mixed group could not eat lunch together in public, the health officer brought them home for lunch. Although the group was in a private home, the county officer's wife observed the letter but not the spirit of racial etiquette by placing Dr. H. at a small separate table less than an inch from the dining room table, where the four men sat and conversed freely "on every subject except race relations." According to Davis, Dr. H. subsequently observed, "She was a clever woman, wasn't she. She saved her husband's job." Despite the irrationality and ongoing influence of segregation, Davis saw progress in the fact that southern whites interacted with blacks on a professional basis.[39]

The black physician was probably H. L. Harris Jr., a consultant who had reported to the Rosenwald Fund in 1931 that it was "useless to attempt to cure syphilis in the rural Negro population in Macon County, Alabama," without more support for a comprehensive program to address the myriad health and other social problems of the black population. The PHS officer was Taliaferro Clark, a Virginian who had succeeded Parran as head of the PHS Division of Venereal Diseases in 1930 and conceived the idea for the Tuskegee Syphilis Study to follow the complete course of untreated disease in a group of black men. The Rosenwald Fund ended its support for the original treatment demonstration project in 1932 as a consequence of declining resources during the depression and refused to fund Clark's request for the new study, for which the PHS assumed sponsorship. The health officer was likely Murray Smith, who began work in 1932 as the head clinician of the PHS's field treatment clinics, which identified and screened participants in the study. Although Davis's article was published fifteen years after the Tuskegee study began, the incident occurred at the beginning of the study and involved its originator (Clark), its first detractor (Harris), and the health officer (Smith) who simultaneously identified potential study participants and led the PHS mass VD treatment program in Macon County, which dramatically reduced rates of infection among rural blacks. The Tuskegee study, while nearly always preceded by the adjective *infamous* in common parlance today, was also at the nexus of the southern health reform alliance that conceived deluxe Jim Crow.[40]

The PHS program of mass VD case finding and treatment among the South's black population, including that of Tuskegee in Macon County, Alabama, was ironically in full swing during the first ten years that the PHS was conducting the Tuskegee Syphilis Study. While the 424 men in the study were denied treatment, the PHS and the Macon County Health Department, headed by Murray Smith, with the assistance of Eugene Dibble, head of the Tuskegee Institute's John A. Andrew Hospital, reduced the incidence of syphilis among Macon County blacks from 40 percent to 10 percent. One of the most successful demonstration sites was directed by future surgeon general Leroy Burney in the South Georgia counties of Camden, Glynn, and McIntosh, where PHS physicians hauled the "Bad Blood Wagon," a mobile treatment unit designed by Burney, to turpentine camps and rural black churches. After Sunday services, preachers led members of the congregation outside to receive blood tests, sometimes offering a raffle ticket to win a pig as an incentive. Within eighteen months, 80 percent of the black population in three counties had been tested, and treatment efforts had begun. The Georgia case-finding pilot program set a precedent for using modern venereal disease control methods and orchestrating a carefully coordinated effort among county, state, and federal health agencies. Similar mobile testing and treatment units were established in seven other southern states, with the potential to double or triple the number of patients reached in high-rate rural areas while maintaining low operating costs.[41]

As health commissioner of New York state from 1930 to 1936 and a medical adviser to President Roosevelt, Parran influenced the authors of the Social Security legislation to include a requirement that 10 percent of federal matching funds to states under Title VI be designated for syphilis control. Immediately after becoming surgeon general in 1936, Parran launched an antisyphilis campaign that would elevate the disease to the nation's top public health priority and pluck the word *syphilis* out of the back-alley shadows and thrust it into the parlors of middle-class society women. Under Parran, the Venereal Disease

Division became the prime assignment for young PHS officers on their way up. The La Follette–Bulwinkle Venereal Disease Control Act of 1938 provided new federal funding to expand testing and treatment. The VD Control Act adopted the Social Security Act's South-focused principles of targeting states with the greatest health needs and lowest per capita income and marked the first of many pairings of northern liberals (in this case, Wisconsin senator Robert La Follette) with southern Democrats (North Carolina congressman Alfred Bulwinkle) to enact reform legislation with great potential to improve southern health.[42]

Parran identified the South and venereal disease as the two most important targets for federal public health efforts and focused heavily on reducing rates of syphilis among the region's blacks. He shared the view of his friend and colleague, Joseph Earle Moore, the leading venereal disease specialist of his day and an early consultant on the Tuskegee Syphilis Study, that "syphilis in the Negro is in many respects almost a different disease than syphilis in the white." Yet both men worked hard to include blacks as patients and providers in New Deal and World War II public health initiatives.[43]

Moore corresponded with Parran and Davis during the 1930s about various strategies to promote improved access to medical care, particularly venereal disease treatment, for blacks in Baltimore. The three men agreed that "the need of the Negro population for service and the need of the Negro physicians for training ought, of course, to be considered in shaping the program from the beginning, rather than after other main items have been crystallized." Moore had attempted to circumvent the Johns Hopkins Hospital's racial bias by requesting funding to establish a syphilis clinic at Provident Hospital, Baltimore's only black general hospital. When no sponsors stepped forward, Parran subsequently arranged for a recurring three-month postgraduate course in syphilis control offered jointly by the District of Columbia Health Department and Howard University, which offered black physicians scholarships under VD-control grants to state health departments. The PHS also assigned its first black commissioned officer to the Baltimore City Health Department during the war, but the department refused to accept a black uniformed officer. Moore's enthusiasm for training black physicians to do venereal disease control was responsible for the mid-1940s integration of the Johns Hopkins Hospital staff and the School of Hygiene and Public Health, where Moore headed the Division of Venereal Disease Control.[44]

Parran made substantial contributions to advancing public health in the United States, particularly among southern, black, and rural populations; he was a pioneer in international health and played a crucial role in founding the

World Health Organization; and he advocated enlightened regional health planning and the expansion of health care access for all in America and worldwide. Yet Parran is most widely known for his role as the head of the PHS during the early years of the Tuskegee Syphilis Study. Syphilis control ultimately received 10 percent of all public health funding under the Social Security Act, but the money pouring into southern state and local health departments did not always convince white southern officials to carry out Parran's imperative of impartial testing and treatment. Moreover, the benefits of New Deal health programs at times came at the price of extending white control into new areas of blacks' lives. Black health workers, program administrators, and educators faced hard choices when their efforts to extend the reach of the New Deal in the black community proved to be an avenue for white intrusion or oppression. As Karen Ferguson has concluded, "White paranoia and racist assumptions about African Americans and syphilis colored the program. Even the most liberal white New Dealers in Georgia shared the view that syphilis was an African American disease caused by black sexual promiscuity and general lack of hygiene."[45]

If the civil rights movement sought to expose segregation and disfranchisement as not just black or southern problems but as problems of national and international proportions, Parran strove to do the same with syphilis. By emphasizing the ravages of syphilis on labor productivity and infant health while claiming that one in ten Americans suffered from the disease (a number that was probably an overstatement but at least suggested the truth of VD's widespread impact), Parran sought to redefine syphilis as not a venereal disease but a communicable illness that, like tuberculosis and typhoid, would readily respond to the scientific application of modern medicine and epidemiology. He also stressed the need to make modern health care universally available to all Americans according to his belief that "every citizen, North and South, colored and white, rich and poor, has an inalienable right to his citizen's share of health protection."[46]

Black reformers, notes Ferguson, "used the new white attention on blacks and venereal disease to promote health-care programs for African Americans and to further their inclusive aims for the black community." Parran also won African American reformers' support by recruiting qualified black doctors and nurses, whom he believed to be "much more successful in caring for their own people than are the well-qualified and well intentioned white nurse and physician. . . . That is why we need more good ones helping on this public health job, and we need them now." Parran would apply this principle even more extensively during World War II, when he actively recruited black nurses to join the Cadet Nurse

Corps. The war would also give the PHS an opportunity to deliver the most devastating blow to venereal disease via the potent combination of penicillin and rapid treatment centers. The wartime health programs that Parran oversaw continued and expanded the principles of the New Deal's emphasis on southern and black health, but the 1940s would bring a quantum leap toward defining health as an essential facet of national defense.[47]

NEW DEAL HEALTH FACILITIES

Although the New Deal dramatically improved sanitation and public health services and made inroads into expanding access to medical care, federal health programs also reflected the increasing centrality of hospitals as conduits for the delivery of medical care. As an indication of the growing priority placed on the development of hospitals as a foundation of good health, much of the debate over the adequacy of health care during the 1930s and 1940s centered on ratios of hospital beds to population. From 1933 to 1945, New Deal and wartime public construction programs significantly expanded the number of black and southern hospital beds (table 2.1). Hospital improvements were a top priority for southern cities for federal works programs such as the WPA, PWA, and Lanham Wartime Housing Act of 1940 (amended in 1941 and 1942 to fund war-related public works, including hospitals on military bases and in war-affected areas). Between 1935 and 1940, the WPA completed 2,000 projects for both military and civilian health facilities. Between 1933 and 1941, grants and loans from the PWA built, enlarged, or modernized 2,056 health facilities with 107,849 additional beds at a total cost of $397 million—7 percent of the PWA budget for nonfederal projects. Under the Lanham Act, the PWA built another 444 hospital projects for military

TABLE 2.1
Federal Aid for Hospital Construction

LEGISLATION	YEAR PASSED	NUMBER OF PROJECTS	FEDERAL FUNDING
Public Works Administration	1933	2,100 total; 668 new	$300 million
Lanham Act	1943	444	$55.5 million
Hill-Burton Act	1946	10,748	$3.7 billion
TOTAL		13,292	$4.0 billion

purposes at a total cost of $66 million. The federal PWA, WPA, and Lanham Act programs accounted for two-thirds of hospital construction nationwide during the Roosevelt administration.[48]

Federal hospital construction programs also represented a new public policy approach to civil rights and health care that presaged Hill-Burton's principles of racial parity under segregation and targeting poor southern states. Even in the South, federal aid was directed, with few exceptions, to hospitals that accepted black patients. Under the influence of James A. Atkins, racial relations officer for the Federal Works Agency, the PWA added nearly eight thousand new beds (7.4 percent of the prewar total) in all-black hospitals or wards in sixteen southern states as well as an undetermined number of beds available to black patients in 2,400 biracial general and 568 special hospitals nationwide (table 2.2). More black health professionals could treat their patients in the new facilities, although pre-1945 hospital construction legislation offered neither patients nor doctors explicit protection against racial exclusion. Nearly 60 percent of the beds for blacks built by the PWA were in mental wards or hospitals (such as 1,170 beds at the North Carolina State Hospital for the Colored Insane), while 15 percent were in tuberculosis and other special hospitals. For example, Cooley Sanitarium in White's Ferry, Louisiana, was completed in 1938 with $121,000 in funding from the WPA. It featured identical white and colored units on either side of a two-story brick, white-columned main building and was fitted with "44 spacious and modern rooms, huge sun porches so arranged that patients get the maximum benefit from sunlight, and adequate laboratories and technical rooms. A bridge spans a small artificial lake on the grounds of the hospital."[49]

The remaining 25 percent of PWA-funded beds for blacks were located in black units of municipal general hospitals, including the 54-bed, $100,000 Norfolk

TABLE 2.2

General Hospital Beds for Blacks in Four Southern States, 1940 and 1950

STATE	1940	1950	CHANGE, 1940 TO 1950	POPULATION CHANGE
Virginia	958	1,745	787 (+82%)	+78,043 (+12%)
North Carolina	1,297	2,176	879 (+68%)	+66,085 (+7%)
Georgia	1,184	1,493	309 (+26%)	−22,165 (−2%)
Mississippi	545	1,720	1,175 (+216%)	−88,084 (−8%)
TOTAL	3,984	7,134	3,150 (+79%)	+33879 (+0.9%)

Source: Ponton, "Hospital Service," 14–15, 50; McFall, "Needs," 235–36.

Community Hospital; the 90-bed, $250,000 Negro Hospital in Galveston; and the five-building, 685-bed complex at Homer G. Phillips Municipal Hospital in St. Louis built at a cost that topped $3 million. In southern cities, the PWA aided extensive renovations of urban teaching facilities that served large indigent black populations, including John Gaston Hospital in Memphis and Grady Memorial Hospital in Atlanta. In booming Birmingham, the only hospital caring for indigent patients was the forty-year-old Hillman Hospital, which received a $300,000 WPA grant in 1938 to construct a five-story clinic addition. The new sixteen-story, 575-bed Jefferson Hospital opened next door only two years later, after prominent Alabama New Dealers including Senators John Sparkman and Lister Hill, Congressman Luther Patrick, and Supreme Court justice Hugo Black influenced the PWA to offer a grant and loan totaling $2 million. The two public facilities subsequently merged to become a teaching hospital for the new Medical College of Alabama. The University of Arkansas Medical School also built a much-needed new main building, located next to Little Rock's City Hospital, with half a million dollars in PWA funds. But the largest PWA hospital project was a mammoth new main building at Charity Hospital in New Orleans, built for $12 million as part of an arrangement between Louisiana governor Richard Leche and President Roosevelt where Leche supported FDR's 1936 reelection in return for tens of millions in WPA funds. The expansion made Charity Hospital "the second largest in the United States and the largest state health facility in the world for the treatment of acute and contagious diseases."[50]

Louisiana exemplified the relationship between the number of public hospital beds and rates of hospitalization among indigent groups, particularly where segregation further limited access to private beds. By 1954, Louisiana had the highest ratio of charity beds per capita in the nation and ranked highest among southern states in overall ratios of hospital beds and rates of hospitalization among blacks as well as whites. Unlike most southern states, Louisiana's large supply of public hospital beds ensured that occupancy rates remained high and that more beds were available to nonpaying patients, including large numbers of African Americans. If North Carolina was the deluxe Jim Crow state par excellence, Louisiana demonstrates both the gross inadequacy of prewar southern health care and the success of efforts to remedy its worst aspects during the 1940s by devoting new public resources to promote health care access for blacks within biracial institutions.[51]

Louisiana's charity hospital system grew out of the nation's second-oldest continuously operating general hospital, Charity Hospital. An individual bequest to the City of New Orleans had established Charity in 1736, and the Louisiana territorial government assumed control of the hospital in 1811. The state founded a second charity hospital in Shreveport in 1876. In 1936, the Louisiana legislature created the State Hospital Board to implement Huey Long's vision of a public state hospital system, and four new state hospitals were built between 1938 and 1941, with two more added during the 1950s. Long (who served as governor from 1928 to 1932 and as a U.S. senator from 1932 until his assassination in 1935) and his successor in the Senate, Allen Ellender, frequently touted their state's public hospital system as a model for indigent care, claiming that poor Louisiana blacks received proportionally more charity care than poor whites and that the quality of care for blacks in the Louisiana charity hospital system was better than anywhere else in the country. Only four states (Mississippi, Louisiana, West Virginia, and Pennsylvania) maintained charity general hospital systems before World War II. Even during the depression, Mississippi appropriated $500,000 biennially to operate its five state charity facilities, but all were in the majority-white southern section. In the majority-black northern Delta counties, with 70 percent of the black population, even public hospitals still did not admit black surgery patients by 1940. Moreover, blacks needing orthopedic surgery had to leave the state. Oklahoma, Maryland, and North Carolina initiated or expanded state indigent care programs in 1945.[52]

In the decade after Long's death, Louisiana constructed four new charity hospitals around the state and erected a massive new main building for the New Orleans Charity Hospital. Douglas L. Smith described the twenty-story, 2,700-bed building as "a truly magnificent structure [with] separate but roughly equal wards for whites and blacks." Completed in 1940, the new Charity was among the earliest and most deluxe of the deluxe Jim Crow hospitals. Its H-shaped biracial blueprint placed blacks in wards on the east side and whites on the west, with private rooms for either severely ill or paying patients in the center of each floor. Wings at either end of the main structure provided teaching hospitals for the Tulane and Louisiana State University medical schools. The new twenty-one-floor, 1,100-bed tower for Grady Memorial Hospital in Atlanta, completed with Hill-Burton assistance in 1958, featured a layout identical to Charity's, and the southern postwar hospital construction boom replicated variations on this partitioned floor plan.[53]

Just prior to the passage of the 1946 Hill-Burton Hospital Survey and Construction Act, out of 7,110 acceptable general hospital beds in Louisiana, 3,113 were in the seven charity hospitals, whose physical plants according to a 1948

TABLE 2.3
Southern State Hospital Admissions per Thousand Children, 1947

	WHITE	NEGRO	DIFFERENCE
Alabama	35.2	10.8	24.4
Louisiana	70.2	47.2	23.0
Maryland	46.8	26.6	20.2
Mississippi	49.4	9.3	40.1
South Carolina	55.9	13.9	42.0
Virginia	39.0	17.8	21.2
Six States	47.8	19.2	28.6

Source: Goldstein, "Longevity," 94–95.

report were "better than is generally found in the private institutions in the state." The charity hospitals nevertheless experienced overcrowding, and at four of the institutions, "the physical facilities . . . are not adequate to support the number of beds they are now required to provide." Half the charity hospital beds were allocated for blacks, who composed just under 30 percent of Louisiana's population. The state charity hospitals admitted 22,324 more black patients than whites in 1946–47, in part because of shorter average hospitalizations for blacks. A 1947 study of hospital admissions of children in six southern states conducted by the American Academy of Pediatrics ranked Louisiana first in rates of both black and white admissions (table 2.3). Louisiana's rate of 47.2 admissions per thousand black children nearly equaled the white rate for the six states as a whole (47.8) but trailed the rate of 70.2 for white Louisiana children.[54]

New Orleans's new Charity Hospital marked a watershed in hospital architecture that would transform both the real-world application of segregation and the day-to-day environment in which health care was delivered. Increased public funding for hospital construction and the growth of scientific biomedicine, including the rapid development of effective drug therapies and technological innovations for diagnosis and treatment, combined to foster a revolutionary expansion and reconceptualization of the facilities where health care was delivered. Until the turn of the twentieth century, hospitals were reviled as places where the poor without family went to die. As they evolved from charitable institutions providing convalescent care into modern, rationalized centers of scientific medicine, insurance actuary Frederick Hoffman predicted in 1916 that hospitals would "soon be used far more for the treatment of the half-sick and to-be-sick than for the already sick and the half-dead. We should have hospitals where people may go at the beginning rather than the end of their sickness." During the Progressive Era, the rise of professional experts, the development of scientific management, and the industrialization of health care fostered the emergence of the field of hospital planning, which advocated the subdivision of space within health facilities to allow the segregation of patients by disease process and isolation for other medically indicated reasons. These developments paralleled the architectural transformation of segregation to accommodate the growing inclusion of blacks in public facilities.[55]

As the science of medicine grew more complex and patient expectations rose during the twentieth century, general hospitals became functionally, mechanically, and technologically more diverse and expensive to build. Instead of the old open wards where the only division of patients was by gender, new demands for separation by disease process and economic status required space for private, semiprivate, and isolation units as well as designated wards for maternity, surgical, premature infant, and other special populations. As hospitals performed a greater variety of services and functions, architectural blueprints began to include modern operating rooms lit with electric instead of natural light and additional space for research, teaching, and group practice as well as social work, public health, and outpatient departments. Hospital planners also had to accommodate an increasing diversity of technological functions, such as laboratory testing, radiology, and electroshock therapy, which required expensive interstitial infrastructure including electrical wiring, additional plumbing and ventilation, and in some climates air-conditioning.[56]

In the mid-twentieth-century South, medical and racial segregation developed alongside and reinforced one another. The advent of biracial general hospitals changed the nature of segregation from separate buildings to partitioning within the same structure. This development had several practical and rhetorical advantages. Southern state and local governments could simultaneously comply with the *Gaines* decision and with segregation laws that required the racial separation of hospital patients. They also achieved cost savings and operational efficiency by allowing black patients to be treated by the same staff and use the same auxiliary services and medical technology as white patients.

The 1943 expansion of a county hospital in Columbia, South Carolina, shows an earlier pattern of segregation that duplicated completely separate hospital buildings and nurses' quarters for blacks and whites on adjacent city blocks. The expansion, however, provided space for black patients and staff, who had been excluded from the existing white hospital. The Chester County Hospital in South Carolina, completed in 1947, exemplifies partitioned segregation within a single structure, with separate parking, driveways, entrances, and waiting rooms for each race. Black patients were housed on the first floor, while white patients were housed on the second floor, with the operating suite, and the third floor, with the delivery room. Both races could use the operating and delivery rooms, but black patients were moved downstairs to the first floor to recuperate.[57]

Although deluxe Jim Crow facilities provided blacks and whites with access to health care that had never before existed in many areas, segregation still continued to take its toll in overt and subtle ways. Hospital architect Isadore Rosenfield spoke passionately about the "tremendous cultural responsibility" of hospital architecture and its effects on patients:

> By honest expression we build in [the man on the street] confidence in the hospital so that he may look toward the possibility of being a patient therein during the span of his life with anticipation of pleasant expectation instead of horror. The friends or relatives of patients on approaching the hospital should not be intimidated with its officious monumentality, but should be made to feel that their friends or dear ones are in the presence of kindliness, considerateness, and scientific certainty. The patient within the hospital, by means of environment, should be made to feel uplifted rather than let down, and of course the doctors, nurses, and other employees working in the hospital should be made to feel that they are in an atmosphere where the exercise of care, kindliness, and service is a natural expectation.[58]

The deluxe Jim Crow architecture of new southern hospitals profoundly influenced the experiences of black patients and health professionals. Separate entrances, admission desks, restrooms, dining areas, wards, and even driveways; equipment labeled *white* and *colored*; and the exclusion of black patients from certain areas of the hospital inevitably undermined the "uplifting" environment that Rosenfield advocated and caused black patients to question the "kindliness, considerateness, and scientific certainty" of deluxe Jim Crow hospitals. The practice of segregating the blood supply, upheld by the American Red Cross blood donation program until 1950, was the most potent symbol of differential treatment of blacks within deluxe Jim Crow hospitals. It also attracted the greatest opposition.[59]

Since many of the new deluxe Jim Crow facilities, such as Grady and Charity, were municipal teaching hospitals with hundreds or thousands of beds, they accepted large numbers of indigent patients and provided much-needed care, but patients' needs and comforts were often subordinated to the educational mission as well as public institutions' unrelenting push to minimize frills and expenditures. Teaching hospitals could be frightening, disorienting places, and patients' experiences were as much determined by class and the pecking order of doctor-nurse-patient as by race. The conventions of segregation were at times indistinguishable from the hospital staff's expectations of unquestioning submission to medical discipline and routine. For example, regardless of race, patients were commonly called by first or last name without courtesy titles, although this practice apparently persisted longer in southern Jim Crow wards.[60]

The federal health programs of the Roosevelt era built on and vastly expanded the PHS's cooperative work with black and southern organizations during the first third of the twentieth century, further cementing the PHS's remarkable reputation as both the most prosouthern and most problack federal agency. By the time Roosevelt died, health had become the least discriminatory sphere of public policy. Swedish sociologist Gunnar Myrdal concluded in 1944 that there was "less discrimination against Negroes—and in some cases no discrimination at all—in respect to the so-called 'out-patient' services of public health institutions" and that "tremendous improvements [in public health] have been achieved in recent years, and . . . Negroes have shared in the benefits." Southern public health programs had in fact catered so heavily to African Americans that Milton Roemer of the Yale University Department of Public Health observed in 1949 that "the personal health services offered by many Southern health department programs are provided overwhelmingly to Negro people." Yet tremendous medical needs remained unmet by the deficiencies or complete absence of public health services in many rural areas, and even the passage of a universal comprehensive health insurance plan would not by itself make a difference in communities where doctors, hospitals, and public health services simply did not exist.[61]

The identification of public health with black health was still as much a function of enduring poverty among rural black southerners and their continuing exclusion from the private health care system as it was a sign of enlightened attitudes among public health officials. The growth of public health services for blacks and poor rural whites may in fact have provided opponents of national health insurance with ammunition to deny the need to improve access to the private system. Yet by providing unprecedented resources for the expansion of health services and facilities, federal, state and local governments enabled black southerners to become more knowledgeable users of health care and to establish patterns of seeking treatment that intensified the demand for integration after the war.

chapter 3

NEW DEAL HEALTH
IN NORTH CAROLINA

N orth Carolina's position as a regional and national leader in public health resulted from several unique resources, particularly the state's visionary health reformers. The State Board of Health was led by some of the nation's most progressive public health leaders, John A. Ferrell, Watson Smith Rankin, and Carl V. Reynolds.

OVERVIEW OF PUBLIC HEALTH IN NORTH CAROLINA

John Ferrell began his career as a county health officer during the 1900s. Under Rankin, Ferrell served as North Carolina's assistant secretary of health and as the state director of the hookworm campaign, advancing to become Wickliffe Rose's second in command at the Rockefeller Sanitary Commission. North Carolina's antihookworm program was so successful that it became a template for health modernization efforts around the world undertaken by the Rockefeller Foundation's International Health Division, which took over and expanded the activities of the Sanitary Commission in 1915. Ferrell served as associate director of the International Health Division from 1914 to 1944, directing its U.S. activities and its office of cooperative state programs. The International Health Division sent Ferrell to the Johns Hopkins School of Hygiene and Public Health, where he earned the first doctorate of public health in the United States in 1919. The International Health Division said of Ferrell on his retirement, "His was the job of laying the mudsills and framework of public health methods and of inspiring others to build for the future." He subsequently served as executive director of the North Carolina Medical Care Commission.[1]

Rankin and Ferrell were contemporaries and intimate friends as well as golf partners; both also served as president of the American Public Health Association, Rankin in 1920 and Ferrell in 1933. Rankin was elected to national office in the American Medical Association and won acclaim as America's most outstanding state health officer. He completed postgraduate training at Johns Hopkins and a residency at University of Maryland's University Hospital in Baltimore before becoming a professor of pathology at Wake Forest Medical School, where he also served as dean from 1905 to 1909. He was appointed North Carolina's first full-time state health officer as the hookworm campaign was getting under way. As a chief apostle of the southern public health movement, Rankin promoted the founding of health departments throughout the region, beginning with the first full-time county health department in the United States in Robeson County. Rankin's racial progressivism was well known, and he made hiring black public health nurses a top priority, with ten by 1917 and one or two in nearly every county by the early 1920s.[2]

Under Rankin and Ferrell's leadership, North Carolina had been the epicenter of the southern public health movement and ground zero for the crusade against hookworm, the "germ of laziness" among poor whites. Yet these efforts had largely bypassed North Carolina's large rural black population, which faced the common southern woes of entrenched segregation, chronic poverty, and severe shortages of medical personnel and hospital beds. North Carolina's 2,100 doctors (only 129 of them black) could attend only a small fraction of the state's 100,000 annual births, more than 70 percent of which were rural. In 1940, the state ranked fortieth in the percentage of doctor-attended births, with only 17.1 percent of rural and 13.6 percent of nonwhite births taking place in hospitals. In 1945, thirty-four of North Carolina's one hundred counties had no hospitals. The state posted the nation's eighth-highest death rate for mothers and the eleventh-highest for infants. Black women in North Carolina were twice as likely as white women to die from complications related to childbirth, and black infants were 1.5 times as likely as white infants to die in their first year. Mortality from birth defects, premature birth, and diseases of infancy was twice as high among black as white babies. Such figures marred the state's self-proclaimed image as a progressive beacon.[3]

In the 1930s and 1940s, Rankin and Ferrell continued to combat North Carolina's looming health problems and increased their efforts among the black population. After sixteen years as state health officer, Rankin retired in 1925 to become director of the Duke Hospital and a trustee of the Duke Endowment, and in 1931 he assumed the position of head of its Hospital and Orphans Section. Beginning in 1927, Rankin also served as one of thirty-five members of the Committee on the Costs of Medical Care, which influenced his subsequent work to address health financing problems in North Carolina. The endowment was founded by James Buchanan Duke in 1924 to establish Duke University and its School of Medicine as well as to create hospitals and orphanages for the poor of all races in North and South Carolina. Funded with the profits of the American Tobacco Company, the Duke Endowment was the only southern philanthropy during the first third of the twentieth century substantially to aid black health. The endowment spent 32 percent of its annual income to build and operate hospitals to make them accessible to the rural poor. By 1940, Duke gave over $1 million annually to 130 hospitals in the Carolinas, and one-third of the patients at these facilities received free care.[4]

The Duke Endowment under Rankin's influence had a major impact on black hospitals and patients. According to a 1944 Duke Endowment report, eleven of North Carolina's twelve black hospitals received Duke funds (the exception was a ten-bed private facility in Raleigh). Seventy-five mixed hospitals contained black wards, of which only fifteen facilities—representing less than 10 percent of black hospital beds—did not receive Duke support. Thus, the Duke Endowment helped maintain the vast majority of hospital beds for North Carolina's black population. Rankin cooperated closely with Duke Medical School's dean, Wilbert C. Davison, to promote coordinated hospital service and medical care in North Carolina with special attention for the needs of blacks in white-run biracial and black-run hospitals. Just after Rankin assumed leadership of the endowment's hospital section in 1931, he and Davison found themselves at the center of a controversy at Lincoln Hospital in Durham. The dilemma resembled that faced by Louis Wright at Harlem Hospital in the 1920s: how to improve the quality of patient care and reduce surgical mortality without alienating the hospital's veteran staff and their supporters in the local black community. Rankin's success in improving the conditions and finances of the hospital as well as maintaining the support of Durham blacks testified to his abilities as a savvy negotiator.[5]

Unlike Ferrell and Rankin, Carl V. Reynolds was from the western North Carolina mountains, and he served as Asheville's chief health officer from 1903 to 1910 and 1914 to 1923. He was elected president of the North Carolina Medical Society in 1924 and was appointed state health officer in 1934. The breadth of public health activity in North Carolina under Reynolds is suggested by a 1940 report on public health administration in North Carolina. In 1930, three-quarters of North Carolina's population of 2.3 million was still rural, and its racial demographics were 70.5 percent white, 29 percent Negro, and 0.5 percent Indian. By 1938, however, two-thirds of the state's one hundred counties were served by full-time health departments. North Carolina's total state expenditures for 1937–38 reached $37.9 million, with the State Board of Health's allocation totaling just over $1 million, more than half of it from federal sources, including the Public Health Service ($337,914, including $281,126 for county health work) and the Children's Bureau ($121,085 for maternal and child health and $105,212 for crippled children).[6]

As state health officer, Reynolds followed surgeon general Thomas Parran's lead and focused on venereal disease control and maternal and child health. Reynolds also helped start North Carolina's school health program to address the massive health needs of pupils. In 1934–35, school health screenings discovered correctible defects in more than four-fifths of both white and colored elementary children and more than two-thirds of high schoolers. In 1939, the state departments of health and education received a five-year start-up grant from the Rockefeller Foundation to set up a school health service program with staff including a black physician and a black health educator. The program trained teachers in health education, provided health education to elementary and high school students, provided protective health measures in schools, and sought the cooperation of parents and community organizations. The success of North Carolina's school health program was noteworthy, since school health programs elsewhere often identified medical problems year after year but had no authority or funding to treat them. In addition, most city school health programs were administered by departments of education rather than health, resulting in a lower priority for medical services for students.[7]

Reynolds was particularly active in the campaign against venereal disease and made North Carolina a national model for state campaigns. The Board of Health operated venereal disease clinics across the state and provided examination and treatment to prisoners and domestic servants. The University of North Carolina established strong connections to the federal agenda for regional health reform generally and venereal disease particularly. Reynolds was instrumental in establishing the University of North Carolina's public health program with President Frank Porter Graham, and the two recruited Milton Rosenau, founder of the

Harvard School of Public Health, to serve as the first director of the Division (later School) of Public Health from 1936 to 1946. During the war, Reynolds was instrumental in establishing Raleigh's Venereal Disease Education Institute, funded jointly by the U.S. Public Health Service (PHS), North Carolina State Board of Health, and the Z. Smith Reynolds Foundation. The institute produced pamphlets and posters that were distributed to millions of civilians and servicemen and were frequently requested by state health departments.[8]

Rankin's, Ferrell's, and Reynolds' empathy for the plight of blacks and the poor set them apart from many whites of their era and region. Thanks in large part to their leadership and success in securing state, federal, and private funds, no other southern state targeted black needs as North Carolina's Board of Health did through programs such as venereal disease control and infant and maternal care. Ferrell told the American Public Health Association in 1933 that "any program for the improvement of health and the lowering of death rates in the South must afford [the] negro health protection." The State Board of Health's more progressive racial attitudes were evident in its monthly *Health Bulletin*, which capitalized the word *Negro* in defiance of conventional white usage.[9]

Such progressivism garnered accolades from black state officials. John Larkins, head of the Bureau of Negro Work in the Department of Public Welfare, praised his home state for recognizing "the needs of its largest minority group, the Negro, and [making] conscientious efforts to alleviate some of its social and economic conditions. The State has pioneered in many phases of work among the Negroes and stands as a beacon and guiding light to other states." Walter J. Hughes, the first black physician to be hired full time by a state board of health, declared in a 1941 Durham address that "North Carolina has done more to promote the health of the Negro than any other state." That year, the PHS recognized the North Carolina Board of Health for its outstanding work among African Americans in connection with National Negro Health Week.[10]

BLACK MATERNAL AND INFANT MORTALITY

During the late 1930s and 1940s, North Carolina's black women were remarkably engaged with the public health system as both patients and caregivers. The public health campaign to reduce maternal and infant mortality occurred at a critical historical moment, before the advent of a multibillion-dollar federal hospital construction program and before civil rights leaders had grown preoccupied with equal access to facilities. Given the prevailing prejudices of the

pre-civil-rights-era South, black women's needs garnered a striking amou
attention from mainstream policymakers and health professionals—more, a
ably, than women's health issues would receive from the civil rights moven
or the hospital-centered delivery system, both of which emerged in the So
following World War II. Although midwife training programs and maternal
and infant clinics were not designed to be "inclusive" in the contemporary
sense, black women took far greater advantage of them than did white women
in terms of both percentage and raw numbers. These alternative paths for the
mass delivery of care to the rural poor offered cost-effectiveness and a sensitivity
to black female patients that could not be matched by the hospitals that would
supplant them. Race, class, gender, and geography converged to shape the health
status of black women as well as the professional identities of the midwives,
public health nurses, and physicians who embodied North Carolina's public
health outreach to those women.[11]

North Carolina's health leaders hoped to reduce infant and maternal mortality rates by encouraging women to receive prenatal care and to give birth in
sterile surroundings with modern technology close at hand. But not only were
hospital beds in short supply, existing facilities were often small and ill-equipped,
particularly for childbirth. Well into the twentieth century, mortality rates for
mothers and infants had been so high in many American hospitals that women
often refused to deliver there. Describing labor, delivery, and newborn facilities
before 1945, Isadore Rosenfield observed that most maternity units were identical to units in the rest of the hospital, and small hospitals did not even segregate
maternity cases in separate units. When separate infant nurseries existed, they
were "frequently improvised, occupy cheerless and hazardous locations and the
infants are herded together one bassinet against the other without any separation between." Infants were taken from their beds to be fed, bathed, and treated
in the same nursery room, and the lack of separation between sterile and septic
activities was "frequently a grave source of cross-infection," particularly when
babies were bathed in one common basin. The absence of isolation facilities
for sick infants endangered the well babies in the nursery, and few nurseries
had separate provisions for premature newborns. Chicago obstetrician Joseph
DeLee's campaign to improve hospital antiseptic methods and strictly segregate
sick mothers and babies to prevent cross-infection increased public confidence
and use of hospital facilities. Yet DeLee blamed continued high rates of maternal
and infant mortality on the lack of prenatal care, which was provided for fewer
than 25 percent of women giving birth in the 1930s.[12]

In a 1997 interview, black obstetrician-gynecologist Andrew Best described the conditions for black mothers and infants at Pitt County Memorial Hospital in Greenville, North Carolina.

> Early on, from the time I came in 1954 for about the following ten years, all the black patients were admitted to the first floor of the east wing of the hospital. Even though we used the same delivery room and the same surgical suites to be bedded and admitted, they were all on one floor of the east wing: whether you had pneumonia or a newborn baby, you were on the so-called colored floor. Dr. Malene Irons, as a pediatrician, got interested in this problem, because in the early days, we had what you called an isolette that you put the prematures in, so they'd have the proper warmth and humidity. The newborn nursery with the iso-lettes was up on another floor. There were some barriers to having a black baby in the isolette in the newborn nursery. That black baby had to come on back downstairs, and shift as they could with the mother.[13]

After 1945, maternity facilities began to feature individual bassinets equipped for the needs of a single infant, including bathing. Hospitals began to isolate sick infants from healthy ones and to segregate premature infants in a separate nursery with incubators. Thus, the conditions Best described for blacks in 1950s small-town North Carolina had been fairly universal for all races nationwide before World War II but probably persisted longer in smaller southern hospitals. As Best observed, innovations in treatment reached black patients last of all. Still, whereas the small, obsolete, largely private hospitals built during the first third of the twentieth century had usually barred black patients, blacks were now welcome at most new, modern hospitals, particularly those constructed with government aid. With modern maternity wards, delivery rooms, and nurseries, conditions for labor and delivery were vastly superior at newer biracial hospitals than at old private whites-only facilities.[14]

Most health reformers blamed high infant and maternal mortality rates not on poverty or a dearth of doctors and hospitals but squarely on black midwives, who during the 1930s attended approximately 80 percent of births to black southern women. After 1900, midwifery was largely the province of black women in the rural South and immigrant women in the urban North. As textile mills drew more and more white farm women out of the countryside, black women stayed behind. A much higher percentage of black women were employed than were white women, but since southern factories excluded African American women until World War II, most picked crops or cleaned houses. In addition to paid labor and caring for their own families, some black women also felt called to deliver babies. Midwives received little financial compensation but enjoyed a degree of prestige and respect in rural black communities similar to that of male preachers.[15]

Midwives were first and foremost participants in the folk culture they shared with their patients. In a 1926 monograph, *Folk Beliefs of the Southern Negro*, Newbell Niles Puckett observed, "While disease in general is not confined to womankind alone, yet, with the Negroes, the great mass of folk-medicine is in their hands rather than in the hands of the men. The women are the great practitioners, the folk-doctors—the old Granny with her 'yarbs an' intmints' does much to keep alive these folk-cures and to make these beliefs in general much more a feminine possession than the context would seem to indicate." Some folk practices employed by midwives were compatible with the theories of medical science. According to Puckett, "almost everywhere the linen bandage used [during childbirth] must be scorched before applying, a practice having some distinct sanitary advantages." Cherry tree bark and the nest of the dirt dauber wasp, commonly prescribed in teas to relieve pain and hasten labor, contained natural blood coagulants. Antihemorrhaging preparations including spiderwebs, soot, and heated alum mixed with sugar were applied to vulva dressings. Other practices had no analogues in institutional medicine, and some clearly conflicted with conventional medical wisdom. To hasten delivery of the afterbirth, midwives directed the woman to stand over a bucket of hot coals with burning feathers. To stop milk production after weaning, women rubbed camphor on their breasts or wore necklaces of old, rusty nails dangling between the breasts and then threw the nails into a fire or an old ants' nest. Puckett noted that while waiting for a new mother's milk to come in, "the Negroes insist on the child having food at once, and slip a piece of fat, greasy, bacon in the child's mouth soon after birth 'ter clean out his system.'"[16]

Folk medicine remained a more influential and compelling system among poor blacks than the "medical scientific approach to health" that proponents of midwifery reform sought to impose. Beginning in the late 1910s, states passed laws to license and regulate midwives. Like most other states, North Carolina prohibited midwives from delivering a baby if the mother had not been examined by a physician or attended a prenatal clinic. A Moore County public health nurse observed, "This obstruction to their practice has bothered more than one of our midwives, who often practice in neighboring counties as well as our own." In

1940, only seventeen of forty-two Moore County midwives (40 percent) complied with a state law that required them to obtain permits to practice, despite the prescribed penalties of fifty dollars or a thirty-day jail term. Enforcement of the midwife licensing law in North Carolina appears to have been lax in comparison to Mississippi, where registered midwives frequently helped identify their unregistered copractitioners. But some Mississippi midwives also resisted compliance with state regulation, engaging in practices such as "a bag to show" for inspections and "a bag to go" for deliveries. Alabama and South Carolina required midwives to take an intensive two-week refresher course every four years.[17]

In North Carolina, the editor of the *Health Bulletin* complained, "One of the chief thorns in the flesh of our nurses always is dealing with the 'bootleg' midwives, that is, those who are too old, too ignorant, too dirty, too diseased to be permitted by the state to carry on this important work for the poor and underprivileged women of the state." Such midwives were, according to the editor, "law only unto themselves." Although the editor's remark reflected stereotypes of blacks as irrational and disrespectful of authority, it also emphasized black women's determination to maintain control over one of the most precious and personal aspects of their lives. The editorial cited an incident where a public health nurse told a midwife who was more than eighty years old and repeatedly practiced without a license that she "wished the old woman was in jail and could never get out. The instantaneous reply from the old woman was, 'My Gawd, honey, I wish so, too. Then I wouldn't have to work and could have plenty of vittles.'" The story highlights the reality of poverty for many midwives while perpetuating racial and class stereotypes of poor blacks as freeloaders.[18]

Irene Lassiter, a white public health nurse, expressed similar sentiments around 1940 in "Problems with Untrained Midwifery in the South," arguing that untrained midwifery was characterized by "Ignorance and Superstition. To the public health nurse these two words stand as mighty mountains . . . that must be destroyed." Lassiter recounted a visit to the home of "Mary Doc," who had "learned her 'calling' from her mother who was a midwife of the dark ages of midwifery." Lassiter traveled "15 miles of good dirt road" but complained that "no midwife would live on a good road—Oh, No!—like the squirrel she must get back into the woods." She described Mary Doc as "between 55 and 60—her exact age is not known. She married at an early age and has nine living children and has had five abortions." Lassiter was thankful that midwives had "no medication to hasten labor—no instruments to cause danger" and emphasized her professional and racial superiority: "We do not attempt to teach midwives the art of obstetrics as taught to the medical student or nurse—they have neither the mental ability nor the money for such." Yet Mary Doc was not completely uneducated, since she had been taught to wash her hands and to recognize danger signs in a mother. In Lassiter's opinion, Mary Doc regarded the public health nurse as an "earthly god—from whom she expects everything from calling a doctor in a difficult labor to buying her eggs and chickens on Saturday that she may buy snuff." Lassiter did not return Mary Doc's admiration, calling such midwives a "necessary evil" and predicting that only with "time and education, with the old midwives dying off can we hope to conquer our problem." Such views of midwifery were inherent in the policies and propaganda of federal agencies such as the Farm Security Administration, which chose to exclude nontraditional practitioners from participation in its medical cooperatives to court the favor of local medical societies and the American Medical Association. Farm Security Administration photographs highlighted the competence of doctors and nurses attending patients but portrayed black midwives as exotic, archaic relics of a primitive practice.[19]

Despite such protests against untrained midwives, black women would continue to rely on traditional midwifery as long as poverty, racist health institutions, poor transportation, and the scarcity of physicians prevented them from having hospital deliveries or even physician-attended home births. Health reformers advocated two complementary solutions: mothers would receive prenatal care for themselves and postnatal care for their infants at clinics in outlying areas, and midwives trained in scientific medicine would deliver babies. The foundation for this strategy had been laid by a biracial coalition of public health workers, black voluntary organizations, and white philanthropies during the 1910s and 1920s. As Susan Smith has noted, the black lay health movement during the four decades before World War II was conducted almost entirely by black women and thus devoted substantial attention to their and their children's health needs.[20]

NEW DEAL MATERNAL AND INFANT HEALTH PROGRAMS

The federal government took over and expanded this private, largely female role after the Roosevelt administration began to perceive poor health among all races of southerners as a national liability. Infant and maternal health had been an early target of federal health funding through the Sheppard-Towner Act of 1921, but the resulting programs benefited blacks in only a handful of southern cities, among them Memphis and Houston. However, Sheppard-Towner provided a model for New Deal maternal and infant care programs offered under the Farm Security Administration and Social Security. The PHS administered most of these funds, with the remainder under control of the Children's Bureau. The act's maternal and child health title gave priority to states with the highest birth rates and to "rural areas and in areas suffering from severe economic distress." It also required states to develop "demonstration services in needy areas and among groups in special need," stipulations that favored the South.[21]

To extend federal health programs to the black population, PHS officials sought the cooperation of black doctors, public health nurses, and community workers. Black physician Walter H. Maddux served as the pediatric consultant to the Maternal and Child Health Division of the Children's Bureau and was "available for assignment to States having a large Negro population." In perhaps no other southern state was this strategy applied more successfully than in North Carolina, where approximately one-tenth of all full-time public health nurses employed by city and county health departments were black. These men and women, the North Carolina Board of Health reported in its *Health Bulletin*, "present to their people the problems that confront them with perfect candor, evading no facts, but, at the same time, letting it be known that the State, through the processes of education and preventative medicine, wishes to help them." Large numbers of African Americans responded. Although blacks represented just over a quarter of the state's population, they accounted for half the caseloads of public health nurses. In 1940, for example, the Beaufort County health officer reported that clinics under his supervision had provided 90 percent of black expectant mothers "the privilege and benefit of medical examination during the year."[22]

As the product of local, state, and federal resources, the maternal and infant clinics represented the priorities of white government authorities. Yet like midwifery, the clinics became identified as a "colored institution." When North Carolina established its first prenatal clinics in 1936, nearly 80 percent of the thirteen thousand patients were African American. By 1940, the Board of Health supervised 171 maternity clinics in seventy-three of the state's one hundred counties; only one-sixth of the twenty-nine thousand patients were white. Only Georgia operated more public maternity clinics within its borders, with 181, and of the 1,229 maternity clinics nationwide, 960 were in the South, which needed the facilities most. White women were apparently more concerned about maintaining segregation with regard to themselves than to their children, seventeen thousand of whom visited well-baby clinics in 1940, as did thirty-six thousand black children. In Moore County, just above the South Carolina border in the south-central region of the state, the prenatal clinic was "made up entirely of Negro mothers and [was] held in the colored school." A handful of poor white mothers were "cared for through visits of the nurses and an occasional visit to the Vass [a town in Moore County] clinic where necessary." Thus, white public health nurses maintained segregation while they provided poor whites with personal, in-home service similar to that enjoyed by the clients of black midwives.[23]

To supplement the services offered to mothers and infants in public health clinics and physicians' offices, the Board of Health taught midwives the basic principles of scientific medicine. Local health officers spoke to midwives at annual meetings to administer health examinations and provide education. About 75 percent of midwives either attended the 225 midwife meetings held statewide or were seen at 1,000 home visits. Estimates of the number of midwives in North Carolina ranged between three thousand and eight thousand, with twenty-two hundred holding valid permits to practice. Midwife education programs were adopted throughout the South, with courses ranging from two weeks for basic instruction to a year for certification as a nurse-midwife. Only three hundred nurse-midwives practiced in the United States in 1950, out of an estimated 20,000 midwives. In addition to meeting the requirements for certification as a registered nurse, nurse-midwives also took courses in public health and a minimum of six months in obstetrics. Nurse-midwives in Alabama, for example, completed nine months of classes and apprenticed with experienced midwives. A North Carolina midwifery permit required the applicant to master sterile technique, observe at least ten deliveries, and assemble an equipment bag with sterile dressings, scissors, scales, and silver nitrate drops (to prevent blindness in infants with congenital gonorrhea). Trainees learned "the very first symptoms of danger to the mother, and to ... secur[e] the services of a competent physician at such times (at all hazard) and at the earliest possible moment." Other topics included the proper way to tie off an umbilical cord and the most nutritious foods for nursing mothers. The training courses not only attempted to fill the gaps in midwives' knowledge but also enabled the white health establishment to exercise stricter control over black female practitioners. Students were urged to cooperate with doctors and nurses and to register babies with written birth certificates, since black midwives were key to state efforts to collect vital statistics.[24]

Even if they completed the state training course, midwives could be stymied by other requirements that had a potential for abuse. A literacy test and proof of graduation from high school effectively disqualified many would-be licensees, especially older black women. Applicants had to obtain character references from "a local physician and two other persons of good standing in the community," a requirement that could easily be interpreted to the disadvantage of "troublemakers." State laws placed midwives firmly under the surveillance of physicians. In North Carolina, a midwife could not take a case without "written permission from a doctor or clinic stating that the patient may be delivered by a midwife." Midwives risked losing their permits if they asserted their medical authority by offering gynecological treatment. Conducting a digital exam to determine the progress of labor or even failing to wear a regulation uniform could bring punishment. White officials at times used the regulation of midwifery, like voting qualifications, to restrict black civil rights. In Mississippi, for example, some midwives who engaged in civil rights activity during the 1960s had their permits revoked.[25]

Physicians, nurses, and midwives reacted to maternal and child health reforms according to differing concepts of professional identity. Public health clinics for rural mothers and children offered many health workers, the vast majority of whom were white, their first contact with African Americans and the conditions in which they lived as sharecroppers and farm laborers. Some doctors and nurses, disgusted by their experiences, advocated sending out midwives as proxies, while others professed respect and even admiration for the black women they encountered as patients and practitioners. White health professionals reacted most negatively to untrained midwives, whom they regarded as ignorant and superstitious menaces, a "law unto themselves" who defied the professional and social authority of doctors and nurses. Obstetricians generally abhorred midwifery as unsalvageable, an opinion shared by many private physicians and not a few public health officers. Public health nurses were more likely to accept trained and licensed midwives on a relatively equal basis.

The negative views expressed by white health professionals illustrate the racial paradoxes of deluxe Jim Crow public health. White doctors and nurses made stereotypical assumptions about the intelligence and morality of blacks that were compounded by biases toward women, the poor, and country folk, yet rural black women flocked to receive public health services. Lassiter's comments show that despite the improved availability of public health services, blacks still experienced overt prejudice at the hands of an overwhelmingly white public health profession. Noted black activist and physician Paul Cornely studied city health services for southern blacks and confirmed that "Negro patients were often treated with condescension, lack [of] sympathy, without respect and dignity, and without attention to many of the minor details for personal comfort and privacy."[26]

Cornely's observations were borne out in the attitudes of white health professionals toward the poor of both races. The February 1941 *Health Bulletin* printed a letter from "one of the ablest county health officers in North Carolina," who asserted that birth control was "the answer to the lowering of the infant death rates because morals are very lax among the Negroes in many parts of this county and our illegitimate birth rate is high." He charged that many black mothers "don't care and in many instances are glad when the baby doesn't live." He not only criticized unwed black women as being morally unfit for motherhood but also cited married mothers who had "such large families that when they lose a baby they say 'the Lord knows best.'" Likewise, when Federal Emergency Recovery Administration field agent Martha Gelhorn visited the white textile mill communities of Gaston County in 1934, she reported that "every social worker I saw, and every doctor, and the majority of mill owners, talked about birth control as the basic need of this class. I have seen three generations of unemployed (14 in all) living in one room; and both mother and daughter were pregnant." Gelhorn advocated having prenatal clinics provide expectant mothers with birth control education, which they could then pass on to other women by word of mouth. But she saw "absolutely no hope for" children already born into large, poor, millworker families: "I feel that our relief rolls will double themselves given time."[27]

The health officer's and Gelhorn's incredulity at the fatalistic "Lord knows best" attitude of women who bore one child a year typified the frustration that white medical, public health, and welfare professionals often exhibited toward their clients, black and white, who were caught in a cycle of poverty, hunger, and large families. Callous racism and classism were not, however, universal among white public health professionals. Even among those who clearly favored their own race and class, more than mere prejudice lay behind frustrated pronouncements that poor people were hopeless and ignorant. Even W. E. B. Du Bois expressed exasperation toward black families who refused to follow the example of the "better class of blacks," who controlled their reproduction by marrying later and pursuing education. Du Bois blamed the detrimentally high fertility rate among the black masses on both the conservatism of black churches that viewed birth control as sinful and the lingering influence of antebellum white masters who had engaged in human husbandry by encouraging their slaves to produce as many offspring as possible to maximize their owners' wealth.[28]

Despite the fact that birth control was prized by many southern women of all races, whether Du Bois's elite Talented Tenth or farm wives desperate to escape the physical and financial strain of constant pregnancy and childbirth, the clash of viewpoints on fertility was part of a larger sea change in cultural attitudes toward death and disease. The almost universal religious fatalism that had undergirded nineteenth-century Americans' valorization and romanticization of death was in retreat during the early twentieth century, as mass sanitation, immunization, and public health education efforts began to convince the public that disease was preventable and curable rather than an unavoidable fate. But the stoic acceptance of morbidity and mortality as well as pregnancy, once the common view of poor immigrants, middle-class Victorians, and cracker farmers alike, was now a holdout among the southern people whose low standard of living ensured that death remained as familiar in the present century as it had been in the last.

The fear of death and the belief that race was an indelible marker of human character and potential receded together, but not always at the same pace. County health officer William H. Richardson, writing in the *Health Bulletin*, insisted that "public health knows no race, no creed." He claimed that "public health, like education, welfare and other activities, is administered for the benefit of the entire population rather than for any particular race or group. The benefits of government are, or at least should be, all inclusive." Reciprocal, respectful relationships were indeed possible among public health professionals, midwives, and their mutual clients. During visits to rural African American communities, public health nurses witnessed the respected role midwives played as healers. One Halifax County nurse wrote with admiration that the midwives "ride over muddy roads on wagons, sometimes in the rain, to receive the new generation of their race and to minister to their needs." Such experiences led some nurses to include black women in their professional sphere and to advocate the reform rather than the eradication of midwifery.[29]

When Lila Blalock, who began practicing public health nursing in Wilson County in 1950, made one of her first field visits to a black country church to promote tuberculosis testing, the congregation "began to shuffle their feet, they began to say Amen." Blalock remembered that "it was a little startling to me at first, because I was fresh out of the [University of North Carolina] School of Public Health, and I had not had experience with that kind of situation." In the first years of her career, Blalock encountered black mothers who put cabbage leaves under the bed to reduce fever and tied nutmeg around infants' ankles to help the babies teethe. Although Blalock was skeptical of such traditional remedies, she proved adaptable and sensitive to her patients' beliefs. To win the trust of a mother whose son frequently missed school with a sore throat, she asked the woman to teach her how to read the signs of the almanac. In turn, she convinced the mother that the signs were favorable to allow her son to be hospitalized for a tonsillectomy. Although Blalock did not place the same credence in folk medicine that many of her patients did, her field experience taught her a sensitivity to black culture that most white private practitioners lacked.[30]

Like Blalock, black midwives who received scientific training combined effective medical knowledge with cultural sensitivity, but their knowledge of black culture preceded rather than followed their public health education. While older midwives with years of experience were likely to view licensing laws and other regulations as unwarranted interference with their right to practice a generations-old trade, younger women eagerly signed up for training courses and gained new confidence in themselves as public health professionals. Unlike formally educated doctors and nurses, whose professional identities were physically located in the buildings where they worked, licensed and trained midwives occupied a liminal space between the spheres of mainstream institutional health care and black folk culture. Their ability to communicate across the gulf between rural African American women and the predominantly white public health establishment made modern midwives particularly effective tools in the campaign to reduce infant and maternal mortality. The new generation of trained midwives joined their white counterparts in condemning old-style midwifery and viewed licensing and regulation as enhancements rather than threats to their professional identity.

In an article in the April 1941 *Health Bulletin*, Johnnie Sue Deloatch contrasted trained midwives like herself with their uneducated predecessors. She declared, "Delivering a baby now with a midwife is no more alike it used to be than ink is like milk." The black and white metaphor reflected the racial dimensions of midwifery reform, which had both positive and negative consequences for black women such as Deloatch. Dr. W. R. Parker, Northampton County's health officer, described her as "one of the county's most reliable and conscientious midwives." Deloatch lamented that "there is many a woman today suffering for some midwife['s] carelessness" and joined public health officials in regarding untrained midwives as menaces. Her conversion to the gospel of public health was so thorough that she referred to traditional midwifery as "the old nasty way," a judgment rooted in personal experience. Deloatch remembered that "when the midwife layed my baby on the floor the cat grabbed his foot with her claws and the baby screamed." Traditional practitioners "did not wash their hands" and greased the birth canal with lard. The old midwives "thought delivering a baby was nasty work so everything mostly they used around it was nasty." During the winter, midwives guarded against colds by forbidding the new mother to undress or wash anything but her hands and face for four days, which meant that "the pitiful little baby had to lie with the mother in all that odor." In Deloatch's opinion, rural folk's confidence in midwives was misplaced despite their service to generations of black women: "Some say our mother lived and didn't die. She didn't die, but you don't know how near death she was."[31]

Deloatch and other new-style midwives found support from doctors and nurses who validated midwives' worth to the cause of health reform. Louise East, supervisor of nurses for Halifax County, was encouraged by the "intelligence and native ability" of the applicants for midwife training. Dr. A. W. Makepeace reported that "intelligent, enthusiastic young women interested in midwifery are being encouraged to enter the field to replace the old and incompetent." He described the training available to midwives in 1941 as "so superior to what obtained a few years ago that the progress made is something of which the State can rightly be proud."[32]

Educated midwives such as Amanda Bunch of Wake County enjoyed the favor of both their communities and the public health establishment. When she died in 1946, the *Health Bulletin* published her eulogy, making her the only midwife so honored during the 1940s. Bunch "was proud to be a midwife and she had a record to be proud of." Since 1934, she had delivered more than a thousand babies. Bunch's racial identity was evident—her "skin was the color of a new penny. There was a little hump in her nose and she thought she was part Indian." In the eyes of the white author, Bunch could have received no greater honor than the "love and esteem [that] were expressed by the immense crowd including many white people that attended her funeral and heaped her grave with flowers." But perhaps the greatest compliment Bunch received was that she had "an extra sense of understanding that did not require going into detail." The fact that she "listened and observed closely and spoke everybody's language" was surely instrumental in her success.[33]

Bunch's cross-cultural aptitude enabled her to enjoy a remarkable rapport with local physicians. "She 'helped-out' the doctors and they helped her out, and when she had to call a doctor he never delayed. Every doctor seemed to feel the same respect and personal affection for her and during her illness this past year they voluntarily gave her their best attention." Bunch apparently achieved a level of professional respect rare among midwives. "At Prenatal Clinics she was welcomed by everybody and the Clinician treated her as an equal and had her feel and listen to interesting conditions. . . . The doctor would often have a little chat with her on the side regarding their latest fishing luck."[34]

Unlike Mary Doc, whose "pay [was] small if she gets any at all," Bunch's defense of fee-for-service practice would have pleased the staunchest opponent of socialized medicine. While midwives charged ten dollars or less for deliveries, rural doctors charged up to seventy-five dollars. "Sometimes she would grumble when she saw a man wasting money while in debt to her and once in a while employed a collector. She said there were no hard feelings but folks shouldn't get too careless." Bunch's insistence on being remunerated for her services may have seemed ludicrous to health professionals who considered themselves professionally and racially superior. But Bunch, secure in her professional identity, disregarded such sentiments and went about earning a living.[35]

The degree of camaraderie Bunch experienced with white male doctors was exceptional and may have been exaggerated by the eulogy's author. Bunch's relationship with these doctors may also have reflected a degree of opportunism or the desire to maintain good relationships with men who could revoke her license. Yet she represented the radical potential of midwifery training to elevate the status of black female practitioners. Underneath the general medical condemnation of midwifery as vastly inferior to a hospital delivery supervised by an obstetrician, at least a few doctors may have recognized that educated black women could compete for a patient base. This interpretation is somewhat premature, since the black poor would not become a central client population in medicine and public health until well after World War II. The typical clients of midwives were not a lucrative patient base for doctors, as reflected by the distribution of black physicians—only 8 percent practiced in rural areas, where 70 percent of the black population lived.[36]

Midwife Maude Callen of Pineville, South Carolina, was the subject of a 1951 *Life* photo essay. In contrast to the stereotype of the backward, ignorant granny midwife, photographer W. Eugene Smith portrayed Callen as the living personification of the modern, scientifically trained, highly competent nurse-midwife that the PHS had been educating with Social Security Act funds across the South. Unlike the highly supervised and regulated practices of most black midwives, who depended on the sanction of white public health doctors and nurses, Callen was held up as an independent practitioner of effective alternative care for the rural poor.[37]

Maude Evelyn Callen was born in 1899 and was one of only three of her mother's thirteen daughters to survive. After her mother died when she was seven, Callen left her home in Quincy, Florida, and went to live with her physician uncle in Tallahassee. His support enabled her to complete degrees at Florida A&M College for Negroes and the Georgia Infirmary in Savannah, where she studied nursing. Members of the Protestant Episcopal Church supported missionary work through the United Thank Offering program, which paid Callen eighty-seven dollars a month to serve as a nurse in Berkeley County, South Carolina, beginning in 1923. In addition to teaching elementary school in the mission's one-room schoolhouse, she taught nutrition classes, performed dental and eye screenings, and administered vaccinations for smallpox, diphtheria, and typhoid fever. In 1927, Callen left to care for tuberculosis patients at Homer G. Phillips Hospital in St. Louis and was certified as a registered nurse.[38]

After returning to South Carolina with her new training, she educated herself on modern midwifery techniques and began teaching local midwives, starting and ending classes with hymns. With no federal or state assistance, Callen held the first prenatal clinics in the county in 1934 and began delivering and consulting on births. She later organized the county's first venereal disease clinic. Callen drove thousands of miles per month at her own expense and walked through remote rural areas making house calls. Official recognition of her skills was belated: the Berkeley County Health Department finally hired her as a public health nurse in 1938, and in 1943, she completed a six-month midwife training course at Tuskegee Institute.[39]

Callen got little official support but set up makeshift clinics with the cooperation of local schools and churches. The *Life* article credited the South Carolina Board of Health as the sponsor of the clinics, but Callen considered herself a missionary and said she got "nothing, nothing" from the state. W. Eugene Smith spent two and a half months following Callen, shooting more than twenty-six hundred photos. Most of the images that the *Life* editors chose to publish showed her not practicing medicine but teaching or acting in a supportive role for patients. Two photos show Callen's efforts to save a seven-month-old baby with a 105 degree fever and extreme dehydration from acute enteritis, including driving twenty-seven miles to the closest hospital. According to Carol Squires, *Life* did not indicate "Callen's frustration with the passive role she had to play in the segregated hospital, with a doctor who had seemingly little regard for her medical abilities." Callen knew how to insert an intravenous needle, but the doctor seemed either unwilling or unable to do so, and the baby consequently died without a transfusion.[40]

Smith followed and photographed Callen at work with the intention of exposing racial inequality in American health care. Smith credited Callen with handling "the delicate matter of racial relationships with magnificent intelligence and grace." Smith volunteered to give blood for the ailing baby after black donors could not be found, but the white nurses at the hospital were offended at the idea of a white man offering to donate blood for a black child. Smith's assistant, Berni Schoenfield, remembered, "The blood was taken [and given] very badly. Most of it ended up on the pillow. Maude had to stand by and watch this botching going on because of the color barrier at the time." In the wake of the story's appearance, *Life* readers sent more than $18,500 to fund a permanent, well-equipped clinic for Callen, and the South Carolina legislature increased funding for public health.[41]

It was indeed a cruel irony of deluxe Jim Crow that rather than convincing white segregationists of the injustice of segregation, the existence of "best black men and women" such as Callen was held up as proof of equal opportunity under segregation, while whites denied that extraordinary abilities and character were required to succeed under existing racial barriers. Smith's *Life* essay on Callen portrayed her as an empowered prototype of the modern nurse-midwife. Like black physician and medical researcher Charles Drew, Callen was an inspiring race superhero whose high level of achievement and sacrifice enabled her to triumph over discrimination yet also illustrated the excruciating toll of racism on black aspirations. As historian Spencie Love observes of Drew, "If one was forced to dedicate one's life to breaking down barriers by proving one's worth through humane contributions, one paid a tremendous physical and psychic cost."[42]

Callen, Bunch, and Deloatch represented the first generation of black women to enter the corridors of white institutional medicine, twenty years before black male physicians desegregated the medical profession. By joining modern health science and traditional folk medicine, these midwives enabled rural black women to benefit from health advances that had previously been available only in white facilities. A black Mississippi midwife's model birthing room demonstration so impressed white observers that they wrote enthusiastic letters to the local board of health. One woman remarked that "considering the arrangement of the room, preparation of the bed, and the neat and sanitary surroundings it was a fair rival to most hospitals." A doctor also praised the midwife's demonstration and predicted that if all midwives conducted their deliveries in a similar manner, black infant and maternal mortality would "be largely reduced."[43]

Puckett identified black midwives' key advantage over white health professionals when he wrote, "Often quite as much attention is paid to the mode of administration as to the drug itself, which reminds one of the African treatment of disease, where no distinction is made between the therapeutic action of the drug and the mode of its administration. In fact, the administration is judged by the Africans to be the most important part." Midwifery offered a mode of administration that countered the effects of racial exclusion and poverty. The campaign to reform midwifery was a two-way street that also enabled poor rural black women to reform government intervention to benefit black health. Educated midwives countered stereotypes of blacks as vectors of disease by aiding white health professionals in promoting clinics, immunization programs, and medical examinations for mothers. Yet changes in politics, demographics, and race relations ensured that midwifery eventually died out, as its critics had hoped.[44]

EMIC AND THE SHIFT TOWARD HOSPITAL BIRTHS

After four years of maternal and infant care clinics sponsored by federal Social Security Act funds, maternal mortality in the United States was reduced by almost one-third and infant mortality by one-sixth. The onset of World War II created both obstacles and opportunities for the state- and federally funded strategy of using trained midwives and rural clinics to reduce infant and maternal mortality. The wartime physician shortage muffled criticism of North Carolina midwives, who were estimated to number between four thousand and nine thousand. One public health doctor admitted that "at the moment midwives are an essential part of the plan for improved care to be offered women of this State at the time of delivery." In 1941, more than twenty thousand North Carolina women of all races delivered with midwives, accounting for more than 25 percent of all births, and more than fifteen thousand women did so four years later. As late as 1950, 34 percent of North Carolina's nonwhite births were still attended solely by midwives, compared to only 2.5 percent of white births. The nonwhite figure included a substantial number of Native Americans, who had nearly twice the birth rate of whites or blacks but were more reluctant than blacks to patronize state-funded maternity and infant clinics. In 1939, despite widespread poverty among Indians, only 25 percent of Indian mothers and one out of six Indian children received care at these clinics.[45]

According to Reynolds, the work of the Maternal and Child Health Department "reached its peak throughout the State about 1941" because of wartime reductions in health personnel, but the federal Emergency Maternity and Infant Care (EMIC) program for servicemen's families stepped in to fill the gap. World War II created a crisis in maternal and infant care in the South. Southern senators ensured that the majority of new military bases were constructed in their home states to aid the region's poor economy. North Carolina was particularly successful at attracting new military construction, and three of the country's largest bases were located in its rural eastern Black Belt, permanently transforming the region's economy. EMIC, which functioned from 1943 until 1949, cared for one in every six babies born in the United States in 1944. North Carolina was one of the earliest states to participate; during the program's first two years, fifteen hundred babies and twenty-two thousand mothers benefited, representing 95 percent of soldiers' wives who gave birth in the state. By the end of 1946, EMIC had cared for nearly thirty-eight thousand maternity cases in North Carolina, one of the country's highest totals. In 1937, only 15.5 percent of all North Carolina births had taken place in hospitals, a figure that rose steadily, largely as a consequence of EMIC and rising wartime incomes, to reach 51 percent by 1944.[46]

EMIC received credit for increasing the number of physician-attended hospital births among American women, particularly rural southern women of both races, who had previously been least likely to give birth under those circumstances. Approximately nine hundred thousand African Americans served in World War II, three-quarters of them in the army, where they represented 10 percent of enlisted troops by the war's end. Black women were among the pregnant wives of servicemen, or "storkers," who crowded the wartime boomtowns. Cornely praised EMIC as "one of the best programs ever developed for mothers and infants" and noted that black women were aided disproportionately because more black soldiers were represented in the four lowest enlisted pay grades targeted under EMIC. Not only was EMIC praised for decreasing North Carolina's perennially high infant and maternal mortality rates, but it also focused attention on the health needs of blacks and the poor.[47]

EMIC subsidized maternity care for home as well as hospital births. Although statistics for EMIC do not indicate race, it is reasonable to assume that black women accounted for a disproportionate number of southern home deliveries under EMIC. In 1944, 15.8 percent of North Carolina and 30 percent of Mississippi women cared for under EMIC delivered at home, compared to 9 percent nationally. It is not clear whether this difference reflected a greater preference for midwives, a more acute shortage of maternity beds, or both. Race was also likely a factor, since although EMIC did not discriminate against black women, black hospitals would have been less able to meet the strict standards required for participation. (Only 24 of 183 black hospitals in the United States were fully accredited.) Black women who wanted to retain black physicians could not do so in southern white hospitals, nearly all of which refused to grant admitting rights to black doctors during the 1940s. Finally, as Elizabeth Temkin has observed, "Wartime prosperity led to a change in patterns of hospital use that funneled the growing demand for maternity care into a smaller pool of hospital beds" in private institutions, which were generally preferred by women who delivered under EMIC. But private hospitals were more likely than public hospitals to bar blacks entirely. In 1947, 9 of North Carolina's 123 hospitals were black-only, 48 were white-only, and 66 admitted both races on segregated wards. Thus, even if EMIC removed the financial barriers to a hospital delivery for the wives of black soldiers, other factors still resulted in a higher percentage of home deliveries among southern black women than in the program nationally.[48]

The dramatic increase in hospital births among both black and white southerners during and after World War II also prompted new attention to accommodations for new mothers and infants. In 1941, only 16 percent of births in Mississippi and 17 percent in Arkansas took place in hospitals, compared to 94 percent in the District of Columbia and 92 percent in New Jersey. By 1943, Mississippi hospital births had risen to 31 percent, while those in Arkansas had grown to 42 percent. Between 1931 and 1943, the number of bassinets in U.S. hospitals rose 49 percent, from 51,492 to 77,134. But during that period, hospital births had risen by 171 percent. Rosenfield commented, "Our hospitals are unprepared for the task [of hospital births] put on them. The increasing demand on hospitals for maternity facilities is being met by cutting down the length of stay." The average length of hospitalization for childbirth decreased from sixteen days in 1931 to ten days in 1943, with wartime overcrowding shortening some stays to as little as five days.[49]

Efforts to reduce maternal and infant mortality during the 1930s and 1940s made prenatal care and trained assistance at delivery available to most women in North Carolina. Whites continued to blame high mortality rates on midwives' ignorance of modern medicine but rarely cited physician error. According to health historian Susan Smith, trained midwives matched and in some cases exceeded the safety record of doctors. For example, in 1939, Moore County boasted no maternal deaths and 293 successful deliveries, 98 by doctors and 195 by midwives. During the twentieth century, the racial gap in infant mortality narrowed most rapidly from 1941 to 1946. While more than a third of black southern births were attended solely by midwives, the South recorded the largest declines in nonwhite infant mortality of any region. These improvements during and after World War II resulted from the racial convergence of income and mothers' education levels as well as the effectiveness of federally sponsored wartime health initiatives, particularly those targeted at the large number of southern military bases.[50]

In 1940, North Carolina had ranked forty-first in maternal mortality; by 1952 it was thirty-fourth, ahead of every other southern state except Virginia. Public health clinics for mothers and infants resumed after World War II, and whites tended to credit the clinics, rather than the improved medical knowledge of midwives, for the change. James F. Donnelly, chair of the North Carolina State Medical Society's maternal welfare committee, boasted in 1953, "Because of the rapid increase in the number of prenatal clinics for indigent patients throughout the entire country, and particularly in this state, more women are receiving good prenatal care now than ever before." Prenatal and well-baby clinics operated in nearly every county, and the number of obstetricians had increased from ten in 1940 to fifty in 1950. The use of antibiotics had reduced the proportion of maternal deaths caused by infection from 28 percent in 1940 to 7 percent in 1950. Another factor in improved maternal and infant health was the passage of the Hill-Burton Act in 1946, which affected the quality of hospital care in the South more profoundly than in any other region. As the U.S. birth rate topped four million in 1954, the largest category of PHS grants to states other than the Hill-Burton hospital construction program was for child health programs. Amendments to the Social Security Act in 1950, 1954, 1960, and 1963 continuously increased the annual appropriations for maternal and child health and services for crippled children, which rose from a combined $1.9 million in 1936–37 (the first year of Social Security) to $87.3 million by 1966–67.[51]

What was lost in the decline of midwifery and the rise of a white-dominated, institution-based health care system of public clinics and segregated hospitals? According to historian David McBride, the rise of public health voluntarism among black doctors, nurses, midwives, and community workers during the 1930s indicated "the divergent responses within the black and white southern communities to the infectious disease problems of blacks." Explanations of racial disparities in morbidity and mortality revealed a significant ideological split between white federal health officials, who continued to cite racial factors, and black community health activists, who viewed high disease rates among blacks "as part of a social totality, a spectrum of health and social problems." Black health workers remained an important force for change within the public health establishment, where they found more opportunities than within mainstream organized medicine. But black doctors and nurses lost invaluable allies in midwives, who most effectively shared the worldview and concerns of rural black women. Not until the 1960s did urban migration, hospital desegregation, and Medicaid bring hospital deliveries within the reach of most black women, though white women had begun to enjoy that privilege at the turn of the century and most took it for granted by the end of World War II.[52]

part two

DELUXE

JIM CROW

COMES

OF AGE,

1938–1945

chapter 4

===

THE SOUTH AND
NATIONAL
HEALTH REFORM

S everal watershed events in 1938 heralded the emergence of deluxe Jim
Crow health policy. In July, the Roosevelt administration simultaneously released the *Report on Economic Conditions of the South* and the Technical
Committee on Medical Care's report on a national health program. In November, the inaugural Birmingham meeting of the Southern Conference for
Human Welfare (SCHW) represented the potential and limitations of southern
biracial liberalism. Closing out a momentous year in December, the U.S. Supreme
Court's decision in *Missouri ex rel. Gaines v. Canada* required segregated public
higher education programs either to provide equal opportunities to blacks or
to integrate. Thus, 1938 was the year the federal government signaled its commitment to all the prerequisites of deluxe Jim Crow policy: Washington would
offer national resources to remedy deficiencies in the southern economy and in
health-care services and facilities but would enjoin southern states to choose
between fulfilling the promise of equal or jeopardizing the legitimacy of separate
in the public sphere.

SOUTHERN LIBERALS AND NATIONAL HEALTH REFORM

Despite the midcentury Democratic dominance of Congress and the presidency, the split between the party's northern and southern wings in effect gave
southern Democrats the swing vote in a three-party system. With the South's
monoracial and unopposed Democratic Party behind them, southern senators

accrued seniority and disproportionate power to limit the New Deal or block it entirely. Could the might of the southern bloc be harnessed to pass instead of obstruct reform? Since Reconstruction, white southerners had regarded all federal aid with suspicion and feared it would pave the way for eliminating segregation. Senator Carter Glass of Virginia complained in 1937, "It is perfectly obvious that the so-called Democratic party at the North is now the negro party, advocating actual social equality for the races; but most of our Southern leaders seem to disregard this socialistic threat to the South in their eagerness to retain Mr. Roosevelt in power."[1]

In July 1938, the Roosevelt administration sought to consolidate its southern support with the release of the *Report on Economic Conditions of the South*, which identified the region as "the Nation's No. 1 economic problem." The report blamed the South's woes on its colonial dependence on the North and called on the national government to underwrite aid to uplift the region, but the authors made virtually no mention of racism as a contributing factor. As historian Bruce Schulman has persuasively argued, the *Report on Economic Conditions of the South* "marked the onset of a concerted national effort to restructure the southern economy." With the election of new southern liberals such as senators Claude Pepper of Florida and Lister Hill of Alabama, "the principle of entitlement—the southern liberal view of the South as a national problem deserving of federal aid—would translate into preferential treatment for the region in the disbursement of funds for highways, airports, and public education." But the most preferential treatment of all was reserved for the South's grossly inadequate health-care system. The 1935 Social Security Act and other New Deal health programs had made great strides in extending health services to medically underserved Americans, particularly the South's large poor, black, and rural populations. Yet the United States remained the only Western democracy without comprehensive national health insurance.[2]

The landmark events of 1938 closed with a case that would haunt southern governors for the next sixteen years until the *Brown* decision. In *Missouri ex rel. Gaines v. Canada*, the U.S. Supreme Court ruled that since the state of Missouri did not provide comparable educational opportunity at a public, in-state black law school, the University of Missouri must open its law school to the black plaintiff, Lloyd Gaines. In a decision that had clear implications for health care, the Court stated, "The admissibility of laws separating the races in the enjoyment of privileges afforded by the State rests wholly upon the equality of the privileges which the laws give to the separated groups within the State." Gaines

crumpled under national scrutiny and refused to enroll at Missouri (he reportedly accepted a two-thousand-dollar bribe to leave the country and was never
heard from again), and another decade would pass before a black student walked
onto a previously all-white southern campus. Yet *Gaines* was the first court victory in the campaign launched by Charles Houston and Thurgood Marshall
of the Legal Defense Fund of the National Association for the Advancement
of Colored People (NAACP) to force southern states to provide racial parity in
funding and services for public education, beginning at the graduate and professional level, where white resistance was lowest. Nathan Margold, the Harvard
law professor who originally conceived the strategy, advised the NAACP not to
strike at segregation head-on but to make segregation so expensive for southern
governments that they would agree to integrate public schools.[3]

On the legislative front, the NAACP lobbied during the 1930s for federal funds
to equalize resources for students and salaries for teachers in black and white
southern schools. This was the purpose of the Harrison-Fletcher Bill, which was
introduced in the Senate in 1936 and renamed the Harrison-Thomas-Fletcher
Bill in 1938. The bill was debated for the rest of the Roosevelt administration but
was never enacted. Southern state governments did, however, heed the *Gaines*
decision as a sign of things to come and began varying levels of efforts to shore
up the quality of black public institutions. Missouri was the exception: Governor
Lloyd Stark's blundering after the *Gaines* decision and resulting alienation of the
black vote helped boost the popularity of young senator Harry Truman, who
ran for reelection against Stark in 1940.[4]

Against this backdrop, Florida and Alabama voters elected two liberal senators
who would embody the political soul of deluxe Jim Crow health policy. Claude
Pepper and Lister Hill were close friends who served together on the Senate
Committee on Education and Labor (after 1946, the Committee on Labor and
Public Welfare). Hill and Pepper had populist political roots in ultraconserva-
tive Gulf South states and became loyal New Deal supporters. Florida voters
elected Pepper in November 1936 to fill a vacant Senate seat. After Roosevelt
appointed Pepper's political mentor and confidant, Senator Hugo Black of Alabama, to the Supreme Court in 1937, Hill, at the time a member of the House of
Representatives, replaced Black in January 1938. Pepper assumed Black's mantle
as the Senate's leading southern liberal and a key defender of Roosevelt's policies. As members of the Southern Policy Committee, a group of southern New
Dealers in Washington who gathered to discuss strategy, Hill and Pepper were
instrumental in convincing Roosevelt to appoint a blue-ribbon commission

to study the economic problems of the South, a decision that figured in his strategy to build political support for the New Deal. In the fall 1938 election, the Roosevelt administration backed Hill and Pepper as part of its attempted purge of conservative anti–New Deal incumbents.[5]

Hill and Pepper's leadership on health reform that would potentially benefit nearly 13 million black Americans must be placed in the context of the senators' racial views. Charles S. Johnson must have had Hill and Pepper in mind when he observed, "The intellectual liberals who know what should be done are torn between their private convictions and their public caution, and the most forthright declarations of the need for change are made by persons who are estimated by the community to have so little weight as to be innocuous." Hill and Pepper publicly subscribed to white supremacy for the sake of political survival but still tried to address black needs, a strategy pioneered by Louisiana governor and U.S. senator Huey Long. While Hill and Pepper filibustered against the 1937–38 federal antilynching bill, they also became charter members of the SCHW, a biracial progressive organization dedicated to improving southern race relations, labor conditions, and social welfare.[6]

The SCHW, organized in response to the challenges posed by the *Report on the Economic Conditions of the South*, adopted a platform that included abolishing the poll tax, raising southern living standards, improving the lot of farmers, keeping America out of war, defending civil liberties, advancing opportunity for "the Negro people," promoting passage of a national health program, abolishing rural and urban slums, and ensuring good schools and future job opportunities (but not forced labor) for all southern children. The SCHW became an ally of the NAACP and helped organize southern voter registration campaigns beginning in 1946. Hill dissociated himself from the SCHW under fire from conservative critics, but Pepper, along with his close ally, Henry Wallace, remained a stalwart supporter of the organization and spoke regularly at conferences throughout the 1940s, sharing the podium with black luminaries such as Walter White, Mary McLeod Bethune, and Johnson.[7]

During their 1944 Senate reelection campaigns, both Hill and Pepper faced criticism for being soft on white supremacy. Pepper had won repeal of Florida's poll tax in 1937; as a senator, he began a principled fight to abolish it nationally through federal legislation, which he called "a serious decision, politically and idealistically. It strengthens my opposition immensely at home. It gives a language to the anti-administration–anti-liberal group—which is hard to answer—the red herring of negro voting—or negro sympathy. Yet it is an essential step towards real democracy." When the anti-poll-tax bill was killed by a southern-led filibuster in 1942, Pepper was the only southern yes vote. Pepper's opponents circulated photos of him shaking hands with the congregation of a black Baptist church after a speech in Los Angeles, while Hill's opponent, James Simpson, ran a viciously racist campaign featuring billboards with the slogan "white supremacy." Despite Hill and Pepper's eleventh-hour proclamations that "the South will allow nothing to impair white supremacy," the *New Republic* exulted, "The victories of Senator Pepper of Florida and Senator Hill of Alabama should give new courage to all who believe in democracy." After the war, Pepper supported civil rights measures that he had previously opposed. Hill underwent no such transformation and remained in the Senate, later signing the Southern Manifesto in opposition to the 1954 *Brown v. Board* decision.[8]

Perhaps Hill and Pepper's most lasting political legacy was to convince their conservative colleagues to embrace federal aid to the South. If left-wing liberals argued for redistribution of wealth from rich to poor individuals, southerners argued for regional redistribution. When Mississippi senator Pat Harrison, with sterling states' rights credentials, proposed the 1938 Harrison-Fletcher Bill for federal aid to elementary and secondary education, he included specific provisions against federal interference and an equalization title that channeled more than 60 percent of the measure's funding to the South. This approach, along with a separate but equal clause, became the standard formula for deluxe Jim Crow legislation. Thereafter, southern senators included these features in all the social welfare legislation they proposed, whether in school health programs, aid to medical education, or health insurance vouchers for the indigent. Southern senators proposed a 1939 amendment to Social Security that distributed federal grants on the basis of need according to a graduated formula, but Congress did not enact legislation with a need-based allocation formula until Hill-Burton and other postwar programs.[9]

Pepper joined fellow southern liberals such as Representative Maury Maverick of Texas and Jonathan W. Daniels, a North Carolina writer, editor, and Roosevelt and Truman staffer, as well as supporters of national health insurance such as Milton Roemer, Frederick Mott, and Michael M. Davis. Pepper was particularly adept at making the case for federal aid to the South, as when he addressed the Senate in 1942: "I foresee a South which will come to the bar of the Congress with clean hands asking justice, which will practice democracy and seek it from its Congress and fellow countrymen. I envisage the doors of fair opportunity in all the Nation being thrown open to the people of the South by an interested, a considerate, and a fair Federal Government. I envisage provision being made for adequate health facilities which will make our beloved southern people healthy and strong in civilian and in military accomplishments." Pepper claimed that there was no source "as dependable or as potentially effective as our Government to help us in the South. I do not want the Government to dominate and to regiment us, but it must help us even more than it has in the past." Crediting Franklin Roosevelt and the national Democratic Party for the South's progress and insisting that "no part of America needs Federal help more than we," Pepper urged his southern colleagues to consider their region's needs and self-interest above their fears of federal interference in race relations.[10]

Senator Allen Ellender of Louisiana joined Hill and Pepper in promoting federal aid to southern uplift. Ellender called on the federal government to "lend assistance in making available to our people a reasonable amount of hospitalization at a price commensurate with ability to pay" and to "render all assistance possible so as to provide for all the people a decent home in which to live—another basic need." Building on the South's tradition of uniquely positive federal-state relations in public health, Pepper, Hill, Ellender, and other southern liberals worked to convince Congress and federal officials that the nation's fate was intimately tied to the South's fortunes as well as to convince southern officials and home-state constituents that federal aid was necessary and desirable, not a sign of the apocalypse. To build support for federal intervention in health and other aspects of social welfare, southern New Dealers warned skeptics such as Senator Glass that continuing a policy of laissez-faire Social Darwinism toward the poor, illiterate, and diseased masses would ultimately retard the growth of the entire region and drag down the prosperous elite.[11]

Whether their gradualism was one of principle or pragmatism, southern liberals wanted to reform but not revolutionize the region and give both black and white workers the basic requirements for full participation in the national economy: better wages, education, health care, and living conditions. These changes would not only erase the economic gap between the South and the rest of the nation that had fueled northern smugness since at least the 1862 publication of Frederick Law Olmsted's *The Cotton Kingdom* but would also enable the poor to pull their own weight. The appeal to a combination of regional pride and antiwelfare sentiment was a common tactic of southern New Deal apologists, but even those who viewed poor whites and blacks as socially or biologically inferior agreed on the need to include them in the government's efforts to rescue the South.[12]

A common refrain of reformers including Michael M. Davis, Aubrey Williams, John P. Davis of the National Negro Congress, and southern senators who sought to uplift the South was the region's role as the nursery of the nation's labor force. Even though the farm population earned 9 percent of the national income, it produced 31 percent of America's children, since birth rates were higher in rural areas than in urban areas. Cities of more than ten thousand people had a ratio of ten adults per seven children, while rural areas had ten adults per fourteen children. In 1940, 51.6 percent of all children under fifteen lived in rural areas, which stood to lose nearly half of these children on reaching adulthood to cities. As Hill put it, "The money is where the children ain't." He elaborated, "The best-financed school systems in 1940 spent $6,000 per classroom, and the poorest-financed systems spent less than $100 per classroom—a variation of 60 to 1. . . . It is shameful, but education in America is a lottery."[13]

Ironically, the poorer, more rural states spent proportionally more of their tax revenues on health and education than did the wealthier states, but the well-off states still spent much more per capita. In 1941, even after the Social Security Act boosted state public health budgets, Mississippi, with the nation's lowest per capita income, outspent twenty-seven other states, including Illinois and Pennsylvania, on local health services per resident. Mississippi topped all other states in the ratio of per capita spending for local health services per one hundred dollars of per capita income. Therefore, according to advocates of regional equalization, federal aid to the South was a fair redistribution of resources since the North had unfairly benefited from the South's natural resources and labor supply. Michael M. Davis declared, "Upon these differences in resources and in facilities rests the justification for methods of equalizing health opportunities for people in different communities and sections of the country." He cited the Rockefeller Foundation's aid to southern governments to fight malaria and hookworm and the Rosenwald Fund's support of Negro public health nurses in southern areas as examples of private support for equalization and asserted that taxes had for decades been used extensively to equalize the access of different geographic areas to public services such as road construction. The same principle, Davis concluded, should be applied to equalizing health care.[14]

The connections among health, segregation, national defense, and regional uplift suffused Senate hearings and floor debates on national health legislation between 1939, when Robert Wagner of New York introduced the first comprehensive national health plan, and 1946, when the passage of Hill-Burton signaled the zenith of political support for health reform and deluxe Jim Crow policy. The

Senate Education and Labor Committee heard blacks and white southerners present compelling but distinct arguments for a need-based calculus in federal health policy that would channel public resources to their constituencies. To white southerners such as Dr. Clarence Poe, a leading segregationist from North Carolina who chaired the Hospital and Medical Care Commission and served on the American Hospital Association's Commission on Hospital Care, medical need was "most appalling among farmers, and among sections of America, the need is most appalling in the South." Likewise, Thomas Parran observed in 1948 that "the problems of rural health are, in large measure, the most extreme expression of the problems of national health." But John Davis, national secretary of the National Negro Congress, asserted, "There can be no improvement of the conditions in the Southern section of our country without a very careful and conscious effort to see that improvement is made equitably for the Negro and white populations."[15]

Health care was also a problem in the slums of the urban North, where Davis argued that "although the situation with regard to the poor white families is almost indescribably bad, the situation with regard to Negroes is even worse." An editorial from the Urban League's *Opportunity* magazine declared, "No group in America is in greater need of medical care than the Negro. . . . The deliberate neglect of the health of Negroes is indirect but effective sabotage of the program for health betterment of the whole nation." Beginning with the 1935 Social Security Act and the 1938 Venereal Disease Control Act and intensifying during the debates over national health legislation throughout the 1940s, health reformers insisted that germs knew neither color lines nor state lines and that federal action to fight disease was imperative.[16]

In *An American Dilemma*, a two-volume chronicle of the effects of racism on American society published in 1944, Swedish sociologist Gunnar Myrdal noted the difficulty of separating the effects of racial discrimination in health care from the effects of blacks' disproportionate concentration in the region and income bracket where access to medical facilities was most limited. Southern liberals used this fact to political advantage by employing aggregate figures to emphasize regional health disparities without further breaking down statistics to reveal the interaction of race, region, and rural-urban residence as factors in morbidity and mortality. Their arguments for federal aid to uplift rural and southern health were predicated on racially nonspecific data that cloaked the more dire needs of urban blacks in the politically salable cause of rural southerners, more than

20 percent of whom had already abandoned their farms and migrated to cities in the five years before Hill-Burton was enacted.[17]

This strategy in health reform dovetailed with the philosophy of liberal groups such as the SCHW that promoted racial equality yet were not primarily concerned with ending southern segregation. Such liberal pragmatism avoided a head-on confrontation with segregation in favor of first building other valuable assets, such as voting rights and the unionization of workers and farmers. A fragile coalition of Roosevelt liberals from the South (Pepper and Hill in the Senate and Will Alexander and Michael M. Davis in the Farm Security Administration [FSA], among many others) and outside the region (particularly Senators James E. Murray of Montana, Elbert Thomas of Utah, and Robert F. Wagner of New York) worked together with the leaders of black national organizations to meet black and rural needs by prioritizing poor and medically underserved areas. Since a direct assault on segregation would doom passage of any proposed legislation, the coalition pursued the equalization rather than the elimination of segregated facilities and wards via federal guarantees of a proportional share of services and funding to black patients based on racial population ratios. This method represented the most viable approach for immediately extending health care to African Americans.[18]

Despite the unreliability of morbidity and mortality statistics during this period, apologists for black and southern health needs adapted the numbers with remarkable alacrity to support their arguments, as illustrated by two reports published simultaneously in 1949 by the Committee on Research in Medical Economics (CRME). As one of the foremost advocates of national health insurance, the CRME had attracted the animosity of the American Medical Association (AMA), and CRME chair Michael M. Davis faced a formidable challenge in trying to secure and maintain the support of diverse and often clashing constituencies. In *How a National Health Program Would Serve the South*, Davis appealed to whites who balked at federal interference with race relations or the existing health-care system. He mentioned race in one sentence out of twenty-four pages, emphasized low income and rural isolation as the cause of regional health problems, and praised southern governments for their sincere efforts to address health needs.[19]

Downplaying race appealed to blacks as well, particularly in regard to sensitive issues such as venereal disease, as Davis had acknowledged in a 1936 letter to Parran. Davis urged Parran to follow his *Survey Graphic* article detailing

Rosenwald-supported syphilis testing among rural southern blacks with another article that broadened the problem of syphilis beyond southern blacks and acknowledged that diagnosis and treatment facilities were also inadequate in rural white areas. Davis averred, "The cooperation of the Negro people and the Negro press is essential, and it is therefore necessary to present the health problems of syphilis as affecting rural areas and not focus on the Negro as a health menace. Otherwise economic disadvantages to the Negro in domestic service and in other work will result and the fear of this will stymie cooperation."[20]

Davis took an alternate approach in *Providing Adequate Health Service to Negroes*, a joint project between the CRME and the Department of Special Research of the NAACP that was published in both pamphlet form and the 1949 Yearbook issue of the *Journal of Negro Education*. The report opened with statistics underlining the wide gap between black and white mortality. Poverty, low levels of health awareness and education, and maldistribution and shortages of health professionals and facilities were the chief limitations on health-care access, but all of them were compounded by racial discrimination, especially for black southerners. "Bad as conditions in the South may be for the general population," the authors alleged, "they are even worse for the Negro fourth of the population."[21]

Advocates of national health reform used visual as well as statistical evidence to forward their cause. At the Resettlement Administration (absorbed by the FSA in 1937), the Historical Section headed by Roy Stryker sent photographers out to defend the agency's programs by documenting their positive effects, in contrast to the more well-known depictions of the ravages of rural poverty by photographers such as Walker Evans and Dorothea Lange. One of the few photo essays of the era centering on African Americans was Arthur Rothstein's August 1937 photographs of the destitute inhabitants of remote Gee's Bend, Alabama, published in the *New York Times Magazine*, *American Magazine*, and *Christian Century*. Stryker usually emphasized white farmers in FSA photographs because they would be more widely published, but FSA photographer Marion Post Wolcott returned to Gee's Bend in 1939 to document the changes brought by additional federal aid, including sanitation measures and maternal and infant clinics.[22]

Representatives of the federal government including Parran, Pepper, and FSA officials had to play defense as well as offense. Despite their positive views on national health insurance and their ties with well-known proponents such as Davis and Isadore Falk, these officials tried to counter accusations of "socialized medicine" by downplaying the government's role in federal health programs. FSA medical officer R. C. Williams claimed that the group medical plan was "governmental only in that its organization is sponsored and . . . partly financed" by the FSA. Since Davis required that the group health plans initially be approved by state and local physicians' organizations, FSA planners could not innovate beyond the relatively narrow limits imposed by participating medical societies. Pepper assured an AMA audience in 1945 that he had never favored socialized medicine and had no intention of limiting patients' choice of a doctor. Parran stressed decentralization as one of Hill-Burton's virtues while promising readers of the *Journal of the American Medical Association* that the U.S. Public Health Service (PHS) was only playing an advisory role and that final authority for the program's administration lay with the states and communities.[23]

BLACK ORGANIZATIONS AND NATIONAL HEALTH REFORM

The assurances of limited federal involvement placated doctors and white southerners but had the opposite effect on most African Americans. Even when New Deal health funding began to flow freely, black activists were not convinced that a rising tide of federal aid to the South would lift all boats. The NAACP's Louis Wright denounced the blight of racism at all levels of the health system: southern policy makers and complicit federal officials had let blacks "rot and die as a result of the murderous neglect of health on the part of [government] agencies solely because of race or color," while white southern physicians treated Negro patients with "indifference bordering on criminal neglect." The dilemma faced by black health reformers was summed up in the CRME-NAACP joint report: "How far is it wise to agree to the postponement of the ultimate goal of complete equality and integration of the Negro into the general public health program, in order to assure at least some improved provisions for Negro Health *now?*"[24]

During an era of hostility to civil rights legislation, whether antilynching and anti-poll-tax measures or a permanent Fair Employment Practices Committee, hearings on the federal health bills of the 1940s gave representatives of every major national black organization an alternative forum to promote equality. Leading NAACP integrationists White and Wright were joined by members of the National Medical Association (NMA), National Hospital Association, National Negro Congress, Urban League, and other black advocacy groups in calling for the equal inclusion of blacks in federally sponsored health programs.

Yet David McBride observes that before *Brown*, "black medical leaders did not place highest priority on integration of hospitals and health centers" but instead emphasized "national health insurance, essentially an economic reform measure." This approach resulted from both pragmatism and self-interest, since integration, a lofty but distant goal, was likely to draw patients away from the black hospitals to which black doctors were loyal yet also confined. Until at least the early 1950s, they prioritized expanding black health services over ending segregation, particularly if support was available to improve black hospitals.[25]

Consideration of a national health program began in earnest in 1938, almost simultaneously with the release of the *Report on the Economic Conditions of the South*, when the Roosevelt administration's Technical Committee on Medical Care issued a report on the nation's health needs (the third such report in ten years) and convened a Washington conference of more than 150 representatives of organized labor, farmers, and health professionals. The Technical Committee was a division of the Interdepartmental Committee to Coordinate Health and Welfare Activities, which included representatives from the PHS, Children's Bureau, and Social Security Board. On November 21–22, 1938, five members of the Technical Committee met in Washington with five physicians from the NMA, including George W. Bowles, president, and John A. Kenney Sr., editor of the NMA's journal. The NMA expressed its support for the administration's National Health Program, except for the expansion of Social Security to include compulsory health insurance, a provision that was too controversial and would jeopardize passage of the rest of the program. The NMA delegation urged that black health professionals should "have the privilege of treating and caring for their people and [should] receive therefore the same compensation" and that "this provision will be made one of the conditions of federal subsidy." The NMA representatives also requested that a black physician be named to the federal bureau charged with administering the national health program.[26]

In consultation with Parran and other advocates of health reform allied with the Roosevelt administration, Senator Robert Wagner, the New Deal's premier liberal legislator, incorporated the Technical Committee's recommendations into a bill to create a comprehensive national health program. Introduced in Congress in February 1939, Wagner's bill established the terms for debate in federal health policy over the next fifteen years. The National Health Plan Bill included proposals for the expansion of public health services, maternal and infant care, hospital construction, indigent hospital and medical care, disability insurance, the training of medical personnel, and the broadening of Social Security to include compulsory health insurance. The Wagner Bill was superseded by the Wagner-Murray-Dingell Bill first introduced in 1943 and the national health plan that Harry S. Truman presented to Congress in November 1945, when he became the first president to support universal national health insurance.[27]

The National Health Plan Bill was the first comprehensive legislative proposal to address racial, regional, and rural health disparities. Wagner's original draft contained provisions to make participating hospitals available "to all groups of the population," to prioritize the needs of rural and low-income areas, and to provide health services to medically needy patients. When John Kenney wrote to Wagner that although the NMA generally supported the bill, "I fail to see that it specifically comprehends the Negro group," Wagner replied that "the clauses of the bill to which you refer are designed to preclude discrimination on grounds of race, creed or color. . . . It is my purpose and hope that through these conditions of allotment, the urgent health needs of the Negro people will be adequately served." Wagner also stated that he was working with the NAACP on amendments "to embod[y] in the bill more specific language protecting Negroes and other minority groups from discrimination."[28]

Representatives from three key black organizations—the NAACP, the NMA, and the National Negro Congress—testified at the Wagner Bill hearings in April and May 1939. Like Hill and Pepper, Wright, chair of the NAACP board of directors from 1931 to 1952, understood the connection between Democratic votes and the federal commitment to health reform. "The remedy is not to take public health out of politics," Wright declared at the NAACP's 1939 annual convention, "but to wage an irresistible fight to get the vote for the 9 million Negroes [disfranchised in the South]. When [they] are free to cast an independent ballot, the NAACP struggle for a public health program administered fairly and without discrimination will be just about over." Wright, an outspoken opponent of segregation and monoracialism, had opposed the Julius Rosenwald Fund's attempt to construct a black hospital in New York and led the NAACP to initiate a national program in 1937 to fight health-care discrimination. Yet neither he nor any other representatives of black organizations who testified at the 1939 Wagner Bill hearings called for the elimination of segregation in federally sponsored health programs.[29]

Although Hill later promoted his Hospital Survey and Construction Bill as a states' rights measure with the intention of protecting segregation, the separate but equal clause commonly attributed to Hill was first advanced by Wright in 1939. Drawing on the *Gaines* decision and the proposed Harrison-Thomas-

Fletcher federal aid to education bill, Wright suggested amending the Wagner Bill to include the statement, "In States where separate health facilities are maintained for separate races, provide for a just and equitable apportionment of such funds to carry out the purposes of this title for hospitals and health centers for minority races." Subsequent hospital construction bills, ultimately enacted in the 1946 Hill-Burton Hospital Survey and Construction Act, incorporated remarkably similar language. Until Congress amended it in 1964, Section 622 (f) stipulated, "Such hospital or addition to a hospital will be made available to all persons residing in the territorial area of the applicant, without discrimination on account of race, creed, or color, but an exception shall be made in cases where separate hospital facilities are provided for separate population groups, if the plan makes equitable provision on the basis of need for facilities and services of like quality for each such group." Wright also called for guarantees that federal health funds were "never to be in smaller proportion to the whole sum than the minority bears to the total population," a principle that the PHS adopted in a formula that allocated planned Hill-Burton hospital beds to blacks and whites based on racial population ratios.[30]

Both cochairs of the Wagner Bill hearings before the Senate Labor and Education Committee claimed that there was no need for Wright's nondiscrimination amendments. While filibustering the federal antilynching bill, Ellender had claimed that "no distinction is made in distributing the funds per capita among the whites and the colored population of [the southern states]. Of course, I am sure many Senators will appreciate our endeavor in the South to maintain the white and the colored races separately has cost us quite a good deal of money, but I know that the investment has been worth while." At the hearings, Ellender offered his frequently cited statistic that blacks comprised 28 percent of Louisiana's population but 40 percent of its charity hospital patients as proof that blacks were being favored rather than discriminated against in the administration of public welfare. Senator James Murray twice asked Wright, "If all the other States treated the Negro as well as Louisiana, [would there] be any need for the precautions which you are suggesting?" Despite Wright's emphatic "Yes," Murray concluded that Louisiana blacks got "better treatment in proportion to the population than whites do." This argument was, of course, based strictly on charity hospital bed ratios and did not account for differences in quality of care in black and white wards or between charity care and the private health system. Nor did it acknowledge the racial disparities in poverty, morbidity, and mortality that necessitated more black charity beds.[31]

The exchange among Wright, Ellender, and Murray makes clear that the meaning of *nondiscrimination* as applied to federal health legislation changed over time. Guaranteeing the inclusion of blacks in federal health programs, even couched in the acknowledgment of segregation, was in 1939 a radical rather than reactionary proposition. That December, the trenchant ironies of deluxe Jim Crow were out in force at the Atlanta film premiere of *Gone with the Wind*. The Reverend Martin Luther King Sr., who only a month earlier had led one thousand protesters on a march to the steps of City Hall to demand voting rights, checked his radicalism at the door of the opening-night Junior League Ball. King led the sixty-member Ebenezer Church choir in a performance of Negro spirituals on the steps of a faux plantation house constructed for the occasion. The choir, including ten-year-old Martin Luther King Jr., was dressed in period slave costumes. John Wesley Dobbs, co-organizer of the voting march with King, was deeply offended and called the performance "unconscionable." The following week, the Atlanta Baptist Ministers Union censured King for performing at the event, which was of course segregated. (The movie's two black stars, Butterfly McQueen and Hattie McDaniel, elected not to attend, fearing possible mistreatment and negative publicity in a rigidly Jim Crow city.) But rather than labeling Rev. King a hypocrite, another interpretation is possible: black leaders during the deluxe Jim Crow era continually had to convince both blacks and whites of their loyalty.[32]

During the spring 1940 hearings on the Wagner-George hospital construction bill, black representatives of the NMA, National Hospital Association, NAACP, and Alpha Kappa Alpha Sorority argued for nondiscrimination amendments that applied to both patients and health professionals. The amendments neither recognized the existence of racially separate facilities, as Wright's 1939 amendment had, nor demanded the abolition of segregation as a condition for aid. The testimony of these black organizations influenced the hospital administrators who met with Parran during the Wagner-George hearings and concluded that "the interests of the colored race would be best served by making provision for them in institutions designed to serve the entire population rather than by the establishment of separate hospitals caring for Negroes only." From that point onward, the main groups pressing for federal aid to hospital construction advocated the ideal of biracial rather than monoracial facilities but still accepted the probability that in the South, patients would be internally segregated (as they were in many northern hospitals). Just as advocates of national health insurance had reluctantly accepted its exclusion from the 1935 Social Security Act to ensure the passage of the broader plan, so now advocates of integration refrained from making it a requirement for their support of federal health reform so that blacks might secure the desperately needed benefits of medical care where none now existed.[33]

The American Hospital Association's Commission on Hospital Care, which was instrumental in generating support to pass Hill-Burton, affirmed the goal of caring for black patients "in hospitals that serve white patients rather than in separate hospitals." The commission allowed that where segregation was legally required, service should be of equal quality for both groups. The commission also advocated that hospitals should admit qualified black physicians to their staffs "on the same basis as are other physicians" and provide equal opportunities for professional education. Black organizations continued to testify in favor of nondiscrimination amendments during the Hill-Burton hearings, but most still accepted legal segregation as a matter of pragmatism, not principle. As Thomasina W. Johnson testified in 1946 on behalf of Alpha Kappa Alpha's National Nonpartisan Council on Public Affairs, "In the matters of health and education, where the need among the minority groups is so great, we face a reality and recognize the State laws [mandating segregation] provided there is equitable and proportionate distribution of services, funds, and facilities on the basis of need. This attitude is to be in nowise interpreted as condoning, approving, or compromising on our basic principle [of opposing] segregation because of race, creed, or color."[34]

Others, however, insisted that full integration was just as important as increasing blacks' access to care. Representing the NAACP, Wright objected to the Senate Labor and Education Committee that the Hill-Burton bill provided for "state control over medical facilities constructed with Federal funds without any safeguards whatsoever to protect Negro patients and Negro members of the medical profession. The inequitable manner in which certain States allocate their own general funds affords ample justification for my concern." Wright had changed his position since 1939, and now, in 1945, he proposed that state Hill-Burton councils include minority representatives and that the legislation contain explicit assurances that "all services and physical accommodations of such hospitals shall be available to persons without regard to religion, sex, race, national origin, or degree of indigency" and that federally sponsored hospitals were obligated to accept all qualified, licensed physicians to the staff and to professional training programs. Drawing on the Negro agent concept applied throughout the New Deal, Wright also suggested that "qualified Negro representatives participate in making inventories of existing hospitals in the states where the Negro population is heavy" as well as in surveying hospital needs and developing state construction plans.[35]

Wright's testimony evokes the tension between the dream of an integrated future and the pressing realities of present discrimination. This tension also underlay the complexity of Du Bois's racial philosophy, which sought to kill racism and its bitter fruit, segregation, while fostering black achievement within Negro-led institutions and avoiding "impotent frenzy." Beginning in the 1930s and certainly by the late 1940s, Wright, W. Montague Cobb, and the orthodox integrationists had concluded that segregation could never protect and could only harm black well-being and achievement. Philanthropic or government aid to relieve the suffering of blacks that had been caused by the illegal, unjust acts of the state could only ultimately perpetuate injustice and suffering if it did not remove the root cause. The new generation of integrationists not only rejected the paternalism of Rosenwald, Rockefeller, and Duke but also went a long step beyond Du Bois and included all monoracial institutions, black and white, within their definition of segregation. After Hill-Burton was enacted, the NAACP adopted a zero-tolerance stance toward segregation in all federally funded programs and refused to endorse legislation that did not explicitly ban segregation. In 1951, in response to the ascendancy of such sentiment, the National Association of Colored Graduate Nurses disbanded and the PHS discontinued National Negro Health Week.[36]

WARTIME HEALTH PROGRAMS
AND THE DRAFT REJECTION CRISIS

While hospital construction awaited passage until after World War II, many other health programs were created or energized during the conflict. As Franklin Roosevelt made the transition from "Dr. New Deal" to "Dr. Win the War," the war effort generally eclipsed domestic reform. The exception that proved the rule was health care, the aspect of social policy (along with labor) most critical to national defense. With wartime federal spending ten times that for peacetime New Deal programs, defense-related health initiatives benefited from unprecedented government largesse. As Daniel Fox observes, American policy supported the expansion of social spending generally and health services spending in particular to dilute the appeal of leftist parties both at home and abroad. The leaders of Western industrialized countries were convinced that medical science could ameliorate many of the scourges of the human condition that had fueled the chaos of three decades of depression and war. Ellender told the Senate, "I am convinced that with a fair amount of education, some reasonable degree of hospitalization, and decent housing we can thereby build adequate bulwarks against communism, nazism, or any allied philosophy."[37]

Americans of all backgrounds reexamined their country's race relations in the light of wartime rhetoric that painted the Allies as the humanitarian defenders of freedom and equality. In 1944, CBS radio stations along the West Coast aired *These Are Americans*, intended to promote acceptance of equal opportunity for African Americans and to allay white fears concerning the imminent changes in race relations. The broadcast asserted that "holding the Negro down means the rest of us stay down with him. . . . Keeping him in ill health hurts America and the cause of democracy for which we are fighting." To a greater extent than ever before, white politicians and health professionals acknowledged black needs as central to improving the nation's overall health. But blacks and whites also clashed over the meaning of the struggle for democracy, as when blacks drew a parallel between Hitler's vision of a pure Aryan blood brotherhood and the American Red Cross's policy of segregating blood.[38]

The racialized concept of disease transmission was further undermined by the increased attention on the South as a staging ground for the war effort. In 1942, the South was a hive of activity. Although the federal defense transportation director had requested the cancellation of all nonessential conventions, the Southern Medical Association decided to meet in Richmond to prepare Dixie's doctors for their heightened wartime responsibilities. Likewise, the SCHW, at its 1942 meeting in Nashville, focused on the theme of the South and national defense on the premise that "a people whose will is weakened by poor health, malnutrition, poverty, [low] income, and bad housing cannot become a bulwark in the defense of the nation." In an article published in *The Nation*, SCHW executive secretary James A. Dombrowski examined "The New South on the March" and concluded, "All over the South today there is evidence of an upsurge of progressive thought and action."[39]

While the SCHW deliberated over the role of education and public health in national defense, among other topics, Birmingham newspaper editor John Temple Graves criticized the SCHW and others who would take advantage of the war to push for integration. The SCHW and its allies had chosen "to go crazy with their championings, scouring the land for trouble, entering loud complaint even against the calling of Negro babies 'pickaninnies,' and making plain beyond question an intent to use the war for settling overnight the whole, long, complicated, infinitely delicate racial problem." He also excoriated "Negro leaders who insist on appeasement as their price of full participation in the war." Graves was a prominent member of the Southern Council on International Relations, headquartered at the University of North Carolina at Chapel Hill, which led a united effort to convince federal military officials to use defense spending to boost the southern economy by granting contracts and locating bases in southern communities. Graves published *The Fighting South* in 1943 to promote the South's patriotic contributions to the war effort, but his definition of patriotism did not fully include black citizens in defense activities.[40]

Key federal officials disagreed, however. Armed conflict alloyed the meanings of military and social security, particularly in the case of the Federal Security Agency. In 1939, the Roosevelt administration reorganized the health, education, and social welfare agencies that had mushroomed among various branches of the federal government during the New Deal and placed them under jurisdiction of the new Federal Security Agency. With a 1940 appropriation that topped $812 million, the agency constituted one of the largest federal agencies and included the Office of Education, the PHS, the Social Security Board, the Civilian Conservation Corps, and the National Youth Administration. A second reorganization plan in 1945 transferred the Children's Bureau (previously in the Department of Labor), the vital statistics division of the U.S. Census Bureau, and the U.S. Employees Compensation Commission to the Federal Security Agency. By 1946, the agency had grown to nearly thirty-six thousand employees with a budget of more than $2 billion. The agency would prove to be the most liberal in the government on issues of both racial equity and health reform, which its officials promoted during and after the war as essential components of national defense.[41]

The Federal Security Agency's first head, Paul V. McNutt, received the title federal security administrator and coordinator of health, welfare, and related defense activities; he also chaired the War Manpower Commission. McNutt's faith in the power of the federal government contrasted sharply with the antifederal attitudes of southern politicians and organized medicine. In 1941, he credited the federal government with completing "some of the biggest and best-run jobs in history during this last 10 years" and stated that unlike private business, "government business lives in a 'goldfish bowl.' . . . Government business is the object of vast public attention before it ever begins to operate at all." In a 1942 speech, McNutt defined racial discrimination as a problem of war production: "At Mobile, Alabama, shipyards maintained discrimination against qualified Negro workers readily available and already housed in the area while they recruited workers from hundreds of miles away and then appealed for aid to provide housing for these workers. . . . In war the nation cannot afford and will not tolerate artificial immobilization of workers. Discrimination based on race, creed or color must go—not because of somebody's ideals, but because discrimination represents waste and industrial slowdown." McNutt and his successor, Oscar R. Ewing, advanced arguments on behalf of black equality that recast the labor, education, and health of blacks as crucial for the war effort and national security.[42]

Just before the attack on Pearl Harbor, Parran had stated in *Survey Graphic* that PHS surveys had revealed that "practically all defense areas are deficient in one or more of the essential facilities which they must have if they are to meet the demands imposed upon them by the emergency situation." Parran estimated that $190 million was needed for hospitals, clinics, and public health and sanitation facilities, with an additional $170 million required for medical care. Although the actual figure spent during the war to construct health facilities was less than one-third of what Parran recommended, federal aid to war-affected areas was particularly critical in the South, where the depression had hit hardest and where thousands of people poured into wartime boom towns to find work.[43]

The war also indirectly helped meet the need for health facilities, since many defense plants developed into self-contained communities that included hospitals as well as fire departments, cafeterias, and recreation areas for plant employees. In southern states such as Arkansas, where six ordnance plants were built during World War II, defense workers were segregated by race within plant facilities, but wartime employment nevertheless improved health-care access for poor, rural whites and blacks by both increasing their income and providing access to health services and hospitalization as employment benefits. After the war, military buildings in war-affected areas were sold or appropriated on a surplus basis and converted to civilian use as health facilities. For example, the neuropsychiatric offices at Duke University and the original buildings for Ochsner Hospital in New Orleans were converted military structures.[44]

Conversely, the construction of military bases was a major disruption and often exacerbated prewar problems of inadequate, crowded housing and a shortage of hospitals and medical professionals. Environmental and living conditions also suffered under the stress of rapid growth in areas still reeling from the Great Depression. While wartime production and the expansion of the defense industry would have long-lasting benefits for the southern economy, many residents of overnight military boomtowns such as Jacksonville, North Carolina, where Camp Lejeune Marine Corps Base was built, had their land confiscated to make way for the new bases and endured extremely crowded living conditions to accommodate the influx of new military personnel and defense workers. In some cases, chicken coops were renovated to house human boarders. Severe labor shortages meant that farmers often had to leave their crops in the field or abandon farming altogether.[45]

Michael M. Davis estimated that wartime service would claim one-third of active doctors and two-thirds of doctors under age forty-five, leaving 100,000 doctors by the end of 1943 versus 160,000 before the war. By the end of 1942, Valparaiso, a hamlet of about 600 people on the northwest Florida Gulf coast, had experienced a tenfold increase in population since the war began as a consequence of Eglin Field, an Army Air Corps training center. There was still no doctor for more than twenty miles, and residents who needed hospitalization had to travel by boat to Pensacola, the nearest town of any size, forty-five miles away. Davis criticized the inefficiency of the Procurement and Assignment Service for Physicians, Dentists, and Veterinarians, which had been established by executive order at the suggestion of the AMA to recruit and deploy health personnel, and he joined McNutt in urging that the responsibility be handed over to the PHS. He argued that in some areas without doctors (including many southern communities), "the only feasible method is to commission a doctor in the U.S. Public Health Service, put him in uniform, and send him to look after the people in that locality," while in areas affected by the massive growth of war production industry, management and organized labor could cooperate to provide incentives for doctors to relocate. Davis noted approvingly that the Mississippi Medical Society had proposed that town and county governments provide medical center buildings to house hospitals, professional offices, and health departments as well as subsidized bus service to transport sick patients from surrounding rural areas, though he made no mention of segregation or how the needs of black doctors and patients would be addressed. Davis also maintained that wartime exigencies justified expanding the PHS's authority beyond strictly preventive measures and that its funding should be increased to support medical care programs in war areas.[46]

Parran's mobilization of the PHS for the war effort proved to be a strategic masterstroke that built bipartisan support for health reform and garnered unprecedented federal funding for a broad-based defense-related health program.

The close wartime alliance between the PHS and the military included PHS oversight of the Civilian Defense medical division, which developed state emergency medical service plans and designated more than three hundred hospitals across the country to receive casualties if necessary. The PHS oversaw a wide array of wartime health programs, including the Army Nurse Corps, the Emergency Maternity and Infant Care program for soldiers' families, and rapid treatment centers for venereal disease patients, that dramatically affected the South.[47]

Military health care, particularly the Veterans Administration hospital system, would prove to be among the first spheres of national life to transition out of segregation. Fort Jackson, an army post near Columbia, South Carolina, illustrates how black military personnel experienced both opportunity and racism during World War II, with implications for wartime health care. Just as health defied the general trend of racial discrimination in civilian public policy, medicine was one of the earliest military fields to provide wartime opportunities to black soldiers, although the policies of the PHS at times ran counter to the army's long-standing acceptance of segregation. In early 1941, Parran created medical sanitation companies to employ black draftees in the Medical Corps, and Fort Jackson organized such a company in early 1942 to provide unskilled hospital labor; two more medical sanitation companies and a detachment of black WACS (members of the Women's Army Corps) were later added. Many of the WACS were well educated and from middle-class families, and two women wrote to the post commander to request better assignments in the hospital, arguing that it was wasteful to use higher-paid WACS for menial jobs that civilians could perform for less. They also negotiated additional nursing training for WACS who lacked skills. But most black servicemen who attempted to advance in health-related jobs encountered ongoing discrimination, such as the black corporal assigned to Fort Jackson's medical section who remained a junior noncommissioned officer despite his college education and prewar experience working in hospitals and as a Works Progress Administration assistant supervisor.[48]

World War II dramatized the need for nurses in national defense. Parran urged black women to join the Army Nurse Corps from its inception in 1942, and the PHS made a concerted effort to publicize the availability of federal Lanham Act funds to train black nurses. Yet black army nurses were not commissioned until later in the war, and the navy excluded them entirely. As of February 1, 1943, 131 Negro nurses served at four stateside locations with segregated health facilities: Fort Huachuca, Arizona; Fort Bragg, North Carolina; Camp Livingston, Louisiana; and the Tuskegee Veterans Hospital in Alabama. An additional unit of 29 Negro nurses was assigned to foreign service. A few black civilian nurses found employment at military facilities such as Fort Jackson Hospital, which employed more than 200 nurses during the war, but most wartime positions were assigned to white commissioned officers in the Army Nurse Corps.[49]

The war provided more opportunity for younger black women to enter nurse training programs than for experienced black nurses to find work. Parran established the Cadet Nurse Corps under the 1943 Bolton Nurse Training Act, which subsidized the education of 85 percent of nursing graduates between 1943 and 1946 and supplied schools of nursing with funds for construction and program enhancement. National radio recruiting appeals generated upward of one thousand responses per day to Parran's promise that "no deserving student need be barred from admission to a school of nursing because of lack of funds." With a goal of recruiting 65,000 women the first year, or 10 percent of all female high school graduates, the $65 million program was incredibly popular, aided by publicity that glamorized nursing and stressed it as essential to the war effort. When the program terminated in 1949, the Cadet Nurse Corps had produced 124,000 nurses with the cooperation of 85 percent of nursing schools, including 21 black and 38 integrated schools that graduated 3,000 black nurses.[50]

The success of the wartime nursing program in recruiting black women resulted in part from the efforts of the National Nursing Council for War Service, which represented the seven main national nursing organizations and launched "an attempt to accelerate the integration of the Negro nurse into the total war effort." This program promoted integration by building on the efforts of Estelle Massey Riddle and Mabel K. Staupers of the National Association of Colored Graduate Nurses with support from the Rosenwald Fund during the second half of the 1930s. The General Education Board funded a Negro nurse consultant to the Coordinating Committee on Negro Nursing, and nursing school directors attended institutes and worked with consultants who promoted full use of federal funds for nursing schools open to Negroes, stressed the benefits of the Lanham Act for nurse training, and outlined U.S. Army and Navy policies regarding Negro nurses generally and their role in postwar rehabilitation. Institutes in 1943 in New York and Chicago attracted representatives from twenty-one nurse-training institutions, mostly southern black hospitals.[51]

In addition to opening at least some new opportunities for black health personnel, the war also shed light on interrelated regional, rural, and racial health deficiencies. Half of southern military recruits were rejected, a rate far higher than the one-third of nonsoutherners who did not qualify. North Carolina ranked worst in World War II draft rejections, with 71 percent of black and 49 percent of white recruits deemed unfit for service. Black men and women were induced to enlist by the promise of medical care as well as of food, clothing, housing, job training, and steady employment that, like government service in New Deal agencies, paid better than most work available to blacks. Some black soldiers may have failed the eye test portion of the military entrance examination not because they could not see but because they could not read. At Fort Jackson, the induction station rejected half of African Americans during one month in 1943. The most common reasons for rejecting draftees of all races were dental defects, followed by eye problems, venereal disease, and illiteracy.[52]

The draft-rejection controversy spotlighted the deplorable state of black and southern health and emphasized the inseparability of racial, regional, and rural-urban health differentials. Even among those accepted for service, southern soldiers received medical discharges at a rate approximately 10 percent higher than that for all soldiers. The highest draft rejection rates occurred among Negro farmers and farm managers, only one-third of whom were inducted. Native Americans, the most rural racial/ethnic group in the United States, were also disproportionately rejected for trachoma and tuberculosis. Military service examinations screened for a variety of mental and educational deficiencies, which accounted for 7 percent of the 9 million draft rejections in 1942–43. Farmers were rejected for illiteracy and feeble-mindedness at nearly four times the rate of nonfarmers, and both medical and mental/educational deficiencies were also much more common among farmers. After the failure of attempts during Roosevelt's first two terms to include national health insurance in the 1935 Social Security Act and the 1939 Wagner National Health Bill, the draft-rejection crisis opened the way for health reform that held great promise for African Americans, the South, and the nation.[53]

Unlike most other domestic policy issues, health care achieved new urgency as a critical aspect of national defense. Parran and other national leaders deemed protecting the health of soldiers and civilians as well as expanding the health workforce essential for national security. The war provided a golden opportunity for liberal health reformers to promote federal public health programs as part of the war effort and to build political capital and credibility among the public and conservatives. Senator Truman chaired the committee to investigate fraud among contractors involved in war production, winning national acclaim and positioning him to become FDR's running mate in 1944. New York mayor and labor champion Fiorello La Guardia served as director of the Office of Civilian

Defense. After the war, he directed the United Nations Relief and Rehabilitation Administration and was elected to the board of directors of the NAACP. In addition to their wartime service and support for health reform, all of these men assumed major leadership roles in postwar international health.[54]

After playing a key role in building support for American intervention through his impassioned defense of measures such as the Lend-Lease Act, Senator Pepper was at the height of his political popularity and was considering a presidential run. In late 1942, Pepper began organizing a Senate subcommittee that would solidify support for national health reform among two of its toughest opponents, southerners and organized medicine. Pepper's Subcommittee on Wartime Health and Education held a series of seven hearings between November 1942 and December 1944, pursuant to Senate Resolution 74, "A Resolution Authorizing an Investigation of the Educational and Physical Fitness of the Civilian Population as Related to National Defense." The Pepper Subcommittee's special interest in southern health problems was demonstrated by its choice of Pascagoula, Mississippi, as a typical wartime boomtown in which to conduct a field investigation of the war's effects on civilian health.[55]

The Pepper Report, issued on January 2, 1945, began with a section on "The 4½ million IV-F's." The authors expressed alarm that at least 40 percent of the 22 million men of military age were unfit for general military duty but denied that the draft-rejection figures indicated that "we are a nation of weaklings." Unlike prewar attempts at federal health reform, the Pepper Report appealed to conservatives by definitively linking health with national defense, documenting the negative impact of health deficiencies on the armed forces and war production capacity, and emphasizing the need to prepare for postwar demobilization and the increased demand for health services. The authors closed with the warning, "We have seen what neglect of opportunities for better health has cost us during this war. We should resolve now that never again, either in war or in peace, will the Nation be similarly handicapped."[56]

Like the hearings on the 1939 Wagner National Health Bill and subsequent 1940s health legislation, the Wartime Health and Education Subcommittee cited maldistribution of health professionals and facilities as well as financial barriers to obtaining care as the two main problems that a comprehensive national health program should attempt to solve by making "the benefits of modern medical and public health science ... readily available in all sections of the country and to all persons regardless of economic status." The Pepper Report briefly criticized racial barriers in access to hospital facilities as well as medical education, but only one black representative, E. I. Robinson of the NMA, testified at the hearings. Blacks stood to benefit substantially from the subcommittee's recommendations, which included increasing federal support to expand and reorganize public health services to achieve complete coverage by full-time health departments as well as providing federal funds to subsidize medical care for all welfare recipients.[57]

In the midst of the Pepper Committee hearings, the Wagner-Murray-Dingell Bill introduced in 1943 constituted the first congressional proposal for federally sponsored health insurance to cover all citizens. Although the Pepper Report made no specific recommendations regarding health-care financing, it extensively analyzed the health needs of low-income citizens, which included most blacks. The committee concluded that the fee-for-service system was "not well suited to the needs of most people or to the widest possible distribution of high-quality medical care." Nonetheless, coverage of the Wartime Health and Education Subcommittee was frequent and largely positive in the *Journal of the American Medical Association*, which published the full text of the Pepper Report on January 6, 1945. A complimentary editorial called it "a more scientific, carefully considered document than has heretofore been available as a result of previous hearings in this field," a reference to the AMA's vehement opposition to all previous Roosevelt administration national health plans. After hearing the testimony of AMA representatives, Pepper called Dr. Roger I. Lee, the group's president-elect, "reasonable and sincere. Some others, not." Pepper appeared at a *New York Times* forum on "Public Health and the Doctor" with Morris Fishbein, the conservative editor of the *Journal of the American Medical Association* and the chief public spokesperson for the AMA during the deluxe Jim Crow era. Pepper later confided to his diary, "I advocated real progressive and sound health program for the nation, so did all the others save Fishbein."[58]

Pepper publicly reached out to AMA doctors, reassuring them at a regional meeting of the AMA's Council on Medical Service and Public Relations, "I have never favored socialized medicine. . . . I have no desire to impair the integrity of the profession or the right of the patient to make a free choice of doctor, dentist or nurse or anything else we think of as Americanism." Despite Pepper's private frustration with the AMA for blocking most of the health legislation that he and his liberal allies supported, the AMA accorded the Wartime Health and Education Subcommittee a considerable degree of respect and positive publicity. As historian Elizabeth Temkin has observed, "Wartime conditions enhanced the acceptability of public welfare measures that in peacetime would have been rejected as uncomfortably close to socialism." The Pepper Committee succeeded where New Deal liberals had previously failed in gaining a national hearing for health reform and galvanizing both liberal and conservative support among the public, Congress, and organized medicine.[59]

Alongside the Wartime Health and Education Committee, the Farm Security Administration also capitalized on the draft-rejection crisis to bolster support for government health programs. In league with the Bureau of Agricultural Economics and the Agricultural Extension Service, the FSA piloted six experimental health programs under the authority of the Department of Agriculture's Interbureau Committee on Post-War Programs. Five of the six programs were located in southern counties. A variety of obstacles plagued these programs, however, and they lasted only three years and never reached projected enrollments. All of the Extension Service and FSA agents who staffed the program in Newton County, Mississippi, were white and were unable to recruit black farmers. Low-income families were most likely to leave their farms to take advantage of wartime jobs in urban areas, and the economic recovery reduced the number of farm families who qualified for FSA loans. The 65 percent reimbursement rate, which had seemed appealing during the 1930s, was no longer sufficient for many physicians, who left, taking along their patients. Between 1942 and 1945, membership in the experimental health programs decreased by about two-thirds, with those remaining representing the most serious health risks. The voluntary nature and limited membership base of local FSA plans had left them vulnerable, but they did stimulate the growth of rural prepaid health plans, which by 1947 were most common in the South.[60]

THE PHS WARTIME VENEREAL DISEASE CAMPAIGN

More successful than the FSA wartime health programs was the PHS campaign against venereal disease, particularly the rapid treatment centers (RTCs) run jointly by the PHS and state health departments. The PHS energetically promoted venereal disease screening, prevention, and education programs for military and civilian populations, with special attention to southern defense areas. In New Orleans and Birmingham, the PHS waged intensive, forty-five-day, community-wide public education programs and provided mass diagnosis and treatment of syphilis with free penicillin. More than a quarter of a million blood tests were administered to the citizens of Birmingham, with about one in six testing positive. The wartime VD control effort applied all the principles of deluxe Jim Crow: targeting the South for regional uplift, provision of care within biracial but segregated facilities, and attention to black health problems that belied an ambiguous combination of racism and a logical focus on the populations at highest risk.[61]

The South was an important testing ground for new VD control techniques. During the 1930s, the PHS Venereal Disease Clinic at Hot Springs, Arkansas, had developed a new, efficient method of administering intravenous drug therapy for syphilis and gonorrhea to large numbers of inpatients with a minimum number of personnel. Using Hot Springs as a model, the PHS RTCs combined the best of hospital care and the public health approach by targeting venereal disease in a setting designed to provide mass treatment and to accommodate patients for the period necessary to effect a cure—up to ten weeks. By 1939, the number of venereal disease treatment centers had tripled to more than 2,400, with 9 million treatments given annually to more than 100,000 patients. New syphilis cases had already declined from 500,000 in 1936 to 220,000 in 1939, and infant deaths from syphilis (disproportionately high among blacks and southerners) had been halved.[62]

During World War II, the PHS combined the success of its civilian RTCs with the World War I model of detaining prostitutes to prevent the spread of disease to troops at nearby military encampments. In the Great War, although Congress had apportioned money for detention homes, the southern communities where two-thirds of military bases were located rarely provided facilities for black women, who were instead placed in jails or on prison farms, often in very poor conditions. State and local statutes provided for both the quarantining of individuals infected with contagious diseases and for the referral of "sexually promiscuous girls" by law enforcement officers for mandatory testing and treatment. Federal funding from the Social Security and venereal disease control programs of the 1930s enabled state and local health departments to provide voluntary treatment to poor venereal disease patients in public clinics. All these precedents lay the foundation for the World War II RTCs, which were considered defense-related projects eligible for construction funding under the Lanham Act.[63]

In 1943, the PHS Venereal Disease Division established twenty-five RTCs to reduce the large number of infectious cases of syphilis in the civilian as well as military populations. Like the FSA health programs, the RTCs were overwhelmingly concentrated in the southern and border states of Louisiana, Mississippi, Virginia, Georgia, Oklahoma, Texas, Florida, and Tennessee. Parran emphasized the RTCs' value in providing administrative training to federal, state, and local officials as well as specialized VD control training to physicians and nurses. Parran intended them to be a showcase for "the new technics in the treatment of syphilis and gonorrhea under the best medical supervision available in this country," thereby "demonstrat[ing] the effectiveness of these methods *en masse* in order that the entire medical profession may profit by the accumulated experience." The PHS required the RTCS to use uniform procedures to collect records of tests, treatment, and clinical observations, so that the RTCS' research function would be "of tremendous significance to the medical profession and will have a profound influence on future venereal disease control activities."[64]

Racism and sexism also influenced the operation of RTCS in the South. The PHS ensured that the facilities admitted patients of all races, who were housed separately within each facility by race and gender, just as they were in most southern hospitals. There is no evidence that accommodations for blacks in RTCS were inferior to or different from those for whites. But health officials were authorized to protect the public by committing individuals against their will to RTCS "to isolate infected women, render them noninfectious, cure them, and in so far as possible, redirect them into useful work." The centers proliferated just as extralegal violence between blacks and whites erupted toward the end of the war. In the immediate postwar period, the South's virtually all-white police force was increasingly hostile toward the blacks pouring into cities. Among the patients at the Leesville Quarantine Hospital outside Camp Polk, Louisiana, a white visitor observed "14-year old Negro girls from share-cropper homes [who had] no particular desire in life beyond owning a pair of yellow rayon slacks and a pair of spike-heeled shoes." Such casual devaluing of young black women's aspirations and autonomy surely influenced admissions statistics. Two-thirds of rapid treatment center patients nationwide in 1944–45 were black, and nearly two-thirds were female, with nonwhite women comprising 38 percent of all patients. In some centers, as many as one-quarter of patients were under twenty-one, and a few were infants.[65]

Despite their drawbacks, the RTCS represented a vast improvement over the previous war, providing free, effective VD treatment and far better accommodations as well as job training, counseling, and other services. Donna Pearce, the supervisor of training for nurses assigned to RTCS, emphasized in the *American Journal of Nursing* that "the majority of patients will be admitted upon a voluntary basis." A variety of factors aside from racism on the part of public health officials may have contributed to the disproportionate percentage of black patients: the concentration of military bases in areas of the South with large black populations, where rates of untreated infection were also higher; discriminatory law enforcement of quarantine and antivice policies among poor and black populations; and a higher proportion of black women in low-income occupations such as domestic service, food service, and prostitution, all of which were targeted for venereal disease screening in southern cities. One of the largest-scale operations among southern RTCs was in heavily black Bolivar County in the Mississippi Delta. The county health department conducted mass syphilis testing of more than 18,000 people: nearly 12 percent were referred to the RTC, and three-quarters of those referred received treatment. The PHS telegrammed Mississippi state health officer Felix Underwood to congratulate him on the admission of a record 3,158 patients to the Bolivar County RTC during August 1949.[66]

After World War II, the RTCs began to emphasize therapy for voluntary patients over the apprehension of prostitutes. Assistant surgeon general Raymond Vonderlehr, head of the PHS Venereal Disease Division during the war, criticized one rapid treatment center that was surrounded by electrified barbed wire and locked gates as too much like "a penal institution, rather than a medical center with a rehabilitation program." Vonderlehr and the PHS emphasized the value of early detection and treatment for conserving financial, medical, government, and human resources. The PHS estimated in 1945 that paresis, a complication of late-stage syphilis, cost taxpayers $11 million annually for institutional care, plus millions in lost taxable income. In some areas, special newspaper sections and posters in public health clinics advertised free treatment at local RTCs, and some of the centers featured patient-friendly recreation and educational programs, including circulating library service. Pearce claimed that the agencies responsible for running the centers had "given much thought to the education and redirection of the patients during their stay at the center and following their departure." The centers paid patients "at a reasonable rate for performing the simple routine jobs essential to the center's operation," thereby providing them with funds "to sustain themselves while obtaining employment" with the assistance of job placement programs.[67]

RTC staff, particularly nurses and medical social workers, were crucial in ensuring the cooperation and successful treatment of patients. Nurses' responsibilities included helping patients to understand doctors' diagnoses and treatment instructions, assisting with referrals to local agencies for assistance after patients' release, and acting as liaisons to the community and referring agencies. Pearce stressed the importance of the "skill and alertness of the nurse in helping to avoid reactions and complications during the intensive phase of the patient's treatment" as well as the value of "her nonjudgmental attitude" in "establishing and maintaining the morale of the individual patient and the *esprit de corps* of the entire center." But to what extent did this "nonjudgmental attitude" character-ize relationships between white staff and black patients? PHS rapid treatment center nurses received their training at the PHS Medical Center in Hot Springs or at the RTC run by the city health department in St. Louis. A medical social worker's account of the St. Louis center provides insight into the process by which the RTCs learned to better serve their patients and meet social as well as medical needs.[68]

In April 1943, medical social worker Margaret Lumpkin was assigned to the St. Louis Medico-Legal Clinic, an RTC to which juvenile and adult females who exhibited signs of "sexual promiscuity" were referred by law enforcement for mandatory VD testing and treatment. Only 10 percent of the individuals brought to the clinic were found to be prostitutes, and 42 percent tested positive for venereal disease, but "all of them had social problems," according to Lump-kin. The referrals included runaways, pregnant girls with no other resources, distraught servicemen's wives, and teenagers simply looking for excitement in the city's taverns and hotels. Lumpkin provided no data on the racial makeup of the clinic or whether it was segregated, but contemporary statistics indicate that black women made up the largest demographic group at most RTCs, and St. Louis was a segregated city. Lumpkin focused on the younger girls, two-thirds of whom were under twenty-one, and 30 percent of whom she described as "underprivileged and misguided girls . . . denied the love and security of a normal home and . . . seeking excitement and attention."[69]

In the early months after Lumpkin's arrival, her clients exhibited many forms of resistance: refusing to eat, making "themselves as disheveled and dirty as pos-sible," and "bringing up many social problems to make hospitalization seem an impossibility." Some "disgruntled" patients "managed to escape from the hospital within a few days" and were "reported to the police department for arrest on a charge of breaking quarantine and, if found, [were] sentenced to 60 or 90 days in the workhouse where treatment was completed." Female patients at other rapid treatment centers also sometimes exhibited rowdy or contentious behavior: PHS officers reported that disturbances erupted between groups of black and white patients at several Florida centers, and on one occasion, law enforcement became involved. In another southern center, fifty black women allegedly fled a ward after claiming to have seen a ghost, which the white correspondent cited as evidence of deep-rooted superstitions and belief in voodoo among "uneducated plantation negroes." Yet such episodes reveal that RTC patients, including black women, exercised some agency and that the limits of their quarantine were not absolute.[70]

Lumpkin's approach involved interviewing patients to evaluate their needs as well as "their capacity for redirection." After treatment was completed, she referred those with additional needs to other social agencies for "continuing service"; nineteen different agencies provided services to 42 percent of the center's patients. In interviews, the girls revealed "their complete lack of understanding of their illness" as well as their "family history and relationships, school and work adjustments, patient's interests, activities, and plans for the future." After a local hospital opened a new RTC, patients from the Medico-Legal Clinic were transported by a station wagon furnished by the hospital instead of "the Police 'Black Maria.'" The hospital also provided a psychiatrist and psychiatric social worker to help "the infected patients who showed unusual emotional disturbance." Lumpkin concluded that her year of experience with patients in the Medico-Legal Clinic had resulted in a "better understanding of the patient group[, which] not only brought about improved patient management but was effective also in clarifying the social needs of these patients." The presence of a medical social worker had also "raised questions about other health, welfare, legal, and military aspects of the program and encouraged interest in experimenting with problems of patient management" as well as better cooperative working relationships among agencies connected with the RTC, particularly the police.[71]

As the country celebrated victory and prepared for demobilization, the PHS announced that rates of venereal disease among civilians had not markedly increased during wartime, as they had in every previous conflict. At their height in fiscal year 1944–45, fifty-four rapid treatment centers provided inpatient care that lasted on average eleven days for syphilis patients and three days for gonorrhea cases. After clinical trials had demonstrated the effectiveness of a single injection of penicillin to treat gonorrhea, inpatient care was no longer necessary, and the burden of gonorrhea cases shifted from RTCs to outpatient clinics and physicians' offices. After the war, Congress authorized funds to continue forty-four rapid treatment centers in thirty-five states, with an additional three hundred hospitals eligible to receive venereal disease patients for intensive treatment. The RTCs were so successful in drastically reducing venereal disease rates in the civilian as well as military population that they became obsolete within a few years, and most had closed by the early 1950s.[72]

Wartime public health measures provided quality medical care to millio
South's low-income rural, black, and military families. These programs ha
ing, beneficial effects on the health and civil rights of southerners and Ameri
generally. Some, including the FSA experimental health programs, were inno
tive but impermanent flashes in the pan; others, among them the Emergency
Maternity and Infant Care Program, had great wartime impact and helped
shape the postwar health picture even after their demise. The war fostered the
dramatic growth in size and influence of both the PHS and its administrative
parent, the Federal Security Agency, which were instrumental in advancing the
civil rights of black patients and professionals in government health programs
during the rest of the Truman administration. Parran's emphasis on applying
federal resources to improve southern health meant that the PHS earned its
extensive wartime experience in campaigns against communicable diseases of
poverty primarily on southern soil.

In 1944, Parran outlined an ambitious plan for the future of the PHS, including
complete public health services, the public provision of medical care, and federal
funding for health professional education and medical research. He promoted
the cause of racial and regional equalization when he stated, "The principle is
accepted that no one in the United States should be denied access to health and
medical services because of economic status, race, geophysical location, or any
other non-health factor or condition. It is a duty of governments—local, State,
or Federal—to guarantee healthful living conditions and to enable every person
to secure freedom from preventable disease." As World War II drew to a close,
the PHS reached the height of its influence in the South and in national policy
making. With the founding of the World Health Organization in 1948 as his
crowning achievement, Parran emerged as the foremost public health leader of
the twentieth century.[73]

The passage of the 1944 Public Health Service Act consolidated the agency's
New Deal and wartime reorganization. Even after demobilization, the PHS
permanently retained its sixteen thousand employees (half of whom were physicians; one-quarter were women), double the number who had served in 1940. By
1944–45, the PHS budget totaled $40.3 million, including $21.8 million in grants
to states for general health, venereal disease control, and tuberculosis control. A
new Division of Tuberculosis Control used fast-film X-rays and grants-in-aid to
carry out mass case-finding and treatment programs in cooperation with health

agencies and voluntary tuberculosis associations. The division also conducted studies to determine TB rates by age, race, and economic status. The war thus focused much-needed attention and resources on tuberculosis, long a leading cause of death and chronic disability among blacks and Native Americans as well as an increasing number of rural southerners. By 1945, the southern states of Texas, Louisiana, Alabama, and Virginia that had topped the list for TB mortality a decade earlier were nearly in line with the national average.[74]

Two federal health agencies emerged from the war to play major roles in southern and national health: the Communicable Disease Center (CDC) and the Veterans Administration (VA). PHS officer Joseph Mountin had spearheaded the establishment of the Malaria Control in War Areas program, based in Atlanta, which was converted on July 1, 1946, to become the permanent CDC. The CDC's postwar emergence as a powerful national arbiter of public health paralleled the transition of the South from the PHS's regional laboratory to a source of national and worldwide health leadership and innovation. Both the CDC and the VA enjoyed generous increases in federal funding that, along with the VA's postwar affiliation with academic medical centers to provide additional residency programs, proved extremely influential in expanding southern medicine generally and black opportunity in particular. The premium placed on providing medical care to veterans exemplified the fullest application of the philosophy of public health as national defense, enabling health reformers and civil rights activists to overcome opposition to federal legislation that increased public funding for health services and facilities.[75]

National defense and the armed forces were an essential vector of desegregation. The presence of federal installations charged with preserving national security greatly undermined states' rights arguments against segregation. Federal military spending directly and indirectly fed the rapid wartime and postwar expansion of medical facilities, public health initiatives, and training programs for health professionals. The provision of health care and education on southern bases and surrounding areas to military personnel and their dependents proved to be a beachhead for integration during the decade before the *Brown* decision.

Wartime health programs also eased desegregation efforts in an atmosphere of personnel shortages and widespread agreement on the need to utilize health personnel to the fullest possible extent. This viewpoint helped to open residency training to blacks just as hospitals were rapidly adding positions, which increased from five thousand nationwide in 1940 to more than twelve thousand by 1947 and twenty-five thousand by 1955. Of all the groups who gained professional training and experience during the war, black nurses were perhaps best situated to capitalize on their rapid advancement to eliminate racial barriers in their field. The training of thousands of new black nurses under federal sponsorship was crucial to their widespread acceptance in the profession after the war, and by 1951, the American Nurses Association and the National Association of Colored Graduate Nurses agreed to merge, fully integrating organized nursing. New educational and employment opportunities for black health professionals not only broadened the reach of health services for black patients but also chipped away at the Negro medical ghetto to create a new cadre of young, scientifically trained doctors, dentists, nurses, midwives, administrators, engineers, and technicians whose professional identity was rooted in the mainstream of medical knowledge and practice. These men and women would prove less loyal to the venerable black health institutions built on racial uplift and beholden to white patronage as well as more willing to challenge white racism, particularly when it threatened their professional advancement. These developments by no means eliminated racial discrimination in health care, but the centrality of blacks in New Deal and World War II southern health programs had far-reaching implications for the nascent civil rights movement and the initial push for federal health reform.[76]

chapter 5

STATE REFORM AND

THE RACIAL DIVIDE

OVER NATIONAL

HEALTH INSURANCE

A t the same time that Thomas Parran, Lister Hill, Claude Pepper, Michael
M. Davis, and Louis Wright pursued national health reform, southern
state officials began to accept responsibility for equalizing public services for
blacks with regard to health and welfare spending. Not only in the American
South but in every industrialized nation, the seemingly unlimited promise of
medical science released a torrent of public and private funding to increase the
supply of medical services by training medical professionals, building and equipping hospitals, and multiplying the number and scope of research laboratories.
Southern efforts, substantially aided by federal funding, were motivated not only
by the sincere desire to improve health care for all southerners but also by political
maneuvering to counter the appeal of leftist groups not to mention a pragmatic
fear of discrimination lawsuits. During the 1940s, southern governors actively
began to upgrade segregated health, education, and other public institutions in
response to mounting legal challenges from the National Association for the
Advancement of Colored People (NAACP), particularly the 1938 *Missouri ex rel.
Gaines v. Canada* decision, which did not directly challenge *Plessy v. Ferguson*
but insisted that its principle of separate but equal be enforced.[1]

WHITE ORGANIZED MEDICINE AND STATE HEALTH REFORM

In contrast to the general atmosphere of acceptance that most wartime health
programs enjoyed, national health insurance polarized American medical professionals according to their beliefs on the proper roles of individuals, society, and

the federal government in preventing and treating disease. Providing temporary assistance during a national crisis was one thing, contemplating permanent structural changes in health-care financing was quite another. Throughout its history, the American Medical Association (AMA) has claimed to speak for the medical profession and has fiercely protected the primacy of the doctor-patient relationship and its economic corollary, fee-for-service medicine. Yet a significant minority of physicians in the American Public Health Association, American Academy of Medicine, the Physicians' Forum, and the National Medical Association (NMA) supported national health insurance and also held egalitarian racial views. Even within the AMA, local and state societies often differed with the policy stands of the national leadership and large sections of the membership challenged the views of Morris Fishbein, editor of the *Journal of the American Medical Association*.[2]

In North Carolina, John Ferrell, Watson Smith Rankin, and Carl V. Reynolds—health reformers with moderate racial views who served on Governor J. Melville Broughton's Hospital and Medical Care Commission—grappled over state policy with the all-white Medical Society of the State of North Carolina (MSSNC), which began publishing the *North Carolina Medical Journal* in January 1940. As physicians and white southerners, members of the MSSNC belonged to two of the most antifederal groups in American society. During the late 1930s, Franklin Roosevelt's administration had earned the ire of white organized medicine by considering various proposals for national health insurance (including one that would have federalized the medical profession as members of the U.S. Public Health Service) and antagonizing the AMA with an antitrust suit. AMA president Rock Sleyster complained of "five years of persecution" during which the Roosevelt administration had been, according to a *North Carolina Medical Journal* editorialist, "exerting its power to frighten people into distrusting the medical profession and demanding a radical change, with the government in charge."[3]

Surgeon general Parran and the "distinctly 'left' hand" of the Public Health Service were favorite targets of the *Journal*. Parran was one of Roosevelt's "Washington disciples," "long-haired men and short-haired women who have wanted to make over the medical profession and force it to become a servant of the state." MSSNC president William Allan alleged in 1940 that "the maneuvers of the New Deal so far have served chiefly to confuse and distract us in our daily tasks of administering to the sick." Some physicians resisted even state and local public health activities, particularly those that threatened to cross the sharply defined line between prevention and curative treatment. Several *Journal* authors protested that mass health department immunizations infringed on the rights of physicians to charge those who could pay for such services. Programs that offered treatment, such as state care for the mentally ill, allegedly undermined doctors' proper authority and responsibility for all types of therapeutic care. The MSSNC charged that the state board of health had revealed a dangerous tendency to interfere with private practice and increase government controls.[4]

But some *Journal* writers allowed that certain types of patients warranted treatment at state expense, such as those who were indigent, mentally ill, or threats to the public health. As doctor's offices and hospital beds stood empty, a few MSSNC physicians, including state health officer Carl Reynolds, suggested that organized medicine would benefit from more comprehensive planning of health services. He advocated closer cooperation between the private and public sectors of health care and pointed to New Deal health and social welfare programs as "recognition that the government has a definite responsibility in the prevention and cure of disease and the preservation of health." Reynolds proposed that the state boards of health and education develop a unified health service in public schools. Only communication and cooperation between private and public interests in health, education, and welfare would "prevent the regimentation of medical men."[5]

Like Reynolds, J. Buren Sidbury appealed to his fellow physicians to actively shape health reform rather than criticize it from the sidelines. He proclaimed that the time had arrived "when the medical profession must assert its leadership in its own household. We cannot sit quietly by and see untrained, unskilled and unscrupulous politicians assume leadership in medical affairs. We will either lead in this campaign or we will be driven as cattle to the slaughter." Sidbury also accorded public health a prominent role in the administration of medical care and espoused a broad-gauged view of social reform. He warned *Journal* readers that "providing adequate medical care for all the people, including the indigent, will accomplish very little toward the solution of their social and economic problems if provision for food, shelter, and work to establish a decent standard of living is not maintained."[6]

By the 1940s, most North Carolina doctors recognized that the state's poor black and white populations faced major obstacles to good health but remained divided on how much government intervention, if any, was warranted to solve the problem. The prewar *Journal* featured writers who were either sympathetic or noncommittal toward socialized medicine, an ambiguous term that did not always connote government-sponsored medical care. For example, Hubert Haywood defined socialized medicine as "that form of medical service which is paid for by individuals or groups ... through insurance companies or associations" and urged the acceptance of voluntary third-party plans. He called for "the whole-hearted cooperation of the physicians" to "make socialized medicine a success" and to perfect "this instrument of good in our state." C. Horace Hamilton, head of the Department of Rural Sociology at North Carolina State College, pointed out that use of the term *socialized medicine* was "designed to decide the issue on the basis of popular prejudice against socialism in general rather than on the basis of facts and logic. If public health care is socialism, then we should place the same label on all other public functions. In other words, we could just as well speak of socialized highways, socialized education, socialized postal service, or socialized fire protection." Socialized medicine did not take on strictly negative connotations in the *Journal* until after the United States entered World War II and authors began to use *socialized* and *totalitarian* synonymously.[7]

In their criticisms of government involvement in medicine, particularly national health insurance, white physicians invoked the fundamentally American values of liberty, individualism, and private enterprise. Most *Journal* writers dismissed calls for new forms of health-care financing, including voluntary health insurance, as leftist propaganda. A 1941 editorial insisted that "the demand for prepaid medicine has been exaggerated. It is quite apparent that a majority of people are not ready [for] nor do they want change in the present method of providing medical care." Mainstream organized medicine emphasized progress against disease, minimized the seriousness of health problems that persisted among poor blacks and whites, and adopted a generally fatalistic attitude toward health reform, in part because racial health disparities were assumed to be biological and behavioral in origin. Allan, an early and influential advocate of eugenic sterilization as a preventive form of public health, predicted that "governmental insurance against sickness, poverty and old age will abolish neither the one nor the other, nor will it affect materially either the sickness or death rate." Another MSSNC member protested that "in spite of the undisputed fact that American health statistics are unsurpassed, the position of the physician in American society has become increasingly difficult, because political theorists have formed legislative action to promote governmental control of medical service." The *Journal* held up the American private-practice system as "the envy of the rest of the world" and credited it for decreasing morbidity and mortality rates. By comparison, twenty-five years of European socialized medicine had created the "debacle" of "constantly mounting incidence and death rates in tuberculosis and other communicable diseases," paying no mind to the vastly different consequences of World War I on the health of Europeans and Americans. To North Carolina's white medics, disease was not a social problem but a professional challenge to be met only by duly trained and licensed physicians.[8]

After World War II began, opponents of national health insurance labeled it an enemy ideology of leftist provocateurs. The author of a 1944 *North Carolina Medical Journal* editorial exclaimed, "It is more than regrettable—it is despicable—that certain politicians should take advantage of the all-out war effort our medical profession is undertaking voluntarily, to attempt to sneak through Congress a bill to make ours a totalitarian state. . . . Let us hope, pray and work that our liberties—civil, professional, and personal—may be preserved, not only from the onslaught of the Germans and the Japs, but from the enemy that is within our gates." Variations on the phrase "The Government in medicine is just another step from democracy toward totalitarianism" appeared in the *Journal* throughout the 1940s.[9]

Most white physicians perceived the potential benefits of national health insurance as insignificant compared to the dangers that it might rob doctors and patients of freedom and spoil the hard-earned fruits of American medical progress. An anti-national-health-insurance physician wrote to Parran in 1945 that "any *compulsory* health insurance program . . . would inevitably impair the quality of medical care received by the people." In response, Parran framed national health insurance as a matter of democracy to rebut the libertarian logic of those who declared their "unalterable" opposition to national health insurance and threatened a boycott if it were adopted: "If we have faith in our form of Government it is incumbent upon all citizens to accede to the majority will and to be governed thereby. It is therefore an alarming symptom that any responsible group—especially a professional group—should take a position of non-cooperation, even of boycott, of a proposed law if such law be enacted." Critics of fee-for-service medicine, Oscar Ewing foremost among them, credited government health initiatives, not physicians, for the sharp improvements in Americans' health status. "Our public health programs protect the health of the people in a thousand ways," Ewing told his employees in the Federal Security Agency, "often so silently and efficiently that most people do not realize that without them they would hardly last out the week." Such statements horrified white southern physicians, who viewed Ewing, Parran, and the alliance of black activists, public health professionals, and federal officials as "a law unto themselves" that threatened doctors' rightful authority and embodied the threat of socialized medicine.[10]

In North Carolina, the primary topic of state health policy debates was how to address the needs of the indigent. Rankin had reprimanded the MSSNC for its failure to treat indigent children, and in 1939, he and the president of the MSSNC testified from opposite positions on legislation to establish a national health program. The MSSNC had done little to improve the availability of health services for blacks or poor whites within the state but often actively opposed measures intended to do so. But during World War II, draftees from the fiercely patriotic South, with its proud tradition of martial prowess, were rejected at higher rates than draftees from the country as a whole, with North Carolina posting the highest rate of any state.[11]

The news that so many southern men were ineligible for combat engendered disbelief and outright hostility. MSSNC president Hubert Haywood saw the draft rejections as "further evidence that we are breeding from the bottom instead of the top. . . . Nutritional diseases, syphilis, mental diseases, alcohol, and poverty are weakening the germ plasms of our people." A *North Carolina Medical Journal* editorial expressed the widely held opinion that the "good people" of the South were fundamentally healthy and that the problem lay with the large and burdensome black population. Black soldiers had been "rejected on one pretext or another," the writer claimed, not because of endemic disease and malnutrition. Rather than probe why so many blacks were deemed unfit for service, the editorialist wanted to restore the state's maligned honor. The "discrimination against Negroes as soldiers" was lamentable not because it was unjust but because "the youth of North Carolina—and of other Southern states also—have suffered as a result of this discrimination the humiliation of being branded as the nation's weaklings." Overlooking the fact that that draft rejections were high among white as well as black North Carolinians, the editorialist pointed to the University of North Carolina's 1945 Sugar Bowl championship football team as proof of the widespread good health among white youth.[12]

THE NORTH CAROLINA HOSPITAL AND MEDICAL CARE COMMISSION

Such was the climate of opinion on black health as North Carolina embarked on an ambitious program to construct hospitals, train medical professionals, and extend insurance coverage. In 1945, medical facilities were scarce for both blacks and whites in North Carolina, which ranked forty-second among states in hospital beds per capita. Blacks represented nearly 30 percent of the state's population but could use only 20 percent of its hospital beds. Of North Carolina's one hundred counties, fifty-five had no hospital beds for blacks, and thirty-four rural counties had no hospitals. Black hospital beds were divided between the chronically underfunded black hospitals, with 635 beds in twelve facilities, and the segregated wards of seventy-five white hospitals, with 1,048 black beds. Both types of facilities were concentrated in urban Piedmont communities such as Charlotte, Durham, and Raleigh. Only 100 hospital beds served the three hundred thousand blacks who lived in the eastern region with the highest percentage black population.[13]

Governor Broughton had corresponded with Senator Pepper after hearing him speak at the March 1943 Southern Governors' Conference in Tallahassee, Florida. Like Pepper, Broughton pursued health reform that appealed politically to southern whites but held great potential for addressing black needs. Five present and past presidents of the MSSNC urged the governor to consider measures to improve "medical care in the post-war period for all groups of citizens," including the expansion of the University of North Carolina School of Medicine to a four-year school with a teaching hospital and state assistance to build or enlarge hospitals to meet the needs in underserved areas. In 1944, Broughton named fifty citizens to a State Hospital and Medical Care Commission, including "doctors, industrialists, business men, leaders in agriculture and labor, representatives of women's and church groups, editors, and humanitarians." Two commission members were black: C. C. Spaulding, president of the North Carolina Mutual Life Insurance Company, served on the executive committee; Charlotte physician Edson Blackman was a member at large.[14]

The Hospital and Medical Care Commission was commonly called the Poe Commission after its chair, Clarence Poe, who also served on the American Hospital Association's Commission on Hospital Care. He had built his reputation as a reformer by advocating scientific farming methods and had actively supported the Rockefeller Sanitary Commission's hookworm campaign. As editor of the *Progressive Farmer*, a periodical with a circulation of over 1 million, Poe had advocated measures to improve rural health, denounced lynching, and urged whites to treat blacks with fairness. But from 1912 to 1915, Poe had been a proponent of segregated rural villages that would promote a virtuous agrarian society and solve the problems of urban blight and racial unrest. Like many white progressives of his day, Poe also supported eugenics. By statute, North

Carolina's Board of Eugenics, which functioned until 1965, comprised the welfare commissioner, the state health officer (Reynolds during this period), the attorney general, and two superintendents at state hospitals. By the early 1950s, Poe moved toward more moderate racial views, and he served as a member of Harry S. Truman's Commission on the Health Needs of the Nation.[15]

Both wartime cooperation to provide broad-based health care and the looming threat of federal health insurance legislation created the receptive atmosphere in which Broughton proposed a comprehensive health plan for "more doctors, more hospitals, and more insurance." The Farm Security Agency and Emergency Maternity and Infant Care programs had innovated in extending health care to masses of southerners, but AMA leaders regarded them as steps toward the complete federalization of medical practice and pushed to eliminate them as soon as victory was declared. Doctors preferred hospital construction, state-funded health insurance, and measures to increase participation in private insurance plans but often disagreed on whether health financing or infrastructure should receive top priority.[16]

Many members of the Poe Commission advocated a state health insurance plan to ward off a federal program. Paul Whitaker alerted his fellow commission members to the "general uprising in this country today for some better form of public-health and medical-care program. If North Carolina does not initiate some program of this kind," he warned, "you might look over the provisions of the Wagner-Murray-Dingell Bill and see how you like them. They propose to tax the people from [$4 million to $10 million]; that is the alternative to some state method of providing medical care." Another doctor asserted in the *North Carolina Medical Journal* that "*hospitalization* is the answer to the indigent patient problem." The state should, he argued, "finance the hospitalization of the indigent patient, and a free medical profession will treat him."[17]

William M. Coppridge, chair of the Committee on Hospitals, led the contingent of physicians who encouraged North Carolina to expand its state hospital system as an antidote to federal intervention. By meeting indigent health needs through hospital construction rather than state health insurance, physicians could expand the physical infrastructure of the health-care system without endangering the free market for their services. Coppridge wrote in the *Journal* in November 1944, "In our opinion the state should confine its aid to providing facilities for diagnosis and hospitalization at this time and leave to the medical profession and to the communities or special groups of citizens the working out of plans for payment of medical care." Coppridge hoped to obtain government aid with no strings attached. "The state should be free," he believed, "to accept direct Federal [construction] grants providing they do not carry with them an element of control."[18]

The black press and some of Coppridge's colleagues in the MSSNC, however, opposed hospital expansion as the wrong solution to the problem of indigent care. Sidbury proposed that with federal, state, or local funding, "hospital care for the indigent and medically indigent could well be met in ... existing hospitals at a per diem rate more cheaply than could be done by building, equipping and running new government hospitals." In a subsequent *North Carolina Medical Journal* article, Thomas L. Carter proposed the opposite solution to Coppridge's, calling on the medical profession to lobby for "compulsory medical and hospital insurance laws" as more effective and less expensive than hospital expansion. Free services from health departments adequately met current needs for indigent care, and a state hospital plan might merely result in duplicating the efforts of existing programs. Hospital expansion, Carter warned, would "encourage a greater number to become indigent." He alleged that competition from federal- and state-funded hospitals was forcing private hospitals out of business and creating a surplus of vacant hospital beds. Instead, he argued that "private institutions, run by doctors, [should] take care of our medical situation." Since North Carolina ranked forty-fifth among states in the care of mental cases, the expansion of state-funded health institutions was unlikely to yield better care and might even make the problem worse. "The Legislature has never granted sufficient appropriations to run its state institutions properly," Carter charged. "If we have failed in the small things in the past, how can we expect so much larger things in the future from the same source?"[19]

The *Raleigh Carolinian*, a black weekly newspaper, joined Carter in opposing the Poe Commission's plan to expand state-run hospitals. The newspaper charged that both state leaders and the AMA were "sidestepping the crux of the medical care problem in this country." Doctors, nurses, hospital beds, and public health facilities were "obvious needs, but the very center of the problem is the cost to the individual and the family of medical care." But despite the opposition of the *Carolinian* and a minority of white doctors, the hospital expansion plan enjoyed widespread support.[20]

The Poe Commission's 1945 report to the General Assembly represented an unprecedented commitment by a southern state government to health-care reform and marked a transitional stage in race relations. The document's authors addressed the health needs of blacks in North Carolina, yet its language and structure, with a separate section on Negro health problems, confirmed continuing support for segregation. The commission's Committee on Negro Health Problems faced the herculean task of changing an abysmal, long-neglected situation. The committee emphasized "the very urgent need for more doctors if the Negro people in North Carolina are to receive even moderate medical attention" and recommended that "hospital units [should] be established for both races at advantageous and convenient locations, and—both white and Negro physicians [should] be available to their patients." The Committee on Hospitals advised that each state-funded community hospital have a black ward. The ratio of beds might be higher than the percentage of blacks in the general population, since "the need of medical services may be found, upon study, to be greater among Negroes than among the white population."[21]

The committee suggested that "hospital associations should be encouraged to extend the Blue Cross program to Negroes" but upheld the positive role of black-owned commercial, fraternal, and burial organizations. The committee objected to plans that claimed an "exorbitant part of [blacks'] small weekly or monthly wages" for coverage but acknowledged that "the benefits have been a relief and a genuine satisfaction to thousands who had no other way to [assure] at least minimum comforts, medical and hospital service, and when the end comes, a respectable funeral." The largest and most famous black insurance company, North Carolina Mutual, had begun as a mutual aid society in 1898. Another black insurance organization, the Tyrrell Hospital Association, was founded in 1941 and had more than four hundred members by 1945. Members paid monthly dues of ten cents and were taxed twenty-five cents to provide hospitalization benefits, including maternity coverage. The Lights of Tyrrell cooperative movement also supported a credit union, store, housing improvement program, and other ventures. One white official called the movement "a commendable venture on the part of the negroes of this county to help themselves." The Lights was, however, primarily "a business enterprise" that was "not reaching the lowest level of negro society." Other black fraternal organizations throughout the South provided sickness benefits to members, and some ran hospitals.[22]

Genuinely hopeful that its proposals would bring about real change in both the health and economic status of blacks, the Committee on Negro Health Problems stated, "The program proposed by the Governor, the State Medical Society, and this Commission will prove to be a real blessing to thousands upon thousands of Negroes [and will] give them courage and determination to lift themselves gradually but surely out of a status of making a bare living into higher income groups." Committee members believed that improving the health of blacks would enable them to earn more, escape poverty, and "become contributors to the support of their various communities and the state." Supporters claimed that the plan would prevent rather than promote reliance on public welfare, but its ultimate purpose was to ensure "that no person in North Carolina shall lack adequate hospital care or medical treatment by reason of poverty or low income." Parran commended the General Assembly's financial commitment to hospitalization for indigent patients, "thus recognizing... the need for making medical services available to all, regardless of race, creed, or economic status."[23]

The long process of improving the availability of health care for blacks and whites alike began when the North Carolina General Assembly approved the Poe Commission's recommendations in 1945 and created a permanent body to implement them. The new Medical Care Commission became the state's principal health policy-making agency. One of the commission's first steps was to consult rural sociologist Selz Mayo of the North Carolina State College Agricultural Experiment Station to investigate black health needs. Mayo identified race as the crux of what would become a thirty-year debate over the quality, accessibility, and efficiency of health-care delivery. "The people of North Carolina are too poor to afford bilateral arrangements in health education, medical care facilities and in methods of paying for their services," he argued. "At the same time, the state is too poor not to provide for one complete system of medical care. Two systems will mean lower standards and poorer services for both the white and the Negro population." Mayo echoed Michael M. Davis's warning against expanding public medical care without providing universal access to the private system through national health insurance, arguing that the failure to provide universal access would further segregate health care on a class as well as racial basis and undermine the quality of care for all patients. Mayo and Davis struck a theme that would be repeated throughout the debates over desegregating health care and medical education: two systems were inefficient, and the increasing pace and breadth of medical knowledge in the postwar era demanded a single, *integrated* system, in all senses of the word.[24]

AMA physicians had considered Roosevelt their worst foe until Truman's administration made health and civil rights reform its twin domestic priorities. After President Truman endorsed a national health program in the form of a revised Wagner-Murray-Dingell Bill, it was furiously debated in Congress and the press throughout his tenure in office. The Truman health plan proposed four major initiatives: a construction program to expand hospital facilities; additional support for public health, especially maternal and child health programs; aid for medical research and education; and compulsory national health insurance for all classes. During the same period, the President's Committee on Civil Rights published *To Secure These Rights* (1947), and in 1948, Truman signed executive orders desegregating the armed forces and ending racial discrimination in federal employment.

Truman and congressional Democrats brought national health insurance to center stage just as the Cold War began to escalate in 1948, and the *North Carolina Medical Journal* repeatedly referred to the Truman plan's seamy red underside. A January 1948 editorial quoted the findings of the U.S. House of Representatives' Harness Committee, which investigated accusations that government officials had written partisan propaganda intended to secure the passage of Truman's health insurance legislation. "American communism holds [compulsory national health insurance] as a cardinal point in its objectives," the committee warned. "In some instances, known Communists and fellow-travelers within the Federal agencies are at work diligently with Federal funds in furtherance of the Moscow party line in this regard." Occasionally, however, a dissenting *Journal* author warned of the consequences of ignoring legitimate health problems, as when a June 1948 article noted, "Unfortunately, many of the leaders of organized medicine have shown a reactionary attitude toward the demand for change and have seen the bugaboo of so-called state medicine behind every tree. At the same time many liberal leaders in the profession are working effectively to bring organized medicine to a more realistic view of things."[25]

BLACK ORGANIZED MEDICINE AND THE BLACK PRESS

As the Red Scare gathered steam and the Truman administration devoted its greatest energy to health-care reform, black organized medicine came into its own on the stages of national and state politics by campaigning to integrate hospitals, medical schools, and physician organizations. By 1950, more than two thousand black physicians belonged to the NMA. They worked hard to win professional respect and recognition from their AMA counterparts but were divided on the issue of federal compulsory health insurance. A 1944 *Journal of the National Medical Association* editorial had blasted the Wagner-Murray-Dingell Bill as "dominated by whimsical, crafty and machine-building politicians" and "a medico-social nightmare." After Truman took office, more black physicians began to support the president's stand on health care as well as civil rights, including NMA president E. I. Robinson and the Howard group including W. Montague Cobb, Paul Cornely, and Charles Drew. Most major black organizations, including the NAACP, National Negro Congress, National Urban League, and National Association of Colored Graduate Nurses, adopted resolutions urging Congress to pass the Wagner-Murray-Dingell Bill. The NMA, however, did not formally endorse national health insurance until 1962, in the form of the King-Anderson Bill, a predecessor of Medicare. When the issue first came up for a vote at the national convention in August 1949, the delegates decided to table the issue as too divisive. In November, the National Negro Press Association reported that NMA president C. Herbert Marshall had announced his support for national health insurance.[26]

Marshall acted in response to the AMA's tempting offer to recognize black medical societies as AMA affiliates if the NMA joined in opposition to the Truman health insurance program. Marshall did not wish to antagonize the AMA, and he emphasized the need to protect patients' choice of physician, one of the few issues on which black and white physicians could agree. But in the same breath that he declared himself "absolutely opposed to socialized medicine," Marshall defended the Truman plan as progressive, not socialistic. Unlike Fishbein, the *Journal of the American Medical Association* editor who fiercely defended the right of the medical profession to dictate health policy, Marshall demurred, "It is not really the doctors who should decide the fate of compulsory medicine. The people should decide." While the AMA reserved doctors' right to set fee schedules, Marshall had the audacity to state publicly, "Medicine has become so specialized that fees have become too high. The cost of medical care is too great [for] the mass of America's population." Andrew Best of the NMA-affiliated Old North State Medical Society echoed Marshall's concerns. "Here was a whole group of people who were unserved and underserved," he said in a 1997 interview. "Whatever it took, even if it took giving up a little bit of authority or preference, [black physicians had] to design some measure to get these people under the umbrella." Best expressed the frustration of many of his colleagues toward white physicians who defended the fee-for-service system and opposed reform: if the white medical profession "hadn't done anything in a hundred years, how can we explain continuing to let them do the same thing?"[27]

The editorial pages of the *Raleigh Carolinian* and the *North Carolina Medical Journal* illuminate the rift between liberal and conservative views of medical need and government intervention during the decade after World War II. In contrast to Best and Marshall, the MSSNC's Coppridge supported "states' rights medicine" as preferable to federal involvement in health care. He praised North Carolina's health-care initiative for "more doctors, hospitals, and insurance" as a proper use of states' rights and promised that the plan would "serve the rich and the poor, the white and the Negro; it is a community plan into which every individual and every institution is invited to join." Coppridge denounced the Truman health plan as "exceedingly loose and careless in its economic provisions, dangerous in its political implications, and demoralizing in its social and individual effects." Allowing the U.S. Public Health Service to administer a national health program would, he insisted, compromise "the freedom and responsibility of the state, community, and individual" to care for the sick. Coppridge preferred to have segregationist state and county governments administer medical care for the indigent, to which the *Raleigh Carolinian* bluntly replied, "States' rights is not the answer to this problem."[28]

In a bitter crusade against the AMA, the black press joined the medical civil rights movement in publicizing the lack of medical care available to African Americans and exposing racial discrimination in health-care institutions, education, and professional organizations from the local to federal levels. The *Carolinian*'s editorialists accused the AMA of using "professional autonomy" as a thin veil for a medical monopoly that excluded the poor and working class, including disproportionate numbers of blacks. One editorial targeted the "moguls of the AMA," who were "more rugged individualists then even the typical captains of industry," an attitude that the *Carolinian* found "outmoded" and believed "shows a narrow-mindedness difficult to comprehend." The *Carolinian* also rejected the *North Carolina Medical Journal*'s rosy assessment of private medicine. Not only was there "something obviously wrong with our system of medical care," one writer asserted, "there is no system." According to the editorialist, AMA doctors were protecting only their freedom, not that of their patients. Rather than equating freedom with individual choice of physician, as the AMA did, the *Carolinian* identified financial barriers as the worst obstacle to patient choice.[29]

After the Korean War shifted the Truman administration's attention firmly away from domestic issues, federally sponsored universal health insurance was essentially dead. In what might be considered a postmortem for the Truman health plan, the *Carolinian* blasted white organized medicine's attempts to discredit national health insurance as a leftist ploy. "The AMA and their allies will have to do more than yell 'socialized medicine' in rebuttal." According to the *North Carolina Medical Journal*, the medical profession had "been forced into a campaign of opposition," not out of selfish motives but because it knew "that control of the practice of medicine by government would lower our standards." To drive this point home to the American public, the AMA had waged a $2.25 million lobbying campaign against federal health insurance, attempting to fund these efforts by billing members $25 and making nonpayment grounds for expulsion, though the AMA quickly dropped the new policy after coming under fire from its members and the media. The *Carolinian* held up the organization's "strong arm methods which will weaken any argument it might offer against 'statism' and arbitrary control of the profession by the Government.... If that is the AMA's idea of democracy in action, then maybe we would be better off with 'statism.'" In the context of growing antiunion sentiment and Truman's clashes with labor leaders, the editorial concluded, "There is little to choose between the leadership of the AMA and the United Mine Workers these days. Neither seems much concerned with the feelings of its individual members or with the welfare of the non-professional public."[30]

Ironically, Truman's support for wage controls to prevent postwar inflation and for allowing unions to include health insurance and other nonwage compensation in collective bargaining agreements under the 1947 Taft-Hartley Act helped spur the expansion of private health insurance as a standard employment benefit. In 1940, only 9 percent of Americans were covered by hospital insurance; by 1950, that number had risen to half. The spread of employer-based health insurance and the growth of the American economy during and after the war further dampened support for universal federally sponsored health care.[31]

But the proportion of Americans with insurance coverage was lowest in the southern states with the largest poor and black populations. Most blacks could afford only weekly installment industrial policies that paid forty cents or less on the dollar in benefits. Oscar Ewing of the Federal Security Agency declared, "The Negro, I assure you, will get much, much more for his money under national health insurance," which would give blacks purchasing power as health-care consumers and increase demand for medical professionals and hospitals in areas with concentrated black populations. A 1951 editorial in the *Carolinian* explicitly compared the AMA's new support for private insurance to white southern officials' belated support for equalizing public schools. "Many features of these voluntary [group health insurance] plans were opposed by the Association up to a few years ago but it has seen the light, just as the southern states have embraced 'substantially equal' school facilities for Negroes when the system of segregation itself came under direct attack."[32]

The AMA's promotion of private health insurance, unlike southern states' pursuit of school equalization, took root and ultimately prevailed as a strategy to block further federal action. The success of the incremental New Deal and wartime health programs that targeted particular populations or diseases and prompted the passage of state health legislation across the South also helped undermine postwar drives for comprehensive reform. In January 1953, the *North Carolina Medical Journal* assured its readers, "The threat of bureaucratic control of medical practice is less now than it has been for many years—although eternal vigilance must be maintained as the price of freedom from socialized medicine."[33]

Leroy Burney (far left), two public health nurses, and surgeon general Thomas Parran (far right) at a mobile syphilis clinic in Brunswick, Georgia, 1939. Parran's campaign against syphilis used both black and white public health personnel to reach the rural South, where rates were highest. (National Library of Medicine)

Eugene Dibble, Louis T. Wright, and C. B. Powell at the 1952 meeting of the John A. Andrew Clinical Society at Tuskegee. Dr. Louis Wright was a vociferous opponent of segregation in health care and served as chairman of the board of directors of the NAACP. Wright declared to the 1938 National Health Conference, "There is no such thing as Negro health. . . . [T]he health of the American Negro is not a separate racial problem to be met by special segregated setups or dealt with on a dual standard basis, but is an American problem which should be adequately and equitably handled by the identical agencies and met with the identical methods that deal with the health of the remainder of the population." (Louis T. Wright Papers, Countway Medical Library, Harvard University; photo by Prentice H. Polk)

Claude Denson Pepper (top) represented Florida in the U.S. Senate (1936–51) and the U.S. House of Representatives (1963–89). Joseph Lister Hill served as U.S. senator from Alabama (1938–69). Hill (bottom right) was sworn in by Vice President John Nance Garner on January 11, 1938. Hill and Pepper, the South's most progressive and influential senators, pursued a South-centered federal health policy that would channel resources to address the region's urgent shortages of doctors and hospital beds. Both Pepper and Hill served on the Senate Subcommittee on Health. With the support of the American Hospital Association, surgeon general Thomas Parran, and most national black organizations, they formed a political coalition that aligned liberal New Dealers, the southern bloc in Congress, organized medicine, and pragmatic black medical activists. The Hill-Burton Hospital Survey and Construction Act was passed in August 1946. (Library of Congress)

The North Carolina Good Health Association
used billboards, newspapers, radio, songs, celebrity
spokespersons, and other media to promote support for
the state's postwar health plan, which became a model for
states across the South and the nation. (University of North
Carolina School of Medicine)

Charity Hospital: original building, and completed new building and surrounding
complex. The biracial Charity Hospital in New Orleans was the single largest Public Works
Administration hospital project and the most deluxe Jim Crow hospital of all. The $12 million
expansion made Charity "the second largest in the United States and the largest state health
facility in the world for the treatment of acute and contagious diseases." The twenty-story,
twenty-seven-hundred-bed main hospital building had wards for black patients on the east
side and whites on the west, with private rooms for paying patients in the central tower. The
teaching hospitals for Tulane and Louisiana State University Medical Schools occupied the two
wings and treated many indigent black patients, who comprised between two-thirds and three-
quarters of total admissions at Charity. (Rudolph Matas Medical Library, Tulane University,
New Orleans)

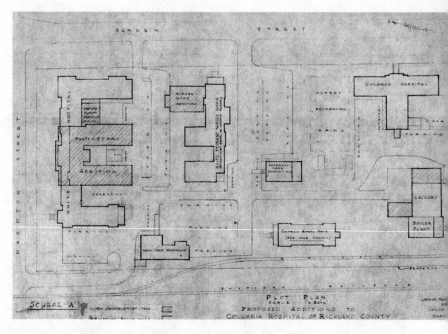

These architectural blueprints illustrate two different phases of deluxe Jim Crow hospital architecture. The plan of Columbia Hospital, Richland County, South Carolina, shows racially separate buildings on adjacent blocks. The existing white hospital did not admit black patients, so they had no access to hospital care until the black hospital and nurses' home was built around 1943. (Records of Lafaye Associates, South Caroliniana Library, University of South Carolina, Columbia, S.C.)

Chester County Hospital in South Carolina opened in 1952 and featured separate driveways, entrances, parking lots, and waiting rooms for blacks and whites. The ground floor included a twenty-bed ward for black patients of all types, who received care on the other floors of the hospital and then returned to the first floor for recovery. (Records of Lafaye Associates, South Caroliniana Library, University of South Carolina, Columbia, S.C.)

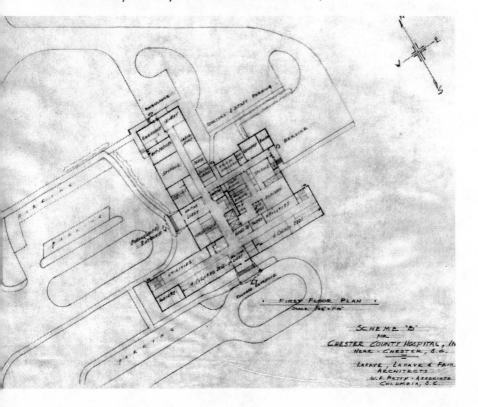

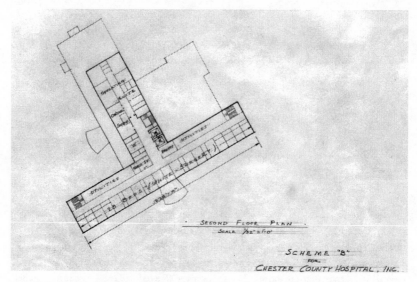

Second floor of Chester County Hospital, South Carolina, with operating room and twenty-eight white surgical beds. (Records of Lafaye Associates, South Caroliniana Library, University of South Carolina, Columbia, S.C.)

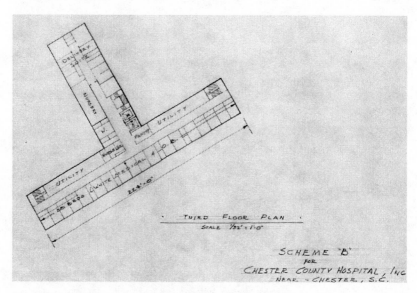

Third floor of Chester County Hospital, South Carolina, with a delivery room, nursery, and twenty-six white beds for medical and obstetrical patients. (Records of Lafaye Associates, South Caroliniana Library, University of South Carolina, Columbia, S.C.)

This cover of the Southern Conference for Human Welfare's *Southern Patriot* from September 1949 protested the Southern Regional Education Compact.

Edward O. Diggs (left) and James Slade (right), the first two African Americans to receive medical degrees from the University of North Carolina, on Diggs's graduation day in 1955. (North Carolina Collection, University of North Carolina at Chapel Hill; photo by Roland Giduz)

part three

DELUXE

JIM CROW

UNDER

HARRY S.

TRUMAN,

1945–1953

chapter 6

HILL-BURTON AND
THE DELUXE
JIM CROW HOSPITAL

During World War II, progressive southern leaders such as Claude Pepper and Lister Hill at the national level and Governor J. Melville Broughton and state health officer Carl V. Reynolds in North Carolina elevated health reform, particularly hospital construction, to the top of the political agenda. A variety of factors had laid the foundation for a large-scale federal hospital construction program that would represent the culmination of deluxe Jim Crow health policy's strange hybrid of New Deal redistributive liberalism and racial parity under segregation. Hospital construction programs funded by the Works Progress Administration, Public Works Administration, Lanham Act, state health agencies, and municipal bond issues had achieved modest gains in the supply of hospital beds, while private-sector construction remained virtually stagnant throughout the Great Depression and World War II. The U.S. Public Health Service (PHS), under the leadership of Thomas Parran, had established itself as an innovative leader in public health policy at the national and state levels and stood poised to administer an ambitious federal grant-in-aid program to promote centralized planning as well as expansion of hospital facilities. Physicians had expressed a willingness to support hospital construction as an alternative to national health insurance, and black medical and civil rights leaders saw the construction plan as a way to both improve blacks' access to care and establish a legal precedent that defined participating hospitals as agents of the state that were bound to provide equal protection under the law.

TOWARD COMPREHENSIVE REFORM:
THE CRISIS OF SOUTHERN HOSPITALS

One of the central debates within deluxe Jim Crow health policy concerned whether reforms should be comprehensive, universal, and federally administered or incremental, targeted to the needs of particular populations, and administered by state and local officials. The federal government's pre-1945 role in health has been described as the "politics of exceptions," designed to provide care to groups with special needs that could not be adequately met in the private medical system. Before the New Deal, health services for merchant marines, entering immigrants, Native Americans, veterans, active military personnel, prisoners, and drug addicts were provided in separately financed and administered federal hospital systems, with the mentally ill cared for primarily in state hospitals. The New Deal added health programs targeted to mothers and children, farm families, venereal disease patients, and the wives of servicemen, groups that included disproportionate numbers of black as well as white southerners. These initiatives contributed to the strengthening of the public tier of the two-tiered, public-private health system: by 1943, PHS hospitals alone treated well over a million patients annually, about 10 percent of those as inpatients. But did this approach represent a pragmatic stepping-stone toward more comprehensive reform, or did it stave off further change by enabling opponents of national health insurance to deny the need for national action? Was it best to continue to create programs tailored to the needs of various demographic groups and classes of patients, or was comprehensive health reform that covered all Americans more efficient, cost effective, and just?

Commencing with the Wagner National Health Plan in 1939 and continuing into the 1950s with the Wagner-Murray-Dingell Bill and the Truman health plan, World War II marked a strategic shift toward broader, more inclusive health reforms featuring a "strong, top-down senior partner model of governance in which the federal government took full responsibility for setting and administering policy." This pattern was also evident in the philosophical evolution of civil rights reform from self-help to integration, as black physicians and activists began to favor more comprehensive federal legislation to circumvent southern white racism and because federal dollars were more plentiful. Such changes, of course, did not go unquestioned. Senator Allen Ellender of Louisiana spoke for all southern Democrats (and most Republicans) when he insisted that any federal aid program must include a clause protecting against federal interference: "Full control and authority for carrying out the programs must be at the State level. I want no part of any plan that will be conducted and managed from Washington." Although from a postintegration perspective, such statements may seem to have been motivated primarily by a desire to preserve segregation, public sector involvement in health at this point had been almost entirely limited to state and local governments. Even Michael M. Davis, one of the most racially progressive and strident advocates of federal involvement in health care, stated that "along with emphasis on national action must go equal stress upon the necessity of decentralized administration. Medical care cannot be run by remote control." Adaptability to local conditions and the preservation of responsible action and freedom at the grassroots level were (and still are) positive reasons to minimize federal oversight.[1]

Advocates of federal aid to hospital construction needed to determine the quantity and quality of the nation's existing supply of hospital beds and then make projections about how many new and renovated structures were needed and where they should be located. New York hospital planner and architect Isadore Rosenfield called the nation's hospitals "ancient, outmoded, obsolescent, uneconomical, and badly equipped structures. It would be an understatement to say that one-half of them ought to be replaced." Another observer described hospitals in the 1940s as "museums in which we exhibit the failures of medical sciences" and "mausoleums erected to the memory of somebody. They are full of marble, brass, bronze, chipped beef, chapels, research laboratories, and stuff."[2]

The South's paucity of resources in the face of widespread unmet need for hospital care strengthened the case for comprehensive planning to maximize the impact of federal aid. The small size, racial segregation, private ownership, and heavy reliance on patient fees that characterized most southern hospitals compounded a regionwide crisis in health-care access. The South had the highest proportion of beds in facilities of fewer than one hundred beds as well as in private and proprietary facilities, which together contributed to lower occupancy rates despite the nation's lowest ratios of hospital beds to population (table 6.1). During economic downturns, even more private hospital beds stood vacant—in 1933–34, four in ten were empty. Rosenfield compared this phenomenon to a man who was "very hungry with not a cent in his pocket, at the same time knowing that the 'Ritz' has a dozen vacant seats in the dining room." Fluctuations in occupancy also made it difficult to estimate the true number of needed hospital beds.[3]

TABLE 6.1

General Hospital Beds per Thousand Population in Forty-eight States and the District of Columbia, 1943

1 TO 2 BEDS	2 TO 3 BEDS	3 TO 4 BEDS	4 TO 5 BEDS
Alabama 1.0	Florida 2.5	Arizona 3.1	California 4.2
Arkansas 1.5	Idaho 2.8	Colorado 3.8	Delaware 4.3
Georgia 1.6	Indiana 2.3	Connecticut 3.7	District of Columbia 5.0
Kentucky 1.7	Iowa 2.7	Illinois 3.1	Massachusetts 5.0
Mississippi 1.4	Kansas 2.8	Maryland 3.6	Michigan 4.1
Oklahoma 1.7	Louisiana 2.9	Minnesota 3.7	Montana 4.6
South Carolina 1.8	Maine 2.7	Missouri 3.0	Nevada 5.0
Tennessee 1.7	New Jersey 2.9	Nebraska 3.1	New Hampshire 4.3
	New Mexico 2.1	North Dakota 3.3	New York 4.0
	North Carolina 2.0	Oregon 3.4	
	Ohio 2.6	Pennsylvania 3.0	
	South Dakota 2.0	Rhode Island 3.6	
	Texas 2.1	Utah 3.1	
	Virginia 2.3	Vermont 3.2	
	West Virginia 2.6	Washington 3.3	
		Wisconsin 3.5	
		Wyoming 3.6	

Source: Rosenfield, *Hospitals*, 5; Ponton, "Hospital Service for Negroes," 14–15, 50.

Small hospitals with fewer than one hundred beds represented about two-thirds of all U.S. hospitals but contained only 13.5 percent of total beds. Generally, a hospital's bed capacity was inversely proportional to the average daily cost per patient. For example, patient per diem costs for New York municipal general hospitals in 1943 ranged from $4.89 (at 2,594-bed Bellevue) to $6.75 (at 214-bed Gouverneur). By comparison, the two private 65- and 90-bed white hospitals in the rural eastern North Carolina community of Wilson reported spending $7.17 and $7.80 per patient in 1945. Small black hospitals such as Wilson's 41-bed facility spent the least of all ($2.88), reflecting not greater efficiency but seriously lowered quality of care due to inadequate resources and a much lower percentage of paying patients. Large hospitals were also cheaper per bed to build than small ones. The South's preponderance of small, inefficient, private hospitals further increased construction and operating costs and decreased the amount of care provided per bed.[4]

Despite the desperate need for care, the South's hospitals were least able to provide charity care and derived the highest proportion of their budgets from patient fees. Care was more available to poor patients who lived in wealthier, more hospital-rich states, with the richest providing thirteen hundred days of hospital care per thousand population and the poorest only two hundred. The Carolinas were the exception: there, the Duke Endowment promoted a more systematic approach to hospitalization beginning in the 1920s by subsidizing the cost of patient care and conducting comparative statistical analyses of medical and administrative services that helped hospitals check per diem costs. In addition, the Duke Endowment and Duke University Medical School in 1930 established one of the first graduate hospital administration programs in the United States, based on Davis's proposal to the Rockefeller Foundation to apply business management methods to enable hospitals to serve patients and communities more efficiently.[5]

Aside from these beginnings of coordinated hospital service in the Carolinas, southern health care was a Wild West frontier. The medical sector of the economy has long been, in economic terms, a textbook example of a "disorganized market," with producers and sellers out of sync with consumers; even though there is a significant documented need or desire for a particular good or service, it cannot be produced on a cost-effective scale until there are both sufficient demand and reliable means of financing to justify it. Therefore, the product remains in limited production and unaffordable to most consumers. Medical economists Frederick D. Mott and Milton I. Roemer observed that the "divergence of the lines of organization of medical care from those of medical science . . . has been most extreme in the rural section of our country." The overwhelmingly rural South was in greatest need of regional planning to maximize access to scarce resources of insurance, medical personnel, and hospital beds. Aside from low per capita income that restricted individual ability to purchase health care, other factors related to but distinct from poverty further disrupted the southern market for health services—greater resistance to group practice, low capitalization of health-care facilities, lack of health information among isolated and illiterate rural dwellers, and the persistence of segregation.[6]

Hospitals and health professionals in the urban Northeast enjoyed the greatest degree of what economist Holly Raider calls "structural autonomy," enabling them to generate more profits, innovation, and efficient output. Structural autonomy results from an industry with a small number of firms competing in disorganized markets of buyers. In the disorganized market of health-care buyers before the widespread post-1950 adoption of employer-based health insurance, individuals purchased care primarily on a fee-for-service basis. In the South, there was less competition (or none at all) among a smaller number of health-care providers, since the supply was severely limited by the dearth of professional schools as well as the underdevelopment of southern education generally from the primary to graduate levels. Therefore, southern health care had less economic incentive to improve the quality or efficiency of services to patients or, paradoxically, to control costs.[7]

When Davis testified before the Wartime Health and Education Committee in 1942, he explained why previous attempts to address the shortage and maldistribution of physicians (and thereby increase competition among them) had failed. The committees that determined the local need for medical professionals were made up entirely of doctors, who tended to underestimate demand and were reluctant to induce physicians to relocate or to increase competition among existing doctors. He therefore advocated "vigorous and prompt action" by government and citizens as well as by the medical profession "to correlate the future Army recruiting of doctors with civilian medical needs, and to redistribute some doctors to meet acute local needs especially in war-production areas."[8]

The quality as well as the quantity and distribution of hospital beds was worst in the South. The U.S. Census listed 6,139 hospitals nationwide in 1940, with 76 percent (4,690) registered by the American Medical Association (AMA). According to AMA requirements, registration standards included "modern safe buildings maintained in a sanitary condition," with complete facilities and equipment for diagnosis and treatment (for example, laboratories for pathology, diagnostic tests, and autopsies) as well as radiology, nursing, dietetics, pharmacy, and medical records departments. Surgical and obstetrical units were to provide "a modernly equipped operating room" and a delivery room and nursery. Registration was considered evidence of only basic adequacy, while approval by the American College of Surgeons was a mark of higher-quality hospitals. Only 39 percent of hospitals with just over half the nation's beds were approved by the American College of Surgeons, and hospitals with fewer than twenty-five beds were ineligible. (Table 6.2 lists the number and type of beds in the United States.) The highest standards were reserved for teaching hospitals, which were required to have a daily average census of at least two hundred patients and 70 percent occupancy. Since the majority of southern and nearly all black hospitals were small and underequipped, many of them were unregistered, most were not approved by the American College of Surgeons, and only a handful in urban areas qualified as teaching hospitals. Before World War II, southern white hospitals, though segregated, had been at closer par with their black counterparts than they would be afterward, when the entire nature of medical practice as well as the brick and mortar that housed it underwent a fundamental and costly transformation. The fault line of race that had divided southern hospitals opened into a huge chasm after the war, leaving black hospitals increasingly unable to compete for patients.[9]

As the hospital expansion movement determined the quality and quantity of beds needed nationwide, it raised the banner of comprehensive regional planning. Regional health planning had been a favorite tool of Progressive reformers, such as the 1910 Flexner Report's proposal to allot one medical school per metropolitan area. Taking cues from Herbert Hoover's philosophy of government-business cooperative planning by experts to scientifically manage the economy, health planners attempted to apply principles of vertical integration and rationalized industrial production to coordinate health-care resources and maximize their efficiency.[10]

TABLE 6.2

Type and Number of Beds in U.S. Hospital Facilities, 1942

HOSPITAL TYPE	NUMBER BEDS	PERCENT
All beds (registered)	1,383,827	100
All government beds	1,015,781	73
All nongovernment beds	368,046	27
Beds approved by American College of Surgeons	767,384	55
General hospital beds (governmental, private, and voluntary nonprofit)	594,260	43
Nervous and mental	646,118	47
Tuberculosis	82,373	6

Source: Rosenfield, *Hospitals: Integrated Design*, 5.

Total population: 130,000,000

In the mid-1930s, while Thomas Parran was health commissioner of New York state, New York City completed one of the first comprehensive surveys of a major city's hospital needs. Parran, the PHS, and the American Hospital Association would promote state surveys and regional hospital planning on a nationwide basis beginning with the hearings of the Senate's Wartime Health and Education Committee and subsequent hearings on hospital construction legislation. The PHS Hospital Facilities Section served as a consultant unit on planning, design, and administration of hospitals and other health facilities. The section advised federal agencies on war emergency construction but also worked closely on postwar planning with national hospital, medical, and architectural organizations. The PHS collaborated with the American Hospital Association Commission on Hospital Care in the ongoing effort to pass federal hospital construction legislation to remedy deficiencies in health facilities and to develop a coordinated hospital system. The Hospital Facilities Section also worked with PHS district offices and state health agencies to provide policy and technical guidance for statewide health facility surveys and developed a model hospital survey bill for state legislatures.[11]

Under the PHS Coordinated Hospital Service Plan (fig. 6.1), the smallest, most remote facilities were health centers that would handle preventive medicine, health education, and outpatient and home medical care. The rural hospital with between fifty and one hundred beds would admit primarily uncomplicated cases requiring hospitalization but not specialized care and would act as a referral center for the district and base hospitals. If rural hospitals were part of an integrated hospital network, rural areas would need only one bed per thousand population, since most patients would not be severely ill and, as a result of wartime changes in medical practice, turnover would be as much as twice as rapid as in prewar general hospitals. Nationwide medical and hospital insurance and integrated regional planning of hospital facilities could reduce the required ratio of beds to less than 3.5 per thousand population. The quality of rural health care could also be improved by the spread of group practice, which Rosenfield proposed could include a surgeon, internist-pediatrician, obstetrician-gynecologist, and a junior member to assist and do laboratory and X-ray work.[12]

Despite the similarities in the regional hospital plans advanced by the PHS and others, there was widespread disagreement on just how many rural hospitals were needed, if any at all. About 40 percent of U.S. counties lacked hospitals, but these counties contained only 13 percent of Americans, and nearly half of those counties had populations of fewer than ten thousand. Since the area and

FIGURE 6.1

PHS Coordinated Hospital Service Plan

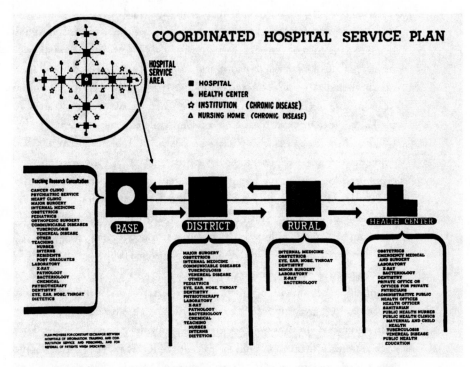

Source: U.S. Public Health Service, *Planning Suggestions for Acute General Hospitals from Fifty to Two Hundred Beds* (Washington, D.C.: U.S. Government Printing Office, 1942).

population of counties varied widely and many rural hospitals also served adjacent counties, even many residents of counties without hospitals were within reasonable range of health facilities, particularly as automobile ownership and good roads proliferated. The American Hospital Association and AMA went so far as to claim that only thirteen counties across the nation were more than thirty miles from a good general hospital. Citing the AMA's figure that 25 to 35 percent of American hospital beds lay unoccupied, J. Buren Sidbury of the Medical Society of the State of North Carolina contended that there was "no point in building a hospital where there are not enough people to support it."[13]

Given the financing obstacles, scattered population, and difficulties in recruiting medical personnel faced by rural areas, some reformers advocated the practice of sending rural patients needing hospitalization to larger urban hospitals as more efficient and conducive to better-quality care. Henry Southmayd, director of the rural hospital division of the Commonwealth Fund, wrote in 1941, "The disparity between city and country hospitals is so marked and so generally recognized by rural social workers, in medical ranks and in the hospital world, and among governmental and voluntary agencies, that the term 'rural hospital' has gained wide currency to denote a particular class of institution." But proponents of rural hospitals argued that rural areas needed and deserved hospitals to foster rural medical service, cater to distinctive rural needs, and enable families to remain close to their loved ones under treatment. Davis wrote to Parran in 1938, "I've come to think that a start on rural hospitalization under the U.S.P.H.S. auspices is the most strategic single step on the whole rural health front." [14]

Immediately after the Pepper Report was issued in January 1945, Senator Lister Hill began to hold hearings on his Hospital Survey and Construction Act to move forward on the Pepper Report's first recommendation that "federal grants-in-aid to States be authorized now to assist in post-war construction of hospitals, medical centers, and health centers, in accordance with integrated State plans approved by the United States Public Health Service." Hill (but not Pepper) worked closely with conservative Republican senator Robert Taft of Ohio, who contributed substantially to revising the legislation prior to passage and helped determine the formula for allocating federal grants-in-aid to states based on population but limited by existing hospital facilities and per capita income. Hill and Taft's collective political acumen secured the passage of Hill-Burton by uniting, if only briefly, proreform factions (the PHS, the American Hospital Association, liberal Democrats, and national black organizations) with previous opponents (the AMA, Republicans, and southern Democrats). Federal aid to hospital construction, for which Pepper had introduced the first proposal in March 1938, was approved by both houses of Congress in August 1946 as the Hospital Survey and Construction Act, commonly known as Hill-Burton in recognition of its Senate sponsors, Hill and Ohio Republican Harold H. Burton. [15]

Internal White House correspondence reveals the conflict of priorities over Hill-Burton between the Truman administration's allies and detractors. The administration's version of the bill had given need-based federal funding of up to 75 percent of the total construction cost, which favored poorer states. Truman, Parran, and other White House officials closely involved with the bill wanted to circumvent state governments and require applicants to deal directly with the federal government, which these officials felt would be more accountable than the states. After Hill reported the Truman administration's original version, Taft introduced amendments to vest administrative control in the state agencies and reduce the authority of the surgeon general, a change Parran and Truman not surprisingly protested. In the House, the bill was amended to reduce the federal contribution to one-third. General Philip B. Fleming, head of the Federal Works Agency, objected to checks on the surgeon general's authority through the creation of a Federal Hospital Council and court review. Fleming even cited the short-lived Federal Emergency Relief Administration as a program that had to be abandoned because of abuses that developed under discriminatory state officials. He also objected that "the powers of the Surgeon General are actually subordinated to those of the State agency" since the surgeon general was required to approve any application that met the legislative requirements, while the state agency designated to administer Hill-Burton could arbitrarily withhold its approval.[16]

When it came time for Truman to sign the bill, Senator James Murray, a Montana Democrat, urged the president to veto it because it had been "amended by Republicans in order to put Federal hospital funds in the complete control of the Governors in all of the Republican states" and had become "an instrument of the Republican Party to seize the Congress." Farm Security Administration administrator Watson B. Miller raised the "danger that Federal funds may not be used in the areas of greatest need and may not relieve existing disparities between different types of communities and population groups." The concerns of black national leaders and medical activists had been fully represented in the Truman administration's version of Hill-Burton, but the version of the bill that passed reduced the federal government's share of funding as well as its administrative authority. Congress would subsequently increase the federal share to the original level of 75 percent.[17]

FROM EQUALIZATION TO INTEGRATION

In the 1920s, black medical reformers had pursued both equalization and full integration but had not usually seen the two goals as incompatible. When the first all-black Veterans Administration hospital had opened in 1923 at Tuskegee, Alabama, it was hailed as a major coup not only for black veterans but also for the black physicians and nurses who would staff the hospital and provide training opportunities to other black professionals. Such training could either improve the quality of care at existing black institutions or produce competitively qualified black applicants who might find new opportunities at white institutions. Black institutions, whether public or private, courted both government and philanthropic support. As they did so, black leaders struck the chords they believed white patrons wanted to hear, but these leaders also hoped one day to break free of white sponsorship and the lip service to segregation it required.[18]

In the 1930s, while many of the NAACP and NMA's rank-and-file southern members subscribed to a separatist self-help philosophy that focused on building and expanding black institutions, northern blacks in cities such as Chicago and New York began to turn away from Booker T. Washington's ideology of racial uplift within private black hospitals. Some agreed with Wright's position that large grants from the Rosenwald and Rockefeller philanthropies to build black hospitals had done more harm than good by perpetuating segregation in health care. Yet even Wright had at first modeled his approach to nondiscrimination in health legislation on federal education legislation, which guaranteed inclusion and parity for blacks while tolerating racially separate institutions. And even in the North, new black hospitals were still being established—for example, as late as 1957 in Cleveland.[19]

The new availability of federal funding to construct health facilities tempted cash-strapped black institutions and dampened the appeal of a hard-line stance against segregation, particularly when such funding promised to establish or strengthen beneficial partnerships with white institutions. In the fall of 1945, Meharry Medical College submitted its first application for a PHS grant to build a health unit in a black Nashville neighborhood. The proposed facility would cooperate with the city and county health departments and provide clinical training to Meharry medical, dental, and nursing students. At that time, the only black public health unit associated with a university teaching program was the Somerset Health Center, located in the Eastern Health District in Baltimore, where white public health, medical, and nursing students at Johns Hopkins did field training and black city health department employees received continuing education. When Somerset was dedicated in June 1944, Baltimore commissioner Huntington Williams called the center "one of the most important City Health Department new developments associated with the Johns Hopkins School of Hygiene and Public Health."[20]

Although the Meharry project had the approval of the PHS and the Social Security Agency, the Bureau of the Budget denied the request in the initial PHS budget. Meharry president M. Don Clawson protested to President Truman that while Howard was "generously supported by federal funds," the only federal funding Meharry had received was to train medical military personnel during World War II. Clawson reminded Truman that "collectively, [Meharry alumni] represent one of the most powerful professional and political groups in America." Clawson also urged his college classmate Robert E. Hannegan, chair of the Democratic National Committee, to request Truman's approval for the health center. Public support for Meharry was justified because its graduates provided health services to more than 50 percent of all black Americans, according to Clawson. U.S. representative J. Percy Priest of Nashville also contacted Truman to urge approval for the health center, but the item was rejected in the final budget. Truman assured Priest, however, that Meharry would be eligible for federal funding under pending legislation to aid medical education.[21]

But such federal aid would not materialize during Truman's administration. The Hill-Burton Act became law during a brief window of opportunity that opened between the war's end and the disintegration of the extremely fragile southern-liberal-black alliance. During World War II, black integrationists such as Wright, Charles Houston, and Thurgood Marshall in the NAACP and W. Montague Cobb and Paul Cornely in the NMA began to advocate making zero tolerance for segregation a condition of black support for federal legislation. They were joined by white liberal Democrats such as Wagner and Murray, who tried to ban segregation outright in Hill-Burton and other federal health legislation, while southern Democrats clung to the earlier, more conservative definition of *nondiscrimination* as inclusion and parity for black patients without requiring integration. After Roosevelt's death, liberal Democrats finally made black civil rights a top priority. But a Republican Congress, joined by conservative Democrats, ushered in an anti–New Deal backlash, and the AMA increased its political opposition to anything that might become an entering wedge for socialized medicine.[22]

The war's end brought a surge of antisegregation activism, represented by the theme of the National Negro Congress's 1946 convention, "Death Blow to Jim Crow." The Congress included among its "eleven points for freedom" passage of the Wagner-Murray-Dingell Bill and "adequate housing, health protection and education without segregation or discrimination." In 1947, the NMA, with a membership of more than two thousand black doctors, joined forces with the NAACP, Urban League, and other black organizations to fight racial discrimination in medical societies, medical education, and hospitals. The first target of health-care integrationists was the hospital system run by the Veterans Administration (VA).[23]

The VA stood at the confluence of the military and medical establishments, the first two institutions in American society to integrate. The quality of care for blacks in the VA hospital system was much better overall than in public, segregated hospitals, particularly in the area of mental health treatment, which was offered for blacks at Tuskegee and five other southern neuropsychiatric VA hospitals. Compared to the state mental institutions, VA facilities were newer, less crowded, and better staffed and equipped, and they provided more privacy and a wider range of therapeutic and recreational activities. Another key difference was that "industrial therapy," or the employment of patients in field, mechanical, or custodial work, was prohibited at VA hospitals, whereas it was common practice, particularly for black patients, at state institutions.[24]

Despite their better quality of care for black patients, the VA hospitals remained segregated. In 1947, of 128 VA facilities, 14 in the South and 1 in Albuquerque, New Mexico, were white-only, and 28 others placed blacks on separate wards. In sixteen segregated states, the VA provided just over 20,000 beds for roughly 4 million white veterans and 5,000 beds for 1 million black veterans, so the ratio of beds was approximately equal. But black veterans seeking care often had to travel long distances, since the 1,931-bed Tuskegee facility was the only VA hospital providing general medical and surgical care to black veterans in Arkansas, Mississippi, Alabama, and Georgia. The VA general hospitals in North Carolina, Kentucky, and Texas also excluded minorities.[25]

Returning black veterans energized the civil rights movement and demanded equal treatment for themselves and their families. Black leaders such as I. S. Leevy, founder of the Lincoln Emancipation Clubs in Columbia, South Carolina, pushed the Columbia VA hospital to hire black physicians and nurses. At the same time, the NAACP blocked proposed new all-black VA hospitals in Mound Bayou, Mississippi, and Franklin County, Virginia, as perpetuating segregation rather than expanding black opportunity. Under the progressive leadership of Paul Magnuson, the VA seemed ready to accept integration. In March 1947, officials selected Harlem's Lafargue Clinic as the designated facility for psychiatric treatment of veterans of both races, marking the first time that a predominantly black medical facility had been selected to provide integrated, federally sponsored care. The clinic's board of directors, which included novelist Richard Wright, called the decision "the clearest and most outspoken gesture made by the Federal Government against discrimination in the treatment of veterans."[26]

Yet the next month, the VA hospital at Oteen, North Carolina, dismissed fourteen black nurses rather than hire a racially mixed staff to care for the sixty-six black veterans on the tuberculosis ward. The hospital had recruited the nurses after the National Association of Colored Graduate Nurses lobbied VA medical director Paul R. Hawley to hire black nurses without discrimination in VA hospitals. But the hospital could not find another sixteen black nurses to maintain an all-black nursing staff, so it hired only white nurses, since local law forbade black and white women from living together in the onsite nurses' quarters. Black patients (but not black staff) were welcome at all VA hospitals by 1950, and in October 1953 the VA ordered all its hospitals (except the sole all-black facility at Tuskegee) to desegregate. The first of several new integrated VA hospitals in the South opened in Salisbury, North Carolina, in December 1953. Despite the protests of fifty-six southern congressmen, who petitioned the VA in 1957 to reinstate segregation in its hospitals, black veterans were thereafter treated equally without regard to race.[27]

Some southern blacks remained skeptical of whether the long-term goal of eliminating segregation was worth sacrificing opportunities to meet immediate needs by improving black-run facilities. In the late 1940s, many southern NAACP branches remained numerically small, clubby, and dominated by elite blacks who were little concerned with the struggles of their poor counterparts. Until the NAACP assigned Ruby Hurley to establish a southeastern regional office in 1951, many southern chapters remained moribund, and the belief that integration was the best way to guarantee black equality and opportunity had not fully penetrated the Deep South. Southern black physicians were particularly hesitant to support new "integrated" facilities that would threaten black doctors' practices by accepting blacks only as patients, not professional staff. Howard's dean of medicine, Numa Adams, charged that "the Negro doctor faces an unfair competition with the white physician, who controls the Negro clinical material, limits the economic opportunity of the Negro physician and shuts him out of an opportunity to learn. Not only this but the white physician does not hesitate to take charge of hospitals for Negroes and refuse to permit the Negro qualified doctor to participate in staff activities in a hospital for his own people." New Deal hospital construction programs had added more than eight thousand beds for blacks in dozens of southern communities, but these facilities had been almost exclusively for indigent patients. The postwar drive to expand training opportunities for black medical students and physicians as well as rising affluence that increased the number of insured blacks who could afford private care pushed white policy makers to apply deluxe Jim Crow principles to build a new type of facility: publicly funded teaching hospitals for southern black physicians and their private patients.[28]

While most such projects involved the construction of new buildings or additions to existing facilities, southern cities also sometimes reserved new construction for white hospitals and refitted outdated white facilities for blacks. Carver Memorial in Chattanooga, Tennessee, a public general teaching hospital for blacks, opened in June 1947 in the building formerly occupied by the all-white Erlanger Hospital. Carver's new white superintendent, a former administrator at Erlanger, came with the bargain. With fifty beds and "the best equipment now obtainable" but no emergency facilities, Carver was the specific target of Cobb's lament that whites were "giving old clothes to Sam" by renovating cast-off white facilities for black use. Although the local paper heralded Carver as "presumed to be the only hospital operated with municipal funds for private patients of colored doctors in the United States," at least three other municipal hospitals offered black physicians both private and ward accommodations for their patients: the black unit at Knoxville General as well as Kansas City General No. 2 and Homer G. Phillips in St. Louis.[29]

Others were soon proposed. After the Medical College of Alabama opened in Birmingham in 1945, Dean Roy Kracke favored establishing a Negro hospital as part of the medical center to meet the needs of local black physicians and their patients and to provide training opportunities. Kracke communicated with the Birmingham and Jefferson County Negro Hospital Association regarding the location of a site for the hospital and available funds to purchase property and begin construction. The state legislature, however, would not approve the hospital, and in 1954, the association donated the funds it had raised to Holy Family Hospital, a Catholic institution four miles west of downtown Birmingham that was both patronized and staffed by African Americans. A new private black hospital was subsequently built with Hill-Burton funds, matched by six hundred thousand dollars from the Sisters of Charity.[30]

During the early 1950s, three new all-black teaching hospitals opened with public support. The first, in 1950, was a $2 million 105-bed facility at Florida A&M College in Tallahassee, one of the country's larger black colleges. Of the more than two thousand new teaching hospitals built under Hill-Burton, Florida A&M had the only one located at a historically black college or university. Florida A&M had no medical school, despite school officials' attempts to found one during the late 1940s, but it did have a nursing school and established a school of pharmacy in 1951 under the leadership of President George Gore Jr. The executive secretary of the Florida Higher Education Board of Control, J. C. Culpepper, said in 1956 of the new construction during the preceding six years at Florida A&M, "No state in the union has made this effort in behalf of Negro higher education in that period." The new hospital was "recognized as one of the best hospitals for Negroes in America" and included an outpatient clinic and student health center.[31]

In June 1952, Georgia governor Herman Talmadge dedicated another all-black deluxe Jim Crow teaching hospital in Atlanta. The Hughes Spalding Pavilion, adjoining the existing black unit of Grady Memorial Hospital, cost $1.85 million, with 60 percent of funding from Hill-Burton, 20 percent from the state, and 10 percent each from city and county funds. The impressive facility was the result of a biracial drive initiated by the National Urban League. Under the leadership of Lester Granger, the Urban League pursued a cooperative approach to reform that focused on cultivating moderate white southern leaders and inviting them to join in promoting positive social change. Beginning in 1947, the league's Atlanta director, Grace Towns Hamilton, rallied black leaders to lobby city officials and Grady's administration to build a facility for private patients that would provide residency training for black physicians. (Although several services explored plans for training programs, only the surgery department, headed by Asa Yancey, developed one, beginning in 1958.) Jesse O. Thomas, the organization's southern field secretary, used his weekly Urban League column for the *Atlanta Constitution* to call for the equalization of city funding for black schools, hospitals, parks, and recreation centers.[32]

The hospital was planned and brought to completion by Benjamin Mays, president of Morehouse College, and Hughes Spalding, the hospital's namesake. Spalding was a prominent white Atlanta attorney, civic leader, and board member of the Coca-Cola Company who chaired the Fulton-DeKalb Hospital Authority, which controlled Grady. The handsome five-story cream-brick-and-green-marble building featured no wards but 33 bassinets, 116 beds in private, semiprivate, and 4-bed rooms, a central oxygen supply, and air conditioning. It also included its own kitchen, laundry, and morgue, although an underground tunnel connected to the main building at Grady. Only two years after Spalding opened, Grady began construction on a twenty-one-floor tower with 1,100 beds and seventeen operating rooms. Like Charity Hospital in New Orleans, the H-shaped building was symmetrical, with emergency rooms, wards, and cafeterias for whites on one side and blacks on the other; only the radiology and operating rooms were shared. The Grady Hospital complex now reflected each phase of deluxe Jim Crow architecture: the old completely separate municipal hospital buildings for blacks and whites built on opposite sides of Butler Street in 1918 and renovated with Public Works Administration funds in the late 1930s, the brand-new Hughes Spalding Pavilion for black private patients, and the biracial but partitioned New Grady, finished in 1958 as the last major monument to deluxe Jim Crow.[33]

Southern states had made such substantial progress toward equalizing hospital beds for blacks that by the early 1950s, black activists' focus of concern shifted from the exclusion of blacks from federal health programs to the entrenchment of segregation in the separate wards of mammoth new biracial public facilities such as Charity and Grady. In a 1952 editorial, "The Crushing Irony of De Luxe Jim Crow," the *Journal of the National Medical Association* opined that despite the thousands of new hospital beds for blacks, "*de luxe* Jim Crow is just as objectionable as any other kind. It is merely a new line of defense against the slow, but irresistible advance of liberal change." Addressing the national NAACP convention in June 1953, Cobb attacked Hill-Burton for presenting "the threat of foisting on generations unborn the entrenched ghetto hospital system, through the construction of new segregated hospitals."[34]

Encouraged by their victory in integrating the VA hospitals, the national leaders of the NMA and NAACP embraced integration as a wonder drug for fighting racial inequality in health care. The national NAACP adopted a new policy in 1952 that forbade any chapter to support private or public funding for all-black hospitals or wards. NMA physicians in Miami and in Charlotte and Raleigh, North Carolina, fought proposed publicly funded black hospitals or wings in white hospitals. The South Carolina NAACP led black voters narrowly to defeat a proposed $2.25 million bond issue to improve Columbia Hospital because it provided only $150,000 to improve facilities available to blacks. But internal regional and philosophical divisions among black reformers came to light in Memphis.[35]

When the Memphis NAACP chapter supported a new black public teaching hospital, the national organization threatened to revoke its charter. Although the local chapter rescinded its support, Memphis voters passed a 1952 municipal bond issue to construct the E. H. Crump Hospital, which opened in 1956. Crump was funded by the city but tailored to the needs of black professionals and their private patients. As historian Keith Wailoo writes, new black hospitals "responded to the rising socioeconomic ideals of African Americans" in the postwar South's growing middle class. These facilities both "preserve[d] Jim Crow medicine [and] incorporate[d] large numbers of African American consumers and practitioners into the burgeoning health care system." Even private white-run voluntary hospitals such as Duke University Hospital in Durham responded to increased demand for private accommodations for paying black patients by incorporating such accommodations into expansion plans.[36]

Deluxe Jim Crow hospitals resembled the pattern of hospital segregation practiced in many northern cities, except that Hill-Burton enabled southern blacks to be cared for in new, updated facilities instead of in the basements of deteriorating city hospitals. However, Hill-Burton guaranteed the inclusion of blacks only as recipients of health services, not as providers, since Hill had blocked a proposed amendment to guarantee all licensed physicians access to Hill-Burton facilities. (The amendment had been designed to provide admitting rights to chiropractors, osteopaths, members of group practices, and other practitioners who, along with minority physicians, faced discrimination in this arena.)[37] The absence of the amendment ensured that white hospital administrators controlled policies governing physician admitting rights. Although Cornely noted in 1956 that the black wards in new southern hospitals had improved the rates of staff integration to about 25 percent, a level comparable to northern hospitals, many Hill-Burton hospitals and virtually all non–Hill-Burton hospitals still refused admitting rights to black physicians. Black patients in Hill-Burton hospitals often could not retain black physicians of choice. Residencies did, however, begin to open to blacks, as federally funded positions with the VA and various specialties under the National Institutes of Health pumped funds into the system and enforced nondiscrimination. New black medical and nursing graduates also benefited from a tight labor market and the growth of medical specialization. The nationwide trend of rapidly expanding hospitals with an urgent need for more house staff despite little increase in the production of medical graduates was even more pronounced in the South as a consequence of Hill-Burton and the region's small number of medical schools.[38]

Cobb lamented the lack of commitment to full integration among his fellow black physicians, who remained professionally and financially invested in the black hospitals where they trained and practiced. S. W. Smith of the NMA emphasized the need to assure nondiscrimination in staff and patient admissions policies at all tax-supported institutions yet told his fellow black physicians, "It is incumbent upon us to set about to build and maintain hospitals for ourselves, since the government will never build hospitals sufficient to care for all of the sick." Many black doctors feared that integration would drain existing black institutions of patients and resources. George Simkins, the principal plaintiff in the landmark hospital desegregation lawsuit, *Simkins v. Cone*, recalled that when he first began seeking support from Greensboro black medical professionals in the late 1950s,

> some of the younger fellows wanted to open up these hospitals, and some of the older fellows didn't. . . . These fellows didn't want to lose their income from operating [at the black hospital, L. Richardson], and they knew if they had been admitting to Cone and Wesley Long [the all-white defendant Hill-Burton hospitals], they would have to be board certified to do any operations, so they weren't too much for it. They also figured that if you opened up Cone and Wesley Long, it would hurt L. Richardson. Patients would stop going to L. Richardson. I went around with a petition, and got guys that I knew who would sign up—I put their names on there first. Then I would approach the older fellows, and those that were reluctant, when they saw all the younger fellows down there, some of them signed, and some of them wouldn't sign.[39]

The majority of plaintiffs in the *Simkins* suit were black patients and dentists rather than physicians. Black physicians first filed formal complaints with the PHS's Hospital Division in 1951 against segregation in federally funded hospitals. Not until 1956, ten years after the passage of Hill-Burton, did black doctors in Wilmington, North Carolina, and Luling, Louisiana, file the first hospital desegregation lawsuits, *Eaton v. James Walker Memorial Hospital* and *In re: Board of Commissioners of St. Charles Hospital Service District*. Until the mid-1950s, the NMA's southern members remained focused primarily on gaining the right to treat black patients within new biracial but segregated hospitals rather than on eliminating the segregation of patients.[40]

HILL-BURTON'S IMPACT ON THE SOUTH

The Hill-Burton Act was debated in Congress and passed into law at the height of the South's paradoxical status as the nation's neediest yet most politically powerful region. Hill-Burton's passage marked the climax of an unlikely political synergy among blacks, southern whites, and nonsouthern liberals. Federal aid to hospital construction represented a fleeting compromise that combined the pragmatic promise of parity under segregation with New Deal liberalism to achieve a mutually desired goal: the expansion of hospital care for black and white southerners in medically underserved communities. But by the late 1940s, such sentiments had grown outmoded as a consequence of increasing calls for an end to segregation by northern liberals, civil rights organizations, and the Truman administration combined with American liberalism's rightward shift to replace redistributive social justice with economic growth and national security. By 1954, when the U.S. Supreme Court declared segregation in public elementary and secondary education unconstitutional in the landmark *Brown* decision, a sweeping expansion and modernization of southern hospitals was well under way.[41]

From 1947 to 1971, Hill-Burton underwrote the creation of a modern health-care infrastructure with $3.7 billion in federal funding and $9.1 billion in matches from state and local governments. Space for nearly half a million beds was constructed in 10,748 projects, including nursing homes and other specialized facilities. By 1971, Hill-Burton had also contributed $100 million toward building nearly 1,300 local health centers and another $100 million toward 28,000 beds in mental and tuberculosis hospitals, the vast majority of which were public facilities. Federal construction grants substantially increased the number of government-owned hospitals and the overall proportion of beds in public hospitals, particularly teaching institutions affiliated with medical schools.[42]

Hill-Burton contributed to a series of major transitions in the South and the nation. Teaching hospitals represented 21 percent of all Hill-Burton projects and 30 percent of total federal funding expended during the program's history (table 6.3). Health services researcher James E. Rohrer notes that "advancement of medical education and training by aiding in the construction of teaching facilities was an important secondary effect of Hill-Burton. . . . Subsequent shifts in Hill-Burton funding increased the share of resources devoted to large, acute care hospitals, many of which also had medical school affiliations." Although usually located in urban centers, southern teaching hospitals also functioned as tertiary care centers for rural patients. Urban teaching hospitals fulfilled large numbers of required black beds for state Hill-Burton plans and drew on concentrations of indigent patients as clinical material.[43]

The scores of large, modern teaching hospitals fostered the growth of institution-based, capital- and technology-intensive medicine in the South, including the burgeoning new academic medical centers at the state universities of Alabama, North Carolina, Texas, and Florida as well as the expansion of facilities at private medical schools such as Duke and Wake Forest. Funding from the VA and the National Mental Health Act also underwrote construction on southern

TABLE 6.3

Types of Facilities Aided by Hill-Burton in the United States, 1947–1971

TYPE	NUMBER OF PROJECTS	BEDS	HILL-BURTON FUNDING
Teaching hospitals	2,223 (20.7%)		$1.1 billion (29.7%)
Public-owned	5,280 (49.1%)	189,543 (40.3%)	$1.5 billion (41%)
All races admitted (segregated and integrated)	10,644 (99%)		
All-white	84		
All-black	20		
Inpatient	9,670 (90%)	470,329	$3.3 billion
General	5,787 (73%)	344,453	$2.6 billion
Long-term	1,733 (16%)	97,358	$523.1 million
Mental		21,034	$78.5 million
Tuberculosis		7,484	$27.7 million
Outpatient	1,078 (10%)		$453.2 million
TOTAL HOSPITAL PROJECTS	10,748	470,329	$3.75 billion
Health centers	1,281	n/a	$99.7 million
TOTAL PROJECTS	12,029	470,329	$3.82 billion

Source: U.S. Congress, Senate, Committee on Labor and Public Welfare, Subcommittee on Health, *Hill-Burton Hospital Survey and Construction Act*, 11–13; Morais, *History*, 181.

Note: Because categories overlap, the totals do not represent the sum of the numbers presented in the table. Inpatient projects include numbers for rehabilitation facilities, public health centers, and state health laboratories.

medical school campuses, such as the $12 million, five-hundred-bed Birmingham VA hospital built in 1947 adjacent to the Medical College of Alabama.[44]

As an outgrowth of Senator Pepper's Subcommittee on Wartime Health and Education, Hill-Burton was among the first and most successful examples of a new postwar brand of federal reform that garnered bipartisan support by blending centralized planning, economic development, and a rationale for domestic spending based on national defense. Writing in 1980, Lawrence J. Clark, a health administrator and policy analyst, and his coauthors judged the act "one of the most ambitious efforts for the development of social capital to that time." Senator Hill observed that the Hill-Burton Act was "unique for its recognition—for the first time in any Federal legislation—of the principle that the low-income States should receive the greatest proportion of Federal aid and for its preference to rural areas and small communities." By mid-1949, the eleven former Confederate states had received 93 percent of federal Hill-Burton appropriations. That year, Hill amended the program to double its annual appropriation from $75 million to $150 million and increased the federal share, originally 33 percent for all projects, to a range from 33 to 66 percent based on the state's per capita income. By 1962, the South still received more than 40 percent of Hill-Burton aid.[45]

Hill-Burton spread hospital-based health care, already standard in the urban North by the 1920s, to the South, where half of all Hill-Burton hospitals were built during the program's first decade. Hill-Burton's allocation formula achieved its intended goal of redistributing federal tax revenues from wealthier to poorer states to build hospitals in impoverished, underserved, and rural areas. The program benefited blacks as well as whites, particularly in North Carolina, where Hill-Burton arguably realized its fullest potential. In the South overall, Clark and his coauthors found that "net redistribution of beds [by 1970] to the lowest ranking states [in 1950] would have been only about half as great had it not been for the systematic market-countering effects of Hill-Burton." Five of the top seven recipients of Hill-Burton funding per capita were southern states, which benefited from a formula that allocated federal funds to the five poorest states at a per capita rate 3.56 times that for the five richest states.[46]

But medical sociologist Paul Starr contends that within states, middle-income (and thus most often white) communities benefited disproportionately from Hill-Burton, since they were best able to meet the requirements for matching funds. Edward H. Beardsley cites Arkansas and Oklahoma as prioritizing black needs, and all of the southern states accorded the most attention to their poorest rural areas. Of the fifteen top recipients of Hill-Burton funding from 1948 to 1970, nine were southern states (Mississippi, Alabama, North Carolina, Arkansas, Georgia, South Carolina, Kentucky, Tennessee, and Louisiana) with a combined African American population of 7 million (52 percent of the nation's African Americans) in 1940.[47]

Although Hill-Burton promoted the racial and regional redistribution of hospital beds, its deluxe Jim Crow hospitals ultimately helped the urban poor more than their rural counterparts. Historian Numan V. Bartley argues that "the massive health problems of the southern rural poor were ultimately ameliorated not by doctors but by the depopulation of the rural South." Hill-Burton substantially reduced southern rates of maternal and infant mortality by increasing the number of physician-attended hospital births, particularly among rural blacks. But economists William J. Collins and Melissa A. Thomasson note that "even as the colossal Hill-Burton program pumped federal funds into the health care system . . . the secular decline in infant mortality stagnated for nonwhites from 1950 to 1965 and for whites between 1955 and 1965." Collins and Thomasson conclude that the largest single factor contributing to the racial gap in infant mortality before 1970 was the racial difference in education levels of women between twenty and forty, followed by income, urban residence, and geographic distribution of physicians. This conclusion conflicts with Beardsley's beliefs that the first two postwar decades saw rapid gains for southern black mothers and infants and that city dwellers closed the racial gap more rapidly than did rural residents. Whether in 1950 or in 1970, black mortality rates stood approximately where white rates had fifteen to twenty years earlier.[48]

Health policy scholars have criticized Hill-Burton as a poor substitute for government-sponsored comprehensive health insurance and cited it as evidence of the subordination of public health needs to conservative politics. They contend that Hill-Burton's generous levels of funding would have been better spent on comprehensive public health services. Yet capital improvements to health facilities were one of state and local governments' greatest needs and expenses. The growth of Hill-Burton and smaller construction grant programs to build mental health facilities and sewage treatment plants constituted the most pronounced trend in federal public health spending during the 1950s. In 1950, PHS grants to states for nonconstruction programs roughly equaled Hill-Burton grants; by 1960, facilities construction received three times as much grant funding as all other programs. Construction programs offered a prime example of how postwar federal spending broadened the scope of public health beyond the traditional limits of state and local health departments. Hill-Burton brought hospital care under the aegis of public health, and its Hospital and Medical Facilities Study Section offered the first formal federal support for health services research to plan and evaluate medical care systems on a population basis.[49]

Hill-Burton's graduated, need-based allocation formula paved the way for federal sponsorship of southern health, education, and welfare programs as well as costly new infrastructure that made Sun Belt prosperity possible while allowing southern states to maintain low taxes. Texan Oveta Culp Hobby, secretary of the Department of Health, Education, and Welfare under President Dwight

Eisenhower, applied the Hill-Burton formula to all department grants. This strategy soon spread beyond health to programs such as highway and airport construction, and by 1955, southern states drew 20 percent of their revenues from federal sources, well above the national average of 14 percent. Mississippi, the epicenter of antifederal sentiment and the backlash against *Brown*, tied for fourth with Arkansas among states with the highest percentage of their budgets from federal funds. Today, despite the marked improvement of the southern economy over the past sixty years, many southern states receive more in federal aid than they pay in federal taxes. As the culmination of the New Deal, which targeted federal resources to the South, Hill-Burton was the last and perhaps the most progressive expression of redistributive midcentury liberalism.[50]

chapter 7

HILL-BURTON IN

NORTH CAROLINA

Until 1963, Hill-Burton remained the only federal program governed in the South by a legislative separate but equal clause, which did not, in its original context, preclude segregation within funded hospitals as long as patients were admitted on an equal basis. The clause allowed individual facilities to exclude on the basis of race only in the context of overall parity within planned area facilities.

THE MOST DELUXE
JIM CROW STATE OF ALL

North Carolina arguably gave the most serious thought of any state government to the health needs of black southerners. In response to public alarm over North Carolina's rank of forty-second in hospital beds per capita, forty-fifth in doctor-to-population ratio, and worst in rates of World War II draft rejections, Governor J. Melville Broughton in 1943 proposed a comprehensive health plan for "more doctors, more hospitals, and more insurance." Broughton went on to serve on the Federal Hospital Council, which formulated regulations barring racial and religious discrimination in Hill-Burton. Both North Carolina's Commission on Hospital and Medical Care and the American Hospital Association's Commission on Hospital Care affirmed the goal of providing equal quality care for black patients "in hospitals that serve white patients rather than in separate hospitals." The commissions also advocated that hospitals admit qualified black physicians to their staffs on the same basis as other physicians and provide equal opportunities for professional education.[1]

Under Broughton and Poe's leadership, North Carolina pursued an attenuated form of segregation in health care that mitigated but did not eliminate some of the worst aspects of the old racially separate hospital system. Blacks gained access on a rationed basis to white-run hospitals with state-of-the-art facilities staffed by more, better-trained personnel than could be found in the aging private black hospitals. North Carolina's state health plan also provided free care for the many residents who could not afford hospitalization, including most black citizens. The Duke Endowment and the U.S. military had already recognized the practical benefits of providing care in biracial hospitals. During the 1930s, the Duke Endowment had pioneered the provision of equal-quality care for black patients in white-run, racially mixed hospitals. During the war, integrated nursing staffs cared for black and white patients in southern military hospitals, including those at Fort Bragg, North Carolina; Fort Scott, South Carolina; Camp Livingston, Louisiana; and Lawson General Hospital at the Atlanta Naval Air Station.[2]

Rural sociologist Selz Mayo's vision of "one complete system of medical care" reflected regional and national trends that recast the administrative and spatial organization of hospitals to promote efficiency and adapt to rapid social, economic, and technological change in the delivery of health-care services. On the national level, the American Hospital Association, the U.S. Public Health Service (PHS), and architects specializing in hospital planning advocated more enlightened design that served both medical and social needs. Hospitals constructed after World War II, including the many new veterans' hospitals, contained a higher proportion of private and semiprivate rooms and smaller wards with four or eight beds. Fewer patients to a room and more space between beds reduced nurses' patient loads and prevented cross-infection, a problem that often plagued older hospitals with large wards. More private rooms provided isolation for severely ill and contagious cases. As the PHS noted in its manual, *Design and Construction of General Hospitals*, "Unless there is a definite local need for four-bed rooms, smaller accommodations generally provide greater flexibility for assignment and care of patients by condition, sex, and age." Yet such configurations could also foster segregation on the basis of race and class in new southern hospitals.[3]

The new model of modern, racially mixed but internally segregated facilities was incorporated into the blueprints of North Carolina's postwar hospital construction boom. When the University of North Carolina drew up plans in 1949 for a teaching hospital funded by Hill-Burton, the administration and the board of trustees envisioned "from the very first" a facility that would be "for both white and Negro patients, with separate wards, dining facilities, and so forth. This concept has been carried out in all the planning of the hospital." Some communities, such as Roanoke Rapids, used the trend toward private rooms to dodge the issue of patient integration entirely when applying for Hill-Burton funds to replace the existing community hospital. Doris Cochran, the wife of a local black physician and civil rights activist, served on the planning committee for the new hospital, completed in 1972. She remembered that "the Hill-Burton funds were mentioned tirelessly," and to meet nondiscrimination requirements yet avoid placing together patients of different races, all rooms in the new hospital were private or semiprivate. Despite the added expense, Rocky Mount and other towns built hospitals on the same premise. The availability of Medicare funding further encouraged the conversion of many hospitals to single-patient rooms.[4]

North Carolina's key role in defending and later dismantling the doctrine of separate but equal in federal health policy makes the state an instructive model of postwar federal-state relations in health care and civil rights. Several prominent North Carolinians testified before Congress on behalf of the Hill-Burton bill. Tar Heel congressmen Alfred L. Bulwinkle and J. Bayard Clark, whom surgeon general Thomas Parran credited with ensuring passage of the Hill-Burton Act in the House, led southern lawmakers in insisting that separate but equal facilities be permitted as an exception to the act's nondiscrimination clause. As one of the first four states to qualify for Hill-Burton funds and the first state to begin building, North Carolina set an example for other states by carefully guarding against federal intervention, especially that which threatened the racial status quo. Hill-Burton funded a total of thirty-one racially separate facilities in North Carolina, four of them for blacks. Nationally, twenty all-black and eighty-four all-white Hill-Burton hospitals were constructed before 1964.[5]

During the first five years of Hill-Burton, North Carolina's share of federal funds topped $17 million, which the North Carolina General Assembly supplemented with another $17 million for hospital construction and the expansion of the University of North Carolina School of Medicine. Participation in the Hill-Burton program augmented the state's reputation as a leader in health reform. H. C. Cranford, executive director of the nonprofit North Carolina Good Health Association, publicized the state's success in raising local matching

TABLE 7.1
Hill-Burton in North Carolina

1945: Ranked forty-second in hospital beds per capita

1947: Rockefeller Foundation planning grant to University of North Carolina for statewide medical center

1947–52: $17 million in federal Hill-Burton funds matched with $17 million in state funds (most generous of any southern state)

Fourth state to submit Hill-Burton plan

First state to begin construction

Built more Hill-Burton hospitals than any other state

Fifth in total federal funds expended

Seventy-seven city/county bond issues for matching funds

---

funds for hospital construction in *Hospitals: The Journal of the American Hospital Association*. The Good Health Association provided professional fund-raising and promotional assistance in securing private donations as well as passing tax and bond measures. The association produced pamphlets, newspaper ads, street banners, movie trailers, billboards, cartoons, and radio announcements, enlisting the help of famous entertainers and artists. Parran praised North Carolina for being "in the vanguard with respect to advancement of medical education and expansion of medical care facilities." Edward H. Beardsley credits North Carolina's legislature with being more generous toward hospital construction and the state's planning agency with being more far-sighted than those of any other southern state (table 7.1).[6]

North Carolina's early success sparked a rush of interest in the critical role state health departments could play in mapping out and executing new initiatives. Hill-Burton's promotion of regional health planning and statewide surveys of health needs and resources yielded a variety of outcomes. For example, Louisiana prioritized its state hospital system. During his first full term (1948–52), Governor Earl Long made social spending for health, education, and welfare his top priority, funding his plans with a 50 percent increase in state taxes, including a doubled sales tax. Long would be the state's only prominent politician publicly to endorse President Harry S. Truman during the 1948 Dixiecrat revolt, and the new measures Long enacted reflected those Truman pursued at the national level: pensions for the elderly, an expanded school lunch program, and significant increases in teacher salaries, including the equalization of pay for black teachers. In addition to new public schools and enhancements to the state university system, Long oversaw the refurbishing of the state charity hospitals and the expansion of state mental institutions.[7]

In Alabama and Florida, 1940s health reform centered on campaigns to build new four-year state medical schools, but unlike Louisiana and North Carolina, little specific attention was directed at black needs. *Planning Florida's Health Leadership*, a five-volume report published with funding from the Commonwealth Foundation by the Medical Center Study, provided no racial breakdowns of statistics on hospital beds or health professionals. Except for occasional references to Meharry Medical College, where black Floridians could attend under an arrangement with the Southern Regional Educational Board, the report failed to acknowledge the special needs or obstacles faced by black patients, doctors, or nurses. Since the report relied on membership in American Medical Association–affiliated medical societies to count the state's supply of doctors, black physicians were excluded from the tabulations. Given the attitudes of Florida's health planners, it is not surprising that the state university was the defendant in *Hawkins v. University of Florida Board of Control* (1956), the lawsuit that extended the *Brown* decision to the university level. In 1946, however, all eyes were on hospitals after Congress passed a landmark construction program that would, in very different ways from *Brown*, undermine Jim Crow in southern public facilities.[8]

During Hill-Burton's early years, the North Carolina Medical Care Commission tried to maintain segregation while demonstrating a new commitment to providing care for the indigent. But Hill-Burton's original guarantee that southern states could reap the benefits of federal aid but leave their racial mores undisturbed proved to be a Trojan horse. In their zeal to improve the health of all North Carolina citizens, white reformers unwittingly released forces that would dramatically accelerate the civil rights movement. In spite of the aspects of segregation preserved in state health planning and the Hill-Burton legislation, blacks gained improved access to hospital care; however, a detailed analysis of the act's implementation shows that blacks did not achieve parity with whites, either numerically or qualitatively.

The program raised challenging political questions from its inception. In the pages of the *Journal of the National Medical Association*, authors debated how federal officials would enforce Hill-Burton's provisions to achieve racial parity in funding and facilities and how southern officials and black physicians would in turn shape the practical application of federal health policy at the state and local levels. In 1948, Representative Helen Gahagan Douglas of California doubted that Hill-Burton would benefit blacks because poorer communities would be unable to raise the required matching two-thirds of construction costs or to guarantee funding for ongoing operation and maintenance. In contrast, Dr. Vane Hoge, chief of the Hospital Facilities Division of the PHS, reassured *Journal of the National Medical Association* readers that construction projects would be prioritized according to "percentage of need met by existing facilities," with special consideration for poor and rural areas and "availability to population groups less adequately served by reason of race, creed, or color. All of these factors will operate in favor of the groups with the greatest need of all—the Negroes in the rural South." Black and white liberal reformers were divided on the issue of whether federal aid to hospitals and medical schools would guarantee equality or entrench segregation. The fate of black patients and professionals under Hill-Burton depended on how the federal government chose to enforce the law's nondiscrimination provisions.[9]

Members of the American Medical Association were chagrined when Congress designated the PHS, then a division of the Federal Security Agency, to administer Hill-Burton. Surgeon general Thomas Parran and Oscar Ewing, the agency's head from 1947 to 1953, faced criticism from the ranks of organized medicine and southern politics who feared that aid to hospital construction would provide an avenue for federal interference in health care, race relations, or both. According to Parran, the federal role was "largely that of guidance," but both doctors and Dixiecrats read *guidance* as control. In fact, PHS guidance was very specific and encouraged the bureaucratic standardization of medicine in a wide variety of areas, among them architectural blueprints, day-to-day hospital operations, and safeguards against racial and religious discrimination. State and federal officials wrangled at length over just how far southern states had to go to meet Hill-Burton's requirement for "equitable provision, on the basis of need, for facilities and services of like quality for each [racial] group in the area."[10]

The Hill-Burton program in North Carolina was characterized by tension between the antifederalism of state leaders and the profound need for hospital facilities. Charles Templeton, the North Carolina Medical Care Commission's executive secretary during the late 1950s, was one of many southern officials who feared federal encroachment. Templeton warned other commission members that allowing hospitals to accept "a percentage of Federal funds in excess of 50% would tend to discourage local initiative and would give Federal authorities a greater voice in the planning and construction of facilities. . . . [S]ome of the more progressive states limit Federal participation to 33–1/3%." But the lure of federal dollars was strong, especially in a state with so few hospital beds per capita. Parran reported in 1947 that the PHS was being "deluged with letters inquiring 'How can we get a hospital in our town?'" The Medical Care Commission also received numerous requests from North Carolina counties for more federal and state aid because they were unable to raise enough local matching funds to qualify for the Hill-Burton program.[11]

Correspondence between Samuel C. Ingraham, director of the PHS's District 2 (including the southeastern states from Delaware to Florida), and John A. Ferrell, the first executive secretary of the North Carolina Medical Care Commission, reveals how state and federal officials who administered the Hill-Burton program negotiated the meaning of *nondiscrimination*. But despite the moderate racial views of its members, the Medical Care Commission submitted a Hill-Burton plan that clearly favored whites over blacks. In April 1947, Ferrell requested clarification of Hill-Burton's nondiscrimination requirements. Ingraham responded that the Hospital Facilities Division had ruled that "in an area for which separate hospital facilities are programmed for the exclusive use of a racial group, if funds become available only for that particular group, and funds are not available for other groups, that project may be approved. It would be impossible because of lack of funds to approve a companion project to provide facilities for other racial groups." If whites could raise matching funds and blacks could not, Hill-Burton would fund all-white facilities. Ingraham commented that the decision "should resolve many programming difficulties for those sections of North Carolina for which the 'Non-discrimination Statement' cannot be made." Ferrell sent out several copies of Ingraham's letter, alerting other officials to the availability of funds for racially separate facilities.[12]

Ingraham had to eat his words before the year was out. The PHS adopted a stricter definition of *nondiscrimination* to discourage states that wanted to build all-white hospitals with federal money. Ingraham explained to Ferrell that the PHS had so far received only one state plan for separate facilities. Ultimately, fourteen of the sixteen southern states (all except Texas and Arkansas) submitted state plans to allow monoracial facilities, yet such facilities represented only 1 percent of all projects constructed before 1964. Ingraham encouraged Ferrell to follow the "more expeditious" example of other states that used the official nondiscrimination statement in their comprehensive plans. The statement required individual project applicants to promise to make their facilities "available to all persons residing in the area to be served without discrimination on account of race, creed or color" but still allowed patients to be segregated *within* hospitals.[13]

Despite Ingraham's advice, North Carolina's original state plan included a statement of its intent to provide care in racially separate facilities and an accompanying plan to provide an equal proportion of beds based on racial population ratios in each county. A section on "Minimum Standards for the Maintenance and Operation of Hospitals" required hospital staff to submit quarterly reports with patient statistics by race, with number and rate of fatalities by department. North Carolina's state Hill-Burton plan met all requirements and was approved by the surgeon general in July 1947, when the required ratio of black to white beds was calculated using only proposed facilities. In November 1947, the Federal Security Agency's general counsel interpreted the nondiscrimination requirement to include existing as well as proposed facilities, which favored blacks, since far fewer existing facilities accommodated them. According to the agency's Hospital Facilities Division, the state plan could not call for new white beds to be constructed in a county until enough black beds had been built to match the ratio of existing white beds.[14]

Ingraham apologized that the different interpretation would require North Carolina's state plan to be amended and assured Ferrell, "we are making every effort to obtain Central Office approval for your revised Plan." The Hospital Facilities Division in Washington accepted the amended plan on November 20, 1947, but the PHS Central Office rejected it, citing forty-five of the state's one hundred counties where the number of beds planned was unacceptable. The Central Office directed that the number of beds programmed for nonwhites should be increased in thirty-four counties and decreased in eleven counties. The state commission apparently had not recovered from this blow by the end of April 1948, when Ingraham had to ask Ferrell to submit the revisions to meet the nondiscrimination requirement "as soon as possible" so that final approval for the North Carolina state plan could be granted.[15]

The PHS continued to intervene periodically to enforce the nondiscrimination provisions of Hill-Burton. The black weekly *Raleigh Carolinian* noted in 1951,

Both Negroes and whites will be treated without discrimination at the proposed new tubercular hospital which the State of North Carolina is planning to build at Chapel Hill, but it is because the State had no choice but to bow to integration or lose federal support. Original plans for the hospital [to] be operated in connection with the "liberal" University of North Carolina medical school provided that it would treat only white patients, but . . . the State Tuberculosis Hospital Board signed a stipulation promising there would be no discrimination in the new hospital, and that the huge hospital being built at the UNC medical school with state funds will treat members of all races.

Integration and *no discrimination* here applied only to admitting patients of both races to the same facility, not eliminating racial segregation within the hospitals.[16]

HILL-BURTON AND BLACK HOSPITALS

By expanding and shifting the supply of black hospital beds from all-black to white-run, biracial facilities, did Hill-Burton result in better or worse care for black patients? In 1945, 80 percent of North Carolina's 8,464 hospital beds were reserved for whites, while 20 percent were reserved for blacks. The 1,683 beds for blacks were divided evenly between all-black and biracial facilities, although forty-one of the seventy-four biracial hospitals had 10 or fewer beds for blacks. Two black hospitals that received Hill-Burton funds, the State Hospital for the Colored Insane at Goldsboro and St. Agnes, a private general hospital in Raleigh, illustrate not only the harsh prerenovation conditions black patients faced but also the widely varying long-term outcomes for black institutions.[17]

In the first third of the twentieth century, states centralized care of the mentally ill in institutions and removed responsibility from local communities, since reformers believed that this approach would result in better, more humane, and more effective treatment and improve chances for curing and discharging patients. As local governments took advantage of the opportunity to shift costs to the state by redefining senility as a psychiatric condition and committing patients to state institutions, the number of chronic and elderly mental patients rose dramatically. By 1940, state mental hospitals housed 450,000 inpatients, and by 1950 nearly one-third of those patients were over sixty-five. In addition to overcrowding as a consequence of increasing numbers of committals and a higher proportion of patients remaining hospitalized for more than five years, the state mental hospitals had suffered from gross neglect during the depression and World War II. The resulting deplorable conditions were the subject of both fictional and journalistic exposés of mental institutions, such as Mary

Jane Ward's novel *The Snake Pit*, which was made into a Hollywood movie. In the 1948 book *Shame of the States*, photojournalist Albert Deutsch documented institutions where patients were chained to beds or ate food without utensils, ceilings were leaking and crumbling, and no occupational therapy or recreation was available.[18]

In the South, the combination of Spartan state budgets and segregation only worsened the nationwide crisis in mental institutions. North Carolina, Virginia, West Virginia, Maryland, and Oklahoma maintained state mental hospitals for blacks in completely separate locations from white institutions, and Mississippi, South Carolina, and Florida had separate black divisions within a single complex. Texas's three state mental hospitals were biracial, with separate accommodations for blacks and whites within each facility. One of the few bright spots was care for mentally ill black veterans within the Veterans Administration hospital system, particularly at Tuskegee, and the Veterans Administration would become a major provider of mental health care after World War II. The federal government also sponsored treatment for drug addiction beginning in 1929, when Congress directed the PHS to establish a Narcotics Division (later renamed the Division of Mental Hygiene) and appropriated funds to construct two hospitals for the study and treatment of narcotics addiction as well as the treatment of psychotic military personnel. Both were in the South: the first opened in Lexington, Kentucky, in 1935, and the second opened in Fort Worth, Texas, three years later.[19]

In 1935, North Carolina's legislature passed a resolution authorizing the governor to conduct a comprehensive survey of mental health needs, the first to be undertaken by either a southern state or the Rockefeller Foundation, which funded the study. Although North Carolina was held up as an example that other southern states would follow, the survey uncovered 528:1 patient-doctor ratios in state mental hospitals, whereas the American Psychiatric Association recommended 150 patients per doctor. After the report was released to the General Assembly in January 1937, North Carolina increased appropriations to enlarge its state hospitals, with a total census of 7,347 inpatients. In addition to 699 residents at the School for the Feeble-Minded, 2,104 patients were treated at the State Hospital for the Colored Insane at Goldsboro, 2,299 were treated at Morganton (white), and 2,245 were treated at Raleigh (white).[20]

Within a few months of the release of the survey of mental health in North Carolina, the Bureau of Negro Work in the Department of Public Welfare investigated the State Hospital at Goldsboro, setting in motion a transformation through Public Works Administration and Hill-Burton funding that was nothing short of phenomenal. The investigation uncovered shocking conditions of neglect and use of mental patients as maintenance, child care, and field laborers even after the patients became eligible for discharge. By 1940, the Public Works Administration had built seven new patient dormitories with a total of 1,170 beds, making the black wards "far superior" to those in the white state hospital at Raleigh, according to one 1945 account. Hill-Burton further upgraded the hospital with 487 new beds and two service facilities at a cost of just under $1.5 million, one-third from federal funds and two-thirds from a special appropriation for improvements to state facilities. Twenty years after the 1937 investigation, Goldsboro's new superintendent received praise for his "very excellent and progressive plans for the treatment of the mentally ill at Goldsboro." The expansion of the Goldsboro hospital accounted for 88 percent of beds added and two-thirds of the total expenditures for black hospitals during the first seven years of Hill-Burton in North Carolina. In neighboring Virginia, Hill-Burton also added 1,000 beds for black mental patients. Since mental hospital dormitories cost considerably less per bed to build than general hospital beds, the overall expenditure per bed for black facilities was substantially lower than for biracial or white facilities.[21]

Hill-Burton funding was much more modest and less transformative for Raleigh's St. Agnes Hospital, a private one-hundred-bed facility that built an eighty-six-thousand-dollar service facility under the program. Private black hospitals such as St. Agnes and Lincoln Hospital in Durham received substantial public and philanthropic assistance in return for providing indigent care. They also offered a safe haven from the humiliation of segregation and enabled patients to retain their choice of physician. During the 1950s, Doris Cochran chose to drive eighty miles to deliver her three children at Lincoln rather than endure inferior treatment in the Jim Crow ward at Roanoke Rapids Hospital, only five miles from her home. But when St. Agnes was condemned in 1955, the inspection committee unanimously called its physical plant "a disgrace to the people of Raleigh and of Wake County . . . in considerably worse condition than any place ever inspected by the present Grand Jury." St. Agnes closed permanently in 1961, the same year that a new, integrated, county-owned Hill-Burton facility opened. Only about half of St. Agnes's patients could pay anything for their care, and without sufficient income to offset the heavy load of charity patients, black hospitals increasingly fell behind in making the capital improvements and technological investments necessary for modernization, thereby further hindering their ability to retain paying patients. As was the case in Raleigh, new biracial Hill-Burton hospitals replaced black hospitals in many communities.[22]

Black hospitals also had higher mortality rates than white hospitals, particularly for surgery, in part because black patients were often in such poor health when they were finally admitted that they could not even undergo surgery until they were fed a nutritious diet to gain a minimal level of strength. As more beds for blacks opened in modern, biracial institutions, black patients began to choose them over black hospitals. A critical factor for middle-class blacks was the new availability of private accommodations, since affluence afforded blacks as well as whites an escape from the undesirable conditions of charity wards to which blacks had long been confined. One eastern North Carolina civil rights leader called the private black hospital in his hometown "nothing but a convalescent home" after his wife received treatment there during a high-risk pregnancy in 1950. The hospital's doctors "just were not that equipped, not that up on the job," failing to recognize that the woman was carrying twins. In 1945, the hospital's death rate of 10.5 percent compared very unfavorably with death rates of 2.5 and 2.0 percent at the town's two white hospitals, and the black hospital treated patients at a per diem cost of $2.88, about 40 percent of spending at the two white hospitals. After the civil rights leader's wife collapsed from a kidney stone attack, he rushed her to Duke Hospital, a private 120-bed facility fifty miles away with a 15-bed black ward. Doctors there told him, "You're going to have to bring her to Duke [for the delivery] because if she goes to [the black hospital], she'll die. So will the children, more than likely."[23]

Southern health care stood at the brink of fundamental transformation in 1950, when car accidents in Alamance County in North Carolina's central Piedmont claimed the lives of two black men, Dr. Charles Drew and Maltheus Avery. Historian Spencie Love has disproved the widespread legend that Drew, an internationally renowned pioneer in blood plasma banking and outspoken advocate of health-care integration, died as a result of being refused treatment on racial grounds; Drew in fact died of his severe injuries after three white surgeons treated him in the emergency room of Alamance General Hospital in Burlington. But the Drew legend was based on Avery's remarkably similar circumstances: his death eight months after Drew's sparked outrage among black North Carolinians. After sustaining critical injuries in a car accident, Avery was shuttled among three hospitals. Alamance General evaluated Avery but transferred him to Duke Hospital for specialized care for a serious head injury requiring surgery. Duke's neurosurgeon examined Avery and administered supportive measures, but the hospital's black ward was full, and Avery was refused admission. He was sent on to Lincoln, the only area hospital without racial admitting restrictions, where he died almost immediately.[24]

Hill-Burton funds improved every hospital involved in the Drew-Avery story and supported several new local facilities as well. At the time of Avery's death, a new, million-dollar, 100-bed, county-owned, biracial hospital was under construction in Burlington. The University of North Carolina School of Medicine, which expanded its two-year program to become an M.D.-granting school in 1951, also built a $5 million, 296-bed teaching hospital in Chapel Hill, between Burlington and Durham, where critically injured patients such as Drew and Avery could receive quality care. By 1955, the one black and four biracial general hospitals in Alamance, Orange, and Durham Counties had added 186 more beds for blacks to the 113 available in 1950. Although all these hospitals except Lincoln continued to segregate black patients, increasing the supply of beds relieved demand and eased acceptance of nonpaying and emergency patients. From 1940 to 1960, rates of hospitalization in North Carolina increased 213.8 percent for blacks versus 113.2 percent for whites. Blacks' outrage over white-run facilities refusing care to black patients appears to have peaked in 1952, when the *Raleigh Carolinian*, one of the black newspapers that publicized Avery's death in 1950, ran three front-page stories on the topic during a six-month period. The paper carried no such stories for the rest of the 1950s.[25]

Increasing hospital utilization among blacks helped to promote a shift from mass to minority exclusion from medical care that mirrored the postwar economic shift from majority to minority poverty. Hill-Burton helped to reduce the large number of nonhospital births without physicians, particularly among rural blacks, which had previously contributed to high southern rates of maternal and infant mortality. The proportion of nonwhite births in southern hospitals increased from 24 percent in 1945 to 74 percent in 1960, whereas the white proportion increased from 68 to 97 percent. In many ways, Avery's death is less representative of the direction of southern health care in the 1950s than are the experiences of Drew and the civil rights leader's wife, who were among the growing number of black patients receiving emergency and maternity care in biracial, deluxe Jim Crow hospitals.[26]

RACIAL PARITY IN HILL-BURTON

Southern states' commitment to providing separate but equal facilities for black patients was undergirded by federal enforcement of Hill-Burton's principle of racial parity, which can be quantified by examining patterns of funding and construction in North Carolina. The North Carolina General Assembly provided

$17 million in Hill-Burton matching funds for hospital construction and the expansion of the University of North Carolina School of Medicine, the state's third four-year medical school established in twenty years (after Duke in 1930 and Bowman Gray, affiliated with Wake Forest University, in 1940). In addition, the University of North Carolina received a major Rockefeller Foundation planning grant to establish a statewide medical center. North Carolina health reform was greatly indebted to the region's leading school of public health, located at the University of North Carolina, as well as to Duke University School of Medicine and to strong connections with the PHS, the Rockefeller Foundation, and major North Carolina philanthropies.[27]

North Carolina ultimately ranked first in the number of projects built under Hill-Burton and fifth in total federal funds expended, resulting in a 115 percent increase in beds during the program's first two decades. Hill-Burton qualitatively and quantitatively improved access to health care for southern black and indigent patients by funding the construction of health centers and biracial hospitals, one-third of which were publicly owned. With Hill-Burton aid, North Carolina built eighty-six public health centers, where, according to the North Carolina Advisory Committee to the U.S. Commission on Civil Rights, "the clinical and service elements of the State-wide program favor availability to the Negro." Fifty-four of the new general hospitals constructed under Hill-Burton in North Carolina were biracial but segregated by ward. Conversely, Hill-Burton funded more racially separate projects in North Carolina than in any other state: two new general hospitals and twenty-five additions to existing hospitals exclusively for whites, and two new general hospitals and two additions exclusively for blacks.[28]

Analyzing project-level data from the North Carolina Medical Care Commission and hospital statistics from the Duke Endowment demonstrates Hill-Burton's dramatic impact on North Carolina. In 1945, the number of black general hospital beds was divided about evenly between black and biracial institutions; by 1960, approximately one-third of black beds were in black hospitals, while two-thirds were in biracial hospitals (table 7.2). Although the number of black beds in biracial hospitals more than doubled, by far the greatest numerical increase of any category was white beds in biracial hospitals (4,405). By 1960, the vast majority of both black and white patients were being treated in biracial hospitals, whereas nearly half of white hospitals had either opened their doors to black patients or shut down since the end of World War II.

Hill-Burton did not equalize beds based on racial population ratios, as the state plan and federal guidelines proposed, but it was not capable of doing so

TABLE 7.2
North Carolina General Hospitals, 1945 and 1960

	Black		Biracial			White		Total		
	NUMBER	BEDS	NUMBER	BLACK BEDS	WHITE BEDS	NUMBER	BEDS	BLACK BEDS	WHITE BEDS	TOTAL BEDS
1945	13	840	66	815	4,417	48	2,382	1,655	6,799	8,454
1960	11	919	101	1,758	8,822	15	2,905	2,677	11,727	14,404
% change		+9.4		+108.5	+99.7		+22.0	+59.1	+72.5	+69.8

Source: Number of hospitals is from North Carolina Advisory Committee to the U.S. Commission on Civil Rights, *Equal Protection of the Laws in North Carolina,* 17; beds for each race are from Duke Endowment Hospital Section, "North Carolina General Hospitals Caring for Negro Patients in 1944," MCC; and Duke Endowment, *1961 Miscellaneous Hospital Statistics* (Durham: Duke Endowment, 1961), A-1–A-13, Duke Endowment Archives, Hospital Division Subseries, Box HCCD 16, Special Collections, Perkins Library, Duke University, Durham, N.C.

alone. Blacks represented 27.5 percent of North Carolina's population in 1940, but their share of hospital beds decreased slightly from 19.6 percent in 1945 to 18.6 percent in 1960. The decrease would have been much greater without Hill-Burton as a result of the growing availability of nonfederal sources of hospital construction financing. In addition, the disproportionate growth in the share of white beds reflected the rise of biracial hospitals in which predominantly white paying patients subsidized predominantly black charity patients.[29]

Tables 7.3 through 7.6 depict the effect of the Hill-Burton Act on thirty-nine North Carolina counties that had comparatively high concentrations of black residents and sixty-one counties that had lower concentrations. Statistics were tabulated for both the twenty-five counties with the highest percentage of blacks and the twenty-five counties that had the highest number of blacks. Some counties fell into both categories, resulting in a total of thirty-nine counties with high concentrations of blacks. In 1940, these counties included 693,822 African Americans (71 percent of North Carolina blacks) and a total population of 1,841,650 (52 percent of all North Carolinians).

The twenty-five counties with the highest *percentage* of blacks, sparsely populated and concentrated in the rural northeastern and south-central sections of the state, contained 19 percent of the state's total population but 35 percent of African Americans, who made up between 43 and 65 percent of these counties' populations. PHS official Vane Hoge's prediction that Hill-Burton's emphasis on poor, underserved areas would benefit rural blacks was true for these counties, half of which had no hospitals in 1947. Hill-Burton built thirteen new hospital buildings and sixteen new health centers, with at least one facility in all but three of the high-percentage black counties. Only two counties, Hoke and Jones, still had no general hospital or health center by 1954.

The twenty-five counties with the highest *numbers* of black residents were concentrated among the wealthier, more densely populated urban Piedmont counties containing the cities of Charlotte, Durham, Raleigh, Winston-Salem, and Greensboro as well as counties containing the cities of Wilmington in the east, Fayetteville in the south, and Asheville in the west. These counties, comprising just under a third of North Carolina's black and total populations, received disproportionate shares of federal and local matching funding, while the lion's share of state funding (62 percent) went to the sixty-one counties with predominantly white, rural populations. Although hospital beds were already concentrated in urban areas, residents of these wealthier counties benefited from the greater availability of local matching funds and constructed 48 percent of

TABLE 7.3

Hill-Burton Projects in North Carolina, 1947–1954: Counties by Racial Composition and Project Type

Project type	High number black counties (n=25)		High percentage black counties (n=25)		Total high concentration black counties (n=39)		Low concentration black counties (n=61)		Total counties (n=100)	
	NUMBER	BEDS	NUMBER	BEDS	NUMBER	BEDS	NUMBER	BEDS	NUMBER	BEDS
Addition	15	1,025	9	302	18	1,088	19	821	37	1,909
New building	12	1,572	13	1,064	19	1,894	28	1,886	47	3,780
Nursing home	13	1,045	8	268	17	1,177	21	794	38	1,971
Service facility/ staff housing	7	n/a	4	n/a	8	n/a	6	n/a	14	n/a
Health center	15	n/a	16	n/a	24	n/a	33	n/a	57	n/a
TOTAL NUMBER	62	3,642	50	1,634	86	4,159	107	3,501	193	7,660
TOTAL PERCENT		47.6		21.3		54.3		45.7		

Source: Number of Hill-Burton projects, beds constructed, and costs are from North Carolina Medical Care Commission, "One Hundred Ninety-two Projects Aided by the Commission during the First Seven Years of Construction," November 24, 1954. Records of the Office of the Vice Chancellor for Health Affairs, Henry T. Clark Series, Box 17, 1953–6, Folder, University Archives, Wilson Library, University of North Carolina at Chapel Hill; hospital-level data for race of patients admitted and number of beds for each racial group are from 1961 Miscellaneous Hospital Statistics (Durham: Duke Endowment, 1961), A-1-A-5, Duke Endowment Archives, Hospital Division Subseries, Box HCCD 16, Special Collections, Perkins Library, Duke University, Durham, N.C.

TABLE 7.4

Hill-Burton Funding in North Carolina, 1947–1954:
Counties by Racial Composition and Funding Source

FUNDING SOURCE	HIGH NUMBER BLACK COUNTIES (N=25)	HIGH PERCENTAGE BLACK COUNTIES (N=25)	TOTAL HIGH CONCENTRATION BLACK COUNTIES (N=39)	LOW CONCENTRATION BLACK COUNTIES (N=61)	TOTAL COUNTIES (N=100)
Federal	11,861,612	4,894,967	13,521,436	15,182,744	28,704,180
State	6,181,472	4,589,158	7,922,965	12,868,370	20,791,335
Local	18,933,945	3,849,562	20,151,324	11,865,539	32,016,863
TOTAL	$36,977,029	$13,333,687	$41,595,725	$39,916,653	$81,512,378

Source: Number of Hill-Burton projects, beds constructed, and costs are from North Carolina Medical Care Commission, "One Hundred Ninety-two Projects Aided by the Commission during the First Seven Years of Construction," November 24, 1954, Records of the Office of the Vice Chancellor for Health Affairs, Henry T. Clark Series, Box 17, 1953–63 Folder, University Archives, Wilson Library, University of North Carolina at Chapel Hill; location and type of hospital ownership are from *Annual Reports of the Hospital and Orphan Sections, for the Fiscal Year October 1, 1961–September 30, 1962* (Durham: Duke Endowment, 1962), 22–25; rankings of North Carolina counties by number and percentage black population in 1940 are from University of Virginia Geospatial and Statistical Data Center, *United States Historical Census Data Browser*.

hospital and nursing home beds built under Hill-Burton through 1954. The urban, high-population counties built fewer but larger, more elaborate, more expensive facilities. (The five most expensive projects were for teaching hospitals in or near urban areas.)

The rural counties—whether with high or low percentages of blacks—built smaller, cheaper facilities with proportionally more government funding. The counties with low concentrations of African Americans provided local matching funds for only 30 percent of hospital construction costs versus 51 percent in high-population counties. Poor blacks in the rural, high-percentage counties were least able to raise matching funds but with government aid built proportionally more new hospitals and health centers at lower cost. This outcome upholds the North Carolina Medical Care Commission's claim to be "responsible for an equitable distribution of facilities to all the people in the 100 counties of the State" and to apply state appropriations for hospital construction "only in the economically disadvantaged counties to help them match the Federal share of the cost of construction." Participation in Hill-Burton was much higher in the

TABLE 7.5

Hill-Burton in North Carolina, 1947–1954:
Hospital Facilities by Race of Patients

	BLACK	BIRACIAL	WHITE*	TOTAL
Projects†	7	113	16	136
Beds	552	6,136	972	7,660
Funding source				
Federal	852,860	23,162,884	3,358,457	27,374,201
State	988,226	17,633,456	1,225,999	19,847,681
Local	473,062	22,108,456	8,331,050	30,912,568
TOTAL	$2,314,148	$62,904,796	$12,915,506	$78,134,450
$ PER BED	2,989	9,924	13,199	9,914

Source: Number of Hill-Burton projects, beds constructed, and cost are from North Carolina Medical Care Commission, "One Hundred Ninety-two Projects Aided by the Commission during the First Seven Years of Construction," November 24, 1954, Records of the Office of the Vice Chancellor for Health Affairs, Henry T. Clark Series, Box 17, 1953–63 Folder, University Archives, Wilson Library, University of North Carolina at Chapel Hill; hospital-level data for race of patients admitted and number of beds for each racial group are from *1961 Miscellaneous Hospital Statistics* (Durham: Duke Endowment, 1961), A1–A5; location and type of hospital ownership are from Duke Endowment, *Annual Report of the Hospital and Orphan Sections, 1961–62* (n.p., 1962), 22–25.

  * "white" defined as less than 1% black patients.
  † includes multiple projects at some facilities.

high-concentration counties, where all but six of thirty-one biracial general hospitals received funding. In the low-concentration counties, twenty of fifty-seven biracial general hospitals had not received Hill-Burton funds as of 1954.[30]

Sociologist Jill Quadagno observes, "Hospitals presented a powerful barrier to civil rights objectives" because their segregated practices were protected by the principle that the hospital was a private institution beyond the state's regulatory authority. Although twice as many privately as publicly owned facilities were constructed during Hill-Burton's first seven years in North Carolina, by 1967 local governments had passed seventy-seven bond issues to provide matching funds. As a result, the number of hospitals owned by state and local governments increased 282 percent, while the number of private voluntary nonprofit and proprietary facilities decreased by 30 and 24 percent, respectively. The number of county-owned hospitals increased by 511 percent, while their bed capacity

TABLE 7.6

Hill-Burton in North Carolina, 1947–1954:
Hospital Facilities by Ownership

	STATE*	COUNTY/MUNICIPAL	PRIVATE	TOTAL
Projects†	10	34	92	136
Beds	1,024	1,769	4,867	7,660
Funding source				
Federal	2,779,700	6,901,066	17,693,434	27,374,200
State	5,267,686	4,964,981	9,615,014	19,847,681
Local	0	7,110,957	23,801,611	30,912,568
TOTAL	$8,047,386	$18,977,004	$51,110,059	$78,134,449

Source: Number of Hill-Burton projects, beds constructed, and cost are from North Carolina Medical Care Commission, "One Hundred Ninety-two Projects Aided by the Commission during the First Seven Years of Construction," November 24, 1954, Records of the Office of the Vice Chancellor for Health Affairs, Henry T. Clark Series, Box 17, 1953–63 Folder, University Archives, Wilson Library, University of North Carolina at Chapel Hill"; location and type of hospital ownership are from *Annual Reports of the Hospital and Orphan Sections, for the Fiscal Year October 1, 1961–September 30, 1962* (Durham: Duke Endowment, 1962), 22–25.

 * includes mental, tuberculosis, and cerebral palsy hospitals
 † includes multiple projects at some facilities

grew by 1,500 percent. Hill-Burton dramatically increased the number of beds in publicly owned hospitals in which racial discrimination could be deemed state action and thus unconstitutional under the Fifth and Fourteenth Amendments, but private white hospitals continued to discriminate against black patients and professionals.

In the *Eaton v. James Walker Memorial Hospital* and *Simkins v. Cone* desegregation cases, the defendants were private voluntary hospitals in North Carolina that had accepted public funds. Wilmington's Walker had benefited from a local bond issue, and Greensboro's Moses Cone and Wesley Long had benefited from Hill-Burton, but the courts held in *Eaton* and initially in *Simkins* that accepting government aid did not convert the hospitals to public entities and that the hospitals' discrimination was therefore not "state action." In *Simkins*, the federal appeals court overturned the district court's decision in late 1962,

TABLE 7.7

Charity and Black Patients Cared for by North Carolina
and South Carolina University Hospitals, 1964

	AVERAGE FOR FOUR HOSPITALS	DUKE	BOWMAN GRAY	MEDICAL COLLEGE OF SOUTH CAROLINA	UNIVERSITY OF NORTH CAROLINA
Average beds in use	498	653	479	453	408
Charity days of care	82,293	102,220	57,585	85,762	83,606
% Charity patients	53.5	49.0	35.7	64.0	65.4
% Black patients	26.2	27.5	0.4	44.8	32.2

Source: Duke Endowment, *1964 Miscellaneous Hospital Statistics*, A-1-, Duke Endowment Archives, Hospital Division Subseries, Box HCCD 16.

and the Supreme Court declined to review the case in 1963, thereby upholding the appeals decision and laying the groundwork for the 1964 Civil Rights Act's principle of banning racial discrimination by any recipient of federal funds.[31]

The five most expensive Hill-Burton projects in North Carolina through 1954, ranging from $2.6 to $5.3 million, were for large teaching hospitals in or adjacent to urban, high-population black counties. Four were private, while the fifth was a new state-owned facility for the University of North Carolina School of Medicine. Two of the four private projects did not admit blacks—the 300-bed Moses Cone Hospital and the 107-bed expansion of Durham's all-white Watts Hospital, which was paired with a 35-bed addition to the all-black Lincoln Hospital (also a teaching facility), with federal and local funding allocated based on racial population ratios. The importance of teaching hospitals in providing care to black and indigent patients is illustrated by the three facilities in North and South Carolina affiliated with the Medical College of South Carolina, the University of North Carolina, and Duke University. (The North Carolina Baptist Hospital, affiliated with the Bowman Gray School of Medicine in Winston-Salem, was an all-white private facility that did not receive Hill-Burton funds.) North and South Carolina's three university hospitals that admitted blacks provided 271,588 days of charity care in 1964, roughly half of them for black patients (table 7.7).[32]

In the absence of national universal health financing, the inability of the majority of black patients to pay for their care was at least as important as race per se in determining hospital access for blacks. Postwar economic gains increased both income and health insurance coverage among blacks nationally, and by 1962, about 46 percent of nonwhites and 74 percent of whites had hospital insurance, although the percentage of southern nonwhites was significantly lower. These changes reduced the financial barriers to obtaining the hospital care made more available by Hill-Burton. Postwar prosperity also provided a tax base to support indigent care at the growing number of municipal and teaching hospitals funded by Hill-Burton.[33]

From 1940 to 1960, the incidence of hospitalization in North Carolina increased from 29 to 91 per thousand for blacks and from 68 to 145 per thousand for whites as a result of both the expanded supply of hospital beds under Hill-Burton and improved health-care financing from private hospital insurance and indigent care supported by taxes and philanthropy. The North Carolina General Assembly first appropriated state funds for hospitalization of indigent patients in 1945, at the rate of one dollar per day per patient up to a total of $500,000 per biennium. In 1950, Congress initiated a program of federal grants to states for vendor payments to providers who cared for public welfare recipients. By 1959, federal and state funding provided $3 million annually for the hospitalization of welfare patients in North Carolina. In addition to public and philanthropic support for charity care, the advent of biracial Hill-Burton hospitals included blacks in the cost-shifting system through which hospitals subsidized indigent care via revenues from paying patients. In the fiscal year ending September 30, 1962, North Carolina's 102 public and private biracial hospitals provided 574,085 patient-days of free care (18 percent of total days) versus 98,953 free patient-days (39.9 percent of total days) at ten black hospitals (fig. 7.1). Fourteen white-only hospitals, all but one of them private, dispensed free care for only 10 percent of the days of care provided.[34]

Although liberal senators James Murray and Robert Wagner are usually credited with Hill-Burton's indigent care requirements, Pepper incorporated this concept into the first federal hospital construction bill, S. 3631, "Hospital Construction for the Medically Needy," which he introduced in 1938. Southern policy makers and doctors viewed the question of indigent care (which necessarily included large numbers of blacks) as intimately related to hospital expansion. Senator Allen Ellender remarked during the Hill-Burton hearings, "Our primary purpose should be to devise means to take care of those who cannot take care of themselves. My reason for supporting a bill providing for federal aid to build hospitals is to make it easy for the community in which a hospital may

FIGURE 7.1

Median Percentage Black and Charity Patients in
North Carolina Biracial General Hospitals, 1961

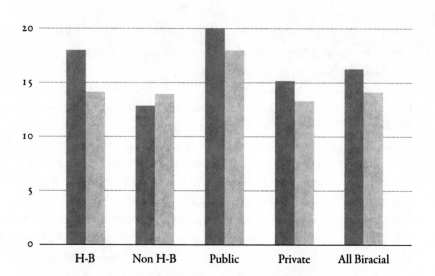

● PERCENT BLACK   ● PERCENT CHARITY

Source: Duke Endowment, *Annual Reports of the Hospital and Orphan Sections, for the Fiscal Year October 1, 1961–September 30, 1962* (Durham: Duke Endowment, 1962), 22–25.

be built to give aid to the indigent." Southern historian David Beito asserts that in Mississippi, "the spread of free care in the 1950s [in Hill-Burton hospitals] cut deeply into the patient base [of black fraternal hospitals] among the poor." Numan V. Bartley asserts, however, that under Hill-Burton, "free care for the poor was almost completely ignored."[35]

Health activists grew increasingly vocal during the 1960s and 1970s, demanding that Hill-Burton fulfill its pledge to provide "a reasonable volume of hospital services to persons unable to pay." Even though virtually all of the law's chief framers had expected Hill-Burton to operate in tandem with federally funded health financing, its primary purpose was hospital construction, not indigent care. One of the greatest ironies of deluxe Jim Crow was that given Congress's continued failure to pass either civil rights or health financing reform in the two decades before the advent of the Civil Rights Act, Medicare, and Medicaid, Hill-Burton hospitals ensured a minimum amount of care for blacks, much of it uncompensated. This development did not result from Hill-Burton's indigent care provisions but rather its separate but equal clause, whose most important practical result was ironically to force states that insisted on the right to build separate facilities to plan for and implement a proportional share of hospital beds and services for blacks, almost entirely within biracial facilities. Thus, North Carolina built the most racially separate facilities under Hill-Burton yet also abided most faithfully by its principle of parity for black patients in both financing care and constructing of facilities.[36]

BEYOND NORTH CAROLINA: RACIAL PARITY OR DISPARITY?

The disintegration during Truman's first term of the agreement to pursue equalization without integration prevented Hill and Pepper from duplicating the success of Hill-Burton during the rest of the 1940s with other federal health reform proposals based on the same formula of federal matching grants to states allocated according to need, local administrative authority, and racial parity but no direct challenges to segregation. Federal enforcement of numerical racial parity in Hill-Burton resulted in the proliferation of modern, well-equipped hospitals that admitted all races of patients but internally segregated them by ward or floor. These multiracial hospitals substantially included blacks in the dramatic postwar expansion, modernization, and geographic redistribution of southern hospital facilities, which without the federal program would have remained racially separate and grossly inadequate for patients of all races.

Without Hill-Burton's nondiscrimination language, which included a separate but equal clause, the targeting of federal hospital construction funds to the South would have been no more effective in reaching black southerners than previous New Deal programs had been. The standard interpretation of the origins of the separate but equal clause labels it a "loophole" that was antithetical to the nondiscrimination statement and claims that as the price of passage, southern segregationists forced liberal integrationists to allow southern states to build racially exclusive facilities. Indeed, the Senate voted down a proposed amendment to deny funds to hospitals that denied admitting rights to qualified physicians on the basis of race, color, or religion. Historian Rosemary A. Stevens asserts that "a major opportunity was lost for including racial desegregation as a condition of federal funding" in Hill-Burton. Yet had desegregation been made a condition of funding, Hill-Burton would probably not have passed at all, since similar attempts immediately after the war to make desegregation a condition for federal aid to medical education helped to defeat these otherwise popular measures. And even if integrationists had overcome very unfavorable political odds to pass Hill-Burton with a desegregation requirement, ensuring compliance would have been extremely difficult, given the subsequent white backlash against the *Brown* decision and the recalcitrance of southern hospitals when desegregation finally did become a condition of federal health funding nearly twenty years later. Although Hill-Burton did not ban all forms of racial discrimination against patients and health professionals, as Wright and other integrationists had hoped, its nondiscrimination clause represented the first national legislative victory for blacks since Reconstruction.[37]

Still, Hill-Burton undeniably failed to meet a post-*Brown* standard of nondiscrimination that rejected the validity of numerical parity at the group level and focused on protecting the right of individuals to use public services and facilities completely without racial restrictions. Black patients and health professionals in deluxe Jim Crow facilities continued to experience racism in a variety of forms, among them separately labeled, inferior quality equipment and facilities and outright exclusion. Within southern Hill-Burton hospitals, Beardsley observes, black patients became accepted routinely with diminishing distinctions in services, but by 1956, of the two-thirds of white-run southern hospitals that admitted blacks, "over half had gotten no Hill-Burton funds and were thus under no compulsion to accord equal treatment to blacks they did admit." Even within Hill-Burton hospitals, the program's tolerance of fixed racial quotas for bed space meant that black patients could be turned away when black wards were full even if white wards were not.[38]

The Senate Subcommittee on Health's 1973 evaluation of the Hill-Burton program concluded that "the establishment of need based on bed-population ratios for large population aggregates failed to recognize the variations in utilization of facilities within a community or of particular services within an institution (e.g., a surplus of obstetrical beds)." The subcommittee also acknowledged that "the spread of third-party payment coverage for hospital costs made it possible for most institutions to go directly to the capital market for construction financing, thereby obviating much of the impact of Hill-Burton state plans on the distribution of facilities." The bed-allocation formulas based on racial population ratios in southern state Hill-Burton plans were more effective in the early years of the program, before the plans were made obsolete by rapid demographic changes (especially rural outmigration to southern and northern cities) and greater availability of nonfederal construction financing through private lenders. Moreover, after 1963, hospitals could issue tax-free bonds.[39]

Despite these caveats, nowhere did the strategy of pursuing parity within segregated institutions come closer to realization than in federal aid to hospital construction. In the pre-*Brown* era, when legislative action to end segregation was politically unthinkable, Hill-Burton both met the South's immediate health needs and provided a transitional infrastructure to promote the acceptance of black patients and health professionals into the mainstream health-care system. By 1954, despite its failure to remove all forms of racial discrimination from southern hospitals, federal aid to hospital construction had definitively shifted the balance of new beds away from private, racially separate hospitals. As the only federal legislation to incorporate a racial parity clause and the first to use a graduated allocation formula based on per capita income that favored the poor southern states and underserved rural communities where most African Americans lived, Hill-Burton materially benefited black southerners as a group more than any other Roosevelt-era program. It represented the last and most progressive expression of New Deal liberalism and the first legislative victory of the twentieth-century civil rights movement.

chapter 8

TRAINING BLACK
DOCTORS AS
PUBLIC POLICY

Abraham Flexner and early black reformers such as John A. Kenney, Eugene Dibble, Numa P. Adams, Midian O. Bousfield, Louis Wright, and Paul Cornely led the early twentieth-century efforts to improve black and southern medical education. In 1942, after the Rosenwald, General Education Board, and Carnegie philanthropies terminated their support for Meharry Medical College in Nashville, the school's white and black representatives as well as white southern policy makers began to seek tax support from southern state governments. These two groups advocated the use of public funds to maximize the number of black M.D. graduates but mutually agreed to sidestep the politically explosive issue of integrating white schools. The National Medical Association (NMA) and National Association for the Advancement of Colored People (NAACP) forcefully opposed this strategy, arguing that equalized funding for separate but equal institutions would entrench segregation forever.[1]

Although the 1890 Morrill Act had provided a model for public support of black higher education in separate but equal land-grant colleges, that model had never been applied to establish graduate or professional schools for blacks. In 1936, the Carnegie Foundation and the NAACP sponsored the publication of *Opportunities for the Medical Education of Negroes*, a report that documented the barriers black applicants faced and stimulated white universities and hospitals to consider admitting blacks. Until World War II, northern schools, notably Harvard, Chicago, Temple, Pennsylvania, and Michigan, together produced fewer than ten black physicians annually, and medical schools used quotas to limit admissions of Jews as well. Before 1940, fifty-five white schools nationwide graduated no more than twenty blacks annually. At the postgraduate level, clinical training was limited to fourteen black hospitals large enough to support internships, and specialty training was virtually unavailable for black physicians. From its founding in 1918 by John A. Kenney until 1969, the John A. Andrews Clinical Society at Tuskegee, held three days each April, was the premier opportunity for southern black physicians to obtain continuing education from nationally recognized physicians and surgeons. For the fifty-eight black doctors who practiced in Mississippi in the late 1930s, the only postgraduate instruction within the state's borders was a two-week series of lectures repeated in nine locations by Walter H. Maddux, a pediatrician who served as a Negro consultant to the Children's Bureau Division of Maternal and Child Health.[2]

After 1920, the only U.S. medical school other than Howard and Meharry to accept minority students with no racial bias was the College of Medical Evangelists (now Loma Linda University), founded in 1909 east of Los Angeles. In 1918, the College of Medical Evangelists graduated its first black physician, Ruth Temple, who joined the school's faculty and became the first African American to gain admitting rights at Los Angeles County Hospital. Like Howard and Meharry, the College of Medical Evangelists survived the post–Flexner Report storm, the only one of Southern California's six medical schools still in operation by 1920. The college's location outside the segregated South and its relatively stable base of financial support from the burgeoning Seventh-Day Adventist denomination made it a unique resource for aspiring black doctors, especially after African American migration to the West Coast accelerated in the wake of World War II.[3]

In the South, the NAACP Legal Defense Fund used graduate and professional education as an entering wedge in its campaign to abolish segregation in education at all levels. The NAACP filed a series of state and federal court cases in the 1930s and 1940s aimed at requiring white public graduate and professional schools to admit qualified black applicants if no separate but equal school for blacks existed. With the aid of the NAACP, Thomas Hocutt in 1933 became the first black student to sue to gain admission to an all-white professional school. Although the state court ruled against Hocutt's plea to enter the University of North Carolina School of Pharmacy, the case had a ripple effect in the North Carolina General Assembly and across the South. C. C. Spaulding, president of the North Carolina Mutual Life Insurance Company, began underwriting NAACP activities in North Carolina, which became "the testing ground for strategies and approaches that would provide the main focus of the school equalization campaign." North Carolina also approved a scholarship program to send black residents to Meharry.[4]

The NAACP was more successful in 1936, when the Maryland Court of Appeals held in *Murray v. Maryland* that the state had not provided equal education to the black plaintiff by offering him tuition to attend any out-of-state law school that would accept him. Since Maryland had no separate black law school, the court ordered the University of Maryland to admit the plaintiff. In *Missouri ex rel. Gaines v. Canada* (1938), the U.S. Supreme Court for the first time upheld the right of qualified black applicants to attend a professional school at a white state university if no separate but equal school for blacks existed. Under pressure from the *Hocutt*, *Murray*, and *Gaines* cases, the North Carolina General Assembly passed the Murphy Act of 1939 to provide black students with "an expense differential"—though not full tuition—"if they enrolled in an out-of-state university for graduate courses that are offered in the University of North Carolina and not offered in the State's Negro Colleges." Virginia and other southern states soon concluded similar agreements with Meharry Medical College. Although a handful of southern black students took advantage of the program, it only superficially addressed the need to educate and train black medical personnel. A growing number of southern and border states also established new graduate and professional programs at public black colleges, but none of these programs were in medicine or dentistry. Florida A&M established its School of Pharmacy in 1951, and North Carolina College in Durham's joint program with the University of North Carolina School of Public Health produced more than one hundred black health educators between 1945 and 1960.[5]

The U.S. entry into World War II shone a national spotlight on the education of black physicians, as prominent leaders such as surgeon general Thomas Parran deemed expanding the health personnel supply essential for national security. As in other areas of health reform, such as public health and hospital construction, the medical staffing crisis was most acute in the South and, within the region, worst among African Americans, particularly rural residents. By 1949, 3,753 black physicians practiced in the United States, with fewer than half (1,572) attending to the 9.6 million African Americans in the thirteen southern states. Blacks comprised 2 percent of all physicians but nearly 11 percent of the total population. In the United States as a whole, one physician practiced for every 755 persons, but the ratio of black physicians to black population was 1:3,681;

in the South, it was 1:6,204. Mississippi and South Carolina had the most acute shortages of black physicians, with one black physician for every 18,132 and 12,561 black persons, respectively.[6]

A REGIONAL MEDICAL SCHOOL FOR BLACKS

Black and white reformers agreed that the South's twenty-six medical schools (one-third of the nation's total) needed to be dramatically expanded to meet the region's need for more medical professionals but were divided about proposed methods of achieving this goal. Most southern whites exhibited a hardening resolve to defend segregation even as they grew more willing to fund health care and education for blacks with tax dollars. A growing minority of white southern progressives, along with nonsouthern liberals in Congress and the Truman administration, joined with black integrationists to pursue the elimination of racial distinctions in medical school admissions. Further divisions among black medical activists along regional and philosophical lines manifested in conflicts between Howard and Meharry, national leaders and rank-and-file members of the NMA and NAACP, and older and younger physicians. The proposal to educate all southern black health professionals at a single regional medical school (by either converting Meharry into a state-supported institution or establishing a new black medical school) exemplified deluxe Jim Crow public policy at the height of its viability. White moderates and members of the Southern Governors' Conference were eager to avoid desegregating white universities and believed that the regional school proposal would comply with the *Gaines* decision, but black integrationists scored an important victory by defeating a bill to grant federal recognition to the regional school plan.[7]

The postwar debate over training more black doctors unfolded as the annual production of black medical doctors dropped to its lowest point during the twentieth century and the number of American medical schools dwindled. In 1940, six of thirteen southern states had no state-funded medical schools, and Florida, Alabama, Mississippi, and West Virginia had no medical schools at all. The rapid postwar expansion of medical education depended on a new willingness among policy makers in Congress and the southern states to fund medical education in general and black medical education in particular. In 1948, Mahlon Ashford of the New York Academy of Medicine wrote a guest editorial on "Medical Education for Minority Groups" in the *Journal of the National Medical Association*. He stated that "the time [has] come for the Minority Group to bring its problems to the attention of the more liberal members of the Majority." Any real progress would "demand resources of power and money beyond the control of a Minority Group. The achievement requires understanding and collaboration upon the part of the Majority."[8]

During what Patricia Sullivan has termed the "days of hope" of the Truman administration, members of Congress broadly supported two proposals: first, direct federal aid to medical education for scholarships, expanded enrollments and new construction; and second, a public medical school for blacks funded by one or more southern states. The American Medical Association was the main opponent of federal aid to medical education but did not block it singlehandedly. Racial politics played a major role in killing each medical education bill that Congress considered between 1945 and 1951. Democratic senators from the Deep South, including Allen Ellender of Louisiana, Claude Pepper of Florida, and Lister Hill of Alabama, led the push for federal aid to medical education. They tried to repeat Hill-Burton's compromise formula of dual separate but equal and nondiscrimination clauses on the grounds that segregation was not discriminatory as long as equal facilities were provided to both races. But after the Truman administration acted decisively on behalf of black civil rights in 1947 and 1948, nondiscrimination clauses became a political minefield that obstructed the passage of the rest of the Truman health plan, including aid to medical education.[9]

At the October 1947 Southern Governors' Conference, Tennessee governor Jim N. McCord cited the *Gaines* decision as the catalyst for state support of black regional education, which, like Hill-Burton, originated in a defense of separate but equal policies but ultimately undermined segregation. McCord predicted that southern law, medical, and dental schools "might as well be abandoned" if blacks and whites were admitted on equal terms, "since such action would effectively destroy their operation." He "not only had in mind the *Gaines* decision but also the moral obligation which every State has to provide opportunities for the medical and dental education of Negroes in the Southern area." To prevent blacks from attending state schools "on equal basis with white students," McCord proposed that "the Southern states set up regional professional schools for Negroes." A subsidy to cover additional travel costs would, he said, "help to clear up the question of 'equal protection' for Negroes." The Southern Governors' Conference met in Tallahassee, Florida, in February 1948 and formally adopted the Southern Regional Education Compact among its fourteen member states: the document called for the "establishment and maintenance of jointly owned and operated regional education institutions in the Southern states in the professional, technological, scientific, literary and other fields."[10]

The centerpiece of the compact was the proposal to take over Meharry Medical College and convert it into a public regional black medical school. The idea had originated with Meharry officials, who had already sought federal support for the school before turning to the southern governors. Since members of Congress from outside the South had refused to contribute tax dollars to a segregated institution, Meharry administrators reasoned that "the fourteen southern states which since 1876 have profited most by the operation of Meharry should at long last support the basic program with tax funds." Despite one evaluation of Meharry as "a well-established, high-class institution with superior physical plant, able teachers, and substantial endowment," the school was on the verge of closing. Meharry president M. Don Clawson claimed that "the growing deficit in the College's annual budget could no longer be made up by private foundations or philanthropies. . . . [I]f this Institution is to continue in existence, tax support at some level must be obtained."[11]

NMA leaders blamed deficits at both Howard and Meharry on "the burden of carrying a hospital to furnish medical care to the indigent of the city and region" and called for public funding of hospitalization costs for the poor to free resources to expand the schools' facilities and increase notoriously low faculty salaries. Medical civil rights activists in the NMA and NAACP believed that federal aid to medical education, with nondiscrimination requirements, was the best way to assist the two struggling black medical schools as well as to open opportunities at predominantly white schools. But fears of an antidiscrimination clause caused the southern governors to advocate the opposite approach, joint funding by state governments. Both Meharry and the southern governors believed that any agreement to provide regional medical education would require congressional approval, which they sought in April 1948. Like Hill-Burton, the regional medical school proposal committed significant new public resources toward meeting both black and white needs within segregated institutions.[12]

According to one of the regional plan's Senate supporters, Utah Democrat Elbert Thomas, the Southern Regional Education Compact would bring "educational facilities which will make over the people of that area . . . and which will to a great extent solve [the problems of] segregation and nonsegregation." Thomas chaired the Labor and Public Welfare Committee and its predecessor, the Labor and Education Committee, and had cosponsored the Harrison-Thomas-Fletcher Bill to extend federal aid to education and equalize spending for black and white southern schools. He claimed that the regional plan presented "an unprecedented opportunity to the Negro advanced students and professional students of the South. . . . As these educational institutions grow stronger and raise their standards, and more students begin to attend them, there will be a larger proportion of black people getting into the nonsegregated schools of the country."[13]

Black leaders and opinion makers across the country were united in their opposition. Representatives of the national black organizations of physicians, dentists, and nurses along with non-health-professional, religious, and civil rights organizations testified against the plan before the Senate Judiciary Committee. The editors of the black weekly *Raleigh Carolinian* charged that "the perpetuation of segregation is the dominating motive in the regional school advocated for Negroes. . . . It must not be forgotten that the same governors who advocate the regional school plan are the governors who are trying to cripple President Truman for his advocacy of civil rights for Negroes." Fisk University president Charles S. Johnson complained that "the action limits rather than expands educational opportunities in the south," citing the paltry proposed biennial budget of three hundred thousand dollars as evidence of the southern states' lack of true commitment to improving black medical education. Among the leaders of the NAACP, NMA, and National Dental Association who blasted the regional medical school plan was Charles Herbert Marshall, who labeled Meharry board members who supported the regional medical school plan "appeasers" who were "offering the school as an outright gift," using a potent analogy to British prime minister Neville Chamberlain's attempted appeasement of Hitler in 1938. Marshall, who served as president of the NMA in 1949, declared in the pages of the *Journal of the National Medical Association* that he was willing to sacrifice Meharry to gain "complete equality" in medical education.[14]

The U.S. House of Representatives passed the regional school bill by a 235–45 vote in May 1948, but the Senate voted 38–37 to return the measure to the Judiciary Committee, effectively killing the bill. Had Pepper, a key proponent of the bill, not been absent, the measure would have passed. In a letter thanking those who had lobbied in support of the regional medical education bill, Clawson made two predictions: first, "when the hysteria accompanying the Presidential election has passed, the regional plan will be debated on its merit as an educational program"; second, "as the work of this Institution, both through its basic program and through all its other activities so promisingly under way, develops and expands, we believe that segregation itself—which has been dragged as an extraneous issue into the current crisis—must eventually vanish." But the debate over the regional plan raged on into the summer. In July 1948, southern segregationists rejected Truman's pro-civil-rights stance in the Southern Manifesto, nominated South Carolina senator Strom Thurmond as their presidential candidate, and walked out of the Democratic Convention. Addressing the NMA's national convention, the organization's president, J. A. C. Lattimore, placed the governors' plan for regional medical education in the context of the Dixiecrat walkout: "The recent ridiculous action of the southern governors on the Civil Rights issue shows how they stand on things vital to the Negro. Some of us are willing to turn over Meharry's millions to the very states which previously have shown that they are not of themselves interested in the Negro doctor—or the health of the Negro people. . . . What Negro doctor would be foolish enough to entrust something as dear to him as his Alma Mater to such a clan of Nazi-minded Americans?"[15]

Caught in the cross fire between the integrationists and proponents of the regional plan was Clifton O. Dummett, dean of dentistry at Meharry and a member of the board of directors. Dummett had initially joined Clawson in attempting to build support for the plan among Meharry alumni and black health professionals generally, and the two spoke about the plan in their presentations to the National Dental Association's August 1948 annual convention. Dummett was named one of three representatives from black institutions (Howard University was noticeably absent) on the Commission on Human Medicine and Health Services of the Regional Council on Education (later renamed the Southern Regional Education Board [SREB]), formed in late 1948 to advise state legislatures on joint interstate education programs in medicine, dentistry, pharmacy, and nursing. When the commission issued its early 1949 report finalizing the plan to provide medical and dental education for black southern students at Meharry, Dummett submitted a minority report protesting the perpetuation of segregation. As the only member of the Meharry administration to criticize the regional plan, Dummett resigned and went on to join the dental faculty at the University of California at Los Angeles. Although Clawson had presided over Meharry's growth during the 1940s, he resigned in 1950. Without federal funding or approval, the SREB designated Meharry as the recipient of joint funding from member states to train southern black medical and dental students in return for a 70 percent subsidy of tuition and fees.[16]

As historian Jennifer E. Brooks comments, New Deal southern liberals believed that "the southern masses could be united across the division of race by emphasizing broad political enfranchisement to achieve shared social and economic interests, not by addressing the question of segregation directly." By the late 1940s, such noninterventionist yet progressive sentiments came under fire from a variety of antisegregation forces. In the debates over the Southern Regional Education Compact, Senator Tom Stewart of Tennessee had lamented, "There seems to be a great deal more interest at the present moment in the apparently all-important matter of segregation than there is in the general welfare, health, well-being, and education of the colored race in the United States." Clawson likewise blamed the plan's failure to obtain congressional approval on integrationists who "persisted in seeing the issue as a maneuver to perpetuate segregation rather than in the terms of medical realities. Thus politics and race were radically injected into what we at Meharry insist is a purely educational problem."[17]

FEDERAL AID TO MEDICAL EDUCATION

In the aftermath of the regional medical school crisis, black physicians included white as well as black institutions in their support for federal funding. According to Marshall, Meharry's closing "would be only a temporary inconvenience because the plight of the Negro would be so vividly portrayed to the public that some agency, and perhaps the Federal Government, would accept the challenge and solve the problem of financial security for this institution, once and for all." By the end of 1949, the NMA favored proposed federal legislation "to provide an emergency five-year program of grants and scholarships for education" of health professionals, not only because it provided $130,000 in annual aid to each of the black medical schools but also because an antidiscrimination clause would support the NMA/NAACP efforts to desegregate the white schools. W. Montague Cobb, editor of the *Journal of the National Medical Association*, warned, however, that an antidiscrimination clause might not be included and that even if it was, the court fight against the white schools might stretch out for years and would put the financial and legal burden on blacks. And southern government officials and congressmen might retaliate by scaling down federal and state contributions to Howard and Meharry.[18]

Black physicians were not alone in turning to Washington to bail out medical education. Congress did not enact direct aid to medical schools during the postwar period, but they received a wide spectrum of indirect funding for construction, research, residency training, and salary support from Hill-Burton, the National Mental Health Act of 1948, the Veterans Administration, and most important, the National Institutes of Health. Such programs helped to raise the number of southern state-funded medical schools from seven in 1940 to twenty-three by 1985, and class sizes at existing public medical schools also ballooned. The average income of medical schools increased from $500,000 in 1940 to $3.7 million by 1958–59 and ten years later had reached $15 million. As Cobb had foreseen, such federal aid did not necessarily open the way for black applicants to white medical schools. Beginning in 1949, Cobb and the NMA repeatedly requested that the American Medical Association and the Association of American Medical Colleges (AAMC) take a public stand against racial discrimination in medical education, but the attitude of both organizations through the 1950s was summed up in the AAMC's response that "it is not within the scope of this Association to take action on matters that are within the jurisdiction of the individual medical school and a matter of internal administration within that school."[19]

But even without federal aid, public universities had already been subject to legal challenges to segregation. Beginning in 1946, Thurgood Marshall widely publicized a call for black students to apply to white medical schools, and when they did, state schools were quicker than their private counterparts to lower racial bars. Between 1948 and 1951, four of the first five southern medical schools to accept blacks were state schools: the Universities of Arkansas, Texas, and North Carolina and the Medical College of Virginia. As the first black students entered southern medical schools, whites resentfully perceived admission as a zero-sum game. The first black student admitted to a historically white medical school was Edith Mae Irby, who enrolled in 1948 at the University of Arkansas Medical School in Little Rock, causing Arkansas governor Ben Laney to storm, "They pushed a white boy aside for this Negro." After the University of North Carolina at Chapel Hill School of Medicine followed suit in 1951, a student echoed Laney's sentiments when he wrote to the *Daily Tar Heel* that the admission of Edward Diggs would "promote the rejection of some hard working Carolina student who has undoubtedly better qualifications than any dark-congo boy."[20]

The political and ethical difficulties of securing the full integration of medical education via federal aid were well illustrated in the career of Senator Thomas, who served with James Murray, Pepper, and Hill as chair of the Committee on

Labor and Public Welfare and its predecessor, the Committee on Labor and Education. Although the U.S. Navy had been providing various forms of medical training since 1822, the modern Naval Medical School (now the Uniformed Services University of the Health Sciences, affiliated with the Walter Reed National Military Medical Center) had been established in 1902 near Washington, D.C., to train navy medical personnel. In 1923, a dental school was added to provide postgraduate training to Navy Dental Corps officers and to prepare hospital corpsmen to serve as dental assistants. Thomas, who had been on the committee to draft the Armed Services Unification Bill, wanted to expand the Naval Medical School model to create a National Service School to train health professionals for both civilian and military agencies such as the armed services, Veterans Administration, U.S. Public Health Service, and all federal agencies that utilized medical personnel. Like Parran and Pepper, Thomas emphasized that expanding the supply of health professionals was a matter of national defense and proposed that the National Service School should be planned by the National Security Resources Board under the Department of Defense. He intended that the federal medical school would admit students without regard to race or sex and would both solve the shortage of health professionals and provide opportunity for minorities without encroaching on southern racial mores at existing schools. Yet Senator Thomas knew that his idea was unlikely to overcome opposition from medical school deans, so he agreed to draft a bill in consultation with the Federal Security Agency.[21]

The bill Thomas submitted in April 1948 specified, "Many qualified individuals, particularly members of minority population groups, are unable to obtain adequate professional training under present conditions." Federal action was justified to assist existing schools and to construct new schools, "with a view to providing opportunities for more qualified individuals to obtain such training regardless of their race, creed, color, or national origin, and by providing scholarships to induce greater numbers of students to train for such professions and to equalize the opportunities for obtaining such training." Yet the Thomas Bill took the same approach to nondiscrimination as Hill-Burton, allowing both all-white and all-black schools to receive funds provided that comparable opportunities existed for qualified minority residents of states that practiced segregation. Although Thomas felt "in my heart and soul an urge to ... make an effort to bring about nonsegregation," he concluded that "in view of what the States are trying to do under the instructions set forth ... by the Supreme Court ..., that would be unwise, and it would bring about the very opposite of what we are trying to do." He alleged that nondiscrimination amendments had been introduced to kill previous medical education bills rather than to help black people, and he urged the Senate not to repeat this mistake. Thomas predicted that the bill would "not be acted upon hastily" and would "have great opposition."[22]

One of the Thomas Bill's supporters was Roy R. Kracke, who represented among medical deans what Hill and Pepper exemplified in the Senate: progressive southern leadership that viewed the health problems of blacks and whites as interrelated and worthy of federal aid. Kracke was the first dean of the Medical College of Alabama, established in 1943 as the first of five new four-year medical schools founded at southern state universities in less than twenty years (followed by North Carolina in 1951, Mississippi in 1955, Florida in 1956, and Kentucky in 1960). Like military bases during World War II, medical schools were prized by southern policy makers as engines of economic development and sources of home-district bragging rights, and they brought in the same influx of abundant federal funds and nonsouthern personnel, both of which would loosen segregation's hold. Kracke, a native of Hartselle, Alabama, and alumnus of the University of Alabama, had served during World War I in the Navy Hospital Corps and trained in laboratory technology at the Naval Medical School. In 1920, he returned to Tuscaloosa as both a part-time instructor in bacteriology and a medical student at the two-year school. He then completed his medical degree at Rush Medical College at the University of Chicago. After graduation, he obtained a professorship at the new medical school at Emory University in Atlanta, where he taught pathology, bacteriology, and diagnostic lab techniques. His research on leukemia gained him recognition in the emerging field of hematology, and his 1941 textbook on hematology and blood diseases became a standard in the field. Kracke accepted the deanship of medicine at Alabama in 1945 at the invitation of Bill Paty, hoping that he and his college roommate and hometown friend, Senator John Sparkman, could improve health care in Alabama. The entire annual operating budget of the medical school, including its teaching hospitals, was $1.5 million.[23]

Kracke was just the sort of "liberal member of the majority" who demonstrated the postwar commitment to expanding opportunities for blacks to study medicine. Kracke's Emory colleague, Eugene A. Stead, was another native southerner who obtained medical training at a top northern medical school (internships and a research fellowship at Harvard) and returned to the South as a leader in academic medicine and an advocate of enlarging the black health-care workforce. While serving as chair of medicine (1941–44) and then dean (1945–46) at Emory, Stead was active in Atlanta politics, urging city officials, labor leaders, and influential blacks to improve medical care through better training for health professionals, particularly black doctors and nurses. As chair of medicine at Duke (1947–67), Stead joined a group of liberal medical faculty there and at the Durham Veterans Administration Hospital who shared "a sense of community activism and a genuine desire to improve the mental health of all people, regard-less of race, sex, age, and class." In the early 1960s, Stead lobbied unsuccessfully for the appointment of hematologist Louis Sullivan as the first black member of the Duke medical faculty. But Birmingham was a much tougher place to fight segregation than Durham, and Kracke could not transcend Alabama public officials' loyalty to segregation, which overrode all other considerations.[24]

Kracke wrote to Hill during the summer of 1948 to express strong support for the Thomas Bill, as the dean had for previous federal aid to medical education bills. "Medical education needs these funds very badly in order to maintain present standards and also to enlarge the output of doctors, dentists and nurses. I have long been very hopeful that federal funds some day might be available for medical education because the cost of instruction in this field, with our present standards, is almost prohibitive to be borne entirely by local units of government." Kracke interpreted the Thomas Bill's racial provisions to mean that "the Medical College of Alabama would have to open its doors to Negro medical students or there would have to be provided within the state comparable educational facilities in this field." Kracke had formed strong relationships with black organized medicine in Alabama and was already pursuing the development of a black medical school at Tuskegee. He noted enthusiastically that "Senator Thomas . . . thinks I should work hard for a medical school at Tuskegee. I am sure he bases that statement upon our recognized need for some new facility to turn out medical personnel for the Negro race. . . . [I]t of course would put our state in a very strong position in the situation of comparable educational facili-ties." At the end of 1948, however, the AAMC dashed Kracke's hopes, opposing the Thomas Bill on the grounds that federal funding "should in no way impose or imply any restriction of the freedom of the medical school . . . in selecting students." The AAMC requested that the dean of each medical school bring the bill to the attention of the university president. University presidents' sentiments on federal aid to education generally were summed up by Isaiah Bowman of Johns Hopkins, who in 1943 warned that "wild-eyed social experimenters" saw the postwar transition period "as an opportunity to invade the whole field of education through Federal grants. Unfortunately these assaults arise in Congress as well as out of it." When Kracke optimistically asked John Gallalee, president of the University of Alabama, if "the University of Alabama could accept funds under the [racial] restrictions as outlined in this Bill," Gallalee's two-sentence reply was negative and blunt.[25]

The defeat of the Thomas Bill marked an impasse for federal medical education legislation. The belated attempts of southern governments to finally keep *Plessy*'s fifty-year-old promise of equality under segregation were inadequate to prevent national NAACP and NMA leaders and the Truman administration from insisting on completely banning segregation in federal health legislation, causing most southern Democrats to withdraw their support. Pepper had no better luck than did Thomas at getting a federal aid to medical education bill passed in 1949. When Pepper submitted his bill, Hill remarked that "a determined fight would be made on the floor to insert" nondiscrimination provisions, but he "anticipated that such efforts would fail." The Pepper Bill did contain a provision that "prevented scholarships from being denied on the basis of race, creed or color." Although the bill was extremely popular among both parties, historian Stephen Strickland attributes its defeat in part to "rumors of the bill's requiring the admission of northern Negroes to southern medical schools [that] circulated in the Senate on the last day of the debate."[26]

Although merely removing the racial bars to admission at white schools would not necessarily increase the number of black physicians in the short term, Cobb and others in the NMA and NAACP continued to focus on this solution. One *Journal of the National Medical Association* editorial, likely penned by Cobb, also advocated opening Meharry to whites in the interest of promoting desegregation at all southern schools. Clawson suggested that Howard should be the test case for "opening up unsegregated opportunity for all people," since the District of Columbia, unlike Tennessee, had no constitution requiring segregation. Integrationists in the NMA were more likely to have attended Howard, the majority of whose alumni either were native to the North or practiced there after medical school. Even at Meharry, only half the entering class in 1948 was from the South. Both black medical schools were less likely to admit southern than northern students; southern blacks who were admitted often failed to return to the South, where discrimination was greater and opportunities were much more limited. Thus, the full integration of medical education would tend to benefit northern more than southern blacks and would still do nothing to guarantee that increasing numbers of black doctors would practice in the most medically underserved areas.[27]

MEHARRY AND THE SOUTHERN REGIONAL
EDUCATION BOARD

The difficulty that many black southern applicants faced in gaining admittance to Howard and Meharry raised a key question in the debate over race and medical education: could black applicants compete on an equal basis with whites, or did the handicaps imposed by unequal education at the elementary through college levels warrant different admissions standards? Would nondiscrimination actually hurt blacks if applied to predominantly black as well as white schools? Senator Thomas cited the testimony of Meharry's President Clawson to argue that nondiscrimination would work against the approximately nineteen hundred black applicants annually to Howard and Meharry, who as a group had less competitive academic qualifications than the nationwide pool of fourteen thousand white applicants. According to Florida governor Millard F. Caldwell, the lead proponent of the regional school plan, "Negro students are given preference at [Howard and Meharry]. Meharry, in Nashville, a segregated medical school, had so many applications from white students that, if processed in the normal way and white students [were] allowed to compete, not more than about five Negro students would have been accepted in the last entering class." The only sure way of educating black doctors and dentists, Caldwell maintained, was to continue segregation at Howard and Meharry. Cobb, the leading proponent of full integration of medical education, had also expressed concern about the poor preparation of black medical school applicants. Howard and Meharry had difficulty filling their classes with top candidates, and even though leading medical schools had by the late 1940s agreed to provide twenty-five openings for Negro students, "qualified applicants had failed to appear." Cobb blamed inadequate preparation at the elementary, secondary, and college levels, where educational spending under segregation was an average of twelve times greater for white students than for blacks.[28]

The alternative to Cobb's push to integrate white medical schools was the education of southern black students at Meharry. Led by Caldwell, the Southern Governors' Conference had created the SREB in 1948 to promote interstate cooperation and sharing of resources to improve and expand expensive graduate and professional programs for both black and white students. Caldwell was a powerful Democrat who chaired President Truman's reelection campaign fundraising committee and served as president of the Council of State Governments and chair of the National Governors' Conference in 1947. He would later serve as the first administrator of the Federal Civil Defense Administration from 1950 to 1952. Medical education was the primary focus of the SREB in its early years, and the board became a key force driving the improvement of premedical preparation for black applicants and, if needed, the remediation of students after their arrival at Meharry. The SREB agreement with Meharry gave preference to students from the sixteen member states. But because these students were from southern segregated school systems of inferior quality, they scored as a group ten points lower on the medical aptitude test than did students admitted from noncontract states. A 1952 SREB report stated,

> Meharry Medical College has clearly made a strong effort to see to it that south-
> ern students have opportunities to study medicine, [but] Meharry is succeeding
> with difficulty in erecting high quality professional training upon the base of
> undergraduate training which students receive at other institutions. It can do
> remedial work only to a limited extent. If it is to continue to accept a higher
> proportion of students from the contracting states, those states must necessarily
> assure themselves that their students receive sound undergraduate training com-
> parable to that received anywhere in the nation.[29]

The SREB was the creation of segregationist southern governors, that "clan of Nazi-minded Americans." Beardsley calls the southern governors' plan a "scheme" that "never came to anything." In a history of Meharry, James Summerville briefly acknowledges that the SREB provided "one-third of a million dollars a year at a critical time in its financial history." In fact the SREB bore out Clawson's predictions over the next three decades, during which southern state governments served as the single-largest source of operating income for Meharry. The SREB disbursed $2.5 million from 1949 to 1961 to aid approximately five hundred black medical students and an additional $1 million for black dental students. By comparison, the NMA's National Medical Fellowships provided $1 million for 326 students during the same period. Meharry was by far the leading school supported by the SREB, and by 1959 it was the only medical school receiving SREB funds.[30]

Representatives of the SREB met with Meharry officials throughout the 1950s and 1960s to assist the school in finding additional financial support, and the SREB periodically liberalized funding guidelines until it was paying Meharry from four hundred thousand dollars to five hundred thousand dollars annually during the 1960s and 1970s. Without the SREB, Meharry would have closed, and the number of black medical graduates would have dropped dramatically.

From 1947 to 1955, buoyed by the increased availability of scholarships under the GI Bill as well as southern state governments and private foundations, the number of black medical students increased by 29.4 percent, while the number of all medical students increased 25.9 percent (table 8.1). SREB support of Meharry helped the production of black physicians to keep pace with the overall expansion of medical graduates. From 1955 to 1963, the number of black medical students enrolled in predominantly white schools fell from 236 to 173, while Howard and Meharry slightly increased their enrollment (table 8.2). Thus, through the first two decades of token desegregation in medical education, Howard and Meharry remained the primary producers of black physicians. Not until the 1970s did the majority of African American medical students enroll at predominantly white schools.[31]

But even if southern governments provided substantial funding for black medical education at Meharry, did they do so only out of a desire to preserve segregation? Despite Governor McCord's 1947 prediction that opening graduate education to blacks "would effectively destroy the operation of our professional schools," the SREB had from its inception substantially included black institutions and educators in its planning and leadership. Key white supporters of the regional plan, including Clawson and Thomas, never saw it as a subterfuge to preserve segregation; rather, they perceived the idea as a way of leveraging the improvement of black medical education with integration as a potential by-product. By 1950, the SREB had definitively moved beyond the original rationale of begrudging compliance with the *Gaines* decision. In *McCready v. Maryland*, in which a black applicant had sued to gain entrance into the University of Maryland School of Nursing, the SREB intervened to expressly state its policy that the Southern Regional Education Compact "shall [not] serve any State as a legal defense for avoiding responsibilities established or defined under the existing State and Federal laws and court decisions." The SREB's purpose was much broader and more progressive than merely shielding southern states and white universities from integration.[32]

The desegregation of southern medical schools beginning in 1948 did not end southern states' support of the SREB program at Meharry. In fact, some states that had already opened their medical schools to blacks subsequently sent students to Meharry through the SREB. Until the mid-1980s, southern states pursued a dual approach to educating black physicians at both Meharry and in-state schools. By that point, medical schools had begun actively recruiting minorities, and the SREB/Meharry program was viewed as counterproductive to the

TABLE 8.1

Black Enrollment in U.S. Medical Schools, 1938–2002

YEAR	BLACK ENROLLMENT	% BLACK STUDENTS
1938	350	1.6
1947	588	2.6
1951	697	2.6
1955	761	2.7
1969	1,042	2.8
1974	3,345	6.3
1984	3,944	5.9
1994	5,092	7.6
1996	5,380	8.0
2002	4,905	7.4

Source: James L. Curtis, *Blacks, Medical Schools, and Society* (Ann Arbor: University of Michigan Press, 1971), 34; *Minorities in Medical Education: Facts and Figures 2005* (Washington, D.C.: Association of American Medical Colleges, 2005), 64.

TABLE 8.2

Black First-Year Students in Predominantly White Medical Schools, 1938–1990

1938	13 percent
1947	16 percent
1951	23 percent
1968	47 percent
1983	61 percent
1990	84 percent

Source: James L. Curtis, *Blacks, Medical Schools, and Society* (Ann Arbor: University of Michigan Press, 1971), 34; Vanessa Northington Gamble, *Making a Place for Ourselves: The Black Hospital Movement* (New York: Oxford University Press, 1995), xii.

goal of increasing diversity at in-state institutions. Today, the SREB continues to aid about forty Meharry students annually: most of those students come from Tennessee, with others from Alabama and North Carolina.[33]

What did the SREB accomplish for black medical education? Under the SREB agreement, southern state governments did not gain control of Meharry, did not receive federal approval or aid from Congress, and did not prevent the desegregation of white schools. By the mid-1950s, medical schools had largely adopted a voluntary policy of opening their doors to black students, unlike public elementary and secondary schools or state universities. By the late 1960s, when many school districts were still circumventing court-ordered desegregation plans, medical schools, including those in the Deep South, were actively recruiting minority applicants. In 1968, John Z. Bowers, president of the Josiah Macy Jr. Foundation, proclaimed, "Today the medical schools are joining the most intensive talent hunt ever launched in this country—the search for Negro students." Yet even if race ostensibly had been removed as a consideration for admission to medical schools, black applicants remained handicapped by their inadequate preparation in segregated southern schools as well as their inability to afford four years of tuition for the scientifically rigorous but more expensive training that was now standard. After the *Brown* decision, the medical school application process was a prime example of the replacement of formal racial barriers with class barriers that disproportionately affected minorities in the form of "new, more rational, legally defensible, and durable restrictions [such as standardized test scores] that have come to define educational policy and practice not simply in the region but also in the nation." Education scholar R. Scott Baker's assertions about the paradoxes of desegregation ring especially true for medical education: "While advantaged blacks entered schools, colleges, and universities, most African Americans, handicapped by generations of segregation and discrimination, were not prepared to compete educationally with whites and remained cloistered in predominantly African-American institutions."[34]

The SREB/Meharry program made maintaining and increasing the supply of black physicians a goal of southern public policy long before the advent of affirmative action or diversity programs, even after the 1954 *Brown* decision and the white backlash it generated. The SREB and Meharry continued to support black medical education after the 1978 *Bakke* decision and mounting challenges to affirmative action during the 1980s and 1990s. Ironically, the SREB became a force for both racial equality and federal funding for medical education, goals that found no quarter among the segregationist southern governors who founded it. Former Florida governor Millard Caldwell, who had convened the conference at Tallahassee to sign the original compact, wrote in 1962 to the SREB's director, Winfred Godwin, to express outrage about his stand in favor of federal aid to education, which was "diametrically opposed to the basic philosophy of the Southern Regional Education Board. The Regional program was conceived as a vehicle for a do-it-ourselves effort—as a means of escaping that which you now advocate. Perhaps it was inevitable—but I am sorry to see it."[35]

More representative of the SREB's direction in the 1960s was George Gore Jr., the president of Florida A&M College from 1950 to 1968 and the first southern black delegate to the National Education Association. Gore, who had founded public black law and pharmacy schools at Florida A&M in the early 1950s, was active in the SREB and served on a committee formed in 1967 to plan new institutions to improve opportunities for southern blacks. By the 1970s, the SREB had sponsored a conference for black educators on "facilitating self-awareness in black colleges," was aiding states in compliance with federal desegregation cases, and facilitated meetings between state higher education officials and representatives from the federal Office of Civil Rights. In the 1990s, the SREB began a minority doctoral scholars program, resulting in more than two hundred minority doctorates in the basic sciences, and conducted a study of factors in the success of the top ten medical schools in retention and graduation of black medical doctors.[36]

At the heart of the postwar debate over race and medical education was the fact that the expansion of both black and southern opportunity in medicine depended on white resources from federal, state, and private sources. The states' rights philosophy of Caldwell's generation, which insisted that southerners should solve their own problems, paralleled older black doctors' preference for self-rule within all-black institutions. These sentiments yielded to the lure of new resources that promised to heal age-old deficiencies: both white southerners and black reformers courted the federal government and white northern philanthropy in hopes of improving conditions for their constituents as well as claiming a place of honor at the American table. But the desire for white and/or federal aid was not incompatible with the quest for self-rule: southern whites and blacks saw themselves as unfairly victimized and viewed aid as reparations, not charity. If the North gave the South and southern whites gave blacks only their just due, they could hold their own on a truly level playing field.[37]

Despite white southerners' commitment to segregation, they funded the education of black doctors and treatment of black patients on an unprecedented scale during the waning years of Jim Crow, providing the foundation for the medical civil rights movement to press forward for full integration during the late 1950s and 1960s. Without southern state support, the percentage of black medical graduates would have declined even further during the 1950s. Without those black doctors, the full integration of medical education since 1970 would have been more difficult, and minority students would have had even fewer role models. Vanessa Northington Gamble's analysis of the Provident Hospital–University of Chicago project to create a high-quality residency for black physicians during the 1930s provides important parallels. The Provident Hospital project was considered cutting-edge by blacks who subscribed to the separatist self-help philosophy, but the black community's transition to an integrationist orientation caused the agreement between Provident and the University of Chicago to be labeled racist. The Meharry-SREB relationship showed that these tensions continued into the 1950s, but Meharry maintained its autonomy even while southern state governments shouldered a large portion of its operating expenses. Like the public funding of separate wards in the modern Hill-Burton hospitals, public funding of black medical education at Meharry gave blacks a foothold from which to make further gains leading to full integration as public policy.[38]

Most black hospitals failed to receive adequate public support and ultimately closed as a consequence of the financial strain of indigent care and of their inability to modernize. Conversely, the two black medical schools remained viable in large part because they received a significant share of the burgeoning state and federal funding for medical education, research, and teaching hospital construction. The equalization of separate but equal, although never complete, proved temporary. It did not result in the permanent entrenchment of segregation, as the southern governors had hoped and black medical activists had feared.

chapter 9

TRAINING BLACK
DOCTORS IN
NORTH CAROLINA

In February 1951, just before the controversy began to heat up over admitting the first African American student to the University of North Carolina School of Medicine, Dean Walter Reece Berryhill received a letter from J. Charles Jordan, president of the Old North State Medical Society. Jordan protested that there were "less facilities provided for the training of Negro medical aspirants in the entire United States than there are for North Carolina's approximately two million white people." Such a situation was "greatly jeopardizing the health of all the citizens of our State," and Jordan demanded that "there must be some provision made for the training of Negro doctors in North Carolina." But Jordan went further to beseech Berryhill and his colleagues, in the name of Christianity and democracy, "to consider immediately and seriously the admission of Negroes to the University of North Carolina, which is being maintained out of State funds provided by all citizens, black and white alike." Education, civil rights, medicine and public policy converged in the desegregation of medical education, which provides important comparisons to the concurrent efforts to overturn institutionalized segregation in K–12 and higher education as well as in the Hill-Burton federal hospital construction program.[1]

POSTWAR CHANGE IN SOUTHERN MEDICAL EDUCATION

North Carolina was embroiled in the southern battle over race yet prided itself on being a national leader in health and education reform. The University of North

Carolina (UNC), the state's flagship university, embodied the conflict between tradition and change in race relations. UNC president Frank Porter Graham was one of the most outspoken southern liberals and a member of President Harry S. Truman's Committee on Civil Rights, which published its prointegration report, *To Secure These Rights*, in 1947. UNC sociologist Howard Odum, famous for his studies of southerners black and white, stood out as an early advocate of including blacks in the public health and welfare systems. Odum's colleague in sociology, Guy B. Johnson, proposed the idea for a landmark collection of essays by prominent black intellectuals across the political spectrum, *What the Negro Wants*, published in 1944 by UNC Press. Edited by Howard University historian Rayford W. Logan, the book was an unequivocal call for equal rights for African Americans and an end to segregation, forever destroying the myth that southern blacks were content with their "separate but equal" status. The School of Public Health, under the leadership of Dean E. G. McGavran, was one of the most vocal opponents of segregation on campus. In 1945, McGavran cofounded the health education program at the North Carolina College for Negroes (NCC) in Durham. Yet the university's upper administration and the majority of its political supporters in the state legislature were committed to maintaining UNC as an all-white institution. During the 1950s and 1960s, the university's controversial role in desegregating southern higher education would be subject to radically differing interpretations. To white progressives, UNC was leading the way toward harmonious race relations; to white segregationists, UNC stood for "the University of Negroes and Communists," in Jesse Helms's memorable formulation; and for many black North Carolinians, the university would never overcome its 160-year history of excluding members of their race.[2]

UNC's drive in the late 1940s to convert its two-year medical school to a four-year degree-granting program owed its success to a legislature that had passed health reform as an affirmation of states' rights and an antidote to Truman's policies supporting universal health insurance and civil rights. At the same time, the campaign undertaken by the National Medical Association (NMA) and the National Association for the Advancement of Colored People (NAACP) to desegregate medical education converged with growing calls to increase the production of black as well as white M.D. graduates. With only nine state medical schools among the sixteen southern states and five states with no M.D.-granting schools at all in 1940, residents who studied medicine out of state often did not return to practice in their underserved home districts. During the Great Depression, Alabama had fewer doctors per capita than any other state, and by

1938, the total number of physicians in Alabama had declined by four hundred. As southern historian Tennant McWilliams observes, even the University of Alabama's two-year medical program "was chasing doctors out of the state," since students had to transfer to another school for the third and fourth years. UNC's two-year program had similar effects in North Carolina, whose twenty-one hundred practicing physicians in 1945 ranked the state forty-fifth in doctors per capita. W. C. Davison, dean of the Duke University School of Medicine, estimated that fifteen hundred additional doctors were needed to provide one doctor per thousand people.[3]

In his 1945 report to the Committee on Negro Health Problems of the North Carolina Medical Care Commission (MCC), Selz Mayo cited the shortage of black medical professionals as a key weakness in the state's health system and called for reforms in medical education that would increase the ranks of black doctors, nurses, and public health workers. Mayo noted that North Carolina ranked fourth among eleven southern states in the ratio of black population per black physician and was one of only two southern states where the number of black physicians had increased (by 45.3 percent) between 1932 and 1942. During that period, the South's African American population had increased, but the number of black doctors practicing in the region had decreased by 12 percent. In Mississippi, the state with the lowest ratio of black doctors to black population, the number of African American physicians had dropped from 71 in 1930 to 55 by 1940, and the state had only 29 black dentists and 11 black pharmacists. Despite North Carolina's gains, fifty-two of the state's one hundred counties still had no black physicians. Among nearly 1 million black residents in 1944, only 129 black doctors remained in active practice, and their average age was fifty-four. Only 8 percent of these doctors practiced in rural areas, where nearly 70 percent of the state's black population lived. Before World War II, public health clinics for maternity and venereal disease patients had employed 19 black doctors, but that number was cut in half during the war. The short supply of African American health professionals was exacerbated by their concentration in urban areas and the central Piedmont section, whereas the majority of the black population was concentrated in North Carolina's rural eastern Black Belt. The western mountain counties typically were less than 5 percent black, except for the city of Asheville in Buncombe County.[4]

According to Mayo, the only logical solution to the critical shortage in black health personnel was to desegregate medical education. "If this state is to have more Negro medical personnel," he concluded, "there should be training facilities within the state. This means very simply a complete medical school for Negroes. Perhaps the state cannot afford to support two schools of high standards, but it can support one. It follows logically that facilities for training Negroes should be in the general system constructed to serve the total population." The Committee on Negro Health Problems incorporated Mayo's conclusions into its final report to the governor and General Assembly, emphasizing "the very urgent need for more doctors if the Negro people in North Carolina are to receive even moderate medical attention."[5]

One of the MCC's first actions was to convene the National Committee for the Medical School Survey to study the feasibility of a state-funded four-year school. W. T. Sanger, president of the Medical College of Virginia in Richmond, chaired the committee, which issued its recommendations in 1946 as the Sanger Report. The report merely validated the existing Murphy Act program for blacks but recommended the expansion of UNC to a four-year, M.D.-granting program to improve the distribution of doctors within the state and to offer more opportunities for white North Carolina residents to study medicine. Yet Jordan was correct that there were indeed "less facilities provided for the training of Negro medical aspirants in the entire United States than there are for North Carolina's approximately two million white people." Although eighteen states in 1946 had no four-year medical schools, North Carolina was not one of them. UNC's two-year program had existed since 1879, and another two-year school, Bowman Gray, had been founded at Wake Forest University in 1902. Bowman Gray expanded to four years in 1941 and led the university's relocation from Wake Forest to Winston-Salem. Duke University Medical School in Durham opened as a four-year program in 1930. All three schools were located in the central Piedmont section of the state.[6]

The Sanger Committee urged the state to "consider education on an inter-state or regional basis in dentistry both for white and Negro students; in medicine for Negro students and in public health nursing for Negro students." The report justified regional medical education as an efficient use of public funds that would meet the need for training more black health professionals while spreading the cost among several states. Efficiency was not, however, the Sanger Committee's primary concern as its members discussed black health education. The maintenance of segregation dictated a separate regional institution rather than the integration of existing white-only state institutions. But the committee did not propose building a new regional medical school for blacks. Instead, the Sanger Report urged North Carolina to join Virginia and other southern states that already contracted with Meharry Medical College. In a section on "Achievement of Quality through Regionalism," the authors reasoned that it was "far more expedient to have a joint, high-class professional and technical institution in a given area than many poor ones." Key to this argument was the assumption that "if every southern state were to attempt medical and dental education for Negroes, there would be insufficient students available to justify the continuance of Meharry Medical College, although it is a well-established, high-class institution with superior physical plant, able teachers, and substantial endowment." The report allowed that "provision should be made to permit a student to go to another institution [besides Meharry] when there is good reason for it."[7]

The MCC convened on August 8, 1946, to consider adopting the Sanger Committee's recommendations. William M. Rich, the African American director of Lincoln Hospital in Durham and chair of the MCC's Committee on Medical Training for Negroes, asked the commission to postpone discussion of the section advocating regional medical education for blacks until his committee could gather further information. One commission member responded by urging the group "to ask the next legislature to provide reasonable funds for at least two years [of medical education for blacks]. We are providing two years for the whites, and we ought to make provision for at least two years for the colored." Rich did not second this suggestion but voiced his support for the expansion of the UNC program. As the commission's only black member, Rich had to exercise diplomacy with his white colleagues. He noted that "a number of my people" had asked him how he would vote on the expansion of the UNC Medical School, especially since the projected cost to the state was $5 million in capital outlay plus $500,000 in annual maintenance. Other commission members "have the idea . . . that, because my people would not get any direct benefit, I would not support it," Rich said before quickly distancing himself from this "very narrow and prejudiced viewpoint." He was "not for any class or race or sect" but "for North Carolina as a whole. [I]f North Carolina Negroes are due anything," Rich proclaimed, "this Commission will see to it that our people do receive it in the same proportion for our group as you provide for yourselves." The MCC adopted the Sanger Report's strategy of sending black medical students out of state and providing a four-year in-state school for whites.[8]

Paul F. Whitaker, a white physician who served with Rich on the Committee on Medical Training for Negroes, argued that a new regional school for training black doctors should be established and located in North Carolina. He testified to the Joint Appropriation Committee of the North Carolina General

Assembly in 1947 that the state already possessed the resources to establish a regional black medical school. Cooperation between black institutions (NCC and Lincoln Hospital in Durham) and the medical schools at UNC and Duke would enable the state to found a black medical school "for a relatively small investment...which will not only train the Negro youth of our state, but could well become a regional facility for the entire South." With an expanded UNC School of Medicine to "furnish the leadership which is its rightful and proper sphere," the regional school would require "only a few full-time Negro medical educators."[9]

Whitaker was a racial moderate who believed that the regional school had "great possibilities for good, and future service to that large and deserving element of our population, the Negroes." Like many white progressives of his day, he saw racial change as a necessarily gradual process. His proposal for a regional black medical school in North Carolina was intended as a long-term rather than immediate solution to the problem of training more black physicians. Whitaker assumed that because only nine blacks from North Carolina entered medical school each year, there were "not enough qualified Negro youths available for the study of medicine." Eventually, "increasing education and opportunity for Negro youth" would remedy "this lack of qualified material." Only then would it make sense for the state to invest its resources in a regional medical school for African Americans. Although Whitaker's gradualist approach to black medical education may have reflected whites' low estimation of black academic ability, black leaders such as the NMA's W. Montague Cobb expressed similar concerns. Shortly after Whitaker made his remarks, the General Assembly approved the initial appropriation to expand UNC's program to four years. In 1947, the legislature rejected a bill that would have appropriated eight hundred thousand dollars to establish a two-year medical school for blacks at NCC.[10]

North Carolina followed the pattern set by Alabama. In 1938, alumni of the University of Alabama's two-year medical school and the Medical Association of the State of Alabama, led by Birmingham physician Seale Harris, mounted a campaign to promote state reform in health care and medical education by documenting Alabama's severe health problems and urging the public and legislators to respond. In contrast to the governor-led effort in North Carolina, state health reform in Alabama had to maneuver around a lethargic legislature by operating at the grassroots level through county medical societies and civic leaders from around the state. To stir debate over Alabama's health needs and prod the state legislature to action, Hopson Owen Murfee, a Prattville civic activist, strategically raised the hot-button issue of which city should be home to the new four-year state medical school. Murfee also urged the state to consider founding two schools to separately train black and white physicians. But as in North Carolina, Alabama's legislature sidestepped the issue of training black physicians and on June 2, 1943, unanimously passed a bill to establish a four-year medical school affiliated with the all-white University of Alabama. The legislature allocated $1 million for construction and an annual budget of $366,750 for maintenance and scholarships.[11]

As UNC officials prepared to expand the School of Medicine, southern white leaders advocated a separate regional black medical school, employing Hill-Burton's logic of using federal funding to make segregated facilities more equal and stave off complete desegregation. Black activists insisted that North Carolina include black students in its plans for medical education. As NMA and NAACP leaders were criticizing the deluxe Jim Crow of segregated wards in new hospitals built with federal funds, black activists and sympathetic UNC faculty insisted that the university open its doors to train black health professionals alongside their white peers.[12]

In his 1947 annual radio address, NCC president J. E. Shephard "pointed to the need for 'some fair and equitable arrangement' by which Negroes will be given an opportunity to acquire medical training." Perhaps in response to pressure from Shephard and other black state leaders, Rich did an about-face and declared himself "definitely opposed to a program which would provide medical education within the state for white students and that would require Negro students to travel about 500 miles outside of the state [to Meharry Medical College] to a regional school to do the same training." The regional school proposition did not conform with the Supreme Court's decision in the *Gaines* case, Rich warned, and he called on the MCC immediately to "take some very definite action on this matter." If the legislature delayed and allowed the four-year school at UNC to open "without any provision having been made for the training of Negroes within the state," Rich was "quite certain that the Negro citizens of the state will take steps to secure equal facilities."[13]

In response to Rich, Paul Whitaker wrote to MCC executive secretary John Ferrell that such action would be against "the best interest of the negro race." As long as segregation remained legal in public schools and "until further time has elapsed," Whitaker did not believe "that after mature thought, the negro citizens who have the genuine interest of both races at heart" would want to raise the possibility of "admitting both races to the University of North Carolina."

Whitaker suggested that Rich and other black leaders "proceed slowly and conservatively" but claimed that he was "not in any way attempting to tell Mr. Rich what to do." Rich softened his position at the November 1947 meeting of the Committee on Medical Training for Negroes, stating that Whitaker had "misinterpreted entirely the intent and spirit of my letter." Since the committee's first meeting in August 1946, Rich had believed that out-of-state medical training for blacks "was of a temporary nature and that something more permanent would be worked out at a later date." The committee had originally asked him to "give the report [on black medical education] more strength and call to the attention of the full Commission the real facts in the case based on the decision of the Supreme Court." The MCC had decided not to bring this information to the attention of the legislature because doing so might have confused legislators' "thinking on the matter of the four year medical school at Chapel Hill." Rich reminded the committee that he had been "in full agreement with this thought." In other words, if the MCC had suggested that the UNC School of Medicine be opened to blacks, the legislature might not have approved the four-year expansion plan.[14]

When the General Assembly took no action on black medical education, Rich heard "echoes from Negroes throughout the state stating their disappointment." Several criticized him personally for "failure to be as aggressive as I might have been." The legislature's inaction on black medical education had caused a backlash "sufficiently acute to justify my calling the matter to the attention of our Chairman." Leaders of the Old North State Medical Society already resented the appointment of Rich, whom they considered "a layman," as the only black representative on the MCC. Originally a banker rather than a physician, Rich had been selected as the business manager of Lincoln Hospital during its reorganization during the early 1930s and had revamped its accounting practices to erase a four-thousand-dollar deficit. He also worked with the Hospital Care Association to establish a hospital insurance program for black patients. The Duke Endowment sponsored Rich to receive training in hospital administration at the premier black hospitals, Provident in Chicago and Flint-Goodridge in New Orleans, where he was mentored by Albert W. Dent, the dean of black hospital men and later a member of the Federal Hospital Council. By the 1940s, Rich had emerged as a national leader in his own right, serving as chair of the National Conference of Hospital Administrators. Despite his close ties to both the Duke Endowment and Durham's black community, he found it difficult to maintain the trust of his black constituents and his white colleagues on the commission. Faced with criticism from both sides, he took a page from C. C. Spaulding and ingeniously raised the specter of a lawsuit as he reassured whites that "no one has expressed or implied that any legal action is contemplated."[15]

As the controversy over the regional medical school mounted, its proponents still hoped "that the negroes will not insist on their individual rights to the Nth degree, but will see that in the Regional School lies their best opportunity." In a letter to the MCC, J. Street Brewer, a Roseboro physician who later served as president of the white North Carolina Medical Society in 1953, claimed to "have given right much thought to the problem of negro medical education in the South." He had concluded that "any negro medical school that any southern state could establish would be of mediocre standards simply because the facilities and the colored teachers are not available now and will not be for many years." Brewer also bemoaned the "recent decision of the U.S. Supreme Court" in *Sipuel v. Board of Regents of the University of Oklahoma* (1948), which reaffirmed the *Gaines* decision. According to Brewer, blacks like the plaintiff in *Sipuel* jeopardized the "mutual effort" to "bring enlarged opportunities to the negro race." He dreaded the day "when some 'ornery cuss' will rise up, like some disgruntled lawyer or politician and 'demand his rights.'" Brewer counted on Rich to "use his influence as a leader among his people to get them to accept the Regional School which I am sure they will find to be the best thing for them."[16]

In the late 1940s, the tide of national opinion began to turn in favor of black applicants to medical schools. Mainstream magazines including *Collier's* and the *Saturday Evening Post* featured articles that criticized the color line in medical education. Under President Truman, the Committee on Civil Rights, the Commission on Higher Education, and Oscar Ewing in *The Nation's Health: A Ten-Year Program* (1948) exhorted medical schools to admit more qualified black applicants. The federal security administrator promised black physicians at Freedmen's Hospital in Washington, D.C., "As we expand medical training facilities for white doctors and nurses, we shall expand them for Negro nurses and doctors. And Government scholarships will be available for qualified young Negro men and women as well as for white young men and women." Under Ewing's leadership, the Federal Security Administration made increasing the number of black doctors a priority and facilitated a joint effort between the Children's Bureau, Meharry Medical College, Tuskegee Institute, and the Alabama and Tennessee state health boards to train black doctors, dentists, and nurses in pediatrics and maternity care.[17]

Another close Truman ally, Arkansas prosecuting attorney Sidney McMath, played an important role in desegregating medical education. McMath was a prolabor racial moderate who had helped Truman hold the Arkansas delegation loyal against the Dixiecrats during the summer 1948 Democratic convention. McMath was also a reform candidate for the state's governorship. The previous January, University of Arkansas officials had announced that the university would accept qualified black applicants to its graduate and professional programs, making Arkansas the first southern state university since Reconstruction voluntarily to remove the racial bar in admissions. Despite the objections of Dixiecrat incumbent governor Ben Laney, the university acted without the threat of a lawsuit, unlike Missouri in the *Gaines* case or Oklahoma in *Sipuel*. In February, law applicant Silas Hunt became the first black student admitted to a white southern university.[18]

McMath also helped the medical school secure major funding for a new classroom-research building and a new department of neuropsychiatry, which helped him and medical dean H. Clay Chenault to convince university president Lewis W. Jones to admit the first black medical student, Edith Mae Irby, in the fall of 1948. Jones had been one of three southern members of the President's Commission on Higher Education who had sharply dissented from the majority's condemnation of segregation, but Chenault had stated that it was "physically impossible in a medical education program to offer any measure of segregation, especially in the pre-clinical years." Irby, a native of Hot Springs, had scored twenty-eighth on the Association of American Medical Colleges' medical school aptitude test, putting her in the top 10 percent of the 230 Arkansas residents who took the exam. The *Little Rock Arkansas Gazette* editorialized that by admitting Irby on the basis of merit alone, "the Board of Trustees has spiked the guns of the South's constant critics, and of those impatient radicals who seek to batter down the whole institution of segregation at a blow." Although Irby attended classes relatively free of harassment, state law required her to use a separate dining room and rest rooms. She could find meals and lodging only with the help of black newspaper publisher Daisy Bates, who would later play a key role in the 1956 Little Rock desegregation crisis. After a year as the first black intern at the University of Arkansas University Hospital and six years of general practice in Hot Springs, Irby completed an internal medicine residency at Baylor and began medical practice in Houston in 1962. She served as president of the National Medical Association in 1986.[19]

After Irby's admission to Arkansas, the University of Texas Medical Branch in Galveston admitted its first black student in 1949, and bars began to fall at other schools. In 1938–39, of 350 black students enrolled in U.S. medical schools, only 45 (13 percent) were enrolled at schools other than Howard or Meharry, and all of those schools were located outside the South. By the 1951–52 academic year, enrollment of black students had risen to 697, including 164 (24 percent) at non–historically black schools. Fifty-one of the nation's 79 medical schools had at least one black student enrolled. Most of this increase had taken place since 1947–48: in only four years, the total number of black medical students had increased by 106, 69 of them not at Howard or Meharry. In the South, however, only 10 black students were enrolled at five historically white schools in 1951–52: the Universities of Arkansas, Texas, North Carolina, and Louisville and the Medical College of Virginia. The shortage of African American dentists was even more severe, and in 1947 only 313 black dental students were enrolled, most at Howard and Meharry, although Howard's College of Dentistry was not accredited by the American Dental Association's Council on Dental Education until 1948. As schools of medicine, dentistry, nursing, pharmacy, and public health expanded to meet the postwar demand for health professionals, competition for admission eased somewhat and may have mitigated racial, religious, gender, and class barriers, thereby promoting desegregation.[20]

DESEGREGATING THE UNIVERSITY
OF NORTH CAROLINA SCHOOL OF MEDICINE

Mayo's radical proposition to integrate medical education in North Carolina would be realized in 1951, only six years after his report to the Hospital and Medical Care Commission. NAACP legal counsel Thurgood Marshall charged that the request for federal aid for "the plan to ship colored students from one state to another for graduate training is in violation of the U.S. Supreme Court's decision [in the *Gaines* and *Sipuel* cases]. Accordingly, we urge all qualified colored youth desiring a medical education to apply to the existing publicly supported medical schools in their respective states rather than submit to this unlawful plan." Back in North Carolina, black students complied with Marshall's suggestion. In December 1947, less than a month after Rich assured the MCC that no legal action was being contemplated, Dewey Monroe Clayton became the first African American to apply to the UNC School of Medicine. Since the application form included a blank marked "race" and requested a photograph, black applicants who were forthright about their racial identity had that information used against them. In his letter of application, Clayton stated, "Since early childhood it has been my desire to become a physician. The primary reason for my desire to study medicine is because of the severe shortage of physicians in my area, especially my state. This is supplemented by the fact that so few persons of my race venture into the field of medicine." Clayton had not been accepted at either Howard or Meharry, which he blamed on "the fact that so many students apply," contradicting whites who claimed that not enough qualified students existed to support additional medical schools for blacks. Howard and Meharry had 1,200 applicants and only 150 slots available. Berryhill, the dean of the School of Medicine, replied to Clayton in February that the entering class of 1948 had been filled and that Clayton had not been admitted because he had not provided transcripts or letters of recommendation. If Clayton's college record and recommendations were "up to the standard required for admission to medical school," Berryhill promised to assist Clayton in gaining admission to Howard or Meharry.[21]

During the ensuing two years, two more African Americans applied to medical school at UNC, James Henry Henderson in 1948 and James Edward Thomas in 1949. In the face of growing legal challenges to segregation in higher education, UNC handled applications from black students with kid gloves. Early in 1950, law school dean Henry Brandis asked Berryhill how the medical school was handling black applicants. Berryhill replied that after consulting the state attorney general, he had instructed black applicants to apply to NCC in Durham for a grant for out-of-state educational costs. Despite their caution, both Berryhill and Brandis shortly found their schools embroiled in NAACP lawsuits. A group of black applicants sued the law school in 1950, and Thomas sued the medical school the following March. University administrators then instructed Berryhill to process medical school applications from blacks "without discrimination and entirely in accordance with procedures for processing all applicants."[22]

The medical school lawsuit came "as no surprise" to the *Raleigh Carolinian*, one of North Carolina's leading black weeklies. "The University and the State of North Carolina have had ample time," an editorialist argued, "to solve this problem sensibly and gracefully without the necessity of a lawsuit. The university and state can hardly win this case even on a temporary basis, as in the case of the law school, since there is no medical school for Negroes maintained by the State of North Carolina, or even a private medical school within the state." The *Carolinian* suggested that "the trustees and officials of the University of North Carolina really prefer that the issue be settled by a court decision rather than by their own action, since they have been 'considering' the matter for several years without apparently getting anywhere with it. To have the question adjudged by a Federal court will take the onus off everybody connected with the University and the State government, and nobody who depends on the good will of the legislature or the voters will have stuck his neck out." In late March 1951, the *Carolinian*'s prediction came true when the U.S. Court of Appeals reversed the lower court's decision in the law school case and ordered UNC to admit the black plaintiffs.[23]

Faced with the Thomas suit on the heels of the law school defeat, UNC administrators and the board of trustees decided to change the university's official admissions policy before the court ordered them to do so. The board voted 61–35 in April 1951 to process applications to all of the university's graduate and professional schools "without regard to color or race" as long as such schools were not separately provided for blacks within the state. At that point, the constitutionality of *Plessy v. Ferguson*'s "separate but equal" doctrine had not yet been challenged. Board members from the eastern Black Belt counties of Bertie and Warren led the opposition to the resolution. State representative C. Wayman Spruill warned that the action would "cause bloodshed in this state." Former Speaker of the North Carolina House John Kerr Jr. responded to the trustees' decision by declaring North Carolina to be one of the "13 sovereign" states and protesting that "the United States Supreme Court can't mandamus (order) us to do anything." He urged the legislature to deny appropriations to any institution not practicing segregation.[24]

The School of Medicine never admitted Thomas but instead chose Edward O. Diggs, one of seven African Americans who applied to UNC's graduate and professional schools for the fall of 1951. Diggs would be the first black student to complete the four-year medical degree at UNC. Diggs's admission occasioned comment in the southern press, with the *Atlanta Constitution* noting that UNC president Gordon Gray was a "distinguished conservative Southerner." According to one newspaper account, Diggs "wouldn't have anything to do with the National Association for the Advancement of Colored People. In return, the N.A.A.C.P. doesn't like him too much because he indicated he wouldn't enter court action if U.N.C. refused him." Of four black applicants to the School of Medicine, all but Diggs were found "unquestionably not competitively qualified." One of the rejected applicants asked Governor Kerr Scott to call a special session of the board of trustees to reconsider his admission. Rather than rejecting such an audacious request out of hand, Scott carefully consulted the attorney general before replying that the applicant's qualifications had not been competitive, and "therefore there would be no occasion to submit your application to the Board of Trustees of the University."[25]

The events surrounding Diggs's admission to medical school highlighted the rift between the university's upper administrators, who resisted change, and its faculty, many of whom favored desegregation. E. M. Hedgpeth, chair of the medical school admissions committee, was the only dissenter as the six other committee members voted to admit Diggs. Berryhill joined Hedgpeth in rejecting Diggs for admission and stated to Gray that "had Diggs been a white man rather than a Negro in his particular circumstances he would not have been found competitively qualified." In an unusual move, however, the six Diggs supporters on the admissions committee wrote to Berryhill to ask that their concerns be made part of Diggs's admission record. The members cited the chair's contradictory statement that more impressive applications than Diggs's had not yet been considered and their own conclusion that "Mr. Diggs' academic accomplishments were outstanding—well above the accepted standards of this school" and above those of two-thirds of the 1951 entering class.[26]

Diggs reportedly insisted "that his application to the white school was not made with the primary interest of crashing the segregation party." Reactions among Carolina students were mixed. One letter to the *Daily Tar Heel* complained that Diggs had unfairly displaced a more deserving white applicant, while another student wrote that "we will welcome Edward Diggs as the pioneer that he is." Both friends and critics of the university acknowledged that the decision to admit Diggs was motivated by fear of the courts rather than a new egalitarian outlook. As the *Raleigh News and Observer* noted, "The University, its attorneys and sponsors of the proposal stressed the law and the attitude of the U.S. Supreme Court left the University and the State no choice but to give Negro medical students equal consideration."[27]

In contrast to the *News and Observer*, the *Carolinian* took umbrage at what it called "a token compliance with the Federal Constitution." In an accusatory editorial, the paper alleged that UNC's admission of a single black medical student was part of a plot to preserve segregation: "The authorities of the University have not been acting in good faith in meeting the problem of equal opportunity for Negroes in graduate and professional training. They have instead applied a great deal of ingenuity, to put it mildly, in trying to circumvent the spirit of the Federal court decisions. The admission of a Negro applicant to the medical school appears, in the light of the later developments, to have been only . . . a sparring for time to work out 'within the pattern of segregation,' if possible, a way to keep all other schools and departments of the University sealed off."[28]

President Gray did little to dispel such allegations. In his explanation of the board of trustees' decision to lift racial restrictions in admissions, Gray stated, "It would be unsound and unwise—educationally and economically" to duplicate "certain highly specialized and highly expensive graduate and professional courses in the consolidated University and in the Negro Colleges." Medicine was perhaps the most specialized and expensive field of all, and medical schools commanded massive resources that empowered them to act as either catalysts or obstacles to change. But Gray denied that the University of North Carolina had "any legal or moral obligation to assume the total responsibility of providing graduate instruction for all qualified citizens of North Carolina—both white and Negro. The doctrine of 'separate but equal' educational facilities is still the law of the land."[29]

Although Berryhill did not favor the desegregation of medical education, he acquiesced when Diggs was admitted. In 1953, after the medical school had admitted a second black student, James Slade, Gray asked the deans of the medical, law, and graduate schools to report on whether their experiences with black students had been "on the whole satisfactory or unsatisfactory." Berryhill replied that his experiences had been satisfactory but qualified his answer by noting that "we are really just now reaching the difficult period in our experience with negro students because the first one is now in the junior year and is coming in contact with patients. There has been no difficulty as long as the [two] negro students were in the basic science laboratories and dealt only with other students, faculty and laboratory animals." After the medical school began assigning students to patients, faculty had encountered "some rather difficult problems" that differentiated medicine from other graduate and professional programs. When Diggs began his clinical work with patients, he protested his assignment only to Negro patients when white students were assigned to patients of both races. But after Berryhill had "a very frank discussion" with Diggs "on the mores of this State at this time and probably for years to come he appeared to accept the policy in a realistic fashion."[30]

When black undergraduates entered UNC in 1955, the university acted much as it had during the integration of its graduate and professional schools a few years earlier. Cabell Phillips, writing in the *New York Times Magazine* in March 1956, described the atmosphere on campus that spring: "The University is highly sensitive to the political winds that blow from the Capitol in Raleigh, twenty-eight miles away. . . . The university's faculty and administrators are under a relentless and skeptical scrutiny in everything they do. Thus, the university officers approached their new bi-racial responsibility with the gingerly reluctance with which one lifts the lid on a teeming beehive." Phillips's evaluation of UNC's motives echoed the *Carolinian*'s evaluation of the 1951 medical school lawsuit: "Their decision was to try to satisfy the court order by obeying the letter of the law, but not to offend political opinion by observing its spirit as well. In other words, they would take the Negro students, but do nothing to make them welcome."[31]

Slade attended the university during the height of the integration controversy. He recalled that with a few notable exceptions, UNC faculty and students generally accepted him, and he received his medical degree in 1957. He had applied because he felt that he "could do as good a job as those guys at Duke and Carolina and other places. It was a challenge." After being accepted at UNC and Meharry, Slade turned down Murphy Act funds to attend UNC. He did not notify the press but "just told my family and the people at the college who had sent my references in. We didn't make it a big event." Segregated campus housing meant that Slade shared an entire dormitory floor with two black law students, while white students on some halls lived three to a room. Diggs advised Slade on how to negotiate an all-white campus, but reactions to the newly arrived black students were unpredictable. On Slade's second attempt to eat at the UNC Hospital cafeteria, the cashier told him to sit in the corner. When he sat down midway across the room, some of his white classmates joined him, effectively settling the cafeteria's seating policy.[32]

The *Brown* decision was announced in May 1954, just before Slade completed his first year in medical school. He remembered wondering "if it was ever going to reach down to a place like Edenton [his home town in eastern North Carolina]. Of course, eventually it did." One of the most outspoken opponents of the school desegregation decision was a professor who taught Slade, Wesley Critz George, "one of the most respected members of the medical faculty" as well as president of the state's largest and most influential segregationist organization. He had founded the Patriots of North Carolina with three former Speakers of the North Carolina House (Kerr, W. Frank Taylor, and John G. Dawson), a UNC trustee (John H. Clark), and prominent businessmen, educators, and lawyers from around the state. Patriot members came from every one of the state's counties and ran well into the tens of thousands. According to the *New York Times Magazine*, the group was "pledged to fight 'usurpation' of state legisla-

tive functions by the Federal courts and the 'mongrelization' of the white race."
George believed that school integration was a "Communist-clerical conspiracy to
promote miscegenation and thereby the ultimate downfall of American civilization." He published his scientific defenses of racism in UNC's student newspaper
as well as in a book, *The Biology of the Race Problem*, which was widely adopted
by activist racist groups, including the White Citizens' Councils.[33]

Despite George and other faculty members who shared his views, Slade
recalled that "all of the professors were open-minded. They didn't bend over
backward, but they didn't try to hinder you at all." He encountered racism not
in the classroom but in clinical training: "The only weak spot in training at
Chapel Hill was in obstetrics because they wouldn't allow the black students to
[attend] deliveries, except on black patients, and there weren't very many black
patients in OB at Chapel Hill." Slade's other experiences were far more reward-
ing, however. For example, "There was no discrimination in pediatrics. You
had one ward, and where [patients] were located depended on which sickness
[they] had." Slade went on to practice pediatrics for more than three decades in
Chowan and surrounding counties, where he won recognition for his dedicated
service in public health clinics.[34]

After the UNC board of trustees' decision to admit Diggs, university counsel
L. P. McLendon had commented to the *Raleigh News and Observer*, "It is not a
question of what the University would like to do, but what it had to do." University officials scrambled to piece together a new admissions policy that would
please both the courts and UNC's political supporters. UNC controller W. D.
Carmichael, Chancellor Robert House, and dean of the graduate school W. W.
Pierson recommended to President Gray "that he apprise the Board of Trustees
of the existing confusion in the State's graduate program for its Negro citizens
[and] that during the period of these discussions applications by Negroes to the
University of North Carolina graduate or professional schools involved in the
discussions not be acted upon." At that point, fifteen black North Carolinians
were studying medicine outside the state with Murphy Act funds. The "existing
confusion" over black graduate education in North Carolina lasted for several
more years, while whites searched for ways to evade the Supreme Court's orders
to desegregate public education from the elementary to graduate levels. Not until
1956, when the court decided *Florida ex Rel. Hawkins v. Board of Control*, was the
Brown decision extended to guarantee African Americans equal access to state
graduate and professional schools. Nevertheless, even with advanced degrees,
southern blacks continued to face employment discrimination. As one black

newspaper editorial noted, "It will do little good to open the doors of Southern graduate schools to Negro students if the Southern economy, stepped up only because of defense production, excludes them and their families."[35]

Although opportunities for blacks to study medicine and other health fields would not be fully equal until the late 1960s and early 1970s, the UNC School of Public Health (SPH) by that point had been involved in black education for twenty-five years. As one faculty member remembered, "Public health was upsetting the hell out of everything. [The university administration] couldn't understand." In 1945, the same year that Mayo wrote his report to the MCC, the SPH helped to establish a Department of Health Education at NCC. Over the next fifteen years, SPH faculty members assisted in training more than one hundred black health educators at NCC. When UNC and NCC public health students began meeting together in Durham and Chapel Hill, SPH faculty member Lucy Morgan introduced them to each other. "We sent them together to the field," she recalled, "and then we had open houses when the people came in from the field, black and white together. Then it got bitter for a while, and we used to pull down the shades sometimes when we had meetings in Chapel Hill."[36]

In the midst of the 1956 anti-integration crisis, the State Board of Health's Public Health Nursing Section temporarily discontinued its orientation program for registered nurses, and the SPH stepped in. Of fifty nurses who were expected to enroll in the summer 1956 program, four were black graduate nurses. Three NCC undergraduates also wished to take one course. Ruth Hay of the SPH Department of Public Health Nursing recommended that UNC give clearance "for these qualified graduate nurse students employed in North Carolina." The students would live in NCC dormitories and receive extension credit through NCC.[37]

McGavran, dean of the School of Public Health, wrote in support of Hay's idea to Henry Clark, head of the Division of Health Affairs. "Since [the black students requesting to enroll] are all North Carolina residents and employees," McGavran could "see no objection or violation of University policy." Since the course was only available at UNC, he even suggested awarding credit through the university, effectively integrating the SPH. But McGavran encountered opposition from other university officials, such as Pierson, who argued that the board of trustees' April 1951 vote to admit black students in graduate and professional programs that were not offered in the state's black institutions no longer represented university policy. Instead, the board of trustees was governed by the General Assembly's actions during the spring of 1955. State senator Thomas

Pearsall, architect of North Carolina's plan to resist the *Brown* decision, declared that "the mixing of the races in the public schools . . . cannot be accomplished and should not be attempted." The legislature adopted the Pearsall Resolution as an amendment to the state constitution.[38]

Pierson also used the SPH's cooperative efforts with NCC as an argument against allowing black students to enroll in public health nursing courses at UNC, since the NCC catalog already included a public health nursing program. He conceded that "it might be argued in a strictly formalistic way" that if NCC did not offer such courses during the summer, "the special program is not duplicated in another public institution at that time, and . . . applications of eligible persons should be acted upon without reference to race." But the university remained enmeshed in legal battles against integration, and Pierson did not know whether anyone in the administration was "as yet prepared to give a formal answer" regarding the enrollment of black students. He worried that "we should be embarrassed if an issue was made concerning our obligation in reference to the unrepealed Pearsall Resolution."[39]

McGavran chose to put a positive spin on Pierson's analysis, writing to Clark that "the comment in my memorandum of January 13 is substantiated." Allowing black students to enroll in a summer public health nursing program at UNC did not "involve University policy" as McGavran saw it, since the students would receive credit at NCC and not at UNC. He concluded, "I judge that Dean Pierson's memorandum means we have your approval and the approval of Chancellor House for proceeding to enroll any qualified student for the summer work in Public Health Nursing." In a handwritten note on McGavran's final memo, Clark allowed, "I guess so, but am a bit confused by Pierson's letter." The status of black students in UNC's School of Public Health remained uncertain until 1960, when the SPH began formally to admit black applicants and NCC discontinued its program in public health education.[40]

During the second half of the twentieth century, more and more black health professionals received their training at historically white institutions. In 1951, only 23.5 percent of black entering medical students enrolled at predominantly white schools; that figure rose to 47 percent in 1968, 61 percent in 1983, and 84 percent by 1990. New generations of black physicians depended less on black institutions for their education and professional advancement. Desegregation affected medical education much as it did public education in general. As historian David Cecelski has noted, "Instead of reconciling black and white schools on equal terms, white leaders made school desegregation a one-way street. Black communities repeatedly had to sacrifice their leadership traditions, school cultures, and educational heritage for the other benefits of desegregation." Once integration opened hospitals and medical training, many black patients and professionals chose to patronize white-run institutions over black facilities that lacked sufficient resources to modernize.[41]

Graduates of African American schools such as Howard and Meharry sensed that the medical profession was waning in its dedication to the black community. Andrew Best, a Meharry-trained black physician and civil rights activist in Greenville, North Carolina, since 1954 and an officer in the Old North State Medical Society, contended that "our training and background [at historically black medical schools] gives us a different perspective than the training over yonder [in Chapel Hill]. When those young doctors finish Duke and Chapel Hill and whatnot, it shows." He remembered faculty at Meharry who emphasized that a physician's humanitarian obligations came ahead of money. Under segregation, black physicians' earning potential had been limited by the geographical, economic, and racial composition of their practices, which necessarily included many nonpaying patients. Charity was not optional but essential for survival, since a small, close-knit community could shut down a physician who seemed to evade his duty. Slade concurred with the idea that integration, combined with the increased cost of medical education, may have undermined traditional ties of charity between black physicians and their patients.[42]

With the full desegregation of health care and the advent of Medicare and Medicaid in the mid-1960s, black physicians found themselves better able to care for their patients but forced to survive in a system where whites still controlled the majority of power and resources. As the practice of medicine required increasing amounts of training, capital, and technology, old-school physicians with solo practices and little office equipment gave way to group practices with access to sophisticated diagnostic tests. By opening opportunities in more lucrative towns and cities, desegregation led to selective migration that reduced the number of black physicians in rural areas. After older black physicians died or retired, poor, rural communities had difficulty finding replacements. Best, Slade, and Salter Cochran, an obstetrician/gynecologist in Roanoke Rapids, spent most of their careers as the sole black doctors in their counties and were not joined by other minority practitioners until the late 1980s or early 1990s.

Best was among the many blacks who resented UNC's long-standing exclusion of African Americans. The university's School of Medicine did not achieve more than token integration until 1970, when Dean Ike Taylor began the Medical

Education Development Program to attract minority students. The University of Pennsylvania had appointed the nation's first dean for minority affairs two years earlier. In the mid-1970s, Best helped to establish a second state-funded medical school at East Carolina University in Greenville, located in the heart of the state's rural eastern Black Belt and given a mandate to train primary care and minority physicians. Opponents of the measure echoed the attitudes of the Sanger Committee nearly three decades earlier, arguing that a second school would be an inefficient use of state resources. UNC's resistance to integration in the 1950s would come back to haunt Berryhill, who waged his last major political battle against the East Carolina Medical School. The outcome of that battle signaled the transformation of African Americans into a viable force in state politics and changed the course of health-care education in North Carolina for decades to come.[43]

chapter 10

RACIAL DISPARITIES

AND THE

TRUMAN HEALTH PLAN

W hen Harry S. Truman assumed the presidency in April 1945, Thomas Parran had been surgeon general for nearly a decade. Parran was the federal official who most advanced the cause of deluxe Jim Crow health policy as an integral part of the New Deal and helped to define its emphasis on southern uplift, equitable access to health care, and targeting the needs of the medically underserved. As the senior U.S. representative during two years of planning meetings and president of the International Health Conference that established the World Health Organization (WHO), Parran applied and expanded these principles in formulating WHO's goals: "To provide in each country, and throughout the world, an equal opportunity for health for everyone—without regard to race, color, economic condition, religious or political belief." The six health issues that WHO prioritized were identical to those that Parran had pursued in the South: malaria, maternal and child health, tuberculosis, venereal disease, nutrition, and environmental sanitation. In his last months as surgeon general, Parran wrote in the *American Journal of Public Health* that America's tremendous technological power in medical science, together with its "well known humanitarian zeal," required that "adequate medical care for all must be the cornerstone of any program designed to meet the health needs of the nation, and this means that medical care must be based on need for services rather than on ability to pay. One of the first problems we must solve, therefore, is that of finding a more efficient method of financing medical care."[1]

Parran remained as surgeon general for the first three years of Truman's administration, but his days were numbered after Oscar R. Ewing took over the Federal
Security Agency in August 1947. Ewing, a Harvard Law graduate from Indiana,
was an international corporate lawyer earning one hundred thousand dollars
a year who had risen in New York political circles to become vice chair of the
Democratic National Committee in 1940. Though their goals for national health
policy were nearly identical, Ewing and Parran clashed almost immediately.
Parran refused Ewing's request to award a National Institutes of Health grant
to Walter Kempner, an academic medical researcher who had treated Ewing's
wife at Duke University. Parran deeply resented a nonprofessional's attempt to
influence a grant-making decision by the U.S. Public Health Service (PHS), but
Ewing increased the pressure further by refusing to approve Parran's appoint-
ments to advisory boards for PHS agencies. Parran refused to back down and
resigned from the PHS in February 1948 to become the founding dean of the
University of Pittsburgh School of Public Health. Yet another veteran New
Dealer left the Truman administration, and the PHS shifted its emphasis away
from the communicable diseases of poverty, particularly syphilis, that had riveted
the agency's attention on the South under Parran.[2]

Ewing characterized his choice for Parran's replacement, Leonard Scheele, as
"just as cooperative as anyone could be," which spoke volumes about Ewing's
and Parran's similar but incompatible temperaments as strong-willed, at times
unyielding leaders who were reluctant to share their authority. Scheele's apoliti-
cal style contrasted dramatically with Parran's activism, and Scheele withheld
his support from the final attempt to pass the Wagner-Murray-Dingell national
health insurance bill in 1948, focusing instead on the less controversial goal of
beefing up National Institutes of Health funding for chronic disease research.
He refused Ewing's invitation to join in a televised debate against the American
Medical Association (AMA), preferring to remain professionally nonpartisan and
warning PHS officers to follow suit.[3]

Despite their differences, Parran and Ewing were avowed supporters of national health insurance who melded wartime patriotism with their goals for
domestic health policy in an attempt to forge what they hoped would be a
new stainless-steel liberalism. Ewing wielded more influence than anyone in
postwar Washington except perhaps Truman. The Federal Security Agency

featured eleven bureaus, thirty-six thousand employees, and a $2 billion annual budget. Ewing told *Parade* magazine in May 1948, "The same zeal and unity of purpose with which Americans contributed to winning the war should be directed toward fighting disease and preventable death and improving the nation's health."[4]

Like Paul V. McNutt's stint as chair of the Wartime Manpower Commission and Claude Pepper's congressional leadership in passing the Lend-Lease Act and chairing the Wartime Health and Education Committee, Ewing's war-era credentials bolstered his credibility and political clout as an advocate of liberal reform. As the special assistant to the U.S. attorney general, Ewing had won the conviction on sedition charges of William Dudley Pelley, leader of a racist vigilante organization, the Silver Shirts, based in Asheville, North Carolina. Ewing had also prosecuted the federal treason case against newspapermen Robert Henry Best and Douglas Chandler, who were charged with broadcasting news favorable to the Nazi war effort over German radio. Both were convicted, and Pelley was sentenced to fifteen years and Chandler to life in prison. Ewing would bring to his postwar administration of the Federal Security Agency the tenacity that had characterized his work as a prosecutor.[5]

Until Ewing's arrival in 1947, a hands-off attitude toward segregation had been a core principle of deluxe Jim Crow policy. More moderate health reformers had also supported deluxe Jim Crow health programs, particularly hospital construction, as prophylactic measures against national health insurance. Ewing boldly seized on federal health programs as an opportunity to champion universal health insurance and the rights of African Americans to equal access to health care and professional opportunities. He became the first high-ranking federal official to publicly and forcefully argue for full integration. Although he oversaw the Social Security Agency and Department of Education, the PHS and national health policy absorbed the majority of his attention and passion. Ewing told the Conference of State and Territorial Health Officers in 1947,

> I don't think we can be complacent until we can feel that we have done a job
> that has prevented every preventable death from one end of this country to the
> other. Somebody said that our poor showing on comparative figures is perhaps
> due to the fact that health conditions among our Negro populations are so bad.
> But that is a challenge, not an excuse. We have no right to be complacent about
> that. The life of the poorest Negro is just as important to him as yours is to you
> or mine is to me. His death means just as much grief and sorrow to his family as

your or my death would mean to our loved ones. We have no right to let up until we have done our utmost to make America more than the healthiest country in the world. I am interested in the last 140,000,000th person in the United States. Only when we are sure that that 140,000,000th person has all the health that medicine and science can give him have we any right to relax. Until then we must fight on.

As head of the Federal Security Agency from 1947 to 1953, Ewing maintained a heavy schedule of speeches and public appearances across the country (though rarely in the South, where he was persona non grata), pushing deluxe Jim Crow policy as far toward racial equality and national health insurance as was within his power.[6]

Ewing stood apart as a member of a small fraternity of New Dealers who joined black physicians in vociferously protesting the racial gap in American life expectancy and demanding that the government act to redress it. The Southern Conference for Human Welfare (SCHW) published a photo-illustrated 1945 pamphlet, *Would You Smile?* that asked readers to place themselves in the position of black Americans. Among the statements following the phrase "If you were a Negro" were "With inadequate medical care, bad housing, and low-paying jobs to which you would be shunted—You could expect to die 10 years before a white American born on the same day. And you could expect your children to die 10 years before white children born the same day. You would know that there are only 3,500 doctors, 1,500 dentists, and 1,200 lawyers out of more than 13 million Negro Americans."[7]

Although black health reformers had been calling attention to higher rates of death and disease among blacks for decades, former vice president Henry Wallace was the first white politician of national standing to make the racial gap in life expectancy a major presidential campaign theme. Using the slogan "Ten Extra Years," Wallace, a close friend of Pepper's, called for the enactment of federal and state bans on racial discrimination and segregation, with suspension of federal aid as the penalty. He charged that "those who stand in the way of the health, education, housing and social security programs which would erase that gap [between black and white life expectancy] commit murder." Although a staunch Truman supporter, Ewing echoed Wallace's passionate call to close the racial disparity in rates of death and disease, a theme that ran through Ewing's massive 1948 volume, *The Nation's Health: A Ten-Year Program.* He declared in the *Journal of the National Medical Association,* "We must cut [the racial disparity in life expectancy] down until there is no disparity at all, and we should not have to wait half a century before we have done so."[8]

In June 1948, Ewing addressed the annual national conference of the National Association for the Advancement of Colored People (NAACP) on the first anniversary of Truman's historic speech as the first president to address the organization. Ewing's speech marked another critical juncture for federal policy on health and race relations. When Ewing expressed his "deep respect and feeling of warm friendship for the National Association for the Advancement of Colored People," he spoke with sincerity as the top domestic policy official in the first administration actively to cultivate the organization's support. Ewing quoted a verse from John Donne's "For Whom the Bell Tolls" and stated, "When we find further that a full *tenth* of our population is, for the most part, not only relegated to the most desperate poverty but to the very meanest of educational, health, and other opportunities, then the tolling of the bell becomes a veritable clamor."[9]

In another address at Freedmen's Hospital, Ewing lamented that "when you come to that area which concerns the Negro, your facts and figures come suddenly to life to reveal a picture of needs, misery, and desperation almost beyond belief." Although the same arguments for the Truman health plan applied to both races, racial discrimination compounded medical need. Ewing criticized Robert Taft and Lister Hill's Senate proposals for federal grants to states to subsidize care for the medically indigent as "nothing but the ancient idea of the dole for those who are on public assistance." Ewing optimistically predicted that national health insurance would erase the ten-year racial disparity in life expectancy within a decade. He admitted that the new Hill-Burton hospital program allowed segregation within biracial hospitals but emphasized that the federal government "can, and does, establish non-segregation in the hospitals which it owns and directly operates."[10]

Ewing fulfilled this claim by opening the federally operated Gallinger Hospital in Washington, D.C., to Howard University Medical School interns. Senator John Rankin of Mississippi protested Truman's executive order to allow Negro doctors to admit and supervise patients at Gallinger as an attempt "to humiliate the doctors and the white patients who are bound to patronize Gallinger Hospital" and a plot of "certain communistic elements to stir race trouble all over the country." Wisconsin Republican senator Frank B. Keefe, who chaired the Subcommittee on Labor and Federal Security Agency Appropriations, challenged Rankin's statement: "We have been trying for years to build up the medical school of Howard University [to meet accreditation requirements] and all that has ever been suggested was that the colored segregated sections of Gallinger Hospital be opened for clinical purposes to the students and doctors of Howard University." But Ewing wanted what Rankin feared, stating that "in all services operated in common, patients would be assigned to each medical school in regular rotation, according to order of admission, without regard to race." Rankin fumed, "There is a hotbed of communism at Howard University. It is doing the Negroes of this country more harm than any other institution I know."[11]

In his 1948 NAACP speech, Ewing reflected on the accomplishment of integrating Gallinger: "I have been amazed at the amount of publicity which the episode received. On all sides it has been hailed as a great victory for the colored race—a mighty blow against racial discrimination." He admitted, however, that "nothing very fundamental is solved by one Government-controlled hospital in the District of Columbia. What we must aim for is to fight racial discrimination on every front—in every State of the Union." Ewing identified African Americans as primary beneficiaries of the president's health plan, which sought to "bring the cost of adequate medical care within reach of almost every citizen—white and Negro alike" and would focus on "the rural areas and small communities where so much of our Negro population is concentrated." Ewing cited the recent expansion of maternal and child health services in rural areas as an important advance for black mothers and children but urged further extension of public health protection to reach the millions of black residents of the twelve hundred rural counties still without public health services. Ewing also assured the NAACP audience that the Truman administration's program to recruit and train more medical personnel "would be operated with special reference to the needs of our ten percent Negro population. It would aid in abolishing one of the most flagrant abuses of our present medical training system." Ewing campaigned so ardently for Truman that he offended the National Urban League just before the 1948 election. When Ewing declared to the Urban League's national conference that any Negro who did not vote for Truman was "betraying his race," executive director Lester Granger retorted, "This is the first time in the history of our annual conference that such a thing has happened, and I cannot allow this occasion to pass without deploring the impropriety and misuse of your invitation."[12]

The trajectory of Ewing's career at the Federal Security Agency illustrates the variety of forces that dogged the Truman administration's domestic policy agenda, particularly its health plan. Both the AMA and its North Carolina affiliate claimed that Washington liberals such as Parran, Pepper, and Ewing had trumped up a health crisis as an excuse to expand federal power. As conservative Democrats and Republicans increased their cooperation to roll back the New Deal, Truman administration liberals increasingly found themselves on the defensive. Conservatives used similar strategies to block national health insurance and the civil rights movement. In both cases, opponents gained popular support by appealing to the powerful symbolism of the anticommunist crusade and by portraying proposed reforms as unwelcome change imposed by a tyrannical minority. Along with the SCHW and the NAACP, Pepper was part of the Popular Front that had thrived during the New Deal but had to defend itself in the late 1940s against charges of communism amid rising domestic and international tensions. Senator Theodore Bilbo of Mississippi called the SCHW the "number one enemy of the South," and the House Un-American Activities Committee issued a June 1947 report alleging that the SCHW was "merely a pliable instrument in the hands of the Communist wirepullers." The *Saturday Evening Post* had already billed the Florida senator as "Pink Pepper" in 1946, and by the end of the decade, he had become a pariah for his advocacy of national health insurance, Truman's civil rights reforms, and especially a pro-Stalinist position in foreign policy. He was defeated for reelection in 1950 with no small help from the AMA. In a speech during what proved to be his last year in the Senate, Pepper declared, "I cast my lot with human rights rather than for the preservation of state wrongs, let the consequences be what they may."[13]

Even more than Pepper, Ewing earned both the strong admiration of black physicians and the ire of the AMA. The National Medical Association praised the Federal Security Agency as "the most liberal Government agency" and touted Ewing's record of expanding career opportunities for black professionals within federal agencies, particularly the PHS. The PHS commissioned black officers and accepted black interns at the marine hospitals, and two African Americans served in high-ranking positions: Walter H. Maddux, medical officer in the Division of Chronic Diseases, and Hildrus A. Poindexter, an expert on child health and tropical disease who directed the PHS mission in Liberia and later served in Suriname, Iraq, Libya, Jamaica, and Sierra Leone.[14]

In contrast, the AMA-affiliated *North Carolina Medical Journal* complained about "the distinctly 'left' hand of the U.S.P.H.S. and other federal bureaus [that were] marching up and down the land—and even visiting foreign lands— stumping for compulsory federal sickness insurance and government control of medicine." White organized medicine's feelings toward Ewing were captured

TABLE 10.1

Federal and State Contributions to Public Health Spending, 1935, 1950, and 1964 (in millions of dollars)

	1935			1950			1964		
	FED.	STATE/LOCAL	TOTAL	FED.	STATE/LOCAL	TOTAL	FED.	STATE/LOCAL	TOTAL
Maternal/child health	0	7	7	20	10	30	59	151	209
School health	0	10	10	0	31	31	0	160	160
Other public health	7	112	119	68	291	359	224	395	619
TOTAL	7	119	136	88	332	420	283	706	988

Source: Congress and the Nation 1945–1964 (Washington, D.C.:Congressional Quarterly, 1965), 1114.

Maternal and child health includes programs for crippled children.

in the title of a 1950 *Saturday Evening Post* profile, "The Man Doctors Hate." Beginning with the question "Who's the most tactless man in Washington?" and proceeding through an unapologetic hatchet job, Paul F. Healy called Ewing "the peripatetic barker for the Truman welfare state" and "a popular whipping boy" on Capitol Hill. Even the lead photograph of Ewing was extremely unflattering, catching him open-mouthed, in midgesture. Like conservative AMA leaders, southern Democrats loathed Ewing for his close ties with Truman and his liberal views on the proper role of the federal government. Primarily out of personal spite against Ewing, these southerners joined forces with Republicans, backed by the AMA, to vote 60–32 in 1950 to block a proposed reorganization plan to elevate the Federal Security Agency into a cabinet-level Department of Health, Education, and Security.[15]

Despite such setbacks, Ewing and liberal health reformers had much to celebrate by 1950. With Ewing's backing, PHS representatives had forced states to give greater attention to the health needs of minorities, such as when the PHS disapproved North Carolina's state Hill-Burton plan because it did not include enough hospital beds for blacks. Although the PHS changed its interpretation of Hill-Burton's nondiscrimination clause three times during the program's first year, it convinced southern states to provide care to blacks in biracial rather than racially separate hospital facilities. Another important achievement under Ewing and Truman was passage of the 1950 amendments to the Social Security Act that substantially liberalized benefits and expanded coverage to include an additional 10 million citizens, including regularly employed agricultural workers and domestic workers.[16]

Parran's postwar goal of "providing modern [public] health services for the one-third of our counties and the 40 million of our people now lacking them" had been largely achieved as federal support for state and local health departments reached its apogee. Since the 1933 inauguration of major federal aid to public health and sanitation, total spending (excluding facilities construction, medical research, and medical care programs) had increased from $7 million in 1935 to $88 million in 1950 and would reach $283 million by 1964 (tables 10.1 and 10.2). State and local spending for public health also rose substantially, from $119 million in 1935 to $332 million in 1950 and $706 million by 1964, but the ratio of federal to nonfederal funds steadily mounted throughout the period. By 1960, the total annual PHS appropriation had quadrupled since the war to $840 million.[17]

Federal programs spurred state efforts, and by 1950, mental hygiene, heart

TABLE 10.2

Federal Funding for Public Health Programs, 1950–1964
(in millions of dollars)

	1950	1955	1960	1964
Grants to states				
General	14.1	13.1	24.7	14.0
Maternal and child health	11.2	11.9	17.4	27.3
Crippled children	7.6	10.6	17.1	27.7
Venereal disease	12.4	3.0	6.4	5.9
Tuberculosis	6.8	6.0	5.3	2.9
Environmental sanitation	1.0	3.7	2.7*	4.5†
Mental health	3.3	2.3	4.9	6.7
Cancer	3.2	2.2	2.2	3.4
Heart disease	1.8	1.1	2.9	6.1
Alaska‡	1.3	1.2	0.0	0.0
Chronic diseases	0.0	0.0	0.0	11.6
Radiological health	0.0	0.0	0.0	1.8
TOTAL PHS GRANTS TO STATES (excluding construction)	62.7	55.1	83.6	111.9
Hill-Burton hospital construction	57.1	74.6	143.4	152.0
Non-H-B construction	0.0	0.0	46.8§	90.0**
PHS GRANTS TO STATES (all sources)	119.8	129.7	273.8	353.9
Communicable disease center	7.5	4.6	8.7	8.4
Vocational rehabilitation	24.7††	25.6	48.6	87.6‡‡
TOTAL	152.0	159.9	331.1	449.9

Source: Annual Reports of the Federal Security Administration (1950) and the Department of Health, Education, and Welfare (1955, 1960, 1964). Figures for state grants are based on checks issued and may be slightly lower than appropriated amounts.

* For water pollution control. The PHS received an additional $15.7 million for sanitary engineering activities other than grants-in-aid.

† For water pollution control. The PHS received an additional $4.2 million for environmental health, $12.9 million for air pollution control, and $9.0 million for milk, food, interstate, and community sanitation other than grants-in-aid.

‡ For mobile health units.

§ $6.5 million for construction of mental health facilities in Alaska, $40.3 million for construction of waste treatment works.

** For construction of waste treatment works.

†† Medical rehabilitative services accounted for approximately $4.0 million, or one-sixth of the total.

‡‡ Medical rehabilitative services accounted for approximately $20.0 million, or just under one-quarter of the total.

FIGURE 10.1
Full-Time Local Public Health Services, 1950

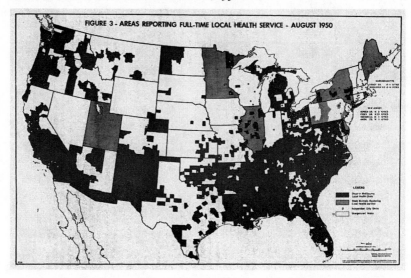

Source: Josephine R. Campbell and Kathryn J. Connor, *Variations in State Public Health Programs during a Five-Year Period* (Washington, D.C.: U.S. Public Health Service, Bureau of State Services, Division of State Grants, 1952), 31.

disease, and chronic disease programs had been inaugurated in all states but one. State dental, industrial hygiene, and malaria and mosquito control programs also expanded, but venereal disease control had receded, and tuberculosis was the only infectious disease that remained a high priority. The force of full-time tuberculosis control personnel in state health departments more than doubled from 1946 to 1950, and they had moved decisively into rural areas. Of the six states with the most staff in TB programs, three were southern: Tennessee (fifty-three), Georgia (thirty-five), and Virginia (thirty-five). With one-quarter of the nation's population, the eleven former Confederate states received one-third of PHS appropriations for general public health services. By 1948, the South enjoyed the broadest full-time public health coverage of any region (fig. 10.1).[18]

Such programs had contributed significantly to closing the mortality gaps between races, regions, and rural and urban dwellers (table 10.3). From 1933 to 1950, the death rate for blacks had been nearly cut in half, except in the rural South, but probable underreporting in the 1930s may have obscured gains there as well. In 1933, age-adjusted mortality for black urban southerners had been twenty-eight per thousand population; by 1950, black mortality was between

TABLE 10.3

Age-Adjusted Mortality by Race, Region, and Rural-Urban Residence, 1931–1933 and 1950

Deaths per thousand persons: age-adjusted

RESIDENCE AND GROUP	1931–33 SOUTH	1931–33 NORTH	1950 SOUTH	1950 NORTH
Urban				
Nonwhite	27.81	22.62	15.07	14.19
White	16.33	14.18	9.73	10.09
Rural				
Nonwhite	17.22	23.81	12.88	12.08
White	11.22	12.02	8.34	8.72
Nonwhite rate more than white rate, percent				
Urban	70.3	59.5	54.9	40.6
Rural	53.5	98.1	54.9	38.5

Source: Goldstein, "Longevity," 90.

Rates adjusted to the age distribution of the total continental population of the United States in 1950. South includes Alabama, Arkansas, the District of Columbia, Florida, Georgia, Kentucky, Louisiana, Maryland, Mississippi, North Carolina, Oklahoma, and South Carolina. North includes Illinois, Indiana, Michigan, Massachusetts, New Jersey, New York, Ohio, Pennsylvania, and West Virginia. Beginning in 1950, the U.S. Census defined *urban* as having ten thousand or more inhabitants, *rural* as having fewer than ten thousand.

twelve and fifteen for rural and urban, North and South—exactly where white mortality had stood in 1933. Rural-urban and regional differences were now negligible, and racial disparities remained but were much narrower (overall mortality was about 1.5 times higher for blacks in the South and 1.4 times higher in the North). The campaign to equalize black, rural, and southern health had achieved remarkable success.

Parran, Pepper, and other liberal health reformers had succeeded during World War II in uniting the country behind at least some of their goals for national health reform by casting health as an integral aspect of national defense, and Ewing continued to emphasize the close relationship between the social and military aspects of national security. "We know how to split the atom," he said in a 1950 speech, "but we have not yet learned to feed hungry people even when there is a surplus of food in the world. . . . If we, here in the United States, revitalize our revolutionary credo, we can meet the challenge of communism head-on; we can build the moral equivalent of the H-Bomb." The strategy of enlisting social welfare policy in the nation's defense against communism would become a hallmark of Old Left consensus liberalism during the Cold War. Yet by the early 1950s, the vast New Deal expansion of public health services had reached a plateau. Foreign affairs once again pushed domestic issues aside as communist revolutionaries toppled Chiang Kai-shek's government in 1949 and the United States entered the Korean War the following year.[19]

Despite Ewing's depth of experience as Truman's right-hand man in domestic social policy, Ewing's 1952 campaign for the Democratic presidential nomination was doomed from the start. Ewing emphasized the progress Americans had made under the Roosevelt and Truman administrations and told the Boston Chamber of Commerce, "In 1932 the people of America were looking for bread; in 1952 they're looking for a parking place." Ewing also repeatedly attacked General Dwight Eisenhower as either ignorant or willfully duplicitous regarding health and welfare issues. "It is tragic," declared Ewing, "to see the distinguished military leader pushed this way and that by various selfish groups without his having any apparent knowledge of the facts involved. In this instance, the high priced public relations hirelings of the American Medical Association seem to have made a captive of the General." Ewing sarcastically observed, "Candidate Eisenhower's sudden solicitude for the welfare of our older citizens is indeed touching. Only a few years ago he said: 'If all Americans want is security, then they can go to prison. They'll have enough to eat, a bed, and a roof over their heads.'" Ewing harshly criticized Republican opposition to measures benefiting the elderly under Social Security and warned, "It will be a sad day for our older citizens if Eisenhower and a Republican Congress are elected in November."[20]

After Eisenhower's election and the Supreme Court decision in *Brown v. Board of Education*, an antifederalist backlash ensued, affecting not only public education but also other areas where segregation was endangered, including health care. At the height of the McCarthy hearings in 1953, the U.S. government withdrew its appointment of Cecil Sheps to the WHO as a result of Sheps's suspected communist leanings. Sheps, a UNC professor of public health who had been instrumental in establishing a statewide medical center at Chapel Hill, had served as one of WHO's first international health researchers. He weathered the attack on his patriotism, but it symbolized the extent to which public health and universal health care had fallen into disrepute after Truman left office. Even proposals to fluoridate local water supplies were suspected of having communist origins. Until a more favorable political environment for health-care and civil rights reform emerged in Congress, Ewing was the first high-ranking federal official to fully commit himself and his agency to reducing economic and racial inequities in health care.[21]

RACIAL DISPARITIES AFTER DELUXE JIM CROW

Had national health insurance been adopted in the early 1950s, it probably would have been implemented within the bounds of segregation. After hopes for universal health coverage died in 1953, black organized medicine shifted its attention to the desegregation of hospitals and mainline medical societies, especially after the *Brown* decision pointed to a renewed federal commitment to civil rights. White physicians in the Medical Society of the State of North Carolina expressed their alarm over "the explosive potentialities of the implementation of the recent Supreme Court decision in attempting to hasten [the] healthy, certain, and evolutionary development" of equal opportunity for blacks in North Carolina. Beginning in the mid-1950s, southern black physicians were finally able to join the AMA when state affiliates amended racial restrictions on membership under pressure from both the national organization and black doctors at the local level. After five years of discussions with leaders of the Old North State Medical Society, the Medical Society of the State of North Carolina finally voted to offer "scientific membership" to black doctors in May 1955, allowing them to attend educational presentations and business meetings but barring them from the society's social functions.[22]

Despite the relatively smooth progress of gradual desegregation in health care and medical education, southern whites responded to *Brown* by heightening their resistance to integration, particularly any federal intervention to enforce civil rights for black citizens. Under deluxe Jim Crow, southern apologists and many black leaders had downplayed race and emphasized the region's poverty to elicit the nation's sympathy; now, the South's racism was a national disgrace as the news media depicted to audiences around the globe the violence and gross human rights violations that unfolded in Little Rock, Arkansas, and "Bombingham," Alabama. Such exposure proved essential for motivating the president and Congress to act decisively on behalf of federal civil rights legislation. But as the South lost face and relinquished its "most-favored region" status, the issue of racial and regional disparities in health was eclipsed as well.

Medical civil rights leaders, southern liberals, and national figures such as Oscar Ewing, Michael M. Davis, and Henry Wallace had consistently emphasized the racial and regional dimensions of death and disease rates, and the Hill-Burton program had required states to carefully measure and analyze the supply and distribution of health professionals and facilities within their borders. But in the decades that followed, race and region virtually disappeared as categories of analysis in health-care policy and political debate, even during the tumultuous Great Society years. Health care was largely absent from the 1960s civil rights agenda. Physicians and policy makers commonly assumed that medical science was universal and that practice had become standardized nationwide, and they had little sense of local or regional variations in health outcomes. The work of John E. Wennberg and the development of health-care quality assessment as a discipline within health services research during the 1980s revealed major variations in the utilization and costs of health care among regions, localities, and institutions. But such studies focused primarily on bringing rising health-care costs down and improving the efficiency of the health-care system, not on addressing disparities among racial or geographic population groups as a social justice or civil rights problem. Not until 1985, with the release of secretary of health and human services Margaret Heckler's *Report of the Secretary's Task Force on Black and Minority Health*, did racial health disparities per se again receive a level of scrutiny from public officials equal to that of the deluxe Jim Crow era. Subsequently, however, discussions of racial and ethnic health disparities have been decoupled from the historically unique circumstances of the South's dominance of Congress as well as federal health policy during the deluxe Jim Crow era. No similarly powerful political force has yet emerged to compel a recognition of health disparities as a national problem.[23]

This amnesia and lack of progress in addressing health differentials during the past three decades has been accompanied by the telescoping of racial disparities that began in the early twentieth century, receded at midcentury, and accelerated again after integration. Based on his work with the Committee on the Costs of Medical Care, Isadore Falk estimated in 1934 that private individually purchased medical service was out of reach for 75 to 90 percent of the population, including virtually all 12 million U.S. blacks. In 1940, only 9 percent of Americans were covered by hospital insurance; by 1950, fully half were. The proportion of insured Americans reached 83 percent in 1975 and had improved little by 2001, when 41.7 million Americans (15 percent of the population) were uninsured; 53 percent of the uninsured were racial minorities. Thus, while the number and percentage of Americans outside the modern private health system declined dramatically during the intervening period, the percentage of minorities among those who could not afford medical care rose significantly. Likewise, although the infant mortality rate declined substantially for both blacks and whites, the rate for blacks was 1.6 times that for whites in 1950 but 2.5 times as great by 2000. At the beginning of the twenty-first century, the best-off Americans still lived thirty-three years longer on average than the worst-off.[24]

The most drastic example of this telescoping of health disparities is syphilis, which has become increasingly concentrated in the South and among African Americans, who experience the disease at rates thirty to fifty times those among whites. By 1998, according to surgeon general David Satcher, 50 percent of new cases of syphilis were reported in less than 1 percent of U.S. counties, two-thirds of them in the South. Although Satcher considered the concentration of syphilis in a handful of southern counties "a real golden opportunity" to focus control efforts, this phenomenon resembles the early twentieth-century southernization of communicable diseases that had previously affected a broad demographic and geographic swath of Americans but later became concentrated among rural southern minorities. Likewise, acquired immunodeficiency syndrome (AIDS) was initially most prevalent in the urban North and West Coast but has subsequently devastated rural black and Latino populations, especially women. By 1998, more cases of HIV infection were diagnosed among black and Hispanic heterosexual men than among gay white men.[25]

One major reason that the problem of significant racial disparities in morbidity, mortality, and life expectancy persists into the twenty-first century is that legally sanctioned segregation, despite its myriad deleterious social and psychic effects, was not the principal cause of racial disparities in health, nor was access to medical care the primary determinant of life expectancy during most of the twentieth century. Consequently, the greatest narrowing of twentieth-century health disparities was achieved not after the integration of health care in the mid-1960s but under deluxe Jim Crow health policy, which paired measures that materially improved the health of all medically underserved populations with rhetoric that prioritized the equalization of health differentials as essential for protecting the nation's economic and military security.

conclusion

DELUXE JIM CROW

IN EDUCATION VERSUS

HEALTH CARE

The act of separation and the act of segregation in
and of itself denies [black schoolchildren] equal
educational opportunities which the Fourteenth
Amendment secures. Here we abandon any claim . . .
of any constitutional inequality which comes from
anything other than the act of segregation itself.

Robert Carter, attorney for the plaintiffs in *Brown v.
Board of Education of Topeka, Kansas*, December 9, 1952

T he rise and fall of the ideology of equalization among both blacks and
whites provided the backdrop for racial change during the era of deluxe
Jim Crow. Beginning in the 1930s, the southern movement to equalize black
and white schools was black-led (primarily by the National Association for the
Advancement of Colored People [NAACP]), never secured federal funding, and
garnered only lukewarm commitment at the state level from whites primarily
bent on protecting segregation. Blacks, however, gave educational equalization their wholehearted support: the Louisiana Farmers' Union, for example,
endorsed the Harrison-Fletcher Bill in 1938. The Farmers' Union agent who
testified at the Senate hearings heard from a member who wrote that aid for
rural schools was "one of the most important things you could have done for
us especially in West Feliciana Parish." By contrast, even the southern Senate
sponsors who coveted regional equalization of education balked at the price of

threatening segregation. But white self-interest in black health was much greater than in black education because, unlike illiteracy, most forms of disease were still contagious. Moreover, white employers had far more motivation to keep the black labor force free of sickness than of ignorance, since improved skills and knowledge might help blacks to compete with white workers or organize for better wages and working conditions.[1]

Equalization in education was motivated almost solely by whites' desire to quarantine rather than improve black education; increasing black health-care access not only deflected attacks on segregation but also served a variety of other, broader purposes that sustained white commitment over several decades. Until the 1930s, the South's hospitals had been as racially separate and unequal as its schools, except that in many rural communities, no hospital existed for either race. But white medical schools needed patients for clinical training, so teaching hospitals were often constructed near large indigent black populations and served both as volume providers of charity care and as referral centers for the surrounding region. The greater expense and increasing technological requirements of health care drove cost-conscious white policy makers to eschew wasteful duplication and build more efficient facilities that were shared by both races. Ironically, public policy in hospital construction built small biracial hospitals in rural areas, while in education, the school-consolidation movement gathered rural students into large, comprehensive schools but continued to separate them by race. In addition, the rationale of rural and regional uplift in health emphasized the universal benefits of federal aid to the South and defused whites' concerns about racial conflict, whereas the NAACP's leadership of the campaign to equalize southern education inherently threatened most southern whites. Equalization in education attempted to address both school facilities and teacher salaries but failed on both counts. In contrast, equalization as implemented in health care emphasized facilities construction and the extension of public health services but did not guarantee equal compensation or even staff privileges for black medical professionals, which had been precisely the goal of the earliest proposed nondiscrimination clauses in federal health legislation. Because the success of equalization in hospital care was conditioned on maintaining white control over its administration, equalization benefited black patients much more than black professionals. Although black doctors and especially nurses gained a foothold in white-run hospitals, the staffs at many hospitals that had received federal construction funds remained all-white into the 1960s. For example, Atlanta's

Grady Memorial Hospital did not admit a black intern to its staff until 1963 and did so only under threat of a lawsuit. The hospital continued to separate black and white patients within its walls until 1965.[2]

During the first two decades of federal aid to hospital construction beginning in 1933, the vast majority of existing black hospitals did not receive assistance. By raising the physical and technological standards for hospitals in the postwar era, Hill-Burton and its predecessors sped the demise of black hospitals, which typically ran on shoestring budgets and bore the burdens of outdated equipment and aging physical plants. At first glance, the attrition of black hospitals parallels the mass closings of black schools in the decades after *Brown*. When southern officials attempted to desegregate public education, they were forced to adapt the completely separate and grossly unequal buildings of black and white schools in each district. Black high schools that remained open were usually repurposed to accommodate middle or elementary students, resulting in the loss of cherished sources of identity and pride for the black community. In contrast to education, the availability of massive public aid to hospital construction facilitated a more gradual transition in the architecture of segregation, from the complete exclusion of black patients from most southern hospitals to spatial isolation of each race in completely separate buildings to partitioning of racial groups within shared structures via separate entrances, admitting areas, floors, wards, dining rooms, and restrooms. This intermediate phase of mixing black and white patients in the same structure while maintaining the veneer of segregation made the transition to full integration in health care much smoother than was the case in education, since deluxe Jim Crow institutions promoted more interracial contact among black and white health professionals than was possible among educators.[3]

In addition to promoting sustained rather than sudden change from seg-regation to integration in health care, another effect of the New Deal was to introduce principles of need- and race-based preferences into programs of federal aid. Such clauses were used in health programs to allocate services for blacks based on their percentage of the population. In *An American Dilemma*, Gunnar Myrdal criticized separate but equal clauses as a "compromise formula": "That Negroes and whites share in the benefits from the public economy in propor-tion to their numbers. This norm is in conflict with the Constitution, since it refers to the Negro *group* and does not guarantee *individuals* their right. It has its utility only as a practical yardstick in the fight against discrimination. Its very presence in the public debate, and sometimes in public regulations, is an indication of the existing discrimination." Although black leaders, particularly physicians in the National Medical Association (NMA), primarily had promoted federal enforcement of racial parity in health care during the late 1930s and early 1940s, the NAACP (particularly its northern wing) and the NMA began to unite behind integration after World War II, as the regional medical school crisis demonstrated.[4]

Louis Wright's public testimony on national health legislation illustrates the NAACP's gradual turning away from Charles Houston's original strategy of compelling southern states to equalize as a means of pursuing the ultimate goal of integration. Health policy historian David Barton Smith argues that by "forcing the letter of the law to be adhered to, requiring provisions for costly separate professional training, . . . NAACP strategists hoped to compel the conclusion that integration was the only cost-effective solution." In hospital construction, however, white policy makers could preserve segregation without costly duplication of separate facilities by adopting a new model: the biracial hospital that admitted patients of both races but segregated them internally by ward. As a result, Houston's strategy was more difficult to apply in health than in education, a complication Wright recognized early on. At the 1938 National Health Conference, Wright opposed allocating health funding or services according to racial population ratios and demanded that "any fundamentally sound program of health coverage must be based and administered per unit of health need, and not arbitrarily per unit of population." Yet he appeared to backpedal on this issue during his testimony at the 1939 Wagner National Health Bill hearings, since he proposed a clause stipulating that federal health funding was "never to be in smaller proportion to the whole sum than the minority bears to the total population."[5]

Wright's seeming inconsistency is a classic example of how the practical application of a policy can turn what was intended to be a floor into a ceiling: Wright wanted federal health programs to be administered on the basis of need rather than race, but given the racial realities of both congressional passage of health reform and the likelihood that any reform would be applied in the South by segregationist whites, he opted to propose a minimum guarantee of inclusion for blacks in federal programs. Using Wright's 1939 definition of nondiscrimination as equalization rather than integration, Hill-Burton was the first and only federal program to incorporate a guarantee of racial parity within segregated facilities. NAACP lawyers did not challenge the doctrine of separate but equal head-on as unconstitutional until the 1948 *Sipuel v. Oklahoma State Board of Regents* and *Sweatt v. Painter* cases. Until that time, the NAACP and other black organizations lobbied for a legislative definition of "nondiscrimination" as inclusion and parity in funding and services for blacks in areas that mandated segregation.[6]

As 1946 dawned, the NAACP issued a press release stating that special counsel Thurgood Marshall had pledged a "fight during 1946 for absolute equality of educational facilities and expenditures between Negro and white students in the southern states where segregation is required by law." The NAACP Legal Defense Fund intended to file as many cases as possible "below the Mason-Dixon line to compel equality in local school systems." After Truman took office, the administration proposed four major initiatives to equalize educational opportunity: general aid to states to maintain and operate primary and secondary public schools, aid to school housing, financial aid to low-income college students, and a national survey of community colleges, with the Department of Education within the Federal Security Agency charged with implementing and overseeing these programs. Oscar Ewing promoted Truman's proposals to aid southern education as relentlessly as he lobbied on behalf of the Truman health plan. He credited the president for making "consistent and stubborn efforts" to initiate federal aid to education, which would help address "tragically inadequate" opportunities for southern black schoolchildren as well as provide adequate resources for states that could not afford "to maintain decent education standards for *any* of their children." Only federal funding with a nondiscrimination clause "would make certain that all children—white or colored—within the jurisdiction of the State, would be given an equal opportunity to acquire an American education."[7]

The President's Commission on Civil Rights was a major catalyst for moving beyond the constricted quid pro quo of deluxe Jim Crow and addressing the broader implications of racial equity in health, education, and every other aspect of American life. After the publication of *To Secure These Rights* in 1947, Truman and the President's Commission received mixed reviews for taking a strong stand against racism. Aubrey Williams, an irascible southern radical who had headed the National Youth Administration under Franklin Roosevelt, congratulated Truman after the report of the President's Commission on Civil Rights was issued: "You've done so many great things I hesitate to pick out any one or a half a dozen and set them out from the rest. But from where I am down here in the deep South, your Civil Rights stand has been the greatest single happening in decent leadership that has occured [*sic*] since the Civil War. Nothing that has occured [*sic*] in my life time has given the reactionary over-lords down here such a drubbing as your unequivocal stand for equality and justice."[8]

Despite such encouragement, Ewing, Truman, and the Senate sponsors of federal aid to education faced opposition from both the left and the right. Isaiah Bowman, president of Johns Hopkins University, lamented that "the backwardness of elementary and secondary education in different parts of the country give ample opportunity for sentimental arguments." Although Bowman acknowledged that "national education is a direct contribution to national security," he judged the federal employees who would administer an aid-to-education program to be unequal "in training, character, disinterestedness and intelligence to those who rise to the top in our competitive education system." Civil servants were not educators but partisan bureaucrats who, once "ensconced in a safe berth," would "pontificate about things on which their judgment is worthless." Opponents of socialized medicine said precisely the same about government officials who would administer a national health program.[9]

In Bowman's view, the attempt to "secure uniformity by some universal scheme through the expenditure of money in backward portions of a country so vast as the United States" would yield "noncooperation of local communities and their complete and careless reliance upon Federal support." Likewise, Lester Granger, executive secretary of the National Urban League, objected that Truman's civil rights programs were inflaming animosity among the organization's white southern supporters and negatively affecting grassroots reform among southern blacks. Granger insisted that "constructive efforts in fields of social interest should be far removed from politics." The Urban League wanted to "stimulate the imagination of southern leadership with the vision of what *can* and *should* be done, rather than what is feared *cannot* be done."[10]

Granger and Bowman rejected what political scientist Howard M. Leichter has called "the Alabama syndrome," where liberals justify strong top-down federal control of proposed reform initiatives by casting all states, particularly those in the South, as "political Yahoos obstructing progressive social programs" and unresponsive to the needs of their poorest, least powerful citizens. As Bowman noted, "Everyone supposes that the local political condition may be so bad in some states that state control might be worse than Federal control," but he concluded that federal support would ultimately "mean the eventual abandonment of local responsibility everywhere[.] Such a danger to the very foundations of the schools, surely the most basic of our social institutions, ought to lead to a general state of alarm and of vigorous analysis of every project in or out of Congress for wholesale Federal aid to education."[11]

While Bowman and Granger objected to federal interference, the NAACP criticized Truman for failing to use his influence to ease the path of civil rights legislation. After Truman's reelection in November 1948, Roy Wilkins, the editor of the NAACP's *Crisis* magazine who would become the organization's executive secretary in 1955, wrote to Truman adviser David Niles, "I am sure I do not have to tell you that there has been a considerable change in the mood of colored people since January 1." He further objected that "the Federal aid to education bill and the housing bill contain no safeguards against racial segregation, and if passed in their present form unquestionably will put the power and the money of the Federal government behind segregated patterns of education and housing for years to come." Wilkins joined Cobb, Wright, and other medical integrationists who refused to accept the equalization of segregated facilities under deluxe Jim Crow policy as a legitimate fulfillment of African American civil rights. Even if southern states had ever actually achieved parity in the form of equal funding per capita and demonstrably comparable separate facilities for blacks and whites, civil rights proponents argued that such quantitative physical equality must not be the only basis for determining equal protection under the law, thereby rejecting the core principle of *Plessy v. Ferguson*.[12]

Richard Kluger begins his classic history of *Brown* with the observation that schools were "the largest, costliest, and most important public enterprise . . . in most American municipalities." He overlooks the role of government hospitals or public health programs. Health has been virtually invisible in scholarly as well as popular understandings of the civil rights movement, perhaps because there were no demonstrations or news coverage surrounding the much quieter (and more successful) process of hospital integration. That success was possible because federal aid to hospital construction, particularly the Hill-Burton program, fueled the expansion of hospital care for blacks by providing massive federal support for new infrastructure in health. Levels of state and federal funding also increased steadily throughout the Roosevelt, Truman, and Eisenhower administrations. In Hill-Burton, the federal share was initially capped at 33 percent but eventually increased to a maximum of 75 percent to enable more projects to be built in poor states and communities that had difficulty raising the required matching funds. But only hospital construction enjoyed large-scale federal sponsorship, since Congress never passed legislation to equalize southern education. Segregationists could accept biracial hospitals but not biracial schools. Conversely, neither black leaders nor northern Democrats would support federal aid to southern states that continued to separate pupils in all-black or all-white schools.[13]

The 1938 *Gaines* decision did, however, enable advocates of educational equalization to achieve some success at the state and local levels. During the decade after World War II, southern states substantially narrowed the racial gap in education spending. In 1945, southern white schools received four times as much funding as black schools did for physical plants and twice as much per student. White teacher salaries were one-third higher, and the seventeen states practicing segregation spent $42 million on transporting white students versus $1 million for black pupils. It was no surprise that whites graduated high school at four times the rate of blacks or that one-quarter of black Americans were functionally illiterate. But as the NAACP stepped up the pressure in the courts, state legislatures allocated more funding for equalization. For example, in the 1951 *Briggs v. Elliott* case in Clarendon County, South Carolina (later consolidated with *Brown v. Board of Education* and covered by that decision), the county school board acknowledged existing racial inequalities in school facilities and promised to rectify them under the state's new $40 million equalization program, to be funded with sales tax revenues.[14]

In a 1954 report, "The Bi-Racial Picture in Southern Education and Related Problems," southern state boards of education and chief school officers declared, "The South has been moving toward racial equalization of expenditures." Teacher salaries allegedly had been equalized in most states, and capital outlay expenditures were about two-thirds equalized by 1952 as a result of a flurry of new construction and upgrading of black schools. School and health facility equalization campaigns were sometimes even coordinated. In Memphis, Tennessee, for example, the construction of new black schools included basement space for auxiliary health centers where prenatal, well-child, tuberculosis, dental, and venereal disease clinics were held. The report's authors claimed that instructional expenditures in the South had been 43 percent equalized by 1940 and 75 percent equalized by 1952, even though the racial difference per pupil had risen from twenty-five dollars in 1940 to forty-two dollars in 1952. The degree of equalization differed significantly among states: some purported to have completely equalized expenditures, while others still spent 2.5 times as much on white students as on blacks. The greatest gaps in expenditures by race occurred in rural areas, and differentials tended to be greater in states with larger black populations.[15]

The alleged equalization was based on a leveling off of spending for white schools and an increase in new spending for black schools, and it excluded auxiliary resources and services such as bus transportation, cafeterias, and recreation facilities that had long ago become standard at white schools yet remained unavailable to many black students. Just as politicians can trumpet their success at reducing the annual deficit while doing nothing to pay down the national debt, the 1954 equalization report essentially emphasized a reduction in the racial differential in current education spending while the size of the southern states' regional debt to black schools remained staggering, since it had been accruing for more than fifty years. The disparity between white and black educational expenditures in the South in 1952 was estimated to total $85 million, with another $350 million needed to equalize buildings. The NAACP Legal Defense Fund attorneys for the plaintiffs in the five communities whose cases were decided as part of the *Brown* decision supported their arguments with exhaustive testimony and documentation that demonstrated that black students still endured grossly inferior conditions. Too many black school buildings remained crowded and dilapidated, without basic elements such as textbooks, desks, and indoor toilets.[16]

With direct federal aid to both medical education and primary and secondary education a dead issue by 1950 as a consequence of southerners' refusal to pass legislation with nondiscrimination clauses, the advent of the Cold War provided the Truman administration with another justification for pursuing a greater federal role in education. That year, the National Security Resources Board had designated the Federal Security Agency to oversee the participation of colleges and universities in the national defense manpower program, including the reduction of illiteracy as a key defense-related education problem. Ewing explained the new defense emphasis in education policy to the presidents of black land-grant colleges: "In the past few months events on the international front, as well as at home, have reinforced the Federal Security Agency's long-standing conviction that education is democracy's first line of defense—that all Americans, regardless of race or creed, should have free access to educational opportunity." He cited the growing number of court cases striking down discrimination in higher education and predicted, "The year 1950 may well have heard the death-knell for second-class citizenship in America's institutions of higher education. . . . Every injustice committed here in the United States against racial or religious groups becomes grist to the communist propaganda mill. Whatever their intention, Americans who aid and abet discrimination are writing copy for Radio Moscow." Ewing placed the equalization of educational opportunity in the context of American international prestige, insisting that "our status among the Nations of the world will be determined in no small degree by our success in making the most of our collective talents, without regard to race, religion, or economic position." Federal aid finally made a difference in southern education at the primary and secondary levels, through the back door of assistance to build and operate schools in areas affected by federal installations.[17]

Throughout the 1950s, both supporters and opponents of integration were unsure of the relationship between health and education in civil rights policy. If Ewing, given his strong record as a supporter of black equality, had remained the chief federal official overseeing health and education programs after the *Brown* decision, he likely would have pushed to end all separate but equal provisions. Instead, officials in the new Department of Health, Education and Welfare (HEW) under Secretary Oveta Culp Hobby and her successor, Marion B. Folsom, continued to insist that *Brown* had no direct application to health care and that they had no power to change the original interpretation of Hill-Burton's nondiscrimination clause unless Congress amended the legislation. Attempts by Representatives Thomas M. Pelly of Washington and Adam Clayton Powell of New York to amend a 1957 appropriations bill to deny Hill-Burton grants to facilities practicing segregation were defeated in the House by a 123–70 vote. With the appointment of Arthur S. Flemming as secretary in 1958, HEW began active efforts to promote desegregation in schools but not hospitals, presumably because hospitals were much farther along the path toward integration and because no official pronouncement comparable to the *Brown* decision had been delivered on health care, except for Truman's executive order desegregating the military, which included veterans' hospitals.[18]

Events involving South Carolina's military base schools and the Jackson, Mississippi, Veterans Administration hospital illustrate the uncertain path of federal efforts after the *Brown* decision to enforce desegregation where Washington should have had unquestioned authority: on and around military installations on federal property. In July 1943, Congress had amended the Lanham Act to provide funding to local school districts in war-affected areas for the maintenance and operation of regular school services and for extended school services for children of working mothers. In 1951, Congress expanded the scope and funding for the program to apply to "federally affected areas," including military and other federal installations. The program also favored the South, which by 1952–53 received 41 percent of funding for school construction and 35 percent for operation and maintenance. As in the Hill-Burton program, southern whites administered federal funds for schools in areas where defense installations had rapidly swelled the school-age population. Because the communities surrounding southern bases were segregated and offered poor-quality housing for blacks, many black servicemen chose to live on base. Therefore, a disproportionate number of children living on military property were black, but since there were relatively few schools located on bases, most children of military personnel attended surrounding local schools. The Department of Defense ended segregation at military base schools several months before the *Brown* decision, but off-base schools were not affected, even though they also received federal funds.[19]

In 1945 and 1957, South Carolina's legislature passed resolutions opposing federal aid to education as a threat to segregation that could lead to blacks taking control of white schools. Not until March 1962 did HEW secretary Abraham Ribicoff order that children who lived on federal installations (though not those living off base) could not attend segregated civilian schools, with that order to take effect by September 1963. Between twenty-five thousand and thirty thousand children and more than $3 million in federal funding were at stake in South Carolina alone, and Senator Strom Thurmond accused Ribicoff of "a flagrant act of economic blackmail." When Anthony J. Celebrezze succeeded Ribicoff later in 1962, the new secretary authorized a survey of segregated conditions on military installations and appropriated $2 million to execute it. Following HEW officials' inspections of Fort Jackson and other bases in early 1963, the agency announced that eight new federally operated elementary schools would open on military property, including two in South Carolina at Fort Jackson and Shaw Air Force Base.[20]

During the 1950s and 1960s, South Carolina received billions of dollars in defense funding for six military bases and the Savannah River Plant, which housed a plutonium reactor for manufacturing nuclear weapons. Historian Andrew H. Myers notes that "South Carolina received bountiful federal aid for education [in and around federal installations] despite the public protestations of state leaders" in part because "civil rights activists made an issue over federal aid to education whereas they did not do so for defense spending." Using a strategy first proposed by members of the President's Committee on Civil Rights, George Meany, president of the American Federation of Labor, advocated the denial of federal funds to school districts that failed to comply with the *Brown* decision. Congress considered an amendment to deny federal aid to schools in federally affected areas where segregation persisted. But Cold War fears of communism prevented this strategy from extending to advocating the closing of military bases in states that opposed the *Brown* decision.[21]

Mississippi, which joined South Carolina at the top of the list of states with highest percentage black population, also shared South Carolina's hard-bitten resistance to integration. In 1956, the Mississippi legislature authorized the formation of the Mississippi State Sovereignty Commission to protect segregation and monitor its opponents. Earl Evans Jr., president pro tempore of the state senate and a member of the commission, identified the quandary posed by the more rapid pace of change in health care via federal influence: "It is inconceivable, inconsistent and ridiculous for the people of Mississippi to resist by every 'lawful means' integration of the races in one phase of our social life [public education] and to accept, without a fight, non-segregation in another and equally vital part of our southern way of life [the integrated Veterans Administration Hospital in Jackson]." Just as integrationists had had to compromise to secure the benefits of federal health reform during the 1940s, Mississippi segregationists now pledged their opposition to integration and federal intrusion but capitulated to wide-spread political support for federal aid to construct a new integrated facility to replace the existing overcrowded, dilapidated veterans' hospital.[22]

Mississippi offers an excellent comparison of the results of racial equalization in hospitals versus schools. In education, equalization failed to close the enormous gap between black and white schools because state funding was insufficient and unfairly administered at the local level and because white Mississippi officials refused to consider federal funding that might endanger the segregated school system that equalization was intended to protect. The racial gap in southern hospital facilities, though significant, was less pronounced than in education and was therefore easier to close because in so many communities across the region, both blacks and whites were starting from ground zero. Mississippi's 1940 ratios of hospital beds to population were the lowest in the country for both blacks and whites. The equalization of hospital facilities was more successful because it attracted high levels of federal as well as state and local funding and garnered widespread support from southern whites who believed that segregation was protected and from southern blacks who believed that they would gain equal access to desperately needed hospital care.

Mississippi, the first state to complete a hospital with Hill-Burton support, appropriated $4 million (7 percent of its 1947–48 state budget) in matching funds for the first two years of its building program. Between 1940 and 1950, Mississippi expanded the number of general hospital beds for blacks by 216 percent, increasing the ratio of hospital beds from about 0.5 per thousand black residents to 1.7. David T. Beito notes that "health facilities in the [majority-black Delta] counties of Bolivar, Coahoma, Sunflower, and Washington obtained $4.6 million from the federal government [from 1948 through 1965], [which] enabled the non-fraternal hospitals to upgrade their equipment and add more than 450 beds." Mississippi, the poorest, most rural state with the largest percentage black population and the fewest hospital beds per capita, received the most Hill-Burton funding per capita.[23]

Alongside federal agencies and black reformers, private institutions and foundations also played an important role in desegregating southern health care and education. Although they are often portrayed as reluctant to embrace integration, most of the largest philanthropies had by the 1960s adopted policies of actively promoting desegregation by refusing to grant funds to organizations that maintained official policies of discrimination. The trustees of the Ford Foundation, for example, limited its matching grants in education to institutions that enrolled black students. Emory University, which had played a major role in the Southern Regional Education Board by accepting state funds to train out-of-state white medical students from member states, made the unprecedented move in 1961 of suing the state of Georgia to protect its right to admit a black student to its dental school without incurring taxes on its private endowment—the penalty prescribed by the state constitution if a private university established for whites chose to admit a nonwhite student. The court upheld Emory's right to admit blacks.[24]

If the goal of southern educational equalization had been to raise black schools and teacher salaries on par with those of southern whites, equalization in health aimed to bring access to medical care for both black and white southerners, particularly in rural areas, in line with the rest of the country. The success of racial equalization in health care was predicated on and at times subsumed by a politically savvy rationale of rural and regional uplift that emphasized the universal benefits of federal aid to southern health and defused whites' concerns over racial conflict. Though never fully realized, federally sponsored racial and regional equalization in health policy transcended the limits imposed by white policy makers and ultimately lay the foundation for eliminating formal racial barriers in the health-care system.

The passage of the Civil Rights Act of 1964 and the Medicare-Medicaid amendments to Social Security in 1965 together fulfilled the goals of deluxe Jim Crow reformers by helping to meet the needs of millions of poor and minority Americans who had been excluded from the private health system on the basis of both race and income. But some liberals subsequently considered Medicare and Medicaid failures because they left fee-for-service medicine basically intact. This development fulfilled the 1940s prediction of reformers Selz Mayo and Michael M. Davis that two separate systems and standards of treatment would adversely affect the quality of care for all patients. Other critics argue that Medicare-Medicaid unduly burdened health professionals with complex, restrictive guidelines and administrative responsibilities; promoted wasteful spending and inefficiency; undermined the preexisting system of voluntary charity care; and lowered the quality of treatment for private patients while increasing their tax burden. In his evaluation of Great Society health reforms, policy historian Allen J. Matusow concludes, "Medicare-Medicaid represented a ruinous accommodation between reformers and vested interests, in this case the organized doctors." Although most observers agree that Medicare and Medicaid together increased the accessibility of health care for the poor, Matusow claims that the services provided were not necessarily better than or even equal to the more cost-effective charity medicine that doctors and hospitals had rendered before federal intervention. As a visit to any hospital's emergency room will demonstrate, today's health-care system still bears the imprint of deluxe Jim Crow: we have expanded access to medical care through political compromise, but even nearly half a century after federally mandated racial integration, a two-tiered system preserves segregation on the basis of class rather than race.[25]

Deluxe Jim Crow Organizations

ORGANIZATION	TYPE	DESCRIPTION	LEADERSHIP
American Hospital Association (AHA)	Medical	organization to promote the interests of hospitals, critical in passing Hill-Burton	Rufus Rorem, George Bugbee
American Medical Association (AMA)	Medical	professional organization of physicians, opposed national health insurance	Morris Fishbein (*JAMA* editor)
American Public Health Association (APHA)	Medical	professional organization of public health professionals, supported national health insurance	Paul B. Cornely (president 1968), Thomas Parran (president 1936)
American Red Cross (ARC)	Medical	Segregated blood supply during World War II	Charles Drew, medical director of dried blood plasma campaign
Communicable Disease Center (CDC)	Federal Agency, Medical	Federal public health research agency, Atlanta	Joseph Mountin (established Malaria Control in War Areas program), Raymond Vonderlehr (director 1947–51)
Commission on Interracial Cooperation (CIC)	Southern reform	Southern liberal initiative to promote racial harmony	Will Alexander

ORGANIZATION	TYPE	DESCRIPTION	LEADERSHIP
Committee on the Costs of Medical Care (CCMC)	Medical, Research	Conducted first broad statistical study of American health care, urged comprehensive regional planning and government-funded insurance	Michael Davis, Rufus Rorem
Committee for Research in Medical Economics (CRME)	Medical, Research	Founded by medical economist Michael M. Davis to promote research on health care financing and access, supported national health insurance	Michael Davis
Department of Interior	Federal Agency, Medical	Oversaw Indian health (pre-1955), Howard University and Freedmen's Hospital (pre-1941)	Harold Ickes (secretary)
Farm Security Administration (FSA)	Federal Agency	Oversaw rural health cooperatives for farm families receiving FSA assistance	Will Alexander (administrator), Michael Davis (consultant), Frederick Mott (medical officer), Milton Roemer (medical officer), R. C. Williams (medical officer)
Federal Hospital Council (FHC)	Federal Agency, Medical	Created as an advisory body to the surgeon general in the administration of the Hill-Burton Act	Members: Melville Broughton, Michael M. Davis, Albert Dent, Frank Porter Graham

ORGANIZATION	TYPE	DESCRIPTION	LEADERSHIP
Federal Security Agency	Federal Agency, Social Welfare	Created in 1941 with oversight of Department of Education, Social Security Administration, PHS, Howard University, Freedmen's Hospital	Oscar Ewing, Paul McNutt
Freedmen's Hospital (Washington, D.C.)	Medical	federally supported, only D.C. hospital where black physicians could admit patients	
Gallinger Hospital (Washington, D.C.)	Medical	public hospital in D.C., admitted black patients on segregated basis, Ewing opened to black interns in 1947	
Harlem Hospital	Black, Medical	public hospital in New York City	Louis Wright (chief surgeon)
Howard University	Black, Education, Medical	Black medical school, Washington, D.C.	Numa Adams (first black president), Edwin Embree (board member), Abraham Flexner (board member and chair)
Meharry Medical College	Black, Education, Medical	Black medical school, Nashville, Tennessee	John J. Mullowney, M. Don Clawson, Harold West

ORGANIZATION	TYPE	DESCRIPTION	LEADERSHIP
National Association for the Advancement of Colored People (NAACP)	Black	led fight to integrate medical care and open opportunities for black health professionals, supported national health insurance, adopted zero tolerance of segregation in 1946	W. Montague Cobb, Charles Houston (Legal Defense Fund), Thurgood Marshall (Legal Defense Fund), Walter White, Louis Wright (chair)
National Dental Association (NDA)	Black, Medical	organization of black dentists, supported national health insurance	Clifton O. Dummett
National Association of Colored Graduate Nurses (NACGN)	Black, Medical	organization of black nurses, fought discrimination against black nurses in military, supported national health insurance	Mabel Staupers
National Hospital Association (NHA)	Black, Medical	organization to promote the interests of hospitals, supported national health insurance	
National Medical Association (NMA)	Black, Medical	admitting rights for black doctors, supported national health insurance (post-1948), pro-integration	W. Montague Cobb (*JNMA* editor), John Kenney (*JNMA* editor), Herbert Marshall (first NMA president to support national health insurance)
National Negro Congress (NNC)	Black	supported national health insurance, pro-integration	John Davis

ORGANIZATION	TYPE	DESCRIPTION	LEADERSHIP
National Urban League (NUL)	Black	supported national health insurance, pro-integration	Lester Granger
North Carolina State Board of Health (NCSBH)	State Agency	brokered extensive federal-state-philanthropic cooperation	Watson Smith Rankin, John Ferrell, Carl Reynolds
North Carolina Medical Care Commission (NCMCC)	State Agency	State agency over-seeing hospital construction, medi-cal care	John Ferrell (executive secretary), William Rich, Paul Whittaker
North Carolina State College (NCSC)	Education	State college, Raleigh	Selz Mayo (Department of Rural Sociology)
President's Commission on the Health Needs of the Nation (PCHNN)	Federal Agency, Medical	Truman appointed to study health needs of the nation	Oscar Ewing
President's Committee on Civil Rights (PCCR)	Federal Agency, Black	Truman appointed to study civil rights, published *To Secure These Rights* (1947)	Frank Porter Graham
Rockefeller Foundation	Philanthropy	Funded southern health and educa-tion projects, includ-ing antihookworm crusade	John Ferrell

ORGANIZATION	TYPE	DESCRIPTION	LEADERSHIP
Rosenwald Fund	Philanthropy	Funded black health and education projects, including improvements to Meharry Medical College, study of rural southern syphilis that preceded Tuskegee Syphilis Study, Rosenwald Fellows program for advanced training of black medical teachers	Will Alexander (board), M. O. Bousfield (associate director), Michael Davis (director of medical services), Edwin Embree (executive secretary), Abraham Flexner, Rufus Rorem
Senate and Labor Education Committee (1946: Labor and Public Welfare)	Federal Government	Held hearings and brokered passage of federal health legislation	Allen Ellender, Lister Hill, James Murray, Claude Pepper, Elbert Thomas
Southern Conference for Human Welfare (SCHW)	Southern reform	Mississippi senator Theodore Bilbo called it the "number one enemy of the South"; joint investigation with NAACP of 1946 Columbia, Tennessee, mob violence against blacks; June 1947 House Un-American Activities Committee report alleged SCHW was communist-front organization, published *Southern Patriot*, with many health articles.	Will Alexander, Frank Porter Graham, Charles S. Johnson, Claude Pepper, Eleanor Roosevelt, Aubrey Williams
Southern Governors' Conference (SGC)	Regional Organization	Organization of southern governors	Melville Broughton, Milton F. Caldwell

ORGANIZATION	TYPE	DESCRIPTION	LEADERSHIP
Southern Policy Committee (SPC)	Political	Unofficial group of southern New Dealers in Washington, urged FDR to publish *Report on the Economic Conditions of the South*	Allen Ellender, Lister Hill, Claude Pepper
Southern Regional Council (SRC)	Southern reform	Southern liberal initiative to promote racial harmony	Will Alexander, Charles S. Johnson, Aubrey Williams
Southern Regional Education Board (SREB)	Education	Founded to avoid desegregation of southern universities, became progressive force for training black doctors and promoting civil rights enforcement	
Tuskegee Institute	Black, Education	Site of PHS Tuskegee Syphilis Study, origin of National Negro Health Week in 1915, site of Tuskegee veterans' hospital, polio clinic, training center for black physicians, medical director Dr. Eugene Dibble was lone black supporter of black veterans' hospital in 1940s and testified before PCHNN in 1952	Eugene Dibble, John Kenney

ORGANIZATION	TYPE	DESCRIPTION	LEADERSHIP
U.S. Army Medical/Nurse Corps (AMC)	Medical, Military	Enlisted black doctors and nurses	Colonel M. O. Bousfield (commanding officer, Fort Huachuca, Arizona Station Hospital)
U.S. Public Health Service (PHS)	Federal Agency, Medical	Federal agency overseeing national health policy	Roscoe Brown, Leroy Burney, Vane Hoge, Joseph Mountin, Thomas Parran, Leonard Scheele, Raymond Vonderlehr
University of North Carolina (UNC)	Education	State university, Chapel Hill	Frank Porter Graham (president), Gordon Gray (president), Edward MacGavran (dean of School of Public Health), Carl V. Reynolds (School of Public Health faculty), Milton Rosenau (first dean of School of Public Health), Cecil Sheps (School Public Health faculty, Director of Program Planning in Division of Health Affairs)
World Health Organization (WHO)	International agency, Medical, Research	Chartered in 1948 in conjunction with but separate from the United Nations	Leroy Burney, Thomas Parran, Cecil Sheps

Deluxe Jim Crow Individuals

NAME	PRINCIPAL ROLE	AFFILIATIONS	PERSONAL RELATIONSHIPS
Will Alexander	Head, Resettlement/FSA	CIC (director), Dillard University (founder and first president), federal Resettlement Administration (deputy director), FSA (administrator), Rosenwald Fund (board member), SCHW (board member), SPC, SRC (board member)	Dent, Embree, M. Davis, Hill, C. Johnson, Mott, Parran, Pepper, Roemer
Midian O. Bousfield	Editor, *JNMA*	NMA, Rosenwald Fund, U.S. Army Medical Corps	Cobb, J. Davis, M. Davis, Drew, Embree, C. Johnson, Kenney, Roemer, Sheps
J. Melville Broughton	Governor, N.C.	FHC, Southern Governors' Conference	Caldwell, Graham, Hill, Parran, Pepper, Rankin, Reynolds, Rosenau
Roscoe Brown	Chief specialist, PHS Bureau of Special Programs	NMA, PHS	Cobb, Drew, M. Davis, Kenney, Moore, Mott, Mountin, Roemer, Sheps, Vonderlehr, R. C. Williams, Wright

NAME	PRINCIPAL ROLE	AFFILIATIONS	PERSONAL RELATIONSHIPS
Leroy Burney	Director, mobile VD clinics in Ga.; chief, PHS Bureau of State Services; Indiana state health officer; assistant surgeon general; U.S. surgeon general (1957–61)	NIH, PHS, WHO	Parran, Vonderlehr
Millard Caldwell	Governor, Fla.; chair, Truman 1948 campaign; president, Council of State Governments; chair, National Governors' Conference; administrator, Civil Defense Administration (1950–52)	Southern Governors' Conference	Broughton, Hill, Kracke, Pepper, Thomas, Truman
M. Don Clawson	President, Meharry Medical College	Meharry, Southern Governors' Conference	Caldwell, Hill, Kracke, Pepper
W. Montague Cobb	Anatomist, Howard University; editor, *JNMA*; founder, joint NMA-NAACP desegregation campaign	Howard, NAACP, NMA	Cornely, Drew, J. Johnson, Kenney
Paul Cornely	Professor of public health, Howard University	APHA (first black president, 1968), Howard, NMA, PHS	Cobb, M. Davis, Drew, J. Johnson, Kenney, Roemer, Sheps, Wright
John P. Davis	Testified on behalf of national health legislation, urged equalization of southern education	National Negro Congress, SCHW	Bousfield, Wright

NAME	PRINCIPAL ROLE	AFFILIATIONS	PERSONAL RELATIONSHIPS
Michael M. Davis	Medical director, Rosenwald Fund; director, CCMC; director, CRME	CCMC (director), CRME (director), Rosenwald Fund (medical director)	Alexander, Cornely, Dent, Embree, Graham, Mott, Parran, Roemer, Rorem, Sheps, R. C. Williams
Albert Dent	President, Dillard University; administrator, Flint-Goodrich Hospital	FHC, NHA	Alexander, Broughton, M. Davis, Graham, C. Johnson, Rich
Charles Drew	Chief of surgery, Howard Medical School; medical director, Freedmen's Hospital, Washington, D.C.; opposed exclusion of black physicians from AMA and residencies; opposed segregation of blood supply in U.S. Army and American Red Cross	American Board of Surgery (examiner); American Red Cross dried plasma banking project (director); Blood for Britain blood banking project (director); dean's committee, Tuskegee VA Hospital; NMA surgical section (chair)	Bousfield, Cobb, Cornely, J. Johnson, Kenney, Wright
Allen Ellender	U.S. senator, La.	SPC	Hill, Murray, Pepper, Thomas
Edwin R. Embree	President, Rosenwald Foundation	GEB, Howard University, Rosenwald Fund	Alexander (coauthors of *The Collapse of Cotton Tenancy*), M. Davis, Flexner, C. Johnson,
Oscar Ewing	Administrator, Federal Security Agency (1947–53)	DNC (chair and 1952 Democratic presidential candidate)	Caldwell, E. Roosevelt, Truman
John Ferrell	Executive secretary, NCMCC	APHA, NCSBH, PHS, Rockefeller	Moore, Parran, Rankin, Reynolds

NAME	PRINCIPAL ROLE	AFFILIATIONS	PERSONAL RELATIONSHIPS
Abraham Flexner	Educator; medical education reformer	Carnegie, GEB, Rockefeller, Rosenwald Fund, Howard (board member, 1930–35)	
Frank Porter Graham	President, UNC; U.S. senator, N.C.	CCR, Federal Hospital Council, SCHW, SPC	Broughton, Ferrell, Hill, Pepper, Rankin, Reynolds, E. Roosevelt, Rosenau
Lester Granger	Executive director, National Urban League	Navy (advisor to Secretary of the Navy James Forrestal)	E. Roosevelt, Truman
Gordon Gray	Secretary of the army; president, UNC	UNC	Graham, Rankin, Reynolds
Lister Hill	U.S. senator, Ala.	Senate Subcommittee on Health, SPC	Ellender, Kracke, Mountin, Parran, Pepper
Harold Ickes	Secretary of interior	Freemen's Hospital, Howard	Alexander, Flexner, C. Johnson
Charles S. Johnson	Sociologist and president, Fisk University	Rosenwald Fund, SCHW (board member), SRC (board member), Urban League (founding editor of *Opportunity*)	Alexander, Embree, Graham
Joseph L. Johnson	Dean, Howard Medical School (1946–55)		Cobb, Cornely, Drew, E. Roosevelt
John Kenney	Editor, *JNMA*	NMA, Tuskegee	Bousfield, Cobb, Cornely

NAME	PRINCIPAL ROLE	AFFILIATIONS	PERSONAL RELATIONSHIPS
Roy Kracke	Dean, Medical College of Alabama		Caldwell, Hill, Kenney, Pepper, Thomas
Selz Mayo	Professor of rural sociology, N.C. Agricultural Experiment Station		Ferrell, McGavran, Rankin, Reynolds, Rosenau
Joseph Earle Moore	Professor of medicine and public health administration, Johns Hopkins (prointegration)	APHA, Hopkins, NRC, PHS	M. Davis, Flexner, Parran, Vonderlehr
Frederick Mott	Medical economist	FSA (medical officer), PHS	Alexander, M. Davis, Roemer, R. C. Williams
Joseph Mountin	Officer, PHS	APHA, CDC (established wartime MCWA), PHS	Cornely, M. Davis, Ferrell, Hill, Moore, Mott, Murray, Parran, Pepper, Rankin, Reynolds, Roemer, Vonderlehr, R. C. Williams
James Murray	U.S. senator, Mont.; sponsor, Wagner-Murray-Dingell bill	Senate Subcommittee on Health	Ellender, Hill, Pepper, Thomas
Thomas Parran	U.S. surgeon general	APHA, CDC, NIH, PHS, WHO	Alexander, M. Davis, Embree, Ferrell, Hill, Moore, Mott, Mountin, Murray, Pepper, Rankin, Reynolds, Roemer, Vonderlehr, R. C. Williams

NAME	PRINCIPAL ROLE	AFFILIATIONS	PERSONAL RELATIONSHIPS
Claude Pepper	U.S. senator, Fla.; worked with Parran on revised Lanham Act and Wartime Health and Education Committee; leading spokesman for national health insurance and federal aid to South	Senate Subcommittee on Health, SCHW, SPC	Caldwell, M. Davis, Ellender, Hill, Miller, Murray, Parran, Wallace
Watson Smith Rankin	State health officer, N.C. Board of Health	APHA, Bowman Gray School of Medicine, CCMC, Duke Endowment, NCSBH, PHS	M. Davis, Ferrell, Parran, Reynolds, Rich
Carl Reynolds	State health officer, N.C. Board of Health	APHA, NCSBH, PHS	M. Davis, Ferrell, Graham, Mountin, Parran, Poe, Rankin, Rich, Roemer, Rosenau
William Rich	Administrator, Lincoln Hospital, Durham	Duke Endowment, Lincoln Hospital, NCMCC, NHA	Dent, Ferrell, Rankin, Reynolds
Milton Roemer	Medical economist and rural health expert, Yale	FSA (medical officer), PHS (associate in medical care administration)	Alexander, Cornely, Davis, Mott, Parran, Sheps, R. C. Williams
C. Rufus Rorem	Medical economist	AHA (associate secretary), CCMC, Rosenwald Fund (associate medical director), University of Chicago (assistant dean)	Alexander, Dent, Embree, Mott, Parran, Roemer, Sheps

NAME	PRINCIPAL ROLE	AFFILIATIONS	PERSONAL RELATIONSHIPS
Eleanor Roosevelt	Wife, President Franklin Roosevelt; social reformer	SCHW, Howard (trustee), Urban League	Ewing, Flexner, Hill, J. Johnson, Miller, Pepper, Truman
Milton Rosenau	Dean, Harvard School of Public Health; founding dean, UNC School of Public Health	APHA, Harvard, UNC	Graham, Mayo, Rankin, Reynolds
Cecil Sheps	Faculty member, UNC SPH (1947–53); director, Program Planning in Division of Health Affairs	UNC, WHO	Cornely, Graham, Mayo, Rankin, Reynolds, Roemer
Elbert Thomas	U.S. senator, Utah; chair, Senate Committee on Labor and Public Welfare		Ellender, Hill, Kracke, Murray, Parran, Pepper
Harry S. Truman	U.S. president (1945–53)	Democratic Party, President's Committee on Civil Rights, President's Committee on the Nation's Health	Caldwell, Ewing, Granger, Hill, Murray, Pepper, Thomas
Raymond Vonderlehr	Head, PHS Division of VD; assistant surgeon general; site director, Tuskegee Syphilis Study; director, CDC (1947–51)	CDC, PHS, Tuskegee	Bousfield, M. Davis, Kenney, Moore, Mountin, Parran

NAME	PRINCIPAL ROLE	AFFILIATIONS	PERSONAL RELATIONSHIPS
Henry Wallace	Secretary of agriculture; vice president, ran on "Ten Extra Years" in 1948	Department of Agriculture, SCHW	Alexander, Pepper, A. Williams
Aubrey Williams	Executive director, National Youth Administration; deputy director, Works Progress Administration; enabled Birmingham Slossfield Clinic to get major federal grants during 1940s	FERA, SCHW (board member), SPC, SRC (board member)	Graham, E. Roosevelt, Pepper, Wallace
R. C. Williams	Helped organize FSA medical cooperatives	FSA (medical officer), PHS	Alexander, Davis, Mott, Parran, Roemer
Louis Wright	Chair, NAACP (1936–52); chief surgeon, Harlem Hospital; blocked Rosenwald Fund from building black hospital in NYC	NAACP	Cobb, Drew

U.S. and Southern Populations by Race and
Rural-Urban Residence, 1900–2000

	TOTAL POPULATION	RURAL	URBAN	BLACK	WHITE	AMERICAN INDIAN
U.S. 1900	76,212,168	45,997,336	30,214,832	8,833,994	66,809,196	237,196
%	100.0	60.4	39.6	11.6	87.9	0.3
South 1900	24,523,527	20,102,642	4,420,885	7,922,969	16,521,970	74,749
%	100.0	82.0	18.0	32.3	67.4	0.3
U.S. 1920	106,021,537	51,768,255	54,253,282	10,463,131	94,820,915	244,437
%	100.0	48.8	51.2	9.9	89.7	0.2
South 1920	33,125,803	23,825,748	9,300,055	8,912,231	24,132,214	75,914
%	100.0	71.9	28.1	26.9	72.9	0.2
U.S. 1940	132,164,569	57,459,231	74,705,338	12,865,518	118,214,870	333,969
%	100.0	43.5	56.5	9.8	89.8	0.3
South 1940	41,665,901	26,375,418	15,290,483	9,904,619	31,658,578	94,139
%	100.0	63.3	36.7	23.8	76.0	0.2
U.S. 1960	179,323,175	54,054,425	125,268,750	18,871,831	158,831,732	551,669
%	100.0	30.1	69.9	10.5	88.6	0.3
South 1960	54,973,113	22,812,863	32,160,250	11,311,607	43,476,636	127,568
%	100.0	41.5	58.5	20.6	79.1	0.2
U.S. 1980	226,545,805	59,494,813	167,050,992	26,495,025	188,371,622	1,420,400
%	100.0	26.3	73.7	11.7	83.1	0.6
South 1980	75,372,362	24,958,104	50,414,258	14,047,787	58,960,346	372,230
%	100.0	33.1	66.9	18.6	78.2	0.5
U.S. 2000	281,421,906	59,061,367	222,360,539	34,658,190	211,460,626	2,475,956
%	100.0	21.0	79.0	12.3	75.1	0.9
South 2000	100,236,820	27,229,281	73,007,539	18,981,692	72,819,399	725,919
%	100	27.2	72.8			

Source: U.S. Census Bureau, Population Division, *Historical Census Statistics on Population Totals by Race, 1790 to 1990, and by Hispanic Origin, 1970 to 1990, for the United States, Regions, Divisions, and States*, Working Paper Series 56 (Washington, D.C.: U.S. Bureau of the Census Population Division, 2002). South is sixteen-state definition.

ABBREVIATIONS

AJPH *American Journal of Public Health*

Black Student Admissions Records of the Office of Health Affairs, Dean of the School of Medicine, Walter Reece Berryhill Series, Subgroup 1, Series 3, Office of Student Affairs, Minority Students: Black Student Admissions Folder, University Archives, University of North Carolina at Chapel Hill

Ewing Papers Oscar R. Ewing Papers, Harry S. Truman Presidential Library, Independence, Mo.

FSLA Florida State Library and Archives, Tallahassee

HB *Health Bulletin*

JAMA *Journal of the American Medical Association*

JNMA *Journal of the National Medical Association*

MCC North Carolina Medical Care Commission Records, North Carolina State Archives, Raleigh

NCMJ *North Carolina Medical Journal*

NCSA North Carolina State Archives, Raleigh

Parran Papers Thomas Parran Jr. Papers, University Archives, University of Pittsburgh

Pepper Papers Claude Pepper Papers, Claude Pepper Library, Florida State University, Tallahassee

RC Raleigh Carolinian

SHC Southern Historical Collection, Wilson Library, University of North Carolina at Chapel Hill

Truman Papers Harry S. Truman Papers, Harry S. Truman Presidential Library, Independence, Mo.

UNCA University Archives, Wilson Library, University of North Carolina at Chapel Hill

INTRODUCTION

1. *Baltimore Afro-American*, August 13, 1927, in *The Marcus Garvey and Universal Negro Improvement Association Papers*, ed. Robert A. Hill, vol. 6, *September 1924–December 1927* (Berkeley: University of California Press, 1989), 582; Williams, *Thurgood Marshall*, 182; "Crushing Irony," 386–87; Brandt, *No Magic Bullet*, 4.

2. Kluger, *Simple Justice*, 212.

3. Carl V. Reynolds, "Annual Report of the North Carolina State Board of Health," *HB* 61.6 (1946): 12; Walker Percy, "The Southern Moderate," in *Signposts in a Strange Land*, ed. Patrick Samway (New York: Farrar, Straus, and Giroux, 1991), 95–97.

4. Ferguson, *Black Politics*, 8, 222–23.

5. Starr, *Social Transformation*, 281.

6. Williamson, *Crucible of Race*, 322–23.

7. Plank and Turner, "Changing Patterns," 586.

CHAPTER 1. THE ROOTS OF DELUXE JIM CROW

1. Elna C. Green, ed., *Before the New Deal: Social Welfare in the South, 1830–1930* (Athens: University of Georgia Press, 1999); Eric Foner, *Reconstruction: America's Unfinished Revolution, 1863–1877* (New York: Harper and Row, 1988), 216; Duffy, *Sanitarians*, 159–61; U.S. Public Health Service, *1945 Annual Report*, 335.

2. Walls, "Hot Springs Waters," 430–35.

3. George Chauncey, *Gay New York: Gender, Urban Culture, and the Making of the Gay Male World, 1890–1940* (New York: Basic Books, 1994), 36; John Kasson, *Amusing the Million: Coney Island at the Turn of the Century* (New York: Hill and Wang, 1978), 11–17; Kenneth T. Jackson, *Crabgrass Frontier: The Suburbanization of the United States* (New York: Oxford University Press, 1985), 116–20, 132; Walls, "Hot Springs Waters," 430–35.

4. Mullan, *Plagues and Politics*, 54–58, 63–65; Duffy, *Sanitarians*, 221–34; Harry M. Marks, "Vital Statistics in a Federalist Republic," paper presented at Public Health and the State Conference Columbia University, New York, September 2005; Starr, "The Boundaries of Public Health," in *Social Transformation*, 180–97.

5. Williamson, *Crucible of Race*, 72–76, 247–48, 323; Samuel Kelton Roberts Jr., *Infectious Fear: Politics, Disease, and the Health Effects of Segregation* (Chapel Hill: University of North Carolina Press, 2009), 107–38.

6. Williamson, *Crucible of Race*, 72–76, 247–48, 323; Hubert B. Haywood, "President's Address: Medical Problems in North Carolina," *NCMJ* 2.6 (1941): 276; Wailoo, *Drawing Blood*, 141–49; Allan Chase, *The Legacy of Malthus: The Social Costs of the New Scientific Racism* (Urbana: University of Illinois Press, 1977), 166–75, 270–73; Barkan, *Retreat of Scientific Racism*, 1–4; Love, *One Blood*, 183–85; Schoen, *Choice and Coercion*; McBride, *From TB to AIDS*, 15–19.

7. Marks, "Vital Statistics," 3, 7; William J. Harris, "The Importance of Vital Statistics Legislation in the South," *Southern Medical Journal* 8.10 (1915): 831; Duffy, *Sanitarians*, 180; Alan M. Kraut, *Silent Travelers: Germs, Genes, and the "Immigrant Menace"* (New York: Basic Books, 1994); Judith Walzer Leavitt, *Typhoid Mary: Captive to the Public's Health* (Boston: Beacon, 1996).

8. Ettling, *Germ of Laziness*, 4, 83, 172–76; Wailoo, *Drawing Blood*, 140. Ettling insists that Stiles's findings on racial differences in infection rates were "value-neutral" (176) and that southern polemicists, not Stiles, stereotyped blacks as disease carriers. Wailoo, however, cites Stiles's article, "Hookworm Disease in Its Relation to the Negro," *Southern Medical Journal* 2.11 (1909): 1125–26, which states that hookworm infection was more severe among whites than blacks and that the Negro was a "much more frequent soil polluter" and was therefore responsible for "killing thousands and causing serious disease among tens of thousands of others."

9. Harry M. Marks, "Epidemiologists Explain Pellagra: Gender, Race, and Political Economy in the Work of Edgar Sydenstricker," *Journal of the History of Medicine and Allied Sciences* 58.1 (2003): 35; Elizabeth W. Ethridge, *The Butterfly Caste: A Social History of Pellagra in the South* (Westport, Conn.: Greenwood, 1972).

10. Humphreys, *Malaria*, 51–65; Packard, *Making*, 72–75.

11. Duffy, *Sanitarians*, 229–30, 257; Mott and Roemer, *Rural Health and Medical Care*, 50–51; Fee, *Disease and Discovery*, 143–46; U.S. Public Health Service, National Office of Vital Statistics, "Births and Deaths by Specified Race, United States, Each Division and State, 1944," *Vital Statistics—Special Reports* 25.11 (October 3, 1946): 199.

12. Ruth Rice Puffer, "Measurement of Error of Death Rates in the Colored Race," *AJPH* 27.6 (1937): 607.

13. Among the many historians weighing in on just when the influence of scientific racism began to decline are McBride, *From TB to AIDS*; Gamble, *Making a Place for Ourselves*; George W. Stocking Jr., *Race, Culture, and Evolution: Essays in the History of Anthropology* (New York: Free Press, 1968); Christian W. McMillen, "'The Red Man and the White Plague': Rethinking Race, Tuberculosis, and American Indians, ca. 1890–1950," *Bulletin of the History of Medicine* 82.3 (2008): 608–45.

14. Baker et al., "African American Physicians"; Gifford, *Evolution*, chap. 8; Beardsley, *History of Neglect*, 129–31; Susan Smith, *Sick and Tired*; McBride, *From TB to AIDS*, 10–15, 32–33, 76.

15. Duffy, *Sanitarians*, 222, 232–33, 250; Gamble, *Making a Place for Ourselves*, 129, 130; Charles S. Johnson, "Julius Rosenwald," *Opportunity*, April 1935, 111; "Negro Health," *Time*, December 14, 1942.

16. Flexner, *I Remember*, 212–13; Brown, *Rockefeller Medicine Men*, 47.

17. Ettling, *Germ of Laziness*, chaps. 2, 5; Link, "'Harvest Is Ripe.'"

18. Johnson, "Julius Rosenwald," 111; Beardsley, *History of Neglect*, 114–17; Rice and Jones, *Public Policy*, 22–27.

19. Howard N. Rabinowitz, "From Exclusion to Segregation: Southern Race Relations, 1865–1890," *Journal of American History* 63.3 (1976): 325–50; David Strong, Pamela Barnhouse Walters, Brian Driscoll, and Scott Rosenberg, "Leveraging the State: Private Money and the Development of Public Education for Blacks," *American Sociological Review* 65.5 (2000): 673–75.

20. Strong et al., "Leveraging the State," 675; Beardsley, *History of Neglect*, 41, 127–29, 172–73.

21. Beardsley, *History of Neglect*, 119; Brown, *Rockefeller Medicine Men*, 128–30; Gamble, *Making a Place for Ourselves*, 129; Mary S. Hoffschwelle, "Rosenwald Fund," in *Tennessee Encyclopedia of History and Culture*, tennesseeencyclopedia.net (accessed September 12, 2008); Johnson, "Julius Rosenwald," 110–12, 122.

22. Starr, *Social Transformation*, 125–26; Ward, *Black Physicians*, 39.

23. Todd L. Savitt, "Abraham Flexner and the Black Medical Schools," in *Race and Medicine in Nineteenth- and Early Twentieth-Century America* (Kent, Ohio: Kent State University Press, 2007), 252–66; Ward, *Black Physicians*, 20–30; Hine, *Speak Truth to Power*, 186–87; Gamble, *Making a Place for Ourselves*, 124; Brown, *Rockefeller Medicine Men*, 147–49; Rice and Jones, *Public Policy*, 20–21; Beardsley, *History of Neglect*, 77–80, 253–54.

24. Starr, *Social Transformation*, 118; Todd L. Savitt, "Four African-American Proprietary Medical Colleges, 1888–1923," *Journal of the History of Medicine and Allied Sciences* 55.3 (July 2000): 203–55; Darlene Clark Hine, "The Anatomy of Failure: Medical Education Reform and the Leonard Medical School of Shaw University, 1882–1920," *Journal of Negro Education* 54.4 (1985): 512–25; John H. Felts, "Abraham Flexner and Medical Education in North Carolina," *NCMJ* 56.11 (1995), 535; Bonner, *Iconoclast*, 70–71, 188–89; J. A. C. Lattimore, "Address of the Outgoing President," *JNMA* 40.6 (1948): 232; Rice and Jones, *Public Policy*, 20; Gamble, *Making a Place for Ourselves*, 36–37, 124; "Howard University College of Medicine," unpublished manuscript, 1993, Howard University Archives, Washington, D.C.; "Dr. Harold D. West New President of Meharry," *JNMA* 44.4 (1952): 316–17. See also Morais, *History*; Cobb, "Medical Care"; Cobb, "Progress and Portents."

25. Flexner, *I Remember*, 13, 19–20.

26. Bonner, *Iconoclast*, 75–79, 154–65; Egerton, *Speak Now against the Day*, 233–34.

27. Savitt, "Abraham Flexner," 256–59; Starr, *Social Transformation*, 116–19; "State Board Statistics for 1910," *JAMA* 56.21 (1911): 1558–75.

28. "State Board Statistics for 1910"; "State Board Statistics for 1920," *JAMA* 76.18 (1921): 1231–48.

29. Bonner, *Iconoclast*, 145, 150–51, 188–92; Flexner, *I Remember*, 211; Savitt, "Abraham Flexner," 262–63; Brown, *Rockefeller Medicine Men*, 152–54.

30. Bonner, *Iconoclast*, 144–45, 160–65.

31. Sterling M. Lloyd Jr., "A Short History of Howard University College of Medicine," 2006, medicine.howard.edu/about/history/default.htm (accessed May 16, 2008).

32. Bonner, *Iconoclast*, 162, 189; Eleanor Roosevelt, "Congress Generous to Howard U. and Freedmen's Hospital," syndicated column, April 19, 1947. Howard assumed control of Freedmen's Hospital in 1967 and renamed it Howard University Hospital.

33. Bonner, *Iconoclast*, 260–62; Dummett, *NDA II*, 85.

34. Bonner, *Iconoclast*, 163, 188–92. For insights on the more recent efforts to recruit physicians to the rural South, see the author's oral history series on the history of Florida State University's medical education programs, available at digitool.fcla .edu/R/?func=collections&collection_id=1308 (accessed March 11, 2011) as well as those by the author and William A. Link at the University of North Carolina Southern Oral History Program on the Area Health Education Centers Program, available at www.lib.unc.edu/mss/sohp_interviewee (accessed March 11, 2011).

35. Savitt, "Abraham Flexner," 258; Starr, *Social Transformation*, 355–59.

36. Provenzo, *Du Bois on Education*, 243, 244, 251–52; Sullivan, *Lift Every Voice*, 198–202.

37. Louis Wright, "Remarks before the National Health Conference," July 19, 1938, Louis T. Wright Papers, Box 6, Folder 18, Moorland-Spingarn Research Center, Howard University, Washington, D.C.; Gamble, *Making a Place for Ourselves*, 59–62; Reynolds, "Dr. Louis T. Wright"; "A Short History of Blacks at Harvard Medical School," *Journal of Blacks in Higher Education* 31 (2001): 122–23; James Michael Brodie, *Created Equal: The Lives and Ideas of Black American Innovators* (New York: Quill, 1994), 143–49; Walter Francis White, *The Fire in the Flint* (New York: Knopf, 1924).

38. Gamble, *Making a Place for Ourselves*, 63–69; Adam Biggs, "The Integration of Harlem Hospital: Racial Politics and the New Negro Physician," paper presented at the Southern Historical Association Conference, New Orleans, October 10, 2008; White, *How Far the Promised Land*, 151–53; Ralph Ellison, *Invisible Man* (New York: Random House, 1952); Susan M. Reverby, "Rethinking the Tuskegee Syphilis Study: Nurse Rivers, Silence, and the Meaning of Treatment," in *Tuskegee's Truths*, ed. Reverby, 369.

39. White, *How Far the Promised Land*, 154; Gamble, *Making a Place for Ourselves*, 62–64.

40. Gifford, *Evolution*, chap. 8; Gamble, *Making a Place for Ourselves*, 110–21.

41. Beardsley, *History of Neglect*, 118–19; Gifford, *Evolution*, 163–67; Ward, *Black Physicians*, 39; Paul B. Cornely, "Distribution of Negro Physicians in the United States in 1942," *JAMA* 124.13 (1944): 827; Campbell Gibson and Kay Jung, "Table 4. South Region—Race and Hispanic Origin: 1790 to 1990" in *Historical Census Statistics on Population Totals by Race, 1790 to 1990, and by Hispanic Origin, 1970 to 1990, for the United States, Regions, Divisions, and States* (Washington, D.C.: U.S. Bureau of the Census Population Division, 2002)

42. Duffy, *Sanitarians*, 253; Ferguson, *Black Politics*, 44; Hine, *Speak Truth to Power*, 177–79.

43. Ettling, *Germ of Laziness*; Fee, *Disease and Discovery*, 17–18, 68–70; U.S. Department of Health and Human Services, Office of the Surgeon General, "Previous

Surgeons General," www.surgeongeneral.gov (accessed October 2, 2008); Mullan, *Plagues and Politics*, 63–72; Marks, "Vital Statistics," 8–9; *Transactions of the Twelfth Annual Conference of State and Territorial Health Officers* (Washington, D.C.: U.S. Government Printing Office, 1915), 22–24; *Transactions of the Fifteenth Annual Conference of State and Territorial Health Officers* (Washington, D.C.: U.S. Government Printing Office, 1918), 43–44. Lombardo and Dorr argue that the University of Virginia School of Medicine's prominence as a center of eugenics and racialized medicine influenced three alumni who became senior PHS officials—surgeon general Hugh Cumming and assistant surgeons general Taliaferro Clark and Raymond A. Vonderlehr—to develop the Tuskegee Syphilis Study to test the hypothesis of differential racial susceptibility to infectious diseases. See P. A. Lombardo and G. M. Dorr, "Eugenics, Medical Education, and the Public Health Service: Another Perspective on the Tuskegee Syphilis Experiment," *Bulletin of the History of Medicine* 80.2 (2006): 291–316.

44. University of Virginia Geospatial and Statistical Data Center, *United States Historical Census Data Browser*, 1940 data; Derickson, *Health Security for All*, 79; Shonick, *Government and Health Services*, 20–21; Earle, "Post-1935 Developments."

45. U.S. Congress, Joint Committee on the Investigation of the Tennessee Valley Authority, *Investigation of the Tennessee Valley Authority* (Washington, D.C.: U.S. Government Printing Office, 1939), 9:3735. Among the principal documenters of black and rural health were the *Journal of Negro Education*, the *Journal of the National Medical Association*, the National Urban League's *Opportunity* magazine, the *American Journal of Public Health*, *Hospital Management*, the Southern Conference for Human Welfare's *Southern Patriot*, the U.S. Public Health Service, southern state boards of health, and rural sociology departments of southern universities, including Louisiana State and North Carolina State.

46. U.S. Bureau of the Census, "Table No. 73. Death Rates per 1,000 Population, by Race: 1920 to 1942," in *Statistical Abstract of the United States, 1943* (Washington, D.C.: U.S. Government Printing Office, 1944); Goldstein, "Longevity," 89–91; John Trask, "The Significance of the Mortality Rates of the Colored Population of the U.S.," *AJPH* 6.3 (1916): 254–59, cited in James H. Jones, *Bad Blood*, 37–38.

47. Galishoff, "Germs Know No Color Line."

48. Beals and Plenn, "Louisiana's Black Utopia," 153–55.

49. Beito, *From Mutual Aid*; Neil R. McMillen, *Dark Journey*, 172; Ward, *Black Physicians*, 39, 153–70; Gamble, *Making a Place for Ourselves*, 8–14; Morais, *History*, 127, 140–41; Anderson, "Neglected One-Tenth," 208; Mayo, *Progress Report*, 8; Pohl, "Long Waits"; Cornely, "Distribution," 827; Florence Murray, ed., *The Negro Handbook, 1946–47* (New York: Malliet, 1947), 78–88; Jessie Parkhurst Guzman, ed., *1952 Negro Year Book* (New York: Wise, 1952), 164.

50. Stevens, *In Sickness and in Wealth*, 206–7; Starr, *Social Transformation*, 125–26, 167–68, 359; Earle, "Post-1935 Developments," 1405; Alan Patureau, "He Was Atlanta's Very Own Dr. Spock for Almost 60 Years," *Atlanta Journal and Constitution*, May 25, 1986.

51. W. Eugene Smith, "Nurse Midwife"; Beardsley, *History of Neglect*, 167; Davis, *America Organizes Medicine*, 116; Mott and Roemer, *Rural Health and Medical Care*, 103–7.

52. Starr, *Social Transformation*, 170–71; Ponton, "Hospital Service for Negroes," 14–15; Stevens, *In Sickness and in Wealth*, 175, 194–96; Davis, *America Organizes Medicine*, 240; McFall, "Needs," 236; Southmayd, "Study," 73.

53. Mott and Roemer, *Rural Health and Medical Care*, 15–28.

54. Rosenfield, *Hospitals*, 220–22.

55. Numa P. G. Adams, "An Interpretation of the Significance of the Homer G. Phillips Hospital," *JNMA* 26.1 (1934): 15; "This Is the South's Case History: Poor People, Poor Health," *Southern Patriot* 3.5 (1945): 1; Rice and Jones, *Public Policy*, 21, 34; M. O. Bousfield, "Presidential Address," *JNMA* 26.4 (1934): 153; Murray, *Negro Handbook*, 78–88; "Saint Agnes Hospital Condemned," *RC*, May 14, 1955.

56. Commission on Hospital Care, *Hospital Care*, 163–67; AMA Council on Medical Education and Hospitals, "Hospitalization of Negro Patients," *JAMA* 115.17 (1940): 1461; Gamble, *Making a Place for Ourselves*, 183; Bousfield, "Presidential Address," 152–53.

57. Commission on Hospital Care, *Hospital Care*, 163–67; Beito, "Black Fraternal Hospitals," 134–40; AMA Council on Medical Education and Hospitals, "Hospitalization," 1461; Gamble, *Making a Place for Ourselves*, 183; Duke Endowment Hospital Section, "North Carolina General Hospitals Caring for Negro Patients in 1944," MCC, Series 94.2, Executive Secretary's Office: Hospital and Medical Care Study Commission File, Box 1.

58. E. H. L. Corwin and Gertrude Sturges, *Opportunities for the Medical Education of Negroes* (New York: Scribner's, 1936); Best, interview; Cathy Lee, "Grady Health System," *New Georgia Encyclopedia*, www.georgiaencyclopedia.org (accessed May 16, 2008); Forest Jones, interview by author, July 14, 2008; Allen, "Challenges," 3–7.

59. Irene Dixon to Forest Davenport, November 4, 1922, in author's possession; Euclid P. Ghee, "A Plea for the Admittance of Negro Doctors to Municipal Hospital Staffs," *JNMA* 28.3 (1936): 102–6; F. W. Fortune, "The Negro Physician," *JNMA* 31.3 (1939): 107–10; John A. Kenney, "A Plea for Interracial Cooperation," *JNMA* 37.4 (1945): 121–24; Bousfield, "Presidential Address," 153–55; Adams, "Interpretation," 14.

60. Stevens, *In Sickness and in Wealth*, 50, 137–38, 175; "D.C. Woman Wins Executive Post in N.Y. Inter-Racial Hospital," *Chicago Defender*, January 12, 1946.

61. McIntosh and Kendrick, *Public Health Administration*, 52, 186, 189; Ponton,

"Hospital Service for Negroes," 14–15; McFall, "Needs," 236; Thomas R. Clark, "Limits of State Autonomy," 274–75. McFall's article, the source for the number of beds in 1946, refers to *nonwhites* rather than specifying *blacks*. Both Rosenfield and Davis criticized Ponton for failing to account for the availability of indigent care in his hospital survey. See Davis, *America Organizes Medicine*, 240; Rosenfield, *Hospitals*, 8–9.

62. "Negro Health"; McBride, *From TB to AIDS*, 2, 46–47; Larkins, *Negro Population*, 30.

63. University of Virginia Geospatial and Statistical Data Center, *United States Historical Census Data Browser*, 1940 data; Mott and Roemer, *Rural Health and Medical Care*, 51–53.

64. University of Virginia Geospatial and Statistical Data Center, *United States Historical Census Data Browser*, 1940 data; Mott and Roemer, *Rural Health and Medical Care*, 51–53; "Great Pox," *Time*, October 26, 1936.

65. Howard W. Blakeslee, "Electric Eye Warns Surgeons of Approaching Death's Signs," *Washington Post*, October 20, 1939; Martin Frobisher, "Strains of C. Diphtheriae in Various Parts of the United States," *AJPH* Suppl. 30 (1940): 28; Shannon and Pyle, *Disease and Medical Care*, 26; Joseph W. Mountin and Evelyn Flook, "Distribution of Health Services in the Structure of State Government: Chapter III. Tuberculosis Control by State Agencies," *Public Health Reports* 57.3 (1942): 81–90.

66. *Southern Patriot* 2.5 (1944): 8.

67. Mott and Roemer, *Rural Health and Medical Care*, ix, 31–49, 64–70, 103–14; McIntosh and Kendrick, *Public Health Administration*, 81.

68. Mott and Roemer, *Rural Health and Medical Care*, 3; Hitt and Bertrand, *Social Aspects*, 2, 7–10.

69. Humphreys, *Malaria*, 52–54; Packard, *Making*, 76–77.

70. Brandt, *No Magic Bullet*, 21; Lemann, *Promised Land*, 28–32; James H. Jones, *Bad Blood*, 83–84.

71. Lemann, *Promised Land*, 6; Mott and Roemer, *Rural Health and Medical Care*, 51–53; McBride, *From TB to AIDS*, 37.

72. Collins and Thomasson, "Declining Contribution," 747, 752–58.

73. Duffy, *Sanitarians*, 180–81, 207.

74. Heart disease surpassed TB as the leading cause of black mortality after 1930 but primarily affected men and postmenopausal women (McBride, *From TB to AIDS*, 119).

75. Hildrus A. Poindexter, "Handicaps in the Normal Growth and Development of Rural Negro Children," *AJPH* 28.9 (1938): 1048; Beardsley, *History of Neglect*, 13–14; "The Symptoms," *Southern Patriot* 3.5 (1945): 3; A. W. Makepeace, "Medical Problems Involved in Better Care of Babies," *HB* 56.4 (1941): 10; Mott and Roemer, *Rural Health and Medical Care*, 290, 306.

CHAPTER 2. THE NEW DEAL IN HEALTH

1. Martha Gelhorn, "Report, Gaston County, North Carolina, Nov. 11, 1934," Harry Hopkins Papers, Box 66, Franklin D. Roosevelt Library, White Plains, N.Y.; Anderson, "Neglected One-Tenth," 209.

2. Pauline Redmond Coggs, "Race Relations Advisers—Quislings or Messiahs?" *Opportunity*, July 1943, 112. For the relationships among Deluxe Jim Crow agencies and individuals, see appendix 1.

3. Egerton, *Speak Now against the Day*, 91–93.

4. Weaver, "New Deal," 201–2; Walter B. Hill Jr., "Finding a Place for the Negro: Robert C. Weaver and the Groundwork for the Civil Rights Movement," *Prologue* 37.1 (Spring 2005): 42–51; Williams, *Thurgood Marshall*, 149–50, 317; Dombrowski "New South," 245; "Negroes in Government, 1944," Truman Papers, Negro—General—Negroes in the Government File; Ferguson, *Black Politics*, 83–84, 222–23.

5. Naomi Rogers, "Race and the Politics of Polio: Warm Springs, Tuskegee, and the March of Dimes," *AJPH* 97.5 (2007): 784–95; John W. Chenault, "Tuskegee Center Combats Infantile Paralysis," *Opportunity* 21.1 (1943): 17; Stephen E. Mawdsley, "'Dancing on Eggs': Charles H. Bynum, Racial Politics, and the National Foundation for Infantile Paralysis, 1938–1954," *Bulletin of the History of Medicine* 84.2 (2010): 217–47.

6. Ferguson, *Black Politics*, 6.

7. Collins and Thomasson, "Declining Contribution"; Duffy, *Sanitarians*, 257–58; U.S. Treasury Department, *Report of the President of the United States to the Congress Showing the Status of Funds and Operations under the Emergency Relief Appropriation Acts for the Fiscal Years 1935 to 1941* (Washington, D.C.: U.S. Treasury Department, 1941), 32; Mott and Roemer, *Rural Health and Medical Care*, 385, 392; Florence Kerr, "Health Conservation and the WPA," October 21, 1939, Works Progress Administration Papers, RG 69, Series 737, Box 7, National Archives, College Park, Md.; Mullan, *Plagues and Politics*, 102, 121; Humphreys, *Malaria*, 49–68.

8. Davis, *America Organizes Medicine*, 278–79; Derickson, *Health Security for All*, 44, 79.

9. Duffy, *Sanitarians*, 258; Douglas L. Smith, *New Deal*, 77–83; M. O. Bousfield, "Presidential Address," *JNMA* 26.4 (1934): 155.

10. William Leuchtenburg, *Franklin D. Roosevelt and the New Deal, 1932–1940* (New York: Harper and Row, 1963), 124; Mullan, *Plagues and Politics*, 100; Thomas R. Clark, "Limits of State Autonomy," 262–63.

11. Beardsley, *History of Neglect*, 89–91.

12. Thomas R. Clark, "Limits of State Autonomy," 263–65.

13. Lawrence Greely Brown, "The Hospital Problem of Negro Physicians," *JNMA* 34.2 (1942): 84; W. A. Cleland, "The President's Christmas Message," *JNMA* 3.2

(1953): 5; Richard B. Clark, "George William Stanley Ish," *Encyclopedia of Arkansas History and Culture*, www.encyclopediaofarkansas.net (accessed April 27, 2008). The Arkansas state and Pulaski County medical societies admitted black Harvard-trained physician George William Stanley Ish during the 1920s.

14. Love, *One Blood*, 170–71; Ward, *Black Physicians*, 153–70; Dummett, *NDA II*, 154–55.

15. Barbara Rosenkrantz, "Preventive Medicine and Public Health," in *The Education of American Physicians: Historical Essays*, ed. Ronald L. Numbers (Berkeley: University of California Press, 1980); Ward, *Black Physicians*, 233–36, 266–67; Susan Smith, *Sick and Tired*, 168–69; McBride, *From TB to AIDS*, 69, 85–124; Beardsley, *History of Neglect*, 99; Ferguson, *Black Politics*, 11.

16. B. O. Barnes to W. T. Bost, April 22, 1939, B. O. Barnes to Walter R. Johnson, May 12, 1938, April 22, 1939, Walter R. Johnson to B. O. Barnes, May 29, 1939, all in State Board of Public Welfare, Bureau of Work among Negroes Records, Wilson County Folder, NCSA.

17. de Jong, *Different Day*, 103–5.

18. "Public Welfare Work among Negroes in Wilson County, N.C., 1940," typescript, 8–9, Commission on Interracial Cooperation Papers, Folder 76, Box 3, SHC; James H. Jones, *Bad Blood*, 45–47; Blalock, interview, 11; Ward, *Black Physicians*.

19. Slade, interview, 20, 22–23.

20. Ward, *Black Physicians*, 239–64; McBride, *From TB to AIDS*, 22–33, 48, 58–67, 99.

21. Beardsley, *History of Neglect*, 130–32, 152; "Conferences and Dates," *AJPH* 40.8 (1950): 1066; "APHA Past Presidents," http://www.apha.org/about/aphapastpresidents .html (accessed November 19, 2009); Robert B. Baker et al., "African American Physicians"; W. Michael Byrd and Linda A. Clayton, *An American Health Dilemma: The Medical History of African Americans and the Problem of Race* (New York: Routledge, 2000), 270–75; McBride, *From TB to AIDS*, 48–49; Lydia B. Edwards, "Life as a Doctor: A Pesky Darling Grows Up," 2001, 16, Lydia B. Edwards Papers, Alan Mason Chesney Medical Archives of the Johns Hopkins Medical Institutions, Baltimore; Korstad, *Dreaming of a Time*, 49–53; Michael M. Davis, "What Color Is Health?" *The Standard*, May 1947, 266.

22. Coggs, "Race Relations Advisers," 112; Louis T. Wright, "Remarks before the National Health Conference," July 19, 1938, Louis T. Wright Papers, Box 6, Folder 18, Moorland-Spingarn Research Center, Howard University, Washington, D.C.; Ferguson, *Black Politics*, 82.

23. Weaver, "New Deal," 201–2; James H. Jones, *Bad Blood*, 162–64; Grey, *New Deal Medicine*, 41; Brenda J. Taylor, "The Farm Security Administration and Rural Families in the South: Home Economists, Nurses, and Farmers, 1933–1946," in *The New Deal and Beyond: Social Welfare in the South since 1930*, ed. Elna C. Green

(Athens: University of Georgia Press, 2003), 30–46; Susan Smith, "A New Deal for Black Health: Community Activism and the Office of Negro Health Work," in *Sick and Tired*, 58–82; Temkin, "Driving Through"; William H. Richardson, "Maternity–Child Care for Service Men's Families," *HB* 60.5 (1945): 5–7; *Report of the President*, 32, 52, 240–41, 536.

24. Thomas Parran, "Annual Report of the Surgeon General of the Public Health Service," *AJPH* 27.5 (1937): 214–15; Mullan, *Plagues and Politics*, 104, 107.

25. Beardsley, *History of Neglect*, 41, 127–29, 172–73; "Government Services," *JAMA* 112.5 (1939): 457; Anthony J. Badger, *North Carolina and the New Deal* (Raleigh: North Carolina Department of Cultural Resources, Division of Archives and History, 1981), 92–93.

26. Beardsley, *History of Neglect*, 156–85; "The Patient Is Improving," *Southern Patriot* 3.5 (May 1945): 6; Douglas L. Smith, *New Deal*, 136.

27. Ettling, *Germ of Laziness*; Fee, *Disease and Discovery*, 78.

28. John H. Stanfield, "Dollars for the Silent South: Southern White Liberalism and the Julius Rosenwald Fund, 1928–1948," in *Perspectives on the American South*, ed. Merle Black and John Shelton Reed (New York: Gordon and Breach Science, 1984), 2:117–38; Duffy, *Sanitarians*, 260–61; Beardsley, *History of Neglect*, 89–91, 156–85; James H. Jones, *Bad Blood*, 52–55, 58–60, 83–90; "Patient Is Improving," 6; Paul Cornely, "Trends in Public Health Activities among Negroes in 96 Southern Counties during 1930–1939," *JNMA* 34.1 (1942): 8–11; Ernest R. Alexander, "The Negro Professional Worker," *Fisk News*, March–April 1939, 27.

29. "N.C. Board of Health Gets Award for Its Work with Negroes," *Durham Carolina Times*, November 8, 1941; William H. Richardson, "Public Health among Our Negro Population," *HB* 56.5 (1941): 11; Larkins, *Negro Population*, 32; Susan Smith, *Sick and Tired*, 126; Mayo, *Progress Report*, 13–14; Thomas Parran to Carl V. Reynolds, January 21, 1939, Carl V. Reynolds to Thomas Parran, January 25, 1939, both in U.S. Public Health Service Records (RG 90), General Classified Records, Group III—States, 1936–44, Box 259, 0505—North Carolina, National Archives, College Park, Md.; Ferguson, *Black Politics*, 83–84.

30. Earle, "Post-1935 Developments," 1405; Beardsley, *History of Neglect*, 163–67, 174–76; George M. Cooper, "Helping Mothers and Children," *HB* 57.10 (1942): 10–11; "Pitt and Beaufort Counties Report on Maternal and Child Health Services," *HB* 56.3 (1941): 5; Marcus S. Goldstein, "Longevity and Health Status of Whites and Nonwhites in the United States," *JNMA* 46.2 (1954): 98; Schoen, *Choice and Coercion*, 46–47.

31. "Southern Infant and Maternity Mortality Rates Drop Sharply," *Southern Patriot* 2.8 (1944): 8; McIntosh and Kendrick, *Public Health Administration*, 47, 83.

32. "How Sick Is the South?" *Southern Patriot* 3.5 (1945): 1–8.

33. Duffy, *Sanitarians*, 288; Davis, *America Organizes Medicine*, 92, 95, 165–66.

34. Thomas R. Clark, "Limits of State Autonomy," 264–65; Grey, *New Deal Medicine*.

35. A. McGehee Harvey, Gert H. Brieger, Susan L. Abrams, and Victor A. McKusick, *A Model of Its Kind*, vol. 1, *A Centennial History of Medicine at Johns Hopkins* (Baltimore: Johns Hopkins University Press, 1989), 221; U.S. Public Health Service, *A Manual of Treatment: The Venereal Diseases*, civilian ed., 3rd ed. (Chicago: American Medical Association, 1919), 56, 59; Brandt, *No Magic Bullet*, 40–41; Harry M. Marks, *The Progress of Experiment: Science and Therapeutic Reform in the United States, 1900–1990* (New York: Cambridge University Press, 1997), 113.

36. James H. Jones, *Bad Blood*, 27–28; Baldwin Lucke, "Tabes Dorsalis: A Pathological and Clinical Study of 250 Cases," *Journal of Nervous and Mental Diseases* 43.5 (1916): 395; C. Jeff Miller, "Special Medical Problems of the Colored Woman," *Southern Medical Journal* 25.7 (1932): 733; William R. Johnson, "Report of Visit to State Hospital, Goldsboro," State Board of Public Welfare, Bureau of Work among Negroes Records, Box 231, NCSA.

37. Ferguson, *Black Politics*; Brandt, *No Magic Bullet*, 20–21, 33, 43–44; Wailoo, *Drawing Blood*, 134–35; Lemann, *Promised Land*, 26–28; McMillen, *Dark Journey*, 14; John C. Cutler, "A Review of the National Venereal Disease Control Program," in *Working Conference for Nurses on the Public Health Aspects of Venereal Disease Control*, proceedings of conference at School of Public Health of the University of North Carolina, 1954, 10, North Carolina Collection, Wilson Library, University of North Carolina at Chapel Hill.

38. Brandt, *No Magic Bullet*, 38–40; Parascandola, *Sex, Sin, and Science*, 68–74, 82–84, 90; Mullan, *Plagues and Politics*, 86; Susan Smith, "Spreading the Gospel of Health: Tuskegee Institute and National Negro Health Week," in *Sick and Tired*, 33–57.

39. Davis, "What Color Is Health?" 265–66.

40. James H. Jones, *Bad Blood*, 52–54, 74–95, 117–18, 129–50, 176–78; "Negro Health," *Time*, December 14, 1942; Raymond A. Vonderlehr, "Are We Checking the Great Plague?" *Survey Graphic* 29.4 (1940): 217.

41. Brandt, *No Magic Bullet*, 142–43; Stephen M. Jay, "Burney's Burney: Leroy Edgar Burney (1906–1998)," 8–9, http://hdl.handle.net/1805/578 (accessed May 14, 2011); "Negro Health"; Vonderlehr, "Are We Checking," 217.

42. Ferguson, *Black Politics*, 129.

43. Beardsley, *History of Neglect*, 171; Thomas Parran, "Shadow on the Land: Syphilis, the White Man's Burden," in *Tuskegee's Truths*, ed. Reverby, 66; Susan M. Reverby, *Examining Tuskegee: The Infamous Syphilis Study and Its Legacy* (Chapel Hill: University of North Carolina Press, 2009), 136–39; James H. Jones, *Bad Blood*, 106, 121–23, 179–80; Marks, *Progress of Experiment*, 53–59; Thomas B. Turner, *Heritage of Excellence: The Johns Hopkins Medical Institutions, 1914–1947* (Baltimore: Johns Hopkins University Press, 1974), 510–12.

44. Joseph Earle Moore to Thomas Parran, May 26, 1936, Thomas Parran to Michael M. Davis, May 28, 1936, Michael M. Davis to Joseph Earle Moore, June 4, 1936, all in Parran Papers, Series 90/F-14, FF3; "Postgraduate Training of Negro Physicians in the Clinical Management and Public Health Control of Syphilis," *JNMA* 29.4 (1937): 171; Mullan, *Plagues and Politics*, 122.

45. Ferguson, *Black Politics*, 112–13; Brandt, *No Magic Bullet*, 41–42, 138–60.

46. Ferguson, *Black Politics*, 112.

47. Ibid., 112–13.

48. Douglas L. Smith, *New Deal*, 122; Stevens, *In Sickness and in Wealth*, 168–69; Harry S. Truman, "Special Message to the Congress on Termination of Emergency and Wartime Powers," February 19, 1947, in *Public Papers of the Presidents: Harry S. Truman, 1945–1953* (Washington, D.C.: U.S. Government Printing Office, 1966); *Report of the President*, 30–34, 240–41, 536; Federal Works Agency, *Second Annual Report* (Washington, D.C.: U.S. Government Printing Office, 1941), 189, 315, 460; Federal Works Agency, *Fourth Annual Report* (Washington, D.C.: U.S. Government Printing Agency, 1943), 61.

49. "Negroes in Government, 1944"; "Federal Works Agency—P.W.A., Office of Advisor on Negro Affairs," *JNMA* 32.3 (1940): 136; AMA Council on Medical Education and Hospitals, "Hospitalization of Negro Patients," *JAMA*, 115.17 (1940): 1461; Charles S. Johnson, "The Negro," *American Journal of Sociology* 47.6 (1942): 857; "Cooley Sanitarium, LA," NARA Control Number RG-69-77, Eleanor and Franklin Roosevelt Institute, *New Deal Network* Photo Library, newdeal.feri.org (accessed May 16, 2008).

50. Douglas L. Smith, *New Deal*, 122, 114; McWilliams, *New Lights in the Valley*, 44–45; Jerry Puryear, "University of Arkansas for Medical Sciences," *Encyclopedia of Arkansas History and Culture*, www.encyclopediaofarkansas.net (accessed April 27, 2008); Wall, *Louisiana*, 293.

51. Gordon Peek, T. Campanella, F. W. Pickell, S. Randall Jr., and A. L. McQuown, et al., "Committee Report, Charity Hospital Committee," *Journal of the Louisiana State Medical Society* 106.1 (1954): 64, 68; "The Symptoms," *Southern Patriot* 3.5 (1945): 3.

52. LSU Hospitals Health Care Services Division, "Charity Hospital System Timeline," http://www.lsuhospitals.org/About_LSU-HCSD/history.htm (accessed April 27, 2008); Beito, "Black Fraternal Hospitals," 114; McMillen, *Dark Journey*, 172; Davis, *America Organizes Medicine*, 88; Allen Ellender in *Congressional Record*, February 16, 1938, 2031, February 17, 1938, 2104–7; "The Maryland Medical Care Program," *JNMA* 43.1 (1951): 60–61; Poe, *Final Report*, 16; Thomas Parran, "Parran Evaluates N.C. Good Health Program," *University of North Carolina Alumni Review* 35.7 (April 1947): 219.

53. Douglas L. Smith, *New Deal*, 114; William Ivy Hair, *The Kingfish and His*

Realm: The Life and Times of Huey Long (Baton Rouge: Louisiana State University Press, 1991), 230–31; John E. Salvaggio, *New Orleans' Charity Hospital: A Story of Physicians, Politics, and Poverty* (Baton Rouge: Louisiana State University Press, 1992); Asa G. Yancey Sr., "Grady Memorial Hospital Centennial: History and Development, 1892–1992," *Journal of the Medical Association of Georgia* 81.4 (1992): 625.

54. Mitchell and Bankston, *Hospital and Health Facilities*, 29–31; Goldstein, "Longevity," 94–95.

55. Stevens, *In Sickness and in Wealth*, 17–19, 71–79.

56. Rosenfield, *Hospitals*, 4, 290–91.

57. Cecelski, *Along Freedom Road*, 7–9; Wyeneth, "Architecture of Racial Segregation," 15–17, 28–33; Rosenfield, *Hospitals*, 154–55.

58. Rosenfield, *Hospitals*, 46.

59. Wyeneth, "Architecture of Racial Segregation," 15–17, 28–33; Reynolds, "Professional and Hospital Discrimination," 710–11; Susan E. Lederer, "Lost Boundaries: Race, Blood, and Bodies," in *Flesh and Blood: Organ Transplantation and Blood Transfusion in Twentieth-Century America* (New York: Oxford University Press, 2008), 107–42.

60. Stevens, *In Sickness and in Wealth*, 63; Best, interview.

61. Myrdal, *American Dilemma*, 345–46; Milton Roemer, "Special Health Problems of Negroes in Rural Areas," *Journal of Negro Education* 18.3 (1949): 321–22; Michael M. Davis, "Inter-Professional Health Conference: Tentative Draft of Report," March 7, 1944, 11, Parran Papers, Series 90/F-14, FF3.

CHAPTER 3. NEW DEAL HEALTH IN NORTH CAROLINA

1. Beardsley, *History of Neglect*, 120, 146–49; Link, "'Harvest Is Ripe,'" 3–4; Fee, *Disease and Discovery*, 17–18, 68–70, 75–76; "John A. Ferrell: Humanitarian," *Southern Medical Journal* 37.9 (1944): 527–28.

2. Walter E. Campbell, *Foundations for Excellence*, 20–21; Schoen, *Choice and Coercion*, 46.

3. William H. Richardson, "Public Health among Our Negro Population," *HB* 56.5 (1941): 10; James F. Donnelly, "Committee on Maternal Welfare: A Review of the First 1000 Consecutive Maternal Deaths in North Carolina," *NCMJ* 14.6 (1953): 254; "Current Good Health Crusade Is Deep Rooted," *University of North Carolina Alumni Review*, October 1946, 36–37; Larkins, *Negro Population of North Carolina*, ·30; Mayo, *Progress Report*, 5, 8. The estimate of 2,100 physicians results from 1,937 white physicians on the Medical Society of North Carolina's 1946 roster, plus 129 black doctors in active practice (*JAMA* 124.13 [1944]: 827).

4. Walter E. Campbell, *Foundations for Excellence*, 21–22; Beardsley, *History of Neglect*, 119–26.

5. Duke Endowment Hospital Section, "North Carolina General Hospitals Caring

for Negro Patients in 1944," MCC, Series 94.2, Executive Secretary's Office: Hospital and Medical Care Study Commission File, Box 1; Gifford, *Evolution*, 163–67; Adam Biggs, "The Integration of Harlem Hospital: Racial Politics and the New Negro Physician," paper presented at the Southern Historical Association Conference, New Orleans, October 10, 2008.

6. McIntosh and Kendrick, *Public Health Administration*, 107, 111, 179, 183, 190.

7. Ibid., 80–83; Starr, *Social Transformation*, 188–89.

8. McIntosh and Kendrick, *Public Health Administration*, 45; U.S. Public Health Service, *1945 Annual Report*, 301; Korstad, *Dreaming of a Time*, 24–26.

9. Beardsley, *History of Neglect*, 149; Link, "'Harvest Is Ripe,'" 3–4.

10. Larkins, *Negro Population of North Carolina*, 62; "N.C. Board of Health Gets Award for Its Work with Negroes," *Durham Carolina Times*, November 8, 1941. For discussions of black lay activism and Negro Health Week, see Beardsley, *History of Neglect*, 102–3; Susan Smith, "Spreading the Gospel of Health: Tuskegee Institute and National Negro Health Week," in *Sick and Tired*, 33–57.

11. Throughout this chapter, I compare conditions for women in North Carolina to those in Mississippi as explored by Susan Smith, *Sick and Tired*. Along with Darlene Clark Hine's *Black Women in White: Racial Conflict and Cooperation in the Nursing Profession, 1890–1950* (Bloomington: Indiana University Press, 1989), Smith's work remains one of the most thorough and valuable studies of southern black women as patients, reformers, and health professionals.

12. "Childbirth: Nature v. Drugs," *Time*, May 25, 1936; Rosenfield, *Hospitals*, 123–30. At the Chicago Lying-In Hospital, which DeLee founded in 1895, only 62 babies and 15 mothers died out of a total 2,881 babies delivered in 1935, making it the safest maternity hospital in the nation.

13. Best, interview.

14. Rosenfield, *Hospitals*, 128–30.

15. Meckel, *Save the Babies*, 173–74; Susan Smith, *Sick and Tired*, 120, 199; Jacqueline Jones, *Labor of Love*, 199–214; Beardsley, *History of Neglect*, 167.

16. Puckett, *Folk Beliefs*, 333–34, 337, 385.

17. McBride, *From TB to AIDS*, 111–12; Mrs. Wilbur H. Currie, "Moore County's Maternal Welfare Committee," *HB* 55.5 (May 1940): 8, 11; Susan Smith, *Sick and Tired*, 130; Gertrude Jacinta Fraser, *African American Midwifery in the South: Dialogues of Birth, Race, and Memory* (Cambridge: Harvard University Press, 1998), 36, cited in Squires, *Body at Risk*, 80; Onnie Lee Logan as told to Katherine Clark, *Motherwit: An Alabama Midwife's Story* (New York: Dutton, 1989).

18. "Wished She Was in Jail," *HB* 56.9 (1941): 4.

19. M. Irene Lassiter, "Problems with Untrained Midwifery in the South," typescript, ca. 1940, State Board of Health Papers, Administrative Services Central Files, Miscellaneous Correspondence, Box 1, NCSA; Grey, *New Deal Medicine*, 60, cited in Squires, *Body at Risk*, 54.

20. Beardsley, *History of Neglect*, 101, 114, 126–27, 156–69; Susan Smith, *Sick and Tired*.

21. McBride, *From TB to AIDS*, 74, 108–9; Squires, *Body at Risk*, 52; U.S. Department of Labor, Children's Bureau, *Maternal and Child-Health Services under the Social Security Act: Development of the Program, 1936–1939* (Washington, D.C.: U.S. Government Printing Office, 1941), 4, 7, 12.

22. U.S. Department of Labor, Children's Bureau, *Maternal and Child-Health Services*, 4, 7, 12; Elizabeth Fee, Theodore M. Brown, and Roxanne L. Beatty, "A Well Baby Clinic in Indianapolis," *AJPH* 93.2 (2003): 271; Richardson, "Public Health," 11; Larkins, *Negro Population of North Carolina*, 32; North Carolina Advisory Committee to the U.S. Commission on Civil Rights, *Equal Protection of the Laws in North Carolina* (Washington, D.C.: U.S. Government Printing Office, 1962), 193–95; "Pitt and Beaufort Counties Report on Maternal and Child Health Services," *HB* 56.3 (1941): 5; Richardson, "Public Health."

23. McIntosh and Kendrick, *Public Health Administration*, 85; McBride, *From TB to AIDS*, 74; Beardsley, *History of Neglect*, 163–67; George M. Cooper, "Helping Mothers and Children," *HB* 57.10 (1942): 10–11; U.S. Department of Labor, Children's Bureau, *Maternal and Child-Health Services*, 93; Currie, "Moore County's Maternal Welfare Committee," 7.

24. W. Eugene Smith, "Nurse Midwife," 134–45; Logan, *Motherwit*, 87–90; North Carolina Board of Health, *A Book of Instructions and Illustrations for North Carolina Midwives* (Raleigh: State of North Carolina, 1953); Lassiter, "Problems with Untrained Midwifery"; Susan Smith, *Sick and Tired*, 124–27.

25. North Carolina Board of Health, *Book of Instructions*; Susan Smith, *Sick and Tired*, 124, 131–33.

26. Beardsley, *History of Neglect*, 170.

27. "Maternal and Child Health Service," *HB* 56.2 (1941): 5; Martha Gelhorn, "Report, Gaston County, North Carolina, Nov. 11, 1934," Harry Hopkins Papers, Box 66, Franklin D. Roosevelt Library, White Plains, N.Y.

28. W. E. B. Du Bois, "Black Folk and Birth Control," *Birth Control Review*, June 1932, 166–67; Schoen, *Choice and Coercion*, 52–56.

29. William H. Richardson, "North Carolina Indians and the Public Health Program," *HB* 56.8 (1941): 10; Richardson, "Public Health," 9; Louise East, "Midwife Training Emphasized in Halifax County," *HB* 56.2 (1941): 14.

30. Blalock, interview.

31. Johnnie Sue Deloatch, "Midwife Work in Northampton County—Past and Present," *HB* 56.4 (1941): 9. Another source that contrasts traditional and modern midwifery is *All My Babies: A Midwife's Own Story*, the 1952 documentary and training film about rural Georgia midwife Mary Francis Hill Coley directed by George C. Stoney and produced by the Association of American Medical Colleges and the Geor-

gia Department of Public Health, available at http://www.der.org/films/all-my
-babies.html (accessed September 1, 2010). See also http://cds.aas.duke.edu/exhibits
/reclaimingmidwives.html (accessed September 1, 2010).

32. East, "Midwife Training," 14; A. W. Makepeace, "Medical Problems Involved in
Better Care of Babies," *HB* 56.4 (April 1941): 11.

33. Ida H. Hall, "Amanda Bunch—Midwife," *HB* 61.1 (1946): 13.

34. Ibid.

35. Jacqueline Jones, *Labor of Love*, 214; Susan Smith, *Sick and Tired*, 121; Lassiter,
"Problems with Untrained Midwifery"; Hall, "Amanda Bunch."

36. McBride, *From TB to AIDS*, 5; Mayo, *Progress Report*, 8.

37. Squires, *Body at Risk*, 78–81.

38. Ibid., 81–82.

39. Ibid., 82–83.

40. Ibid., 83–89.

41. Ibid., 78–92; "Sequel: Maude Gets Her Clinic; Life Readers Donate $18,500 to
Nurse Midwife of Pineville, S.C.," *Life*, April 6, 1953.

42. John W. Blassingame, *The Slave Community: Plantation Life in the Antebellum
South* (New York: Oxford University Press, 1972); Squires, *Body at Risk*, 81; Love, *One
Blood*, 174; Glenda Elizabeth Gilmore, *Gender and Jim Crow: Women and the Politics
of White Supremacy in North Carolina, 1896–1920* (Chapel Hill: University of North
Carolina Press, 1996), 62–63, 75–76.

43. Susan Smith, *Sick and Tired*, 145–46.

44. Puckett, *Folk Beliefs*, 358; Susan Smith, *Sick and Tired*, 118–20.

45. U.S. Department of Labor, Children's Bureau, *Maternal and Child-Health Services*, v; "Notes and Comment," *HB* 55.8 (1940): 5; "Maternal and Child Health Service," 5; Makepeace, "Medical Problems," 11; "Current Health Crusade," 37; Donnelly,
"Committee on Maternal Welfare," 255; Richardson, "North Carolina Indians," 9–10.

46. Carl V. Reynolds, "Annual Report of the North Carolina State Board of
Health," *HB* 61.6 (1946): 12; Beardsley, *History of Neglect*, 174–76; Temkin, "Driving
Through," 587–95; William P. Richardson, "Public Health Workers in North Carolina
Look to the Future," *HB* 59.12 (1944): 3–5; Amy Louise Fisher, "Public Health Nurs-
ing Day," *HB* 60.3 (1945): 7–9; William H. Richardson, "Maternity–Child Care for
Service Men's Families," *HB* 60.5 (1945): 5–7.

47. R. L. Carlton, "Public Health in Postwar Days," *HB* 61.4 (1946): 6; Clayborne
Carson, "African Americans at War," in *The Oxford Companion to World War II* (Oxford: Oxford University Press, 1995), 5–8; Temkin, "Driving Through"; Beardsley, *History of Neglect*, 174–76; William H. Richardson, "New Gains Chalked Up," *HB* 60.4
(1945): 9–11; Virginia Smith, "Some Nursing Activities of the Health Department
during the Year 1944," *HB* 60.5 (May 1945): 3–5.

48. McBride, *From TB to AIDS*, 93; Temkin, "Driving Through," 589; Richardson,

"Maternity–Child Care"; North Carolina Advisory Committee, "Equal Protection of the Laws," 18–19.

49. Rosenfield, *Hospitals*, 123–24.

50. Donnelly, "Committee on Maternal Welfare," 253; Susan Smith, *Sick and Tired*, 143; Currie, "Moore County's Maternal Welfare Committee," 10; Collins and Thomasson, "Declining Contribution," 762–63.

51. Donnelly, "Committee on Maternal Welfare," 253–54; Starr, *Social Transformation*, 373; Beardsley, *History of Neglect*, 247; John L. Thurston, "More Opportunities for All through Social Security," April 9, 1952, Ewing Papers, Federal Security Agency—General Correspondence, Box 29; Shonick, *Government and Health Services*, 92.

52. McBride, *From TB to AIDS*, 24, 86, 99.

CHAPTER 4. THE SOUTH AND NATIONAL HEALTH REFORM

1. Alan Brinkley, "The New Deal and Southern Politics," in *The New Deal and the South*, ed. James C. Cobb and Michael Namorato (Jackson: University Press of Mississippi, 1984), 115.

2. Numan V. Bartley, "The Era of the New Deal as a Turning Point in Southern History," in *New Deal and the South*, ed. Cobb and Namorato, 142–43; Schulman, *From Cotton Belt to Sunbelt*, 3–8, 13–14, 47–51, 61.

3. Ann Short Chirhart, "Gender, Jim Crow, and Eugene Talmadge: The Politics of Social Policy in Georgia," in *The New Deal and Beyond: Social Welfare in the South since 1930*, ed. Elna C. Green (Athens: University of Georgia Press, 2003), 86–88; Kluger, *Simple Justice*, 201–3, 211–12, 259, 268–69; Williams, *Thurgood Marshall*, 75–76, 94–98.

4. Egerton, *Speak Now against the Day*, 152–53; Dawson, "Federal Government and Education," 229–35; Schulman, *From Cotton Belt to Sunbelt*, 193–95; Alonzo L. Hamby, *Man of the People: A Life of Harry S. Truman* (New York: Oxford University Press, 1998), 238–39.

5. Egerton, *Speak Now against the Day*, 175–81; Dombrowski, "New South," 245; Claude Pepper Diary, August 26, 1937, Pepper Papers; Claude Denson Pepper and Joseph Lister Hill biographies, Bioguide.congress.gov (accessed June 22, 2004); Hamilton, *Lister Hill*; Claude Pepper, *Pepper: Eyewitness to a Century* (New York: Harcourt Brace Jovanovich, 1987); William E. Leuchtenburg, *Franklin D. Roosevelt and the New Deal, 1932–1940* (New York: Harper and Row, 1963), 266.

6. Egerton, *Speak Now against the Day*, 88, 292–93, 439; T. Harry Williams, *Huey Long* (New York: Knopf, 1970), 704–5.

7. Sullivan, *Days of Hope*, 67–70; "Southern Conference for Human Welfare," ca.

1940, Frank Porter Graham Papers, Box 18, F1280, SHC; Pepper Diary, November 22, 1938; Anthony P. Dunbar, *Against the Grain: Southern Radicals and Prophets, 1929–1959* (Charlottesville: University Press of Virginia, 1981), 218; Numan V. Bartley, "The Southern Conference and the Shaping of Post–World War II Southern Politics," in *Developing Dixie: Modernization in a Traditional Society*, ed. Winfred B. Moore Jr., Joseph F. Tripp, and Lyon G. Tyler Jr. (New York: Greenwood, 1988), 186; Sullivan, *Lift Every Voice*, 303, 313, 317.

8. Sullivan, *Days of Hope*, 107, 114–18, 130, 174; Pepper Diary, January 16, 1943; Harvard Sitkoff, *A New Deal for Blacks: The Emergence of Civil Rights as a National Issue—The Depression Decade* (New York: Oxford University Press, 1978), 132–36; Ric A. Kabat, "From New Deal to Red Scare: The Political Odyssey of Senator Claude D. Pepper" (Ph.D. diss., Florida State University, 1995), 135–42, 199; Pepper Diary, March 24, 26, April 2, 1944, June 14, 1945; "What Happened in Alabama," *New Republic*, May 15, 1944, 663; "The South and Congress," *Southern Patriot* 2.5 (May 1944): 4; "The Court Stands Guard," *New Republic*. April 17, 1944, 531; "Pepper and Hill," *New Republic*, April 24, 1944, 551; "Good News from the South," *New Republic*, May 15, 1944, 680; "Alabama-Florida Primaries," *Southern Patriot* 2.5 (May 1944): 5; James T. Patterson, *Brown v. Board of Education: A Civil Rights Milestone and Its Troubled Legacy* (New York: Oxford University Press, 2002), 98; Sullivan, *Lift Every Voice*, 348.

9. Starr, *Social Transformation*, 350; "A Decade of Hill-Burton," *AJPH* 47.11 (1957): 1446–47; Schulman, *From Cotton Belt to Sunbelt*, 114–33, 280–81 n. 9.

10. Schulman, *From Cotton Belt to Sunbelt*, 193–94; Claude Pepper, "A Plea for Democracy: The Anti–Poll Tax Bill," November 21, 1942, Pepper Papers, Series 203A, Box 1A, Folder 7; Claude Pepper, "Reply of Senator Pepper to Speech of Former Secretary of State Byrnes on Welfare State," June 20, 1949, Pepper Papers, Series 203A, Box 1A, Folder 22; Claude Pepper in *Congressional Record*, March 11, 1949, A1380, March 10, 1949, 2134.

11. Aubrey Williams, "Major Problems in the Rehabilitation of the South," September 26, 1937, Harry Hopkins Papers, Box 13, Franklin D. Roosevelt Library, White Plains, N.Y.; Allen Ellender in *Congressional Record*, April 14, 1943, 3380.

12. Frederick Law Olmsted, *The Cotton Kingdom*, ed. Arthur M. Schlesinger Sr. (New York: Modern Library, 1984); Ferguson, *Black Politics*, 82.

13. John P. Davis, "Remarks at the Panel on 'Children in the South—Their Health and Education' of the Second Southern Conference for Human Welfare," April 15, 1940, Graham Papers, Box 15, F1097; Schulman, *From Cotton Belt to Sunbelt*, 193; Mott and Roemer, *Rural Health and Medical Care*, 12–13; Lister Hill in *Congressional Record*, April 16, 1943, 3464; see also Allen Ellender in *Congressional Record*, April 14, 1943, 3381–82.

14. Shonick, *Government and Health Services*, 34; Davis, *America Organizes Medicine*, 116–17.

15. U.S. Congress, Senate, Committee on Education and Labor, *Hospital Construction Act*, 201; Mott and Roemer, *Rural Health and Medical Care*, xvii; U.S. Congress, Senate, Committee on Education and Labor, *To Establish a National Health Program*, 237.

16. U.S. Congress, Senate, Committee on Education and Labor, *To Establish a National Health Program*, 242, 895–98; Brandt, *No Magic Bullet*, 143–44.

17. Myrdal, *American Dilemma*, 172; Bartley, "Era," 139.

18. Bartley, "Southern Conference," 181–82; Ferguson, *Black Politics*, 83–84, 222–23.

19. Davis, *How a National Health Program*.

20. Michael M. Davis to Thomas Parran Jr., July 22, 1936, Parran Papers, Series 90/F-14, FF3.

21. Davis and Smythe, *Providing Adequate Health Service*; "Principles of a Nation-Wide Health Program," *JAMA* 126.10 (1944): 640–42.

22. Squires, *Body at Risk*, 11–12, 52.

23. Thomas R. Clark, "Limits of State Autonomy," 263–64; "Council on Medical Service and Public Relations: The Atlanta Conference," *JAMA* 127.10 (1945): 600–601; Thomas Parran Jr., "Hospitals and the Health of the People," *JAMA* 133.15 (1947): 1047–49.

24. Gordon, *Dead on Arrival*, 183; Louis Wright in *Congressional Record*, July 12, 1945, A3680; Davis and Smythe, *Providing Adequate Health Service*, 8.

25. Sullivan, *Lift Every Voice*, 228–29; U.S. Congress, Senate, Committee on Education and Labor, *To Establish a National Health Program*, 237–43, 285–90, 891–98; U.S. Congress, Senate, Committee on Education and Labor, *Construction of Hospitals*, 78–91; U.S. Congress, House, Committee on Interstate and Foreign Commerce, *Hospital Construction Act*, 184–88; McBride, *From TB to AIDS*, 142; Ward, *Black Physicians*, 177–82; Beardsley, *History of Neglect*, 246–50, 312–13.

26. Starr, *Social Transformation*, 276; "Recommendations of a Special Committee of the National Medical Association to the Technical Committee on Medical Care, in Conference, U.S. Public Health Services Building, Washington, D.C., November 22, 1938," *JNMA* 31.1 (1939): 35–36.

27. Starr, *Social Transformation*, 277.

28. "The National Health Act of 1939," *JNMA* 31.4 (1939): 154–60; "Address by Dr. Bowles before the Senate Committee," *JNMA* 31.4 (1939): 173–75; "Senator Wagner Says Non-Governmental Hospitals Are Eligible for Support under His Bill: Negroes Are Protected," *JNMA* 31.4 (1939): 175–77.

29. Grey, *New Deal Medicine*, 41; Starr, *Social Transformation*, 281; Louis Wright, Address for the Annual Convention of the National Association for the Advancement of Colored People, 1939, 4, Louis T. Wright Papers, Box 130-6, Folder 24, Moorland-Spingarn Research Center, Howard University, Washington, D.C.; Reynolds, "Dr. Louis T. Wright."

30. Gamble, *Making a Place for Ourselves*, 186–87; U.S. Congress, Senate, Committee on Education and Labor, *To Establish a National Health Program*, 238.

31. Allen Ellender in *Congressional Record*, February 16, 1938, 2031; U.S. Congress, Senate, Committee on Education and Labor, *To Establish a National Health Program*, 240–41; Starr, *Social Transformation*, 284.

32. Gary M. Pomerantz, *Where Peachtree Meets Sweet Auburn* (New York: Scribner, 1996), 133–35; Clayborne Carson, Ralph E. Luker, and Penny A. Russell, eds., *The Papers of Martin Luther King Jr.*, vol. 1, *Called to Serve, January 1929–June 1951* (Berkeley: University of California Press, 1992), 30; Patrick J. Gilpin and Marybeth Gasman, *Charles S. Johnson: Leadership beyond the Veil in the Age of Jim Crow* (Albany: State University of New York Press, 2003); Weare, *Black Business*.

33. U.S. Congress, Senate, Committee on Education and Labor, *Construction of Hospitals*, 79–91; "Hospitalization of Negro Patients," *JAMA* 115.17 (1940): 1461; Morais, *History*, 144–48; Derickson, *Health Security for All*, 68.

34. Commission on Hospital Care, *Hospital Care*, 163–67; U.S. Congress, House, Committee on Interstate and Foreign Commerce, *Hospital Construction Act*, 186.

35. Debates on S. 191, Hospital Construction Act of 1945, *Congressional Record*, December 11, 1945, 11797–99; Louis Wright in *Congressional Record*, July 12, 1945, A3680–81.

36. Provenzo, *Du Bois on Education*, 251–52; Louis Wright, untitled typescript, January 27, 1931, Wright Papers, Box 6, Folder 20; Louis T. Wright, "Remarks before the National Health Conference," July 19, 1938, Box 6, Folder 18, Wright Papers; "National Negro Health Program Ends," *JNMA* 43.3 (1951): 198–99.

37. Alonzo L. Hamby, *Liberalism and Its Challengers* (New York: Oxford University Press, 1985), 47–48; Alan Brinkley, *The War in American Culture* (Chicago: University of Chicago Press, 1996), 322; Fox, "Health Policy," 241, 245; Allen Ellender in *Congressional Record*, April 14, 1943, 3380.

38. Barkan, *Retreat of Scientific Racism*, 1–4; Barbara Dianne Savage, *Broadcasting Freedom: Radio, War, and the Politics of Race, 1938–1948* (Chapel Hill: University of North Carolina Press, 1999), 181; Love, *One Blood*, 183–85.

39. "War Meeting in Richmond 1942," *Southern Medical Journal* 35.8 (1942): 783; "Draft Program for SCHW Meeting, Nashville," January 10–13, 1942, Graham Papers, Box 18, F1285; Dombrowski, "New South," 244.

40. John Temple Graves, "The Southern Negro and the War Crisis," *Virginia Quarterly Review*, Autumn 1942, 500–501; McWilliams, *New Lights in the Valley*, 42; Egerton, *Speak Now against the Day*, 251.

41. U.S. Congress, House, Committee on Appropriations, *Department of Labor, Federal Security Agency, and Related Independent Offices Appropriation Bill, Fiscal Year 1941*," H.R. 1822 (Washington, D.C.: U.S. Government Printing Office, 1940), 50–51;

U.S. Congress, House, Committee on Expenditures in the Executive Departments, *Constituting the Federal Security Agency a Department of Welfare*, H.R. 122 (Washington, D.C.: U.S. Government Printing Office, 1949), 2–3.

42. Paul V. McNutt, NBC Radio Address to a National Unity Rally, Milwaukee, Wisc., July 14, 1941, Address to the National Industrial Conference Board, New York, May 21, 1942, both in Ewing Papers, Box 49, Political File.

43. John H. Tolan, "Our Migrant Defenders," *Survey Graphic* 30.11 (1941): 615; Federal Works Agency, *Fourth Annual Report* (Washington, D.C.: U.S. Government Printing Office, 1943), 61.

44. Carolyn Yancey Kent, "World War II Ordnance Plants," *Encyclopedia of Arkansas History and Culture*, www.encyclopediaofarkansas.net (accessed April 27, 2008); Walter E. Campbell, *Foundations for Excellence*, 155; Guy A. Caldwell, *Early History of the Ochsner Medical Center: The First Twenty-two Years* (Springfield, Ill.: Thomas, 1965), 28–31.

45. Clifton and Bernice Tallman, interview by author, Jacksonville, N.C., May 18, 1995, SHC; Lafayette Parker, interview by author, Jacksonville, N.C., May 18, 1995, SHC.

46. Michael M. Davis, "The Doctor Shortage and What to Do about It," *Harper's*, October 1942; Michael M. Davis, "Statement before Senator Claude Pepper's Sub-Committee on Manpower," November 1942, Parran Papers, Series 90/F-14, FF3; *Mississippi Doctor* 20.4 (1942): 181.

47. Mullan, *Plagues and Politics*, 115.

48. Myers, *Black, White, and Olive Drab*, 11, 18, 23.

49. Mullan, *Plagues and Politics*, 116–22.

50. Ibid.; Estelle Massey Riddle, "The Negro Nurse and the War," *Opportunity* 21.2 (1943): 44–45.

51. Riddle, "Negro Nurse," 92; Hine, *Speak Truth to Power*, 179–80.

52. Rosenfield, *Hospitals*, 14; "How Sick Is the South?" *Southern Patriot* 3.5 (1945): 2; "North Carolina's Draft Rejection Figures," *NCMJ* 6.1 (1945): 39–40; "Current Good Health Crusade Is Deep Rooted," *University of North Carolina Alumni Review*, October 1946, 36–37; Myers, *Black, White, and Olive Drab*, 17–18; de Jong, *A Different Day*, 118–19; Mott and Roemer, *Rural Health and Medical Care*, 135.

53. Mott and Roemer, *Rural Health and Medical Care*, 117–21, 131.

54. McCullough, *Truman*, 256–80; "La Guardia Elected to NAACP Board," *Kansas City Call*, January 18, 1946.

55. U.S. Congress, Senate, Committee on Education and Labor, Subcommittee on Wartime Health and Education, *Wartime Health and Education: Interim Report*, 78th Cong., 2nd sess. (Washington, D.C.: Committee Print, 1945), i, 1–2, 5–6, 22; "Pepper Committee Investigates Southern Shipbuilding Community," *Southern Patriot* 2.7 (1944): 7.

56. U.S. Congress, Senate, Committee on Education and Labor, Subcommittee on Wartime Health and Education, *Wartime Health and Education*, 1–2, 5–6, 22.

57. Ibid., 5, 9–11, 13, 19, 21–22; U.S. Congress, Senate, Committee on Education and Labor, Subcommittee on Wartime Health and Education, *Hearings before a Subcommittee of the Committee on Education and Labor, United States Senate Pursuant to S. Res. 74*, 78th Cong., 2nd sess., pt. 6, September 18–20, 1944, 2015–18.

58. Starr, *Social Transformation*, 261–77; U.S. Congress, Senate, Committee on Education and Labor, Subcommittee on Wartime Health and Education, *Wartime Health and Education*, 5, 9–11, 13, 19, 21–22; "Wartime Health Program Hearings Resume," *JAMA* 126.3 (1944): 178; "Hearings of Pepper Subcommittee on Wartime Health and Education," *JAMA* 126.4 (1944): 244–45; "Wartime Health and Education Interim Report," *JAMA* 127.1 (1945): 36–43; Morris Fishbein, remarks in *JAMA* 127.4 (1945): 228; Pepper Diary, September 18, 1944, February 7, 16, 1945.

59. "Council on Medical Service and Public Relations," 600–601; Temkin, "Driving Through," 593–94.

60. Thomas R. Clark, "Limits of State Autonomy," 266–76; Ziegler, Weinerman, and Roemer, "Rural Prepayment Medical Care Plans."

61. Beardsley, *History of Neglect*, 172–74; Brandt, *No Magic Bullet*, 161–70.

62. Stevens, *In Sickness and in Wealth*, 49; Walls, "Hot Springs Waters," 437; Raymond A. Vonderlehr, "Are We Checking the Great Plague?" *Survey Graphic* 29.4 (1940): 217; "VD Balance Sheet," *Time*, September 30, 1946.

63. Parascandola, *Sex, Sin, and Science*, 68, 120–22; Margaret Lumpkin, "Utilizing Medical Social Service in a Venereal Disease Clinic," *AJPH* 35.11 (1945): 1185.

64. Donna Pearce, "Rapid Treatment Centers," *American Journal of Nursing* 43.7 (1943): 658–60.

65. Ibid., 658; Gail Williams O'Brien, *The Color of the Law: Race, Violence, and Justice in the Post–World War II South* (Chapel Hill: University of North Carolina Press, 1999), 3, chap. 5; Herbert Shapiro, *White Violence and Black Response from Reconstruction to Montgomery* (Amherst: University of Massachusetts Press, 1988), chap. 12; Parascandola, *Sex, Sin, and Science*, 125; U.S. Public Health Service, *1945 Annual Report*, 296–97; "West Virginia Rapid Treatment Center Transferred to State Health Department," *AJPH* 37.8 (1947): 1083.

66. Pearce, "Rapid Treatment Centers," 658–60; "A Quarterly Report July–August–September 1949," *AJPH* 40.2 (1950): 211; Parascandola, *Sex, Sin, and Science*, 125–27.

67. U.S. Public Health Service, *1945 Annual Report*, 296–97; "Telling the Community about the Health Department," *AJPH* 35.10 (1945): 1083; Herbert H. Cowper, "Development of a Voluntary Agency for Venereal Disease Control," *AJPH* 38.8 (1948): 1139; Pearce, "Rapid Treatment Centers," 659.

68. Pearce, "Rapid Treatment Centers," 660.

69. Lumpkin, "Utilizing Medical Social Service," 1185–90.

70. Ibid.; Parascandola, *Sex, Sin, and Science*, 126–27.

71. Lumpkin, "Utilizing Medical Social Service," 1185–90.

72. "VD Balance Sheet"; U.S. Public Health Service, *1945 Annual Report*, 295–301; M. A. Waugh, "History of Clinical Developments in Sexually Transmitted Diseases," in *Sexually Transmitted Diseases*, ed. K. K. Holmes, P. Märdh, P. F. Sparling, and P. J. Wiesner, 2nd ed. (New York: McGraw-Hill, 1990), 13; "Rapid Treatment Center Closes," *AJPH* 40.8 (1950): 1056–57.

73. Thomas Parran Jr., "Proposed Ten-Year Postwar Program of the United States Public Health Service," November 1, 1944, 2, Thomas Parran Jr. Papers, Modern Manuscripts, History of Medicine Division, National Library of Medicine, Bethesda, Md.

74. Mullan, *Plagues and Politics*, 122; U.S. Public Health Service, *1945 Annual Report*, 280–82, 302–3; Shannon and Pyle, *Disease and Medical Care*, 26–27.

75. Mullan, *Plagues and Politics*, 121, 125; U.S. Public Health Service, *1945 Annual Report*, 289–90; Elizabeth W. Etheridge, *Sentinel for Health: A History of the Centers for Disease Control* (Berkeley: University of California Press, 1992).

76. Starr, *Social Transformation*, 358.

CHAPTER 5. STATE REFORM AND THE RACIAL DIVIDE OVER NATIONAL HEALTH INSURANCE

1. Fox, "Health Policy," 245. For more information on the efforts of southern state governments to equalize social welfare spending for blacks, see the files on the Southern Governors' Conference and Southern Regional Education Board in the collections of governors Millard Caldwell, Fuller Warren, Leroy Collins, and Farris Bryant, FSLA.

2. Derickson, *Health Security for All*, 88–89; Beardsley, *History of Neglect*, 130–32, 152; Shonick, *Government and Health Services*, 22.

3. Starr, *Social Transformation*, 305, 342; "Nationalized Doctors?" *Time*, June 21, 1937; "Trust vs. Ethics," *Time*, August 8, 1938; *NCMJ* 1.1 (1940): 48; "Educating the Public," *NCMJ* 1.8 (1940): 388.

4. Shonick, *Government and Health Services*, 21–23; "Let Not Thy Left Hand Know . . . ," *NCMJ* 9.5 (1948): 271; William Allan, "Presidential Address," *NCMJ* 1.6 (1940): 281–82; Beardsley, *History of Neglect*, 171, 247, 275, 298–99; W. Raney Stanford, "The Doctor's Solution of Two Major Problems Confronting the Medical Profession," *NCMJ* 5.11 (1944): 543; "Hospitalization of Negro Patients: A Report from the Council on Medical Education and Hospitals," *JAMA* 115.17 (1940): 1461.

5. Carl V. Reynolds, "Coordination of Public Health and Related Agencies," *NCMJ* 1.1 (1940): 24–25.

6. J. Buren Sidbury, "The Doctor and Socialized Medicine," *NCMJ* 1.1 (1940): 1–2, 7.

7. Starr, *Social Transformation*, 270; Hubert B. Haywood, "President's Message: Socialized Medicine in North Carolina," *NCMJ* 1.11 (1940): 623; Horace Hamilton, "Elements of a State Medical Care Plan" (revised), typescript, March 1945, 5, MCC, Se-

ries 94.2, Executive Secretary's Office: Hospital and Medical Care Study Commission File, Box 1C.

8. "Do the People Want Prepaid Medical Service?" *NCMJ* 2.1 (1941): 47; Allan, "Presidential Address," 281; Nathan B. van Etten, "Fitness for the National Emergency," *NCMJ* 2.6 (1941): 280; "The Effect of Socialization on Public Health," *NCMJ* 2.2 (1941): 145. In 1941, Allan became chair of the nation's first department of medical genetics at Bowman Gray Medical School. For more on Allan's advocacy of eugenics and his role in early human genetics research, see Nathaniel Comfort, "'Polyhybrid Heterogeneous Bastards': Promoting Medical Genetics in America in the 1930s and 1940s," *Journal of the History of Medicine and Allied Sciences* 61.4 (2006): 415–55.

9. "A Happier New Year," *NCMJ* 5.1 (1944): 24; van Etten, "Fitness for the National Emergency," 280; in *NCMJ* 1.2 (1940): 109; 1.7 (1940): 362; 5.1 (1944): 24.

10. Perlstadt, "Development"; Derickson, *Health Security for All*, 89; Thomas Parran to Harold T. Low, December 11, 1945, Truman Papers, OF 286-A: Socialized Medicine; Oscar R. Ewing, Speech to the Federal Security Agency Regional Staff Meeting, December 10, 1951, Ewing Papers, Box 41; Starr, *Social Transformation*, 348, 351.

11. Beardsley, *History of Neglect*, 148.

12. Hubert B. Haywood, "President's Address: Medical Problems in North Carolina," *NCMJ* 2.6 (1941): 276; "Current Good Health Crusade Is Deep Rooted," *University of North Carolina Alumni Review*, October 1946, 37; "North Carolina's Draft Rejection Figures," *NCMJ* 6.1 (1945): 39–40.

13. Poe, *Final Report*, 9; Duke Endowment Hospital Section, "North Carolina General Hospitals Caring for Negro Patients in 1944," MCC, Series 94.2, Executive Secretary's Office: Hospital and Medical Care Study Commission File, Box 1; L. D. Baver, *Medical Care Services in North Carolina: A Statistical and Graphic Summary* (Raleigh: State of North Carolina, 1945), 34–35; Beardsley, *History of Neglect*, 174–77; William Coppridge, "Suggestions from the Committee on Hospitals of the Governor's Commission," *NCMJ* 5.11 (1944): 545; North Carolina Good Health Association radio spot. Figures for the total numbers of hospital beds for blacks in North Carolina vary. The North Carolina State College Department of Rural Sociology's estimate of 1,865 in 1944 is highest; second is the North Carolina Hospital and Medical Care Commission figure of 1,760 in 1945; and lowest is the Duke Endowment's figure of 1,683. The variation of nearly two hundred beds probably results from additional beds in specialized facilities, such as tuberculosis sanitoriums and the State Hospital for the Negro Insane at Goldsboro, which were not included in the Duke Endowment's report.

14. J. Melville Broughton to Claude Pepper, May 10, 1943, Pepper Papers, Southern Governors Conference Series 203B, Box 12, Folder 3; "Current Good Health Crusade," 34–35; Walter E. Campbell, *Foundations for Excellence*, 150; "North Carolina Hospital and Medical Care Commission," *Southern Hospitals* 12.3 (1944): 34.

15. Paul Fogleman, "Was Clarence Poe Ahead of His Times!" *Durham Morning Herald*, February 9, 1969; "Dr. Owen Named Board Chairman," *Raleigh News and Observer*, March 24, 1944; William McClendon, Floyd Denny, and William Blythe, *Bettering the Health of the People: W. Reece Berryhill, the UNC School of Medicine, and the North Carolina Good Health Movement* (Chapel Hill: University of North Carolina at Chapel Hill Library, 2007), 146–47.

16. Susan Smith, *Sick and Tired*, 147; Temkin, "Driving Through"; Duffy, *Sanitarians*, 247; Lewis E. Weeks and Howard J. Berman, *Shapers of American Health Care Policy: An Oral History* (Ann Arbor, Mich.: Health Administration Press, 1985), 38.

17. North Carolina Medical Care Commission, "Minutes—Special Meeting—N.C. Medical Care Commission," August 8, 1946, 59, Office of the Vice Provost for Health Affairs of the University of North Carolina at Chapel Hill Records, Box 1:18, N.C. Medical Care Commission: General, 1946–52 Folder, UNCA; Stanford, "Doctor's Solution," 543–44.

18. Coppridge, "Suggestions," 545, 547, 550–51; Starr, *Social Transformation*, 337, 348.

19. Sidbury, "Doctor and Socialized Medicine," 3; Thomas L. Carter, "A Rural Physician Opposes the Governor's Plan," *NCMJ* 6.1 (1945): 52–56.

20. "The Crux of the Problem," *RC*, April 29, 1950.

21. Edson E. Blackman, "Negro Hospital and Medical Needs in North Carolina," in Poe, *Final Report*, 5–11; Coppridge, "Suggestions," 550–51.

22. Blackman, "Negro Hospital," 11; Weare, *Black Business*, 29, 128; John Larkins to Ellen Winston, July 18, 1945, J. W. Hamilton to John Larkins, July 9, 1945, both in State Board of Public Welfare, Bureau of Work among Negroes Records, Box 231, Tyrrell County Folder, NCSA; Beito, "Black Fraternal Hospitals."

23. Poe, *Final Report*, 16; Blackman, "Negro Hospital," 11; Thomas Parran, "Parran Evaluates N.C. Good Health Program," *University of North Carolina Alumni Review* 35.7 (1947): 219; Walter E. Campbell, *Foundations for Excellence*, 182.

24. Mayo, *Progress Report*, 19–20; Michael M. Davis, "Inter-Professional Health Conference: Tentative Draft of Report," March 7, 1944, 9, Parran Papers, Series 90/F-14, FF3.

25. "More Bureaucratic Propaganda," *NCMJ* 9.1 (1948): 43; Henry Stuart Willis, "Changing Trends in Medicine," *NCMJ* 9.6 (1948): 284.

26. "We and the Wagner Bill," *JNMA* 36.2 (1944): 63; Derickson, *Health Security for All*, 89–92, 95; "Nurses Adopt Resolutions to Send Congress," *RC*, December 21, 1946; Florence Ridlon, *A Black Physician's Struggle for Civil Rights: Edward C. Mazique, M.D.* (Albuquerque: University of New Mexico Press, 2005), 181–83, 188–93; *RC*, August 27, November 12, 1949.

27. Beardsley, *History of Neglect*, 251–52; "NMA Head Backs Truman Program," *RC*, November 12, 1949; Best, interview.

28. William Coppridge, "States' Rights in Medical Care," *NCMJ* 7.10 (1946): 570–74; "Nation Directly Affected," *RC*, July 12, 1952.

29. Starr, *Social Transformation*, 310–20; "Dr. Fishbein Fights Losing Battle," *RC*, January 8, 1949.

30. "Health Needs Again Aired," *RC*, January 3, 1953; "The Beam in Our Eye," *NCMJ* 14.1 (January 1953): 36; Starr, *Social Transformation*, 284–87; "AMA Off the Deep End," January 7, 1950; McCullough, *Truman*, 492–506, 528.

31. Starr, *Social Transformation*, 280; Stevens, *In Sickness and in Wealth*, 259.

32. Derickson, *Health Security for All*, 126; Oscar R. Ewing, "The President's Health Program and the Negro Doctor," speech, June 1, 1949, Box 39, Ewing Papers; "Face the Facts," *RC*, July 14, 1951.

33. "1953," *NCMJ* 14.1 (1953): 35.

CHAPTER 6. HILL-BURTON AND THE DELUXE JIM CROW HOSPITAL

1. Rich and White, *Health Policy*, 17–19; U.S. Public Health Service, *1945 Annual Report*, 327–28; "NMA Head Backs Truman Program," *RC*, November 12, 1949; Allen Ellender in *Congressional Record*, May 4, 1949, A2653; Michael M. Davis, "Inter-Professional Health Conference: Tentative Draft of Report," March 7, 1944, 8, Parran Papers, Series 90/F-14, FF3.

2. Rosenfield, *Hospitals*, 10–13.

3. Stevens, *In Sickness and in Wealth*, 132–33; Rosenfield, *Hospitals*, 9–13.

4. Rosenfield, *Hospitals*, 27, 220–26; "Hospital Survey, Wilson County," 1945, MCC, Series 94.2, Executive Secretary's Office: Hospital and Medical Care Study Commission File, Box 1.

5. Rosenfield, *Hospitals*, 9–13; Gifford, *Evolution*, 155, 62–63.

6. Holly Raider, "Market Structure and Innovation," *Social Science Research* 27.1 (1998): 1–21; Stevens, *In Sickness and in Wealth*, 62–64, 71–79, 195–96; R. M. Carey and C. L. Engelhard, "Academic Medicine Meets Managed Care: A High-Impact Collision," *Academic Medicine* 71.8 (1996): 839–45; Starr, *Social Transformation*, 261–62; Mott and Roemer, *Rural Health and Medical Care*, v.

7. Raider, "Market Structure and Innovation." The Johns Hopkins Hospital in Baltimore provides an ample illustration of the chaotic state of hospital care, particularly for outpatients, in the South during this period. See Charles Flagle, "Some Origins of Operations Research in the Health Services," *Operations Research* 50.1 (2002): 52–60.

8. Michael M. Davis, "Statement before Senator Claude Pepper's Sub-Committee on Manpower," November 1942, Parran Papers, Series 90/F-14, FF3.

9. Rosenfield, *Hospitals*, 16–18; "Essentials of a Registered Hospital," *JAMA* 112.21

(1939): 2166–68; Stevens, *In Sickness and in Wealth*, 214; Rice and Jones, *Public Policy*, 21, 34.

10. Barbara Bridgman Perkins, *The Medical Delivery Business: Reform, Childbirth, and the Economic Order* (New Brunswick, N.J.: Rutgers University Press, 2004), 69–70.

11. Rosenfield, *Hospitals*, 18–19; U.S. Public Health Service, *1945 Annual Report*, 293.

12. Stevens, *In Sickness and in Wealth*, 206–16; Rosenfield, *Hospitals*, 222–26; Isadore Rosenfield and Simon Breines, *Making Better Health Available to All* (New York: Revere Copper and Brass, 1943); Davis, *America Organizes Medicine*, 235, 242.

13. Stevens, *In Sickness and in Wealth*, 119–22, 132–35; J. Buren Sidbury, "The Doctor and Socialized Medicine," *NCMJ* 1.1 (1940): 4.

14. Southmayd, "Study," 20–21, 73; Michael M. Davis to Thomas Parran, November 23, 1938, Parran Papers, Series 90/F-14, FF3.

15. "Council on Medical Service and Public Relations: The Atlanta Conference," *JAMA* 127.10 (1945): 600; U.S. Congress, Senate, Committee on Education and Labor, Subcommittee on Wartime Health and Education, *Wartime Health and Education: Interim Report*, 78th Cong., 2nd sess. (Washington, D.C.: Committee Print, 1945), 14–17, 21; Perlstadt, "Development," 77–91; Lewis E. Weeks and Howard J. Berman, *Shapers of American Health Care Policy: An Oral History* (Ann Arbor, Mich.: Health Administration Press, 1985), 36–42; Thomas R. Clark, "Limits," 262–64; Claude Pepper Diary, March 8, 1938, Pepper Papers; *Congressional Record*, March 8, 1938, 3008; Starr, *Social Transformation*, 348; Stevens, *In Sickness and in Wealth*, 218–19.

16. Philip B. Fleming to Harry S. Truman, August 2, 1946, Watson B. Miller to F. J. Bailey, August 7, 1946, James E. Webb to M. C. Latta, August 9, 1946, Clark Clifford to Harry S. Truman, August 12, 1946, all in Truman Papers, Box 22, White House Bill File, S.191.

17. James Murray, "Memorandum on the Political Evolution of the Hospital Bill, S. 191," Truman Papers, Box 22, White House Bill File, S.191.

18. Gamble, *Making a Place for Ourselves*, 151; David Barton Smith, *Health Care Divided*, 40, 47–49; Ward, *Black Physicians*, 169.

19. Gamble, *Making a Place for Ourselves*, 142–50, 184–90; Reynolds, "Dr. Louis T. Wright."

20. "Priest, Hon. J. Percy," April 3, 1946, Truman Papers, Box 575, OF 103; Huntington Williams to Isaiah Bowman, May 29, 31, 1944, Records of the Office of the President, Box 184, 745 (1944–45) Folder, Hamburger University Archives, Johns Hopkins University, Baltimore.

21. M. Don Clawson to Harry S. Truman, March 11, 1946, M. Don Clawson to Robert E. Hannegan, March 11, 1946, Matthew J. Connelly to J. Percy Priest, April 22, 1946, Phileo Nash Papers, Box 53, White House File, Truman Presidential Library.

22. Starr, *Social Transformation*, 321, 348, 351; Temkin, "Driving Through"; Bartley, *New South*, 64.

23. National Negro Congress flyer, in *Documentary History of the Truman Presidency*, ed. Dennis Merrill (n.p.: University Publications of America, 2004), 11:72–74; David Barton Smith, *Health Care Divided*, 46–50; Beardsley, "Desegregating Southern Medicine, 1945–1970," in *History of Neglect*, 245–72.

24. Alan P. Smith, "The Institutional Care of Negroes with Mental Diseases in the United States," *JNMA* 24.4 (1937): 146–51.

25. Omar Bradley to Robert K. Carr, April 22, 1947, RG 220, Records of the President's Committee on Civil Rights, General Correspondence with Government Departments and Agencies, Box 7, Veterans Administration Folder, Truman Presidential Library.

26. Myers, *Black, White, and Olive Drab*, 57; Cobb, "Medical Care"; *RC*, March 29, August 16, 1947; "Dr. Marshall Telegraphs Senators Morse and Wiley on Behalf of the National Medical Association," *JNMA* 40.3 (1948): 129; "Fed. Gov. OK's Lafargue Clinic," *Amsterdam Star News*, March 8, 1947.

27. "White Nurses Replace Negroes in Vet Facility," *Pittsburgh Courier*, April 27, 1946; Morais, *History*, 142; "Congressmen Want Jim Crow Hospitals, 3 N.C. Congressmen against Jim Crow in VA Hospitals," *RC*, March 16, 1957.

28. Ward, *Black Physicians*, 169–90, 285; Sullivan, *Lift Every Voice*, 400–1; Numa P. G. Adams, "An Interpretation of the Significance of the Homer G. Phillips Hospital," *JNMA* 26.1 (1934): 16; "Professional News," *JNMA* 24.2 (1937): 71; "Federal Works Agency—P.W.A., Office of Advisor on Negro Affairs," *JNMA* 32.3 (1940): 136.

29. "Hospital Exclusively for Colored to Begin Operation Here Tomorrow," *Chattanooga Times*, June 17, 1947; Cobb, "Medical Care," 208; Ward, *Black Physicians*, 179; M. O. Bousfield, "Presidential Address," *JNMA* 26.4 (1934): 155.

30. Roy Kracke Papers, Series 17.1.1, Dean's Administrative Files, 1939–50, Box 1, University Archives, University of Alabama at Birmingham.

31. John T. Givens, "Our Medical Colleges and Medical Education," *JNMA* 40.4 (1948): 10; Neyland, *FAMU*; "Florida A. and M. College Hospital, Tallahassee, Fla.," *JNMA* 42.3 (1950): 186–87; J. B. Culpepper to John Perry, "The Support of Negro Public Higher Education in Florida," July 9, 1956, Governor T. Leroy Collins Papers, RG 102, Series 776A, Box 33, FF2 Race Relations, May–Dec. 1956, FSLA.

32. "For Negroes Only," *Time*, June 30, 1952; Allen, "Challenges," 3–5.

33. Ferguson, *Black Politics*, 86; Cathy Lee, "Grady Health System," *New Georgia Encyclopedia*, www.georgiaencyclopedia.org (accessed May 16, 2008).

34. "Crushing Irony," 386–87; W. Montague Cobb, "The National Health Program of the N.A.A.C.P.," *JNMA* 45.4 (1953): 333–39; David Barton Smith, *Health Care Divided*, 49; Ward, *Black Physicians*, 170–82.

35. Beardsley, *History of Neglect*, 99, 245–51, 255–59; Ward, *Black Physicians*,

176–78; Cobb, "Medical Care," 208; Rice and Jones, *Public Policy*, 109–10; "Memphis NAACP Branch Rescinds Endorsement of Negro Hospital," *JNMA* 44.4 (1952): 314–15; Reynolds, "Dr. Louis T. Wright," 888–89.

36. "Memphis NAACP Branch Rescinds Endorsement," 314–15; Ward, *Black Physicians*, 179; Wailoo, *Dying*, 94–103, 111–14; Walter E. Campbell, *Foundations for Excellence*.

37. In 1947, during the investigations by the President's Committee on Civil Rights, naturopathic physicians in the National Medical Society called for an investigation of discrimination against "the healing arts outside the fold of organized medicine." They charged that "a great injustice is being done by organized medicine's controlled examining boards and their dominent [*sic*] medic-political influence throughout the nation by undermining and persecuting members of the naturopathic healing arts who are in discord with the policies of the medical hierarchy." The society did not, however, mention racial discrimination as a salient issue for alternative practitioners. See Hans Zimmerman to Robert K. Karr, March 20, 1947, RG 220, Records of the President's Committee on Civil Rights, General Correspondence with Institutions, Organizations, etc., Box 12, Truman Library. As a member of the Committee on the Nation's Health, Davis also wrote to the President's Committee on Civil Rights regarding discrimination against physicians who participated in group practice plans (Box 10).

38. "Crushing Irony," 386–87; U.S. Congress, Senate, debates on S. 191, Hospital Construction Act of 1945, *Congressional Record*, December 11, 1945, 11797–99; Beardsley, *History of Neglect*, 185; Stevens, *In Sickness and in Wealth*, 219; Schulman, *From Cotton Belt to Sunbelt*, 201–3; Starr, *Social Transformation*, 351, 358–59; Paul Cornely, "Segregation and Discrimination in Medical Care in the United States," *AJPH* 46.7 (1956): 1079.

39. S. W. Smith, "Deficiency of Bed Space and Suggestions for Remedies," *JNMA* 33.1 (1941): 26–31; Reynolds, "Professional and Hospital Discrimination"; Simkins, interview.

40. Oscar R. Ewing to Eugene A. R. Montgomery, February 15, 1951, Oscar R. Ewing to Robert Lesueur, June 28, 1951, Maurice B. Gatlin to Marion Folsom, February 5, 1957, Department of Health, Education, and Welfare (RG 235), Records of the Public Health Division, Office of the General Counsel, Box 7, Hospital Construction, Segregation and Discrimination File, National Archives, College Park, Md.

41. Schulman, *From Cotton Belt to Sunbelt*, 135–39, 206–7; Rice and Jones, *Public Policy*, 75, 80; Morais, *History*, 181; Gordon, *Dead on Arrival*, 194.

42. Starr, *Social Transformation*, 350; U.S. Senate, Committee on Labor and Public Welfare, Subcommittee on Health, *Hill-Burton Hospital Survey and Construction Act*, 11–13; Beardsley, *History of Neglect*, 247.

43. U.S. Senate, Committee on Labor and Public Welfare, Subcommittee on Health, *Hill-Burton Hospital Survey and Construction Act*, 13; James E. Rohrer, "The

Political Development of the Hill-Burton Program: A Case Study in Distributive Policy," *Journal of Health Politics, Policy, and Law* 12.1 (1987): 142–43; Jacquelyn Hochban, B. Ellenbogen, J. Benson, and R. M. Olson, "The Hill-Burton Program and Changes in Health Services Delivery," *Inquiry* 18.1 (1981): 61.

44. U.S. Senate, Committee on Labor and Public Welfare, Subcommittee on Health, *Hill-Burton Hospital Survey and Construction Act*, 13; McWilliams, *New Lights in the Valley*, 60–61; Roy Kracke, "The Medical Care of the Veteran," *JAMA* 143.15 (1950): 1321–27, cited in McWilliams, *New Lights in the Valley*, 437 n. 23; Walter E. Campbell, *Foundations for Excellence*, 137.

45. Lawrence J. Clark et al., "Impact of Hill-Burton," 532; Lister Hill in *Congressional Record*, October 17, 1949, A6373; Valerie A. Earle, "Post-1935 Developments in Southern State Health Programs," *AJPH* 41.11 (1951): 1407; Claude Pepper, Speech, July 30, 1947, 4, Pepper Papers, Series 203B, Subseries U.S. Senate—Speeches, Box 5, Folder 2.

46. Lawrence J. Clark et al., "Impact of Hill-Burton," 538–42, 548–50.

47. Starr, *Social Transformation*, 350, 373; Beardsley, *History of Neglect*, 184, 342 n. 88; U.S. Senate, Committee on Labor and Public Welfare, Subcommittee on Health, *Hill-Burton Hospital Survey and Construction Act*, 11; Lawrence J. Clark et al., "Impact of Hill-Burton," 538–42, 548–50; University of Virginia Geospatial and Statistical Data Center, *United States Historical Census Data Browser*, 1940 data.

48. Robert Coles, *Farewell to the South* (Cambridge: Harvard University Press, 1972), 170–77; Bartley, *New South*, 156; Collins and Thomasson, "Declining Contribution," 769–70, 752–61; Beardsley, *History of Neglect*, 279–84.

49. U.S. Department of Health, Education, and Welfare Annual Reports, 1955, 1960; Edward Berkowitz, "Historical Insights into the Development of Health Services Research: A Narrative Based on a Collection of Oral Interviews," www.nlm.nih.gov/hmd/nichsr/intro.html#w31-3 (accessed May 5, 2009).

50. Weeks and Berman, *Shapers*, 39; Schulman, *From Cotton Belt to Sunbelt*, 118–19; "The Republican Welfare States," *Atlantic Monthly*, March 2004, 48.

CHAPTER 7. HILL-BURTON IN NORTH CAROLINA

1. "North Carolina's Draft Rejection Figures," *NCMJ* 6.1 (1945): 39–40; "Current Good Health Crusade Is Deep Rooted," *University of North Carolina Alumni Review*, October 1946, 36–37; Poe, *Final Report*, 16; Commission on Hospital Care, *Hospital Care*, 3, 163–67; William M. Coppridge, "Suggestions from the Committee on Hospitals of the Governor's Commission," *NCMJ* 5.11 (1944): 546–47; Edson E. Blackman, "Negro Hospital and Medical Needs in North Carolina," in Poe, *Final Report*, 5–11.

2. "Current Good Health Crusade," 34; "Parran Evaluates N.C. Good Health Program," *University of North Carolina Alumni Review* 35.7 (1947): 219; Beardsley, *History*

of Neglect, 121–22; Morais, *History*, 130; Myers, *Black, White, and Olive Drab*, 18; Ferguson, *Black Politics*, 226.

3. Mayo, *Progress Report*, 19–20; Rosenfield, *Hospitals*, 44–47; U.S. Public Health Service, *Design and Construction of General Hospitals* (New York: Dodge, 1953), 52.

4. W. D. Carmichael to David S. Coltrane, November 3, 1949, Records of the Controller and Vice President for Finance, W. D. Carmichael Series, Subgroup 1, General Administration, Desegregation: Medical Care, 1949–51 Folder, UNCA; Cochran and Cochran, interview; Stevens, *In Sickness and in Wealth*, 253–54; David Barton Smith, "Politics of Racial Disparities," 264; Pohl, "Long Waits," 132.

5. Parran, "Parran Evaluates," 218; Rice and Jones, *Public Policy*, 75; Gamble, *Making a Place for Ourselves*, 187.

6. Parran, "Parran Evaluates," 219–20; H. C. Cranford, "A Formula That Gets Hospitals into Rural Areas," *Hospitals: The Journal of the American Hospital Association* 22.12 (1948): 33; Beardsley, *History of Neglect*, 184.

7. Stevens, *In Sickness and in Wealth*, 220–21; Wall, *Louisiana*, 304–6, 321.

8. Medical Center Study, *Planning Florida's Health Leadership*, 5 vols. (Gainesville: University of Florida Press, 1954).

9. Helen Gahagan Douglas, "What Price Medicine: Current Legislation Dealing with Health before the Present Congress," *JNMA* 40.1 (1948): 17; Vane M. Hoge, "The National Hospital Construction Program," *JNMA* 40.3 (1948): 102, 104; "Federal Aid and Regional Plan Chimerae," 339. Health economist Milton Roemer also expressed optimism that the nondiscrimination clause would benefit southern blacks (Milton I. Roemer, "Recent National Health Legislation," *JNMA* 39.3 [1947]: 118).

10. Thomas Parran, "Hospitals and the Health of the People," *JAMA* 133.15 (1947): 1047–49.

11. Charles S. Templeton, "Memo to MCC," May 7, 1957, MCC, Series 94.8, Director's Office: Agencies and Organizations Correspondence, Box 3, 1957 State Legislature–General Correspondence Folder; Parran, "Hospitals," 1047–48.

12. Samuel C. Ingraham II to John A. Ferrell, April 22, 1947, MCC, Series 94.8, Director's Office: Agencies and Organizations Correspondence, Box 4, Rules and Regulations (State Plan) Governing Approps. for Hosp. Constr. Folder.

13. Samuel C. Ingraham II to John A. Ferrell, November 21, 1947, MCC, Series 94.8, Director's Office: Agencies and Organizations Correspondence, Box 4, Rules and Regulations (State Plan) Governing Approps. for Hosp. Constr. Folder; Rice and Jones, *Public Policy*, 75; Morais, *History*, 181; Gordon, *Dead on Arrival*, 194; U.S. Commission on Civil Rights, *Civil Rights <ap>63: Report of the U.S. Commission on Civil Rights* (Washington, D.C.: U.S. Commission on Civil Rights, 1963), 131.

14. North Carolina State Hill-Burton Plan, "Minimum Standards for the Maintenance and Operation of Hospitals," Thomas Parran to John A. Ferrell, July 8, 1947, MCC, Series 94.8, Director's Office: Agencies and Organizations Correspondence,

Box 4, Rules and Regulations (State Plan) Governing Approps. for Hosp. Constr. Folder.

15. Samuel C. Ingraham II to John A. Ferrell, November 21, 24, 1947, April 27, 1948, MCC, Series 94.8, Director's Office: Agencies and Organizations Correspondence, Box 4, Rules and Regulations (State Plan) Governing Approps. for Hosp. Constr. Folder.

16. "Jimcrow Hospital Nixed, TB Hospital to Be Utilized by All the People," *RC*, September 22, 1951.

17. Duke Endowment Hospital Section, "North Carolina General Hospitals Caring for Negro Patients in 1944," MCC, Series 94.2, Executive Secretary's Office: Hospital and Medical Care Study Commission File, Box 1.

18. Mullan, *Plagues and Politics*, 85–86; Gerald N. Grob, "Deinstitutionalization: The Illusion of Policy," *Journal of Policy History* 9.1 (1997): 48–52; Albert Deutsch, *The Shame of the States* (New York: Harcourt, Brace, 1948).

19. Alan P. Smith, "The Institutional Care of Negroes with Mental Diseases in the United States," *JNMA* 24.4 (1937): 146; *Congressional Record*, February 16, 1938, 2031; U.S. Public Health Service, *1945 Annual Report*, 335.

20. Walter E. Campbell, *Foundations for Excellence*, 50–51; McIntosh and Kendrick, *Public Health Administration*, 131, 186.

21. William R. Johnson, "Report of Visit to State Hospital, Goldsboro," Bureau of Work among Negroes Records, Box 241, Cherry Hospital, Goldsboro, N.C. Folder, NCSA; Maurice H. Greenhill, "The Present Status of Mental Health in North Carolina," *NCMJ* 5.1 (1945): 10, 12; "Professional News," *JNMA* 29.2 (1937): 71; "Federal Works Agency–P.W.A., Office of Advisor on Negro Affairs," *JNMA* 32.3 (1940): 136; North Carolina Medical Care Commission, "One Hundred Ninety-two Projects Aided by the Commission during the First Seven Years of Construction," November 24, 1954, Records of the Office of the Vice Chancellor for Health Affairs, Henry T. Clark Series, Box 17, 1953–63 Folder, UNCA; "Hospital Construction," 328; John Larkins to J. Melville Broughton, May 11, 1956, John Larkins to M. M. Vitols, January 8, 1957, John Larkins, "Notes Regarding State School for Mentally Defective Children," all in Bureau of Work among Negroes Records, Box 241, Cherry Hospital, Goldsboro, N.C. Folder.

22. Cochran and Cochran, interview; Michael A. Dowell, "Hill-Burton: The Unfulfilled Promise," *Journal of Health Politics, Policy, and Law* 12.1 (1987): 154; Stevens, *In Sickness and in Wealth*, 269–70; "Saint Agnes Hospital Condemned," *RC*, May 14, 1955; "Ford Grant Brings New Hope to St. Agnes Hospital," *RC*, October 27, 1956; Rice and Jones, *Public Policy*, 61–62; Beardsley, *History of Neglect*, 256; Pohl, "Long Waits," 113; Gamble, *Making a Place for Ourselves*, 192–94.

23. Gifford, *Evolution*, 163–64; Pohl, "Long Waits," 111–31; Duke Endowment Hospital Section, "North Carolina General Hospitals"; *Medical Care Services*, 34–35;

Poe, *Final Report*; Rice and Jones, *Public Policy*, 21, 34; Gamble, *Making a Place for Ourselves*, 182–96; Henry James [pseudonym], interview by author, August 15, 1994, in author's possession; North Carolina Medical Care Commission, "Hospital Survey, Wilson County," 1945, MCC, Series 94.2, Executive Secretary's Office: Hospital and Medical Care Study Commission, Box 1. For another positive portrayal of Duke's care for African American patients, see Walter E. Campbell, *Foundations for Excellence*, 91–92.

24. Love, *One Blood*, 1, 21–31, 217–27.

25. Anslee Willett, "Technology Brings Comfort to Patients," *Burlington (N.C.) Times-News*, November 11, 1999; North Carolina Medical Care Commission, "One Hundred Ninety-two Projects"; beds for blacks are calculated by multiplying total beds by percentages of Negro patients from *1961 Miscellaneous Hospital Statistics* (Durham: Duke Endowment, 1961), A-1–A-5, Duke Endowment Archives, Hospital Division Subseries, Box HCCD 16, Special Collections, Perkins Library, Duke University, Durham, N.C.; North Carolina Advisory Committee to the U.S. Commission on Civil Rights, *Equal Protection of the Laws in North Carolina* (Washington, D.C.: U.S. Government Printing Office, 1962), 17, 20; "Student Succumbs after Aid Is Refused at Hospital," *RC*, December 9, 1950; "Seriously-Burned Woman Refused Admittance to Two N.C. Hospitals: White, Negro Hospitals Refuse Aid," *RC*, February 16, 1952; "Lawyer Intervened: Hospitals Filled; Youth Is Jailed," *RC*, March 8, 1952; "Prisoner Is Refused Medical Care; Dies," *RC*, August 2, 1952.

26. Starr, *Social Transformation*, 373; Meckel, *Save the Babies*, 173–74; Collins and Thomasson, "Declining Contribution," 769–70.

27. Parran, "Parran Evaluates," 218–19; Donald L. Madison, "Remembering Cecil," *NCMJ* 65.5 (2004): 304; *The Expansion of Medical Facilities and Services in North Carolina—Two Decades of Progress* (Raleigh: North Carolina Medical Care Commission, 1967), 11.

28. *Expansion*, 11; William F. Henderson, "Remarks before the North Carolina Legislative Research Commission," January 5, 1968, MCC, Series 94.8, Director's Office: Agencies and Organizations Correspondence, Box 3, Legislative Research Commission Folder; North Carolina Advisory Committee, *Equal Protection of the Laws*, 18, 23, 26; David Barton Smith, *Health Care Divided*, 194; U.S. Commission on Civil Rights, *Report*, 132; Gamble, *Making a Place for Ourselves*, 187.

29. University of Virginia Geospatial and Statistical Data Center, *United States Historical Census Data Browser*, 1940 data.

30. John A. Ferrell to Ralph Moody, October 3, 1950, MCC, Series 94.8, Director's Office: Agencies and Organizations Correspondence, USPHS General Correspondence Folder. For national context, see "Hospital Construction under Hill-Burton Program," *JNMA* 42.5 (1950): 328.

31. Jill Quadagno, *One Nation Uninsured: Why the U.S. Has No National Health*

Insurance (New York: Oxford University Press, 2005), 82; Stevens, *In Sickness and in Wealth*, 254–55; *Expansion*, 11; Gamble, *Making a Place for Ourselves*, 188–90; Karen Kruse Thomas, "The Wound of My People: Segregation and the Modernization of Health Care in North Carolina, 1935–1975" (Ph.D. diss., University of North Carolina at Chapel Hill, 1999), 175–88; Reynolds, "Hospitals and Civil Rights."

32. North Carolina Medical Care Commission, "One Hundred Ninety-two Projects"; P. Preston Reynolds, "Watts Hospital, 1895–1976: Paternalism and Race in the Evolution of a Southern Institution in Durham, North Carolina" (Ph.D. diss., Duke University, 1986); Reynolds, "Hospitals and Civil Rights"; Stevens, *In Sickness and in Wealth*, 62–63; *1964 Miscellaneous Hospital Statistics* (Durham: Duke Endowment, 1964), A-1, Duke Endowment Archives; Walter Reece Berryhill to Henry Clark, April 11, 1953, Black Student Admissions; North Carolina Advisory Committee, "Equal Protection of the Laws," 17–18.

33. Peter F. Drucker, "The Age of Social Transformation," *Atlantic Monthly*, November 1994, 53–72; Carolanne H. Hoffman, *Health Insurance Coverage* (Washington, D.C.: National Center for Health Statistics, 1964) cited in Collins and Thomasson, "Declining Contribution," 770; Derickson, *Health Security for All*, 126.

34. North Carolina Advisory Committee, "Equal Protection of the Laws," 20; Stevens, *In Sickness and in Wealth*, 268–75; "Current Good Health Crusade," 35; Roy Parker Jr., "Welfare Officials See Progress for N.C. Hospitalization Program," *Raleigh News and Observer*, August 23, 1959; Duke Endowment, *Annual Reports of the Hospital and Orphan Sections, for the Fiscal Year October 1, 1961–September 30, 1962* (Durham: Duke Endowment, 1962), 22–25.

35. Claude Pepper Diary, March 8, 1938, Pepper Papers; *Congressional Record*, March 8, 1938, 3008; Allen Ellender in U.S. Congress, Senate, Committee on Education and Labor, *Hospital Construction Act*, 190–91; Lawrence A. Schneider, "Comments: Provision of Free Medical Services By Hill-Burton Hospitals," *Harvard Civil Rights–Civil Liberties Law Review* 8.10 (1973): 351–83; Beito, "Black Fraternal Hospitals," 136, 140; Bartley, *New South*, 156; Hamilton, *Lister Hill*, 139.

36. For criticism of Hill-Burton's failure to fulfill its pledge that participant hospitals would provide substantial care to indigent patients, see Schneider, "Comments," 352; Dowell, "Hill-Burton," 153–75.

37. Ward, *Black Physicians*, 176; Stevens, *In Sickness and in Wealth*, 219, 399 n. 56, 254; Beardsley, *History of Neglect*, 178–80; Jill Quadagno and Steve McDonald, "Racial Segregation in Southern Hospitals: How Medicare 'Broke the Back of Segregated Health Services,'" in *The New Deal and Beyond: Social Welfare in the South since 1930*, ed. Elna C. Green (Athens: University of Georgia Press, 2003), 119–21; David Barton Smith, *Health Care Divided*, 46–47; Reynolds, "Professional and Hospital Discrimination," 710–11; Gordon, *Dead on Arrival*, 193–94; Starr, *Social Transformation*, 275–77; Reynolds, "Federal Government's Use." On the role of antidiscrimination

clauses in defeating federal aid to medical education, see the remarks of Senator Elbert Thomas of Utah and President M. Don Clawson of Meharry Medical College in *Congressional Record*, May 12, 1948, 5659–68; "Federal Aid and Regional Plan Chimerae," 339.

38. Beardsley, *History of Neglect*, 256–58.

39. U.S. Senate, Committee on Labor and Public Welfare, Subcommittee on Health, *Hill-Burton Hospital Survey and Construction Act*, 17; Clark et al., "Impact of Hill-Burton," 546.

CHAPTER 8. TRAINING BLACK DOCTORS AS PUBLIC POLICY

1. Beardsley, *History of Neglect*, 253–55; White, *How Far the Promised Land*, 152–57.

2. Teddlie and Freeman, "With All Deliberate Speed," 10–12; White, *How Far the Promised Land*, 153–55; E. H. L. Corwin and Gertrude Sturges, *Opportunities for the Medical Education of Negroes* (New York: Scribner's, 1936); Starr, *Social Transformation*, 124; "History of Rush University," http://www.rushu.rush.edu/catalog /aboutrush/ruhistory.html (accessed March 27, 2008); University of Pennsylvania School of Medicine, Office of Diversity and Community Outreach, "A History of Minority Presence at the School of Medicine of the University of Pennsylvania," http:// www.med.upenn.edu/diversityume/timeline.shtml (accessed March 10, 2008); David Barton Smith, "Healing a Nation: How Three Graduates of the U-M Medical School Wrote Their Own Chapter in the History of Civil Rights in America," *Medicine at Michigan* 2.2 (2000): 38–42; Gamble, *Making a Place for Ourselves*, 30–34, 164–68; Ward, *Black Physicians*, 250–51; Walter H. Maddux, "Postgraduate Courses for Negro Physicians in Mississippi," *The Child* 3.8 (1939): 181–82.

3. Richard A. Schaefer, *Of the Highest Order: The Incredible One Hundred–Year History of Loma Linda University School of Medicine* (Hagerstown, Md.: Review and Herald, 2009); Michael J. Bent, "Negro Students Enrolled in Medical Schools in the U.S.," *JNMA* 42.1 (1950): 45; 42.4 (1950): 253; 43.4 (1951): 276–77; Joseph L. Johnson, "Opportunities for Negroes in Undergraduate Medical Education in 1952," *JNMA* 44.5 (1952): 353–55.

4. Jerry Gershenhorn, "*Hocutt v. Wilson* and Race Relations in Durham, North Carolina, during the 1930s," *North Carolina Historical Review* 78.3 (2001): 275–308; Sullivan, *Lift Every Voice*, 168–70; Kluger, *Simple Justice*, 155–58, 187–94.

5. Jerry Gershenhorn, "Stalling Integration: The Ruse, Rise, and Demise of North Carolina College's Doctoral Program in Education, 1951–1962," North Carolina Historical Review 82.2 (2005): 158–61; Kluger, *Simple Justice*, 202–4, 212–13; Egerton, *Speak Now against the Day*, 489–90; Ward, *Black Physicians*, 40–41; Dawson, "Federal Government and Education," 226–27; Gordon Gray, "A Report on Negro Ap-

plications for Admission to the University," July 16, 1951, 5, Records of the Controller and Vice President for Finance, W. D. Carmichael Series, Subgroup 1, Desegregation: Applications, 1948–55 Folder, UNCA; Neyland, *FAMU*; Korstad, *Dreaming of a Time*, 49–53. Missouri and West Virginia were the first states to offer out-of-state scholarships to black graduate and professional students, and North Carolina followed in 1939. Gershenhorn notes, "As a result of the pressure applied by the NAACP victory in the *Gaines* case, by 1945, seven southern states had established professional and graduate schools at fourteen black colleges. . . . In 1945, black colleges operated two medical and dental schools, two pharmacy schools, three law schools, two social work schools, two library science schools, one journalism school, and one veterinary medicine school. Nine southern states provided funding for black students to attend out-of-state colleges for programs of study not available at in-state black colleges. Alabama, Florida, Louisiana, Mississippi, and South Carolina did not provide such out-of-state funding" ("Stalling Integration," 161). Howard University and Meharry Medical College offered degrees in dentistry and pharmacy but not public health.

6. T. Carr McFall, "Needs for Hospital Facilities and Physicians in Thirteen Southern States," *JNMA* 42.4 (July 1950): 235–36; Joseph L. Johnson, "The Supply of Negro Health Personnel—Physicians," *Journal of Negro Education* 18.3 (1949): 346; University of Virginia Geospatial and Statistical Data Center, *United States Historical Census Data Browser*, 1950 data; Johnson, "Opportunities," 353–55.

7. Beardsley, *History of Neglect*, 253–55; Davis and Smythe, "Providing Adequate Health Service," 8; *RC*, May 22, 1948; Egerton, *Speak Now against the Day*, 430–31; M. Don Clawson to Roy R. Kracke, June 2, 1948, Manuscript Collection 51, Emmett B. Carmichael/Alabama Museum of the Health Sciences Collection, 1859–1990, Box 58, Folder H, University Archives, University of Alabama at Birmingham; Claude Pepper Diary, May 14, 1948, Pepper Papers; "Federal Aid and Regional Plan Chimerae," 339; Charles Herbert Marshall, "The Southern Governors' Educational Plan," *JNMA* 40.3 (1948): 122–23; J. A. C. Lattimore, "Address of the Outgoing President," *JNMA* 40.6 (1948): 233. Here I adopt William Chafe's definition of white moderates as those "who welcomed an atmosphere of tolerance but did not initiate or endorse change in the racial status quo" (*Civilities and Civil Rights*, 43).

8. Mahlon Ashford, "Medical Education for Minority Groups," *JNMA* 40.4 (1948): 167–69.

9. Sullivan, *Days of Hope*; Campion, *AMA and U.S. Health Policy*, chaps. 12, 14; Beardsley, *History of Neglect*, 177–78; Egerton, *Speak Now against the Day*, 474–513.

10. "Governor McCord's Recommendation of Meharry as a Regional School," 5, Governor Jim McCord Papers, Box 19, Folder 1, Tennessee State Library and Archives, Nashville; *RC*, November 1, 1947; Marshall, "Southern Governors' Educational Plan," 122–23.

11. Egerton, *Speak Now against the Day*, 430–31; M. Don Clawson to Roy R.

Kracke, June 2, 1948, Manuscripts Collection 51, Emmett B. Carmichael/Alabama Museum of the Health Sciences Collection, 1859–1990, Box 58, Folder H; W. T. Sanger, *Final Report of the National Committee for the Medical School Survey*, July 1, 1946, 27, Office of the Vice Provost for Health Affairs of the University of North Carolina at Chapel Hill Records, Box 1:18, UNCA.

12. John T. Givens, "Our Medical Colleges and Medical Education," *JNMA* 40.4 (1948): 170.

13. William Mulder, "Elbert Duncan Thomas," *Dictionary of American Biography*, supplement 5, 1951–55 (New York: Scribner's, 1977), reproduced in *Gale Biography in Context* (http://ic.galegroup.com/ic/bic1) (accessed May 16, 2011); Elbert Thomas in *Congressional Record*, May 12, 1948, 5659–61.

14. Dummett, *NDA II*, 88; *RC*, May 1, 1948, December 25, 1948; Sullivan, *Lift Every Voice*, 357; Marshall, "Southern Governors' Educational Plan," 122–23.

15. *RC*, May 22, 1948; Beardsley, *History of Neglect*, 253–55; Claude Pepper Diary, May 14, 1948; *Congressional Record*, May 12, 1948, 5667–68; "Federal Aid and Regional Plan Chimerae," 339–40; M. Don Clawson to Roy R. Kracke, June 2, 1948, Manuscripts Collection 51, Emmett B. Carmichael/Alabama Museum of the Health Sciences Collection, 1859–1990, Box 58, Folder H; Lattimore, "Address of the Outgoing President," 233.

16. Dummett, *NDA II*, 85–90; *RC*, December 25, 1948.

17. Jennifer E. Brooks, *Defining the Peace: World War II Veterans, Race, and the Remaking of Southern Political Tradition* (Chapel Hill: University of North Carolina Press, 2004), 53; Tom Stewart in *Congressional Record*, May 12, 1948, 5668; M. Don Clawson to Roy R. Kracke, June 2, 1948, Manuscripts Collection 51, Emmett B. Carmichael/Alabama Museum of the Health Sciences Collection, 1859–1990, Box 58, Folder H.

18. Marshall, "Southern Governors' Educational Plan," 122–23; M. Don Clawson to Roy R. Kracke, June 2, 1948, Manuscripts Collection 51, Emmett B. Carmichael/Alabama Museum of the Health Sciences Collection, 1859–1990, Box 58, Folder H; *RC*, December 25, 1948.

19. Starr, *Social Transformation*, 352; "Medical Education in the United States and Canada: Fortieth Annual Presentation of Educational Data by the Council on Medical Education and Hospitals," *JAMA* 115.9 (1940): 685–701; *AAMC Directory of American Medical Education* (Washington, D.C.: Association of American Medical Colleges, 1986); W. Montague Cobb, "Federal Aid to Medical Education," *JNMA* 42.2 (1950): 87–94; "Medical Deans and Discrimination," *JNMA* 42.1 (1950): 42; Ludmerer, *Time to Heal*; "Council on Medical Education and Hospitals," *JNMA* 43.1 (1951): 65–66.

20. Michael J. Bent, "Negro Students Enrolled in Medical Schools in the U.S.," *JNMA* 42.1 (1950): 45; 42.4 (1950); 253; 43.4 (1951): 276–77; Johnson, "Opportuni-

ties," 353–55; Egerton, *Speak Now against the Day*, 489; *University of North Carolina Daily Tar Heel*, May 1, 1951.

21. Jan Kenneth Herman and André Baden Sobocinski, *A Short History of Navy Medicine*, 4, 18, http://navyhistory.med.navy.mil/Publications/Booklets/Short%20 History.pdf (accessed May 13, 2008); "Timeline: History of Naval Medical Research," http://www.nmrc.navy.mil/pdf/Timeline.pdf (accessed May 13, 2008); "History," http://www.bethesda.med.navy.mil/Careers/Postgraduate_Dental_School (accessed May 13, 2008); Correspondence between Roy Kracke and Elbert Thomas, Manuscript Collection 51, Emmett B. Carmichael/Alabama Museum of the Health Sciences Collection, 1859–1990, Box 63, Folder c, Kracke—Legislative Papers prior to 1949; Elbert Thomas to Harry S. Truman, January 20, 1948, Truman Papers, Box 540, PPF 1988.

22. Correspondence between Roy Kracke and Elbert Thomas, Manuscript Collection 51, Emmett B. Carmichael/Alabama Museum of the Health Sciences Collection, 1859–1990, Box 63, Folder c, Kracke—Legislative Papers Prior to 1949; Elbert Thomas in *Congressional Record*, May 12, 1948, 5659–61.

23. McWilliams, *New Lights in the Valley*, 46–50; David Barton Smith, "Politics of Racial Disparities," 256–60; Chris Fordham, interview by author, Chapel Hill, N.C., April 8, 1997, SHC; Emanuel Suter, interview by Samuel Proctor, August 3, 1982, 43– 47, 61–63, Samuel Proctor Oral History Program, University of Florida, Gainesville; Emanuel Suter, interview by author, September 21, 2006, Paul Elliott, interview by author, Tallahassee, Fla., September 30, 2006, both in Reichelt Oral History Program, Florida State University, Tallahassee.

24. Walter E. Campbell, *Foundations for Excellence*, 151–52, 156, 272.

25. Telegrams from Roy Kracke to John H. Bankhead, Lister Hill, and Claude Pepper, March 19, 1945, Manuscript Collection 51, Emmett B. Carmichael/Alabama Museum of the Health Sciences Collection, 1859–1990, Box 63, Folder c, Kracke— Legislative Papers prior to 1949; Isaiah Bowman, "Annual Report of the President," in *Johns Hopkins University Circular 1942–43* (Baltimore: Johns Hopkins University, 1943), 10.

26. Summerville, *Educating Black Doctors*, 98–99; Winfred L. Godwin, "Report on SREB Regional Contract Program, 1959–60," in SREB Minutes, June 12–14, 1960, President Wayne Reitz Papers, Box 55, Corresp. Southern Regional Education Board, 1959–61, University Archives, University of Florida, Gainesville; SREB Minutes, "Report of Subcommittee on Meharry Medical College," July 7, 1959, Governor Leroy Collins Papers, Series 776, Box 130, Folder 1, FSLA; National Medical Fellowships, *Opportunities for Negroes in Medicine* (Chicago: National Medical Fellowships, 1959); Roy Kracke to Joseph Volker, August 24, 1949, Manuscripts Collection 51, Emmett B. Carmichael/Alabama Museum of the Health Sciences Collection, 1859–1990, Box 68, Folder e, Kracke—Legislative Bills 1949–50; Committee for the Nation's Health, "Bulletin #2, 3-25-51," Pepper Papers, Series 201 U.S. Senate—Correspondence, Box 93,

Folder 1, Health; Strickland, *Politics, Science, and Dread Disease*, 71; Campion, *AMA and U.S. Health Policy*, chaps. 12, 14; Hamilton, *Lister Hill*, 136–38; Lister Hill in *Congressional Record*, March 30, 1949, 3436–37; Allen Ellender in *Congressional Record*, May 4, 1949, A2653; Schulman, *From Cotton Belt to Sunbelt*, 133–20, 127–28.

27. "Federal Aid and Regional Plan Chimerae," 339; *Congressional Record*, May 12, 1948, 5668; John E. Ivey to SREB members, March 6, 1952, John E. Ivey, "Report on Admissions to 1952 Medical Class at Meharry College," both in Governor Fuller Warren Papers, RG 102, Series 235, Administrative Correspondence 1949–52, Box 79, Folder 3, FSLA.

28. *Congressional Record*, May 12, 1948, 5667; Millard F. Caldwell, Detroit speech, n.d., 10, Millard F. Caldwell Papers, Series 576, Box 1, Folder 11, Addresses—1948, FSLA; Cobb, "Medical Care."

29. Robert E. Hannegan to Harry S. Truman, February 2, 1946, Truman Papers, Box 145, PPF 58; Ivey, "Report."

30. Beardsley, *History of Neglect*, 253; Summerville, *Educating Black Doctors*, 98–99; Godwin, "Report"; SREB minutes, "Report of Subcommittee on Meharry Medical College"; National Medical Fellowships, *Opportunities*. The first non–historically black medical school in the nation to establish a scholarship program specifically for minority students was New York Medical College in New York City. Its founder was a surgeon, alumnus, and voluntary faculty member, Walter Gray Crump Sr., who served as a trustee of Tuskegee Institute and Howard University and worked to advance minority education and minority affairs in medicine (New York Medical College, "A Brief History of New York Medical College," http://www.nymc.edu/today/today .asp? [accessed March 21, 2008]).

31. Charles E. Odegaard, *Minorities in Medicine: From Receptive Passivity to Positive Action, 1966–76* (New York: Macy Foundation, 1977), 19; Ward, *Black Physicians*, 42–46.

32. "Governor McCord's Recommendation"; "Colleges: Fewer but Better?" *U.S. News and World Report*, June 20, 1952; SREB Minutes, June 23, 1950, Warren Papers, Box 79, Folder 1.

33. Summerville, *Educating Black Doctors*, 147; SREB Minutes, "Report of Study Subcommittee on Increased Regional Support for Meharry Medical College," July 7, 1959, Collins Papers, Series 776, Box 130, Folder 1; SREB, *Annual Report 1960–61*, Governor Farris Bryant Papers, Series 756, Box 134, Folder 9, FSLA; SREB, *Annual Report 1975–76*, Governor Reubin Askew Papers, Series 126, Box 20, SREB Folder, FSLA; Mark Musick, interview by author, April 23, 2004.

34. Dummett, *NDA II*, 151–54; Gamble, *Making a Place for Ourselves*, xii; Cogan, *Negroes for Medicine*, 69; R. Scott Baker, "The Paradoxes of Desegregation: Race, Class, and Education, 1935–1975," *American Journal of Education* 109.3 (2001): 322.

35. Ludmerer, *Time to Heal*, 253–56; Millard Caldwell to Winfred L. Godwin, September 30, 1963, Bryant Papers, Box 134, Folder 10.

36. Neyland, *FAMU*; Claud Anderson to S. E. Cary, November 15, 1972, Askew Papers, Series 126, Box 20, SREB Folder; Musick, interview.

37. Ferguson, *Black Politics*, 44.

38. Gamble, *Making a Place for Ourselves*, 131–50.

CHAPTER 9. TRAINING BLACK DOCTORS IN NORTH CAROLINA

1. J. Charles Jordan to Walter Reece Berryhill, February 6, 1951, Black Student Admissions.

2. Egerton, *Speak Now against the Day*, 130–33, 267, 271–74; Korstad, *Dreaming of a Time*, 49–53; Ernest B. Furgurson, *Hard Right: The Rise of Jesse Helms* (New York: Norton, 1986), 76–80; *Raleigh Capital Times*, November 22, 1994; *Charleston Gazette*, September 15, 1995.

3. McWilliams, *New Lights in the Valley*, 41; "Current Good Health Crusade Is Deep Rooted," *University of North Carolina Alumni Review*, October 1946, 36–37.

4. Mayo, *Progress Report*, 5, 8; McMillen, *Dark Journey*, 169–70; "Table 44—Characteristics of the Nonwhite Population, for Counties: 1950," U.S. Bureau of the Census, *Social and Economic Characteristics*, 126.

5. Mayo, *Progress Report* 20; Edson E. Blackman, "Negro Hospital and Medical Needs in North Carolina," in Poe, *Final Report*, 5–11.

6. W. T. Sanger, *Final Report of the National Committee for the Medical School Survey*, July 1, 1946, and Watson Smith Rankin, "The Four Major Arguments for Another Four-Year Medical School," both in "Minutes—Special Meeting—N.C. Medical Care Commission," August 8, 1946, Office of the Vice Provost for Health Affairs of the University of North Carolina at Chapel Hill Records, Box 1:18, N.C. Medical Care Commission: General, 1946–52 Folder, UNCA; J. Charles Jordan to Walter Reece Berryhill, February 6, 1951, Black Student Admissions; Walter Reece Berryhill, *Medical Education at Chapel Hill* (Chapel Hill: University of North Carolina School of Medicine, 1979).

7. Sanger, *Final Report*, 27–29.

8. N.C. Medical Care Commission, "Minutes—Special Meeting—N.C. Medical Care Commission," 56.

9. Paul F. Whitaker, "Remarks before Joint Appropriation Com.," February 13, 1947, Office of the Vice Provost for Health Affairs of the University of North Carolina at Chapel Hill Records, Box 1:18, N.C. Medical Care Commission: General, 1946–52 Folder.

10. Ibid.; Cobb, "Medical Care"; *RC*, April 5, 1947.

11. McWilliams, *New Lights in the Valley*, 41–46.

12. "Crushing Irony," 386–87; Beardsley, *History of Neglect*, 184, 247–72.

13. *RC*, May 3, 1947; W. M. Rich to James H. Clark, October 22, 1947, MCC, Series 94.5, Executive Secretary's Office: Special Studies and Committees of the Commission, Box 1, Committee on Medical Training for Negroes Folder.

14. Paul F. Whitaker to John A. Ferrell, October 28, 1947, "Minutes of the Committee on Medical Training for Negroes," November 4, 1947, MCC, Series 94.5, Executive Secretary's Office: Special Studies and Committees of the Commission, Box 1, Committee on Medical Training for Negroes Folder.

15. "Governor Umstead and the N.C. Medical Care Commission," *Journal of the Old North State Medical Society* 3.2 (1953): 10; Gifford, *Evolution*, 166–67; Gamble, *Making a Place for Ourselves*, 119–20; J. L. Procope to Oscar R. Ewing, March 31, 1948, Ewing Papers, Box 37; Weare, *Black Business*; "Minutes of the Committee on Medical Training for Negroes," November 4, 1947.

16. J. Street Brewer to John A. Ferrell, January 24, 1948, MCC, Series 94.5, Executive Secretary's Office: Special Studies and Committees of the Commission, Box 1, Committee on Medical Training for Negroes Folder.

17. Albert Maisel, "So You Can't Get a Doctor!" *Collier's*, May 14, 1947; Henry F. Pringle and Katharine Pringle, "The Color Line in Medicine," *Saturday Evening Post*, January 1948; "To Secure These Rights," *JNMA* 40.2 (1948): 82–83; Egerton, *Speak Now against the Day*, 431; Oscar R. Ewing, "The President's Health Program and the Negro Doctor," June 1, 1949, Ewing Papers, Box 39; Oscar R. Ewing, "Speech to the Conference of State and Territorial Health Officers" [draft], December 2, 1947, 15, Ewing Papers, Box 37.

18. Jerry Puryear, "University of Arkansas for Medical Sciences," Richard A. Buckalew, "Silas Herbert Hunt," C. Fred Williams, "Sid McMath," all in *Encyclopedia of Arkansas History and Culture*, www.encyclopediaofarkansas.net (accessed April 27, 2008).

19. Puryear, "University of Arkansas"; Diana Fisher, "Edith Irby Jones," *Encyclopedia of Arkansas History and Culture*, www.encyclopediaofarkansas.net (accessed April 27, 2008); Egerton, *Speak Now against the Day*, 431–32, 489–90; "First Arkansas Medical Graduate to Enter University Hospital," *JNMA* 44.4 (1952): 316; Lydia E. Brew, *Edith: The Story of Edith Irby Jones, M.D.* (Little Rock: NRT, 1986), 62; "University of Arkansas Medical School Accepts Negro Student," *Southern Patriot* 6.7 (1948): 1; "Logical Answer," *Arkansas Gazette*, August 25, 1948.

20. Michael J. Bent, "Negro Students Enrolled in Medical Schools in the U.S.," *JNMA* 42.1 (1950): 45; 42.4 (1950): 253; 43.4 (1951): 276–77; Joseph L. Johnson, "Opportunities for Negroes in Undergraduate Medical Education in 1952," *JNMA* 44.5 (1952): 353–55; Dummett, *NDA II*, 84–85.

21. *RC*, December 25, 1948; Dewey Monroe Clayton, letter of application to

University of North Carolina School of Medicine, December 2, 1947, Black Student Admissions; Walter E. Campbell, *Foundations for Excellence*, 163; Walter Reece Berryhill to Dewey Monroe Clayton, February 4, 1948, Black Student Admissions.

22. Walter Reece Berryhill to Henry Brandis, February 21, 1950, Black Student Admissions; *RC*, March 10, 1951; Gordon Gray, "Memorandum Relative to Admission Procedures in the Medical School," March 10, 1951, Black Student Admissions.

23. *RC*, March 24, 31, 1951.

24. *Raleigh News and Observer*, April 5, 1951; Teddlie and Freeman, "With All Deliberate Speed," 16; "UNC Trustees Vote to Admit Negro Grads, Opponents Say Resolution to Cause Tragedy," *RC*, April 7, 1951.

25. *RC*, April 28, 1951; *Atlanta Constitution*, April 26, 1951; *Durham Morning Herald*, April 29, 1951; Gray, "Memorandum"; Harry McMullan to Kerr Scott, March 23, 1951, Kerr Scott to Albert T. Whitaker, March 23, 1951, both in Black Student Admissions.

26. Gray, "Memorandum"; G. D. Penick et al. to Walter Reece Berryhill, March 24, 1951, Black Student Admissions.

27. *Durham Morning Herald*, April 29, 1951; *University of North Carolina Daily Tar Heel*, May 1, 1951; *Raleigh News and Observer*, April 5, 1951.

28. *RC*, June 16, 1951.

29. Gordon Gray, "A Report on Negro Applications for Admission to the University," July 16, 1951, 1, General Administration: Controller and Vice President for Finance, Subgroup 1, Desegregation: Applications, 1948–55 Folder, UNCA.

30. Walter Reece Berryhill to Robert House, December 2, 1953, Walter Reece Berryhill to William Friday, July 13, 1955, both in Black Student Admissions.

31. Cabell Phillips, "Another Trial of Integration," *New York Times Magazine*, March 4, 1956, 14; *RC*, March 24, 31, 1951.

32. Slade, interview.

33. Ibid.; Phillips, "Another Trial"; Steven Niven, "Wesley Critz George: Scientist and Segregationist," *North Carolina Literary Review* 7 (1998): 39–40.

34. Slade, interview.

35. *Raleigh News and Observer*, April 5, 1951; W. W. Carmichael to Gordon Gray, "Memorandum re: A Review of the Development of Graduate and Professional Education for Negroes," May 19, 1951, General Administration: Controller and Vice President for Finance, Subgroup 1, Desegregation: Correspondence, 1947–55 Folder, UNCA; Teddlie and Freeman, "With All Deliberate Speed," 16; *Pittsburgh Courier*, February 16, 1952.

36. Korstad, *Dreaming of a Time*, 49–53.

37. Ruth W. Hay to E. G. McGavran, January 9, 1956, Records of the Office of Health Affairs, Subgroup 7, Series 1, Correspondence, Administrative, McGavran, E. G., 1956–57 Folder, UNCA.

38. E. G. McGavran to Henry T. Clark, January 13, 1956, Records of the Office of Health Affairs, Subgroup 7, Series 1, Correspondence, Administrative, McGavran, E. G., 1956–57 Folder; Chafe, *Civilities and Civil Rights*, 49.

39. W. W. Pierson to E. G. McGavran, January 20, 1956, Records of the Office of Health Affairs, Subgroup 7, Series 1, Correspondence, Administrative, McGavran, E. G., 1956–57 Folder.

40. E. G. McGavran to Henry T. Clark, February 11, 1956, Records of the Office of Health Affairs, Subgroup 7, Series 1, Correspondence, Administrative, McGavran, E. G., 1956–57 Folder; Korstad, *Dreaming of a Time*, 53.

41. Gamble, *Making a Place for Ourselves*, xii; Cecelski, *Along Freedom Road*, 7–8; David McBride, *Integrating the City of Medicine: Blacks in Philadelphia Health Care, 1910–1965* (Philadelphia: Temple University Press, 1989), 190; Beardsley, *History of Neglect*, 271.

42. Best, interview; Slade, interview.

43. Chris Fordham, interview by author, Chapel Hill, N.C., April 8, 1997, SHC; Best, interview; Glenn Pickard, interview by author, Chapel Hill, N.C., September 12, 1997, SHC; University of Pennsylvania School of Medicine Office of Diversity and Community Outreach, "A History of Minority Presence at the School of Medicine of the University of Pennsylvania," http://www.med.upenn.edu/diversityume/timeline.shtml (accessed March 10, 2008).

CHAPTER 10. RACIAL DISPARITIES
AND THE TRUMAN HEALTH PLAN

1. *The First Ten Years of the World Health Organization* (Geneva: World Health Organization, 1958), 40–53, 73, 477, 480; Parran, "Surmounting Obstacles"; Derickson, *Health Security for All*, 97.

2. Oscar Ewing, interview by J. R. Fuchs, May 1, 1969, 198–208, http://www.trumanlibrary.org/oralhist/ewing3.htm (accessed May 7, 2008); Walter E. Campbell, *Foundations for Excellence*, 181–85; "After Twelve Years," *Time*, February 23, 1948 (erroneously reporting that Truman had fired Parran).

3. Ewing, interview; Mullan, *Plagues and Politics*, 111, 128–29; Daniel M. Fox, *Power and Illness: The Failure and Future of American Health Policy* (Berkeley: University of California Press, 1993), 53.

4. Paul F. Healy, "The Man Doctors Hate," *Saturday Evening Post*, July 8, 1950; Oscar R. Ewing, "Wanted: Better Public Health," *Parade*, May 2, 1948.

5. Erastus Corning, "Nominating Speech for Oscar Ewing at the 1952 Democratic National Convention," July 24, 1952, Ewing Campaign Brochure, both in Ewing Papers, Box 47, Ewing, Oscar R. 1952 Election Campaign—General Folder; G. Ellis Mott, "Best, Chandler Trials for Treason Due Soon," *Editor and Publisher*, March 15, 1947, 54.

6. Oscar R. Ewing, Speech to the Conference of State and Territorial Health Officers, December 2, 1947, 11–12, Ewing Papers, Box 37.

7. *Would You Smile?* (Atlanta: Southern Conference for Human Welfare, ca. 1945), Phileo Nash Papers, Box 59, Minorities—Negro—Publications—Pamphlets—Graphic Folder, Harry S. Truman Presidential Library, Independence, Mo.

8. Henry A. Wallace, *Ten Extra Years*, Nash Papers, Box 59, Minorities—Negro—Publications—Pamphlets Folder; Oscar R. Ewing, "Facing the Facts on Negro Health," *JNMA* 44.2 (1952): 108.

9. Oscar R. Ewing, Speech to the National Association for the Advancement of Colored People Annual Conference, June 23, 1948, Ewing Papers, Box 38.

10. Oscar R. Ewing, "The President's Health Program and the Negro Doctor," June 1, 1949, Ewing Papers, Box 39.

11. John Rankin in *Congressional Record*, February 23, 1948, 1567, February 25, 1948, 1707, March 1, 1948, 1934.

12. Ewing, Speech to the National Association for the Advancement of Colored People Annual Conference; Healy, "Man Doctors Hate."

13. Kari Frederickson, *The Dixiecrat Revolt and the End of the Solid South, 1932–1968* (Chapel Hill: University of North Carolina Press, 2001), 40–41; Wesley Price, "Pink Pepper," *Saturday Evening Post*, August 31, 1946, 118; Fred Rodell, "Senator Claude Pepper," *American Mercury*, October 1946, 394; Claude Pepper, Notes—Speech to Iowa State Federation of Labor Convention, August 9, 1946, 7–8, Pepper Papers, Series 203B, Box 8, Folder 2, Document 001; "SCHW Called Instrument in Hands of Communists," *Nashville Banner*, January 30, 1946; Egerton, *Speak Now against the Day*, 440; Claude Pepper in *Congressional Record*, March 10, 1949, 2134–36.

14. Morais, *History*, 132; "The Honorable Oscar Ross Ewing," *JNMA* 43.6 (1951): 402–4; "Negroes in Policy-Making Positions in the Federal Government," July 26, 1950, Truman Papers, Subject File: Negro—General—Negroes in the Government; McBride, *From TB to AIDS*, 143.

15. "'Let Not Thy Left Hand Know . . . ,'" *NCMJ* 9.5 (1948): 271; Healy, "Man Doctors Hate."

16. John L. Thurston, "More Opportunities for All through Social Security," April 9, 1952, Ewing Papers, Federal Security Agency—General Correspondence, Box 29.

17. Parran, "Surmounting Obstacles"; *Congress and the Nation 1945–1964* (Washington, D.C.: Congressional Quarterly, 1965), 1114.

18. Josephine R. Campbell and Connor, *Variations*, 1, 3, 6, 25, 31, 60, 118–19; Mullan, *Plagues and Politics*, 111, 128–29; Earle, "Post-1935 Developments," 1403–4; Ziegler, Weinerman, and Roemer, "Rural Prepayment Medical Care Plans," 1584.

19. Oscar R. Ewing, Speech to the Conference of Presidents of Negro Land Grant Colleges, October 18, 1950, 7, Ewing Papers, Box 41; "News from the Field," *AJPH*

40.8 (1950): 1054; Michael M. Davis, "Inter-Professional Health Conference: Tentative Draft of Report," March 7, 1944, 9, Parran Papers, Series 90/F-14, FF3.

20. "Democratic Strategy for <ap>52," *Life*, June 1952; Oscar R. Ewing, Statements to the Press, August 12, September 16, 1952, Ewing Papers, Box 47.

21. Donald L. Madison, "Remembering Cecil," *NCMJ* 65.5 (2004): 481; Elizabeth Fee and Theodore M. Brown, "The Unfulfilled Promise Of Public Health: Déjà Vu All Over Again," *Health Affairs* 21.6 (2002): 39.

22. "Report of the Committee on Negro Membership," *NCMJ* 16.6 (1955): 231–32.

23. Fitzhugh Mullan, "Wrestling with Variation: An Interview with Jack Wennberg," *Health Affairs* (2004), healthaffairs.org/webexclusives/index.dtl?year=2004 (accessed November 3, 2010); John E. Wennberg, "Factors Governing Utilization of Hospital Services," *Hospital Practice* 14.9 (1979): 115–21, 126–27; John E. Wennberg and A. Gittelsohn, "Small Area Variations in Health Care Delivery," *Science* 182.117 (1973): 1102–8; George Weisz, Alberto Cambrosio, Peter Keating, Loes Knaapen, Thomas Schlich, and Virginie J. Tournay, "The Emergence of Clinical Practice Guidelines," *Milbank Quarterly* 85.4 (2007): 691–727; W. Michael Byrd and Linda A. Clayton, "Racial and Ethnic Disparities in Healthcare: A Background and History," in *Unequal Treatment: Confronting Racial and Ethnic Disparities in Health Care* (Washington, D.C.: Institute of Medicine Board on Health Sciences Policy, 2003), 480–89.

24. Derickson, *Health Security for All*, 64; Stevens, *In Sickness and in Wealth*, 259; A. M. Miniño, M. Heron, S. L. Murphy, and K. D. Kochanek, *Deaths: Final Data for 2004* (2006), www.cdc.gov/nchs/hus.htm (accessed November 3, 2010); William J. Cromie, "Research Shows Who Dies When and Where," *Harvard University Gazette*, September 11, 2006; Committee on the Review and Assessment of the National Institutes of Health's Strategic Research Plan and Budget to Reduce and Ultimately Eliminate Health Disparities, Board on Health Sciences Policy, Institute of Medicine of the National Academies, *Examining the Health Disparities Research Plan of the National Institutes of Health: Unfinished Business* (Washington, D.C.: National Academies Press, 2006), 67.

25. David Satcher, "Surgeon General's Column," *USPHS Commissioned Corps Bulletin* 13.11 (1999): 1; P. H. Kilmarx, A. A. Zaidi, J. C. Thomas, A. K. Nakashima, M. E. St. Louis, M. L. Flock, and T. A. Peterman, "Ecologic Analysis of Socio-Demographic Factors and the Variation in Syphilis Rates among Counties in the United States, 1984–93," *AJPH* 87.12 (1997): 1937.

CONCLUSION

1. de Jong, *Different Day*, 107. For a comparison of school and hospital facilities for southern blacks and whites circa 1940, see Myrdal, *American Dilemma*, 337–46.

2. Gamble, *Making a Place for Ourselves*, 7; Ludmerer, *Time to Heal*, 163–65; Ce-

celski, *Along Freedom Road*, 29–30; Charles C. Bolton, "Mississippi's School Equalization Program, 1945–1954: 'A Last Gasp to Try to Maintain a Segregated School System,'" *Journal of Southern History* 66.4 (2000): 783–84; Paul B. Cornely, "Segregation and Discrimination in Medical Care in the United States," *AJPH* 46.7 (1956): 1079–80; W. Montague Cobb, "Hospital Integration in the United States," *JNMA* 55.4 (1963): 337; "Atlanta's Grady Hospital Sued for Discriminatory Practices," *JNMA* 54.5 (1962): 431; Allen, "Challenges," 7–9.

3. Cecelski, *Along Freedom Road*; Wyeneth, "Architecture of Racial Segregation."

4. Weaver, "New Deal," 201–2; Myrdal, *American Dilemma*, 336–37.

5. David Barton Smith, *Health Care Divided*, 50; Louis T. Wright, "Remarks before the National Health Conference," July 19, 1938, Wright Papers, Box 6, Folder 18; Louis T. Wright in U.S. Congress, Senate, Committee on Education and Labor, *To Establish a National Health Program: Hearings before the Committee on Education and Labor on S. 1620*, April 27, May 4, 5, 11, 12, 1939 (Washington, D.C.: U.S. Government Printing Office, 1939), 238.

6. Williams, *Thurgood Marshall*, 174–75; Kluger, *Simple Justice*, 202–4, 212–13, 259, 268–69; Egerton, *Speak Now against the Day*, 152–153; Ward, *Black Physicians*, 170–82.

7. "La Guardia Elected to NAACP Board," *Kansas City Call*, January 18, 1946; Oscar R. Ewing, Speech to the National Association for the Advancement of Colored People Annual Conference, June 23, 1948, 13–14, Ewing Papers, Box 38.

8. Aubrey Williams to Harry S. Truman, November 11, 1948, Truman Papers, Box 531, PPF 1726.

9. Isaiah Bowman, "Annual Report of the President," in *Johns Hopkins University Circular 1942–43* (Baltimore: Johns Hopkins University, 1943), 9–11.

10. Ibid., 11; Guichard Parris and Lester Brooks, *Blacks in the City: A History of the National Urban League* (Boston: Little, Brown, 1971), 343–44.

11. Howard M. Leichter, "The Case against the States," in *Health Policy*, ed. Rich and White, 156; Bowman, "Annual Report," 9–11.

12. Roy Wilkins to David Niles, June 20, 1949, Truman Papers, Box 482, PPF 393; Kluger, *Simple Justice*, 565.

13. Kluger, *Simple Justice*, 8; David Barton Smith, "Politics of Racial Disparities"; Charles S. Templeton, memo, May 7, 1957, Charles S. Templeton to J. C. Eagles Jr., May 28, 1957, both in MCC, Series 94.8, Director's Office: Agencies and Organizations Correspondence, Box 3, State Legislature—General Correspondence Folder.

14. Kluger, *Simple Justice*, 256–57, 346–540; Sullivan, *Lift Every Voice*, 404–6.

15. Southern States Cooperative Program in Educational Administration, George Peabody College for Teachers, "The Bi-Racial Picture in Southern Education and Related Problems: Report of the Second Regional Conference, State Boards of Education and Chief State School Officers," September 5–7, 1954, Atlanta, Governor Dan

McCarty and Acting Governor Charley Johns Papers, Series 569, Administrative Correspondence, Box 38, FSLA; Joseph W. Mountin, "Housing of Health Departments," *Public Health Reports*, May 22, 1942, 786; N. A. Nelson to Joseph W. Mountin, August 27, 1942, U.S. Public Health Service Records (RG 90), General Classified Records, Box 227, 0243—Maryland Folder, National Archives, College Park, Md.

16. Kluger, *Simple Justice*, 256–57, 346–540.

17. Oscar R. Ewing, speech to the Conference of Presidents of Negro Land Grant Colleges, October 18, 1950, Ewing Papers, Box 41; Schulman, *From Cotton Belt to Sunbelt*, 194–95.

18. Jill Quadagno and Steve McDonald, "Racial Segregation in Southern Hospitals: How Medicare 'Broke the Back of Segregated Health Services,'" in *The New Deal and Beyond: Social Welfare in the South since 1930*, ed. Elna C. Green (Athens: University of Georgia Press, 2003), 120–22; Clarence Mitchell to Oveta Culp Hobby, December 22, 1953, Parke M. Banta to Clarence Mitchell, March 10, 1954, Gladys Harrison to Edward J. Rourke, November 16, 1956, Maurice B. Gatlin to Marion Folsom, February 5, 1957, Marion E. Gardner to General Counsel Files, April 5, 1957, all in Department of Health, Education, and Welfare (RG 235), Records of the Public Health Division, Office of the General Counsel, Box 7, Hospital Construction, Segregation and Discrimination File, National Archives, College Park, Md.; "Nix Hospital Plan," *RC*, May 1, 1954; Robert Fredrick Burk, *The Eisenhower Administration and Black Civil Rights* (Knoxville: University of Tennessee Press, 1984), 196; *Congressional Record*, April 3, 1957, 5024–25.

19. Schulman, *From Cotton Belt to Sunbelt*, 195.

20. Myers, *Black, White, and Olive Drab*, 124, 130–31, 177.

21. Ibid., 130–31.

22. David Barton Smith, "Politics of Racial Disparities," 252–56.

23. Bolton, "Mississippi's School Equalization Program," 783–84; Ponton, "Hospital Service for Negroes," 15; Davis, *How a National Health Program*, 5; McFall, "Needs," 236; U.S. Senate, Committee on Labor and Public Welfare, Subcommittee on Health, *Hill-Burton Hospital Survey and Construction Act*, 11; Beito, "Black Fraternal Hospitals," 136–37; University of Virginia Geospatial and Statistical Data Center, *United States Historical Census Data Browser*, 1940 data; Lawrence Clark et al., "Impact of Hill-Burton," 550.

24. Cheryl V. Cunningham, "The Desegregation of Tulane University" (master's thesis, Tulane University, 1982), 8–9; Dummett, *NDA II*, 151–54; Gamble, *Making a Place for Ourselves*, xii.

25. Michael M. Davis, "Inter-Professional Health Conference: Tentative Draft of Report," March 7, 1944, 9, Parran Papers, Series 90/F-14, FF3; Allen J. Matusow, *The Unraveling of America: A History of Liberalism in the 1960s* (New York: Harper and Row, 1984), 228, 230; Starr, *Social Transformation*, 373.

BIBLIOGRAPHY

Duke University, Special Collections Library, Durham, North Carolina: Duke Endowment Archives

Florida State Library and Archives, Tallahassee: Southern Regional Education Board Records

Florida State University, Claude Pepper Library, Tallahassee: Claude Pepper Papers

Howard University, Moorland-Spingarn Research Center, Washington, D.C.: Louis T. Wright Papers

National Archives, College Park, Maryland: Department of Health, Education and Welfare (rg 235), Records of the Public Health Division, Office of the General Counsel; U.S. Public Health Service (rg 90), General Classified Records

North Carolina State Archives, Raleigh: North Carolina Medical Care Commission Records; State Board of Health Records; State Board of Public Welfare, Bureau of Work among Negroes Records

Harry S. Truman Presidential Library, Independence, Missouri: Oscar R. Ewing Papers; Phileo Nash Papers; Harry S. Truman Papers

University of Alabama at Birmingham, University Archives: Roy Kracke Papers

University of Pittsburgh, University Archives, Pittsburgh: Thomas Parran Jr. Papers

University of North Carolina at Chapel Hill, Wilson Library, Chapel Hill
North Carolina Collection
Southern Historical Collection: Commission on Interracial Cooperation Papers; Frank Porter Graham Papers; North Carolina Good Health Association Papers
University Archives: Records of the Chancellor, Paul F. Sharp Series; Records of the Controller and Vice President for Finance, W. D. Carmichael Series; Records of the Office of Health Affairs, Dean of the School of Medicine, Walter Reece Berryhill Series; Records of the Vice Chancellor for Health Affairs, Henry T. Clark Series

BOOKS AND JOURNAL ARTICLES

Allen, Doug. "Challenges to Providing Medical Education to Black Physicians at Grady Hospital." Unpublished term paper for the South in Transition Research Project at Georgia State University, December 13, 2005.

Anderson, Peyton F. "The Neglected One-Tenth: Who Finally Pays the Cost?" *Opportunity* 13.4 (1935): 208–9.

Baker, Robert B., et al. "African American Physicians and Organized Medicine, 1846–1968: Origins of a Racial Divide." *Journal of the American Medical Association* 300.3 (2008): 306–13.

Barkan, Elazar. *The Retreat of Scientific Racism: Changing Concepts of Race in Britain and the United States between the World Wars*. Cambridge: Cambridge University Press, 1992.

Bartley, Numan V. *The New South, 1945–1980*. Baton Rouge: Louisiana State University Press, 1995.

Beals, Carleton, and Abel Plenn. "Louisiana's Black Utopia." *The Nation*, October 30, 1935, 503–5.

Beardsley, Edward H. *A History of Neglect: Health Care for Blacks and Mill Workers in the Twentieth-Century South*. Knoxville: University of Tennessee Press, 1987.

Beito, David T. "Black Fraternal Hospitals in the Mississippi Delta, 1942–1967." *Journal of Southern History* 65.1 (1999): 109–40.

———. *From Mutual Aid to the Welfare State: Fraternal Societies and Social Services, 1890–1967*. Chapel Hill: University of North Carolina Press, 2000.

Bonner, Thomas Neville. *Iconoclast: Abraham Flexner and a Life in Learning*. Baltimore: Johns Hopkins University Press, 2002.

Brandt, Allan M. *No Magic Bullet: A Social History of Venereal Disease in the United States since 1880*. Expanded ed. New York: Oxford University Press, 1987.

Brown, E. Richard. *Rockefeller Medicine Men: Medicine and Capitalism in America*. Berkeley: University of California Press, 1979.

Campbell, Josephine R., and Kathryn J. Connor. *Variations in State Public Health Programs during a Five-Year Period*. Washington, D.C.: U.S. Public Health Service, Bureau of State Services, Division of State Grants, 1952.

Campbell, Walter E. *Foundations for Excellence: Seventy-five Years of Duke Medicine*. Durham: Duke University Medical Center Library, 2006.

Campion, Frank D. *The AMA and U.S. Health Policy since 1940*. Chicago: Chicago Review Press, 1984.

Cecelski, David. *Along Freedom Road: Hyde County, North Carolina, and the Fate of Black Schools in the South*. Chapel Hill: University of North Carolina Press, 1994.

Chafe, William H. *Civilities and Civil Rights: Greensboro, North Carolina, and the Black Struggle for Freedom*. New York: Oxford University Press, 1981.

Clark, Lawrence J., Marilyn J. Field, Theodore L. Koontz, and Virginia L. Koontz. "The Impact of Hill-Burton: An Analysis of Hospital Bed and Physician Distribution in the United States, 1950–1970." *Medical Care* 18.5 (1980): 538–50.

Clark, Thomas R. "The Limits of State Autonomy: The Medical Cooperatives of the Farm Security Administration, 1935–1946." *Journal of Policy History* 11.3 (1999): 257–82.

Cobb, W. Montague. "Medical Care and the Plight of the Negro." *The Crisis*, July 1947, 201–11.

———. "Progress and Portents for the Negro in Medicine." *The Crisis*, April 1948, 112–18.

Cogan, Lee, ed. *Negroes for Medicine: Report of a Macy Conference*. Baltimore: Johns Hopkins University Press, 1968.

Collins, William J., and Melissa A. Thomasson. "The Declining Contribution of Socioeconomic Disparities to the Racial Gap in Infant Mortality Rates, 1920–1970." *Southern Economic Journal* 70.4 (2004): 746–76.

Commission on Hospital Care. *Hospital Care in the United States*. New York: Commonwealth Fund, 1947.

Cornely, Paul B., and Virginia M. Alexander. "The Health Status of the Negro in the United States." *Journal of Negro Education* 8.3 (1939): 359–75.

"The Crushing Irony of De Luxe Jim Crow." *Journal of the National Medical Association* 44.5 (1952): 386–87.

Davis, Michael M. *America Organizes Medicine*. New York: Harper, 1941.

———. *How a National Health Program Would Serve the South*. New York: Committee on Research in Medical Economics, 1949.

Davis, Michael M., and Hugh H. Smythe. *Providing Adequate Health Service to Negroes*. New York: Committee for Research in Medical Economics, 1949.

Dawson, Howard A. "The Federal Government and Education." *Journal of Educational Sociology* 12.4 (December 1938): 226–43.

de Jong, Greta. *A Different Day: African American Struggles for Justice in Rural Louisiana, 1900–1970*. Chapel Hill: University of North Carolina Press, 2002.

Derickson, Alan. *Health Security for All: Dreams of Universal Health Care in America*. Baltimore: Johns Hopkins University Press, 2005.

Dittmer, John. *Local People: The Struggle for Civil Rights in Mississippi*. Urbana: University of Illinois Press, 1994.

Dombrowski, James A. "The New South on the March." *The Nation*. March 3, 1945, 245.

Duffy, John. *The Sanitarians: A History of American Public Health*. Urbana: University of Illinois Press, 1992.

Dummett, Clifton O. *NDA II: The Story of America's Second National Dental Association*. Washington, D.C.: National Dental Association Foundation, 2000.

Earle, Valerie E. "Post-1935 Developments in Southern State Public Health Programs." *American Journal of Public Health* 41.11 (1951): 1403–9.

Egerton, John. *Speak Now against the Day: The Generation before the Civil Rights Movement in the South*. New York: Knopf, 1994.

Ettling, John. *The Germ of Laziness: Rockefeller Philanthropy and Public Health in the New South*. Cambridge: Harvard University Press, 1981.

"The Federal Aid and Regional Plan Chimerae." *Journal of the National Medical Association* 43.5 (1951): 339–40.

Fee, Elizabeth. *Disease and Discovery: A History of the Johns Hopkins School of Hygiene and Public Health, 1916–1939*. Baltimore: Johns Hopkins University Press, 1987.

Ferguson, Karen. *Black Politics in New Deal Atlanta*. Chapel Hill: University of North Carolina Press, 2002.

Flexner, Abraham. *I Remember: The Autobiography of Abraham Flexner*. New York: Simon and Schuster, 1940.

Fox, Daniel M. "Health Policy and the History of Welfare States: A Reinterpretation." *Journal of Policy History* 10.2 (1998): 239–56.

Galishoff, Stuart. "Germs Know No Color Line: Black Health and Public Policy in Atlanta, 1900–1918." *Journal of the History of Medicine and Allied Sciences* 40.1 (1985): 22–41.

Gamble, Vanessa Northington. *Making a Place for Ourselves: The Black Hospital Movement, 1920–1945*. New York: Oxford University Press, 1995.

Gifford, James F., Jr. *The Evolution of a Medical Center: A History of Medicine at Duke University to 1941*. Durham: Duke University Press, 1972.

Goldstein, Marcus S. "Longevity and Health Status of Whites and Nonwhites in the United States." *Journal of the National Medical Association* 46.2 (1954): 83–104.

Gordon, Colin. *Dead on Arrival: The Politics of Health Care in Twentieth-Century America*. Princeton: Princeton University Press, 2003.

Grey, Michael. *New Deal Medicine: The Rural Health Programs of the Farm Security Administration*. Baltimore: Johns Hopkins University Press, 1999.

Hall, Jacquelyn Dowd. "The Long Civil Rights Movement and the Political Uses of the Past." *Journal of American History* 91.4 (2005): 1233–63.

Hamilton, Virginia Van der Veer. *Lister Hill: Statesman from the South*. Chapel Hill: University of North Carolina Press, 1987.

Hine, Darlene Clark. "Black Professionals and Race Consciousness: Origins of the Civil Rights Movement, 1890–1950." *Journal of American History* 89.4 (2003): 1279–94.

———. "The Corporeal and Ocular Veil: Dr. Matilda A. Evans (1872–1935) and the Complexity of Southern History." *Journal of Southern History* 70.1 (2004): 3–34.

———. *Speak Truth to Power: Black Professional Class in United States History*. Brooklyn: Carlson, 1996.

Hitt, Homer L., and Alvin L. Bertrand. *The Social Aspects of Hospital Planning in Louisiana*. Baton Rouge, La.: Health and Hospital Division, Office of the Governor, 1947.

Humphreys, Margaret. *Malaria: Poverty, Race, and Public Health in the United States*. Baltimore: Johns Hopkins University Press, 2001.

———. *Yellow Fever and the South*. New Brunswick: Rutgers University Press, 1992.

Jones, Jacqueline. *Labor of Love, Labor of Sorrow: Black Women, Work, and the Family from Slavery to the Present.* New York: Basic Books, 1985.

Jones, James H. *Bad Blood: The Tuskegee Syphilis Experiment.* New York: Free Press, 1993.

Kluger, Richard. *Simple Justice: The History of* Brown v. Board of Education *and Black America's Struggle for Equality.* New York: Vintage, 1977.

Korstad, Robert Rodgers. *Dreaming of a Time: The School of Public Health, the University of North Carolina at Chapel Hill, 1939–1989.* Chapel Hill: University of North Carolina School of Public Health, 1990.

Larkins, John R. *The Negro Population of North Carolina, Social and Economic.* Special Bulletin 23. Raleigh: North Carolina State Board of Charities and Public Welfare, 1944.

Lemann, Nicholas. *The Promised Land: The Great Black Migration and How It Changed America.* New York: Knopf, 1991.

Link, William A. "'The Harvest Is Ripe, but the Laborers Are Few': The Hookworm Crusade in North Carolina, 1909–1915." *North Carolina Historical Review* 67.1 (1990): 1–27.

Love, Spencie. *One Blood: The Death and Resurrection of Charles R. Drew.* Chapel Hill: University of North Carolina Press, 1996.

Ludmerer, Kenneth M. *Time to Heal: American Medical Education from the Turn of the Century to the Era of Managed Care.* New York: Oxford University Press, 1999.

Marks, Harry M. "Epidemiologists Explain Pellagra: Gender, Race, and Political Economy in the Work of Edgar Sydenstricker." *Journal of the History of Medicine and Allied Sciences* 58.1 (2003): 34–55.

Mayo, Selz C. *Progress Report No. RS-5, "Negro Hospital and Medical Care Facilities in North Carolina."* Raleigh: North Carolina Medical Care Commission, 1945.

McBride, David. *From TB to AIDS: Epidemics among Urban Blacks since 1900.* Albany: State University of New York Press, 1991.

McCullough, David. *Truman.* New York: Touchstone, 1992.

McFall, T. Carr. "Needs for Hospital Facilities and Physicians in Thirteen Southern States." *Journal of the National Medical Association* 42.4 (1950): 235–36.

McIntosh, William Alexander, and John Fox Kendrick. *Public Health Administration in North Carolina.* Raleigh: North Carolina State Board of Health, 1940.

McMillen, Neil R. *Dark Journey: Black Mississippians in the Age of Jim Crow.* Urbana: University of Illinois Press, 1989.

McWilliams, Tennant S. *New Lights in the Valley: The Emergence of UAB.* Tuscaloosa: University of Alabama Press, 2007.

Meckel, Richard. *Save the Babies: American Public Health Reform and the Prevention of Infant Mortality, 1850–1929.* Baltimore: Johns Hopkins University Press, 1990.

Medical Care Services in North Carolina: A Statistical and Graphic Summary. Raleigh:

North Carolina Agricultural Experiment Station, Department of Rural Sociology, 1945.

Mitchell, Charles, and Jesse H. Bankston. *Hospital and Health Facilities in Louisiana.* Baton Rouge: State of Louisiana, 1948.

Morais, Herbert Montfort. *The History of the Negro in Medicine.* New York: Publishers, 1968.

Mott, Frederick Dodge, and Milton I. Roemer. *Rural Health and Medical Care.* New York: McGraw-Hill, 1948.

Mullan, Fitzhugh. *Plagues and Politics: The Story of the United States Public Health Service.* New York: Basic Books, 1989.

Myers, Andrew H. *Black, White, and Olive Drab: Racial Integration at Fort Jackson, South Carolina, and the Civil Rights Movement.* Charlottesville: University of Virginia Press, 2006.

Myrdal, Gunnar. *An American Dilemma: The Negro Problem and American Democracy.* New York: Harper, 1944.

Neyland, Leedell W. *FAMU: A Centennial History, 1887–1987.* Tallahassee: Florida A&M University, 1988.

Packard, Randall M. *The Making of a Tropical Disease: A Short History of Malaria.* Baltimore: Johns Hopkins University Press, 2007.

Parascandola, John. *Sex, Sin, and Science: A History of Syphilis in America.* Westport, Conn.: Praeger, 2008.

Parran, Thomas. "Surmounting Obstacles to Health Progress." *American Journal of Public Health* 38.1 (1948): 168–72.

Perlstadt, Harry. "The Development of the Hill-Burton Legislation: Interests, Issues and Compromises." *Journal of Health and Social Policy* 6.3 (1995): 77–96.

Plank, David N., and Marcia Turner. "Changing Patterns in Black School Politics: Atlanta, 1872–1973." *American Journal of Education* 95.4 (1987): 584–608.

Poe, Clarence. *Final Report of the North Carolina Hospital and Medical Care Commission.* Raleigh: State of North Carolina, 1945.

Pohl, Lynn Marie. "Long Waits, Small Spaces, and Compassionate Care: Memories of Race and Medicine in a Mid-Twentieth-Century Southern Community." *Bulletin of the History of Medicine* 74.1 (2000): 107–37.

Ponton, T. R. "Hospital Service for Negroes." *Hospital Management* 51.1 (1941): 14–15, 50.

Provenzo, Eugene F., Jr., ed. *Du Bois on Education.* Walnut Creek, Calif.: Alta Mira, 2002.

Puckett, Newbell Niles. *Folk Beliefs of the Southern Negro.* Chapel Hill: University of North Carolina Press, 1926.

Reverby, Susan M., ed. *Tuskegee's Truths: Rethinking the Tuskegee Syphilis Study.* Chapel Hill: University of North Carolina Press, 2000.

Reynolds, P. Preston. "Dr. Louis T. Wright and the naacp: Pioneers in Hospital Racial Integration." *American Journal of Public Health* 90.6 (2000): 883–92.

———. "The Federal Government's Use of Title VI and Medicare to Racially Integrate Hospitals in the United States, 1963–67." *American Journal of Public Health* 87.11 (1997): 1850–58.

———. "Hospitals and Civil Rights, 1945–1963: The Case of *Simkins v. Moses H. Cone Memorial Hospital*." *Annals of Internal Medicine* 126 (June 1, 1997): 898–906.

———. "Professional and Hospital Discrimination and the U.S. Court of Appeals Fourth Circuit, 1956–1967." *American Journal of Public Health* 94.5 (2004): 710–20.

Rice, Mitchell, and Woodrow Jones. *Public Policy and the Black Hospital: From Slavery to Segregation to Integration*. Westport, Conn.: Greenwood, 1994.

Rich, Robert F., and William D. White, eds. *Health Policy, Federalism, and the American States*. Washington, D.C.: Urban Institute Press, 1996.

Rosenfield, Isadore. *Hospitals: Integrated Design*. New York: Reinhold, 1947.

Schoen, Johanna. *Choice and Coercion: Birth Control, Sterilization, and Abortion in Public Health and Welfare*. Chapel Hill: University of North Carolina Press, 2005.

Schulman, Bruce. *From Cotton Belt to Sunbelt: Federal Policy, Economic Development, and the Transformation of the South, 1938–1980*. Durham: Duke University Press, 1994.

Shannon, Gary W., and Gerald F. Pyle. *Disease and Medical Care in the United States: A Medical Atlas of the Twentieth Century*. New York: Macmillan, 1993.

Shonick, William. *Government and Health Services: Government's Role in the Development of U.S. Health Services, 1930–1980*. New York: Oxford University Press, 1995.

Smith, David Barton. *Health Care Divided: Race and Healing a Nation*. Ann Arbor: University of Michigan Press, 1999.

———. "The Politics of Racial Disparities: Desegregating the Hospitals in Jackson, Mississippi." *Milbank Quarterly* 83.2 (2005): 247–69.

Smith, Douglas L. *The New Deal in the Urban South*. Baton Rouge: Louisiana State University Press, 1988.

Smith, Susan L. *Sick and Tired of Being Sick and Tired: Black Women's Health Activism in America, 1890–1950*. Philadelphia: University of Pennsylvania Press, 1995.

Smith, W. Eugene. "Nurse Midwife." *Life*, December 3, 1951, 134–45.

Southmayd, Henry J. "Study Proves More Data Needed to Solve Rural Hospital Problem." *Hospital Management* 51.3 (1941): 20–21, 73.

Squires, Carol. *The Body at Risk: Photography of Disorder, Illness, and Healing*. Berkeley: University of California Press, 2005.

Starr, Paul. *The Social Transformation of American Medicine*. New York: Basic Books, 1982.

Stevens, Rosemary. *In Sickness and in Wealth: American Hospitals in the Twentieth Century*. New York: Basic Books, 1989.

Strickland, Stephen. *Politics, Science, and Dread Disease: A Short History of United States Medical Research Policy*. Cambridge: Harvard University Press, 1972.

Sullivan, Patricia. *Days of Hope: Race and Democracy in the New Deal Era*. Chapel Hill: University of North Carolina Press, 1996.

———. *Lift Every Voice: The NAACP and the Making of the Civil Rights Movement*. New York: Free Press, 2009.

Summerville, James. *Educating Black Doctors: A History of Meharry Medical College*. Tuscaloosa: University of Alabama Press, 1983.

Teddlie, Charles, and John Freeman. "With All Deliberate Speed: An Historical Overview of the Relationship between the *Brown* decision and Higher Education." In *Forty Years after the* Brown *Decision: Implications of School Desegregation for U.S. Education*, ed. Kofi Lomotey and Charles Teddlie, 7–51. New York: ams Press, 1996.

Temkin, Elizabeth. "Driving Through: Postpartum Care during World War II." *American Journal of Public Health* 89.4 (1999): 587–95.

U.S. Bureau of the Census. *Social and Economic Characteristics of the Population: North Carolina*. Washington, D.C.: U.S. Government Printing Office, 1951.

U.S. Congress. House. Committee on Interstate and Foreign Commerce. *Hospital Construction Act: Hearings on S.191*. 79th Cong., 2nd sess., March 7–13, 1946. Washington, D.C.: U.S. Government Printing Office, 1946.

U.S. Congress. Senate. Committee on Education and Labor. *Construction of Hospitals: Hearings on S. 3230*. 76th Cong., 3rd sess., March 18 and 19, 1940. Washington, D.C.: U.S. Government Printing Office, 1940.

———. *Hospital Construction Act: Hearings on S.191*. 79th Cong., 1st sess., February 26–28 and March 12–14, 1945. Washington, D.C.: U.S. Government Printing Office, 1945.

———. *National Health Program: Hearings*. 77th Cong., 2nd sess., April 2–16, 1942. Washington, D.C.: U.S. Government Printing Office, 1942.

———. *To Establish a National Health Program: Hearings on S.1620*. 76th Cong., 1st sess., April 27 and May 4, 5, 11, and 12, 1939. Washington, D.C.: U.S. Government Printing Office, 1939.

U.S. Congress. Senate. Committee on Labor and Public Welfare. Subcommittee on Health. *Hill-Burton Hospital Survey and Construction Act: History of the Program and Current Problems and Issues*. Washington, D.C.: Committee Print, 1973.

University of Virginia Geospatial and Statistical Data Center. *United States Historical Census Data Browser*. http://mapserver.lib.virginia.edu.

Wailoo, Keith. *Drawing Blood: Technology and Disease Identity in Twentieth-Century America*. Baltimore: Johns Hopkins University Press, 1997.

――――. *Dying in the City of the Blues: Sickle Cell Anemia and the Politics of Race and Health*. Chapel Hill: University of North Carolina Press, 2001.

Wall, Bennett H., ed. *Louisiana: A History*. Arlington Heights, Ill.: Forum, 1990.

Walls, E. "Hot Springs Waters and the Treatment of Venereal Diseases: The U.S. Public Health Service Clinic and Camp Garraday." *Journal of the Arkansas Medical Society* 91.9 (1995): 430–31, 433–37.

Ward, Thomas J., Jr. *Black Physicians in the Jim Crow South*. Fayetteville: University of Arkansas Press, 2003.

Weare, Walter. *Black Business in the New South: A Social History of the North Carolina Mutual Life Insurance Company*. Urbana: University of Illinois Press, 1973.

Weaver, Robert Clifton. "The New Deal and the Negro: A Look at the Facts." *Opportunity* 13.7 (July 1935): 200–202.

White, Walter Francis. *How Far the Promised Land*. New York: Viking, 1956.

Williams, Juan. *Thurgood Marshall: American Revolutionary*. New York: Random House, 1998.

Williamson, Joel. *The Crucible of Race: Black-White Relations in the American South since Emancipation*. New York: Oxford University Press, 1984.

Wyeneth, Robert R. "The Architecture of Racial Segregation: The Challenges of Preserving the Problematical Past." *Public Historian* 27.4 (2005): 11–44.

Ziegler, Mark, E. Richard Weinerman, and Milton I. Roemer. "Rural Prepayment Medical Care Plans and Public Health Agencies." *American Journal of Public Health* 37.12 (1947): 1578–85.

PERIODICALS

American Journal of Public Health
Congressional Record
Durham Carolina Times
Durham Morning Herald
Health Bulletin (North Carolina Board of Health)
Journal of Negro Education
Journal of the American Medical Association
Journal of the National Medical Association
North Carolina Medical Journal
Opportunity (National Urban League)
Raleigh Carolinian
Raleigh News and Observer
Southern Hospitals

Southern Medical Journal
Southern Patriot (Southern Conference for Human Welfare)
U.S. Public Health Service Annual Reports

ORAL HISTORY INTERVIEWS

Interviews that were conducted by the author are deposited in the Southern Historical Collection, Wilson Library, University of North Carolina at Chapel Hill.

Best, Andrew. Greenville, North Carolina, April 19, 1997
Blalock, Lila. Wilson, North Carolina, February 14, 1994
Cochran, Salter, and Doris Cochran. Weldon, North Carolina, April 12, 1997
Simkins, George. Greensboro, North Carolina, April 6, 1997
Slade, James. Edenton, North Carolina, February 23, 1997

blacks: appeals to white self-interest, 25; blamed for high southern death rates, 12; civil rights activism of, 3, 75, 117, 121, 170, 173–76, 206, 263, 275; concentrated in rural South, 30–31, 63–65, 110; criticisms of black institutions by, 28; demand for health care among, 48, 54, 75, 86, 171, 174–75; disfranchisement of, 18, 115; Great Migration of, 41, 42–44; as healthy carriers of disease, 13; high draft rejection rate among, 26; leveraged state governments to improve health and education, 18; as New Deal bureaucrats, 3, 46–48, 67; poor living conditions of, 11–12, 32–33, 42–44, 53–54, 110, 112, 130; profederal attitude of, 9; rising income of, 3, 122, 171, 174–75, 193, 202–3; treatment of, under New Deal, 50, 56–60, 65–70, 88–89, 113; urban, 42–44, 69–70, 110; in war effort, 97, 122, 124–26. *See also* black press; health professionals: black; hospitals: black; medical civil rights movement; mental health care for blacks; physicians: black

Blalock, Lila, 90–91
Bousfield, Midian O., 19, 28, 36, 50, 208
Bowles, George W., 114
Bowman, Isaiah, 220–21, 271
Bowman Gray School of Medicine, 77, 195, 202, 232
Brewer, J. Street, 237
Brooks, Jennifer L., 215–16
Broughton, J. Melville, 143, 145, 157, 182–83
Brown, Lawrence Greely, 51–52
Brown v. Board of Education (1954), 2, 104, 107, 114, 186, 206, 226, 244, 266, 273–76

Bulwinkle, Alfred, 66, 184
Bunch, Amanda, 92, 93
Burney, Leroy, 65
Bynum, Charles H., 48

Caldwell, Millard F., 222–23, 227
Callen, Maude, 34, 93–95
Carnegie Foundation, 22–25, 208
Carter, Thomas L., 146
Carver Memorial Hospital (Chattanooga), 172
Cecelski, David, 247–48
Charity Hospital (New Orleans), 63, 70–72
Chenault, H. Clay, 238
Chester County Hospital (S.C.), 73–74
Chowan County, N.C., 55
civil defense, 124, 126–27
Civil Rights Act (1964), 4, 5, 202, 205, 278
civil rights activism. *See* blacks
Clark, J. Bayard, 184
Clark, Lawrence J., 178
Clark, Taliaferro, 64–65
Clawson, M. Don, 168–69, 213, 214–15, 216, 221, 222, 223, 224
Clayton, Dewey Monroe, 239–40
Cleland, W. A., 51
Cobb, W. Montague, 1–2, 150, 169, 172, 174, 175, 216, 217, 221, 234
Cochran, Doris, 184, 192
Cochran, Salter, 248
Coggs, Pauline Redmond, 56–57
College of Medical Evangelists, 209
Collins, William J., 180
Columbia, S.C., 170, 174
Commission on Interracial Cooperation, 46
Committee for Research in Medical Economics, 51, 111–12

Eastman, George, 24

Eaton v. James Walker Memorial Hospital (1958), 201–2

education: compared with health care, 17–19, 152, 168, 247–48, 266–79, 274; elementary and secondary, 17–19, 79, 105, 107, 109, 186, 266–67, 270–78; higher, 22, 25–26, 30, 208, 212–13, 226, 245–46; spending for black versus white, 272–74. See also *Brown v. Board of Education*; Harrison-Fletcher Bill; medical education; war- and federally affected areas, federal aid to

E. H. Crump Hospital (Memphis), 174

Eisenhower, Dwight David, 262

Ellender, Allen, 57, 71, 108, 116, 120, 158–59, 203–4, 212

Ellison, Ralph, 28

Embree, Edwin R., 18, 46

Emergency Maternity and Infant Care (EMIC), 57, 96–98, 124, 135

Emory University School of Medicine, 37, 219–20, 278

equalization: and Harrison-Fletcher Bill, 105, 107, 115–16, 213–14, 266–67; in North Carolina, 182–94; racial, 2–3, 103, 105, 110, 116, 174, 228, 260–61, 263–65, 267, 269, 272–74, 277–78; regional, 2–3, 103–4, 107, 109–10, 135, 260–61, 263–65, 267, 278. *See also* deluxe Jim Crow policy; education; Hill-Burton Hospital Survey and Construction Act

eugenics, 12, 144–45, 304n43

Ewing, Oscar R., 122, 142, 187, 237, 251–58, 261–63, 270, 274–75

Fair Employment Practices Commission, 113

Falk, Isadore S., 50, 112, 264

Farm Security Administration (FSA), 50–51, 111, 112, 167; experimental health programs, 129, 135; medical cooperatives, 57, 61, 85, 86, 113

Federal aid. *See* education; equalization; health reform; Hill-Burton Hospital Survey and Construction Act; liberalism; matching grants; medical education; public health; South; war- and federally affected areas, federal aid to

Federal Emergency Recovery Administration (FERA), 45, 49–50, 89, 167

Federal Hospital Council, 51, 167, 182, 236

Federal Security Agency, 121–22, 251–58, 274

Ferguson, Karen, 47, 52–53, 67

Ferrell, John, 56; as North Carolina Medical Care Commission executive director, 188–89; as Rockefeller Foundation officer, 59, 76–77, 80, 139

Fire in the Flint, The (White), 27

Fishbein, Morris, 128, 139, 150

Fleming, Philip B., 167

Flexner, Abraham, 19–25, 208; alleged racism of, 20, 28–29; as Howard University Board of Trustees chair, 24–26; Rosenwald relationship with, 24; Wright, Louis T., compared with, 25, 28–29

Flint-Goodrich Hospital (New Orleans), 33, 236

Florida, 38, 130, 172–73, 186, 191, 211

Florida A&M College, 94, 172–73, 210, 227

Folk Beliefs of the Southern Negro (Puckett), 83

folk medicine, 83–85, 90–92

Ford Foundation, 278

Foreman, Clark, 46

Fort Jackson, S.C., 124–25, 126
Fox, Daniel, 119
Freedmen's Hospital (Washington, D.C.), 23–24
Frobisher, Martin, 40

Gaines v. Missouri. See Missouri ex rel. Gaines v. Canada
Gallinger Hospital (Washington, D.C.), 254–55
Gamble, Vanessa Northington, 19, 28, 228
Gelhorn, Martha, 45, 89
General Education Board. *See under* Rockefeller Foundation
George, Wesley Critz, 244–45
Georgia, 15, 47, 65, 67, 86, 130, 260, 278
Glass, Carter, 104, 108
Gone with the Wind, 117
Gore, George, Jr., 172–73, 227
Grady Hospital (Atlanta), 36, 70, 71, 74, 173–74, 267–68
Graham, Frank Porter, 230
Granger, Lester, 173, 255, 271
Graves, John Temple, 120–21
Gray, Gordon, 79, 241, 243
Griffith, D. W., 27

Hamilton, C. Horace, 141
Harkness, Edward, 24
Harlem Hospital (New York), 27–29, 78
Harris, H. L., 64–65
Harrison-Fletcher Bill, 105, 107, 115–16, 213–14, 266–67. *See also* education
Harvard University, 80
Hawkins v. University of Florida Board of Control (1956), 186, 245
Haywood, Hubert, 12, 140–41, 143
health disparities, 3–4, 9, 30–44, 63, 110–12, 115, 125–26, 263–64; narrow-

ing of, 49, 99, 179–80, 260–61; racial, 13, 15, 43–44, 62–68, 99–100, 112, 116, 179–80, 252–54; regional, 99; rural-urban, 15, 43–44, 179–80; telescoping of, 39–44, 264–65
health professionals: dental associations, 52, 61, 215, 239; dentists, 239; hospital administrators, 117; integration of national organizations, 52, 137; public health nurses, 83–93, 132–33, 246–47; shortage, 2, 33, 59, 123, 127; U.S. Army Cadet Nurse Corps, 67–68, 124–25. *See also* American Public Health Association; National Association of Colored Graduate Nurses; physicians; rural health
—black, 99–100, 137; dentists, 33, 59; health educators, 210; hospital administrators, 38, 236; midwives, 34, 44, 81–85, 87–88, 90–96, 98–100; nurses, 33, 36, 67–68, 124–25, 137, 170–71; public health nurses, 18, 33, 59–60, 67, 77, 86, 246–47
health reform: antidiscrimination clauses in, 115–19, 268–69; Congressional hearings on, 3, 109–10, 113–19; incremental versus comprehensive, 4–5, 113, 115, 153, 158, 180, 183, 228–29; and national defense, 119–30, 135–37, 183, 217, 251–52, 261–62; in southern states, 4, 9, 57–61, 66, 71, 234–35; states' rights in, 4, 38, 115, 151, 230; white motivations for, 20, 59, 67, 71, 109–12, 230, 266–67. *See also* blacks; deluxe Jim Crow policy; equalization; health professionals: black; liberalism; national health insurance; physicians: black
hearings, congressional. *See* health reform

midwives. *See under* health professionals: black

Mississippi, 9, 127, 129, 204; black physicians in, 52, 209, 211; charity hospitals in, 71; integration resistance in, 276–78; maternity and midwifery in, 33, 84, 97–98; mental hospitals in, 191; mortality in, 15, 40; Poindexter's study of black children in, 44; rapid treatment centers in, 130, 132; revenue versus health-care expenditures in, 109

Mississippi Medical Society, 123

Missouri, 105

Missouri ex rel. Gaines v. Canada (1938), 2, 73, 103, 104–5, 115, 138, 210, 212, 235, 239, 272

Moore, Joseph Earle, 66

morbidity and mortality. *See* statistics, morbidity and mortality

Mott, Frederick, 41, 51, 107, 161

Mountin, Joseph, 136

Mullowney, John J., 24

Murfee, Hopson Owen, 234–35

Murray, James, 111, 116, 167, 169, 203

Murray, Peter, 27, 28

Myers, Andrew H., 276

Myrdal, Gunnar, 42, 75; *An American Dilemma*, 110, 268

Nashville, Tenn., 168–69

National Association for the Advancement of Colored People (NAACP), 3, 26, 106, 112, 115, 117, 127, 150, 168, 208, 254, 266, 267; and *Eaton v. James Walker Memorial Hospital*, 201–2; and legal challenge to separate but equal, 2, 105, 138, 209–10, 240–41, 269–72; and *Simkins v. Moses Cone Hospital*, 176, 201–2; and zero tolerance of segregation, 119, 169, 170–71, 174, 272.

See also blacks; *Brown v. Board of Education*; integration; Marshall, Thurgood; medical civil rights movement; *Missouri ex rel. Gaines v. Canada*; White, Walter F.; Wright, Louis T.

National Association of Colored Graduate Nurses, 125, 150, 171; and integration of organized nursing, 119

national defense. *See* health reform: and national defense; war- and federally affected areas, federally aid to

National Dental Association, 215

National Foundation for Infantile Paralysis (NFIP), 47–48

National Health Conference (1938), 27, 49, 269

national health insurance, 51, 62, 104, 107, 111, 204–5, 254, 255–56, 263; black organizations' support for, 114, 117, 126, 150; criticized for communist/totalitarian influence, 141, 149, 256–57, 262; opposition to, 75, 128, 138–43. *See also* American Medical Association; National Medical Association; Parran, Thomas; Pepper, Claude D.

National Hospital Association, 36, 113, 117

National Medical Association (NMA), 16, 28, 168, 269; support of, for public health and health reform, 56, 113–15, 117, 139, 149–50, 256; support of, for Rosenwald Fund, 17, 19. *See also* medical civil rights movement; Old North State Medical Society; physicians

National Negro Congress, 109, 110, 113, 115, 150, 169

National Negro Health Week, 64, 80, 119

National Urban League, 46, 110, 113, 150, 169, 173, 255, 271

28–29, 119, 168; role of, in establishing deluxe Jim Crow policy, 16–19, 28–30, 58, 119; support of, for integration, 278
Phillips, Homer G., Hospital (St. Louis), 38, 70, 172
physicians: American College of Surgeons, 162; home practice of, 33–34; as hospital construction supporters, 145–46, 157; maldistribution of, 162, 248; in private practice, 11, 32, 49, 54–55, 61, 93, 140–41; proportion of surgeons and specialists, 25. *See also* American Medical Association
—black: admitting rights for, 28, 37–38, 69, 118, 171, 175, 182–83, 210–11; civil rights activism of, 37–38, 52, 176, 231–32, 247–49, 267–68; compared with white physicians, 54–56, 67, 171; concentration of, in urban areas, 93; and licensing exam failure rates, 21–22; medical society membership of, 52, 263; numbers of, 29, 33; public health work of, 25, 50, 54–56, 59–60, 86; support of, for national health insurance and comprehensive health reform, 56, 114; support of, for separatism versus integration, 26–27, 114, 167–76; training opportunities for, 18, 24, 28, 36, 66, 136, 171, 175, 182–83, 209, 256. *See also* medical civil rights movement; medical education; National Medical Association; Old North State Medical Society
—northern, 27–28, 36, 52. *See also* American Medical Association
—southern (white) physicians, 88, 92–93; attitudes of, toward black physicians, 28, 51–52; attitudes of, toward national health insurance, 139–43; attitudes of, toward private insurance,

56, 141, 152–53; attitudes of, toward public health, 56, 139–40; and licensing exam failure rates, 21–22; and Mississippi Medical Society, 123; and Southern Medical Association, 120. *See also* Medical Society of the State of North Carolina
Pierson, W. W., 245–47
Pitt County Memorial Hospital (Greenville, N.C.), 82
Plessy v. Ferguson (1896), 11, 138, 221, 241
Poe, Clarence, 110, 144–45
Poe Commission. *See* North Carolina Medical Care Commission
Poindexter, Hildrus A., 44, 256
polio, 47–48
poll tax, 106–7, 113
President's Commission on Civil Rights, 149, 230, 270, 276
President's Commission on the Health Needs of the Nation, 51, 145
Pritchett, Henry S., 22
public health: broadening scope of, 10–11, 180, 256, 258–60, 262; close ties of, with black health, 56, 67, 75, 168–69, 195; disproportionately led by southerners, 30; racial discrimination in, 88–89; southern, 11, 18, 29–32, 57–62, 75, 77, 86–89, 180, 260; training programs in, 59, 87, 88, 91–94, 130–31. *See also* American Public Health Association; maternal and infant health; North Carolina; physicians; rural health; Social Security Act; statistics, morbidity and mortality; U.S. Public Health Service
Public Health Service. *See* U.S. Public Health Service
Public Works Agency (PWA), 49, 68–70, 157, 191–92

Puckett, Newbell Niles, 96; *Folk Beliefs of the Southern Negro*, 83
Puffer, Ruth Rice, 15, 42

Quadagno, Jill, 200

racial uplift. *See* equalization
Raider, Holly, 161
Rankin, John, 254–55
Rankin, Watson Smith, 16, 56, 139, 143; as Duke Endowment Hospital and Orphans Section head, 28–29; Flexner and Wright compared with, 28–29; as North Carolina state health officer, 76–78, 80
rapid treatment centers, 124, 129–34; racism/sexism in, 131
regional health planning, 161, 163–64, 180, 185–86, 263–64
Report on the Economic Conditions of the South (1938), 2, 103, 104–6, 114
Republican Party, 167, 169, 256, 258, 262
Reynolds, Carl V., 2, 60, 78–80, 139, 140, 157
Reynolds, Z. Smith, Foundation, 80
Rich, William, 233, 235–37
Richardson, William H., 90
Robinson, E. I., 128, 150
Rockefeller Foundation: Bureau of Social Hygiene, 63–64; General Education Board, 17, 22–25, 125, 208; Rockefeller Institute, 24; Sanitary Commission / International Health Board, 13, 17–18, 29–30, 76, 79, 109, 144, 191
Roemer, Milton, 41, 51, 75, 107, 161
Rohrer, James E., 177
Roosevelt, Eleanor, 24
Roosevelt, Franklin D., 46, 50, 70, 104, 105, 108, 119
Rorem, C. Rufus, 50

Rose, Wickliffe, 13, 76
Rosenau, Milton, 79–80
Rosenfield, Isadore, 35, 74, 81, 98, 159, 164
Rosenwald, Julius, 17, 24
Rosenwald, Julius, Fund, 17, 24, 27, 42, 46, 47, 51, 115, 208; criticism of, 19, 27–28; support of, for rural southern black schools, 17, 18; support of, for southern black health, 18, 30, 63–64, 109, 125
rural health: Depression's effect on, 45; and efforts to attract health professionals, 24, 35, 123, 248, 303n34; New Deal programs for, 49–51, 65, 75, 86–96, 129, 260; philanthropic efforts to improve, 16–17, 24; problems of, 34, 40–44, 77–78, 110, 112, 126; strengthened by hookworm campaign, 18; urban health compared with, 30–34, 39–44, 48–51, 110, 179–80, 260–61. *See also* health disparities; Hill-Burton Hospital Survey and Construction Act; hospitals; whites: southern and rural

Sanger, William T., 232
Satcher, David, 265
Savitt, Todd L., 21
Scheele, Leonard, 251
Schulman, Bruce, 104
segregation, racial, 10, 11, 45, 46–48, 64, 67, 73, 95, 103, 104, 111, 115–19, 263, 265, 266–70; in military and defense industries, 122, 124–25; in New Deal programs, 50, 69–70, 86–87, 144, 146–47. *See also* blacks; hospitals; whites
Shepherd, J. E., 235
Sheppard-Towner Maternity and Infancy Protection Act (1921), 85–86

Sheps, Cecil, 262
Sidbury, J. Buren, 140, 165
Simkins v. Moses Cone Hospital (1963), 176, 201–2
Slade, James, 55, 243–45, 248
Smith, Douglas L., 71
Smith, Jean Murray, 38
Smith, Murray, 64–65
Smith, Susan L., 85, 98
Smith, W. Eugene, 93–95
Social Aspects of Hospital Planning in Louisiana, The (Hitt and Bertrand), 41–42
socialized medicine. *See* national health insurance
Social Security Act (1935), 104, 107, 110, 258; attempts to broaden, 114–15, 117, 126; child- and infant-care programs of, 86, 93, 96, 99; impact of, on southern health, 50, 57–61
Somerset Health Center (Baltimore), 168
South: antifederalism of, 9, 61, 104, 111, 187–88, 263; children concentrated in, 109; death rates in, 12, 15–16, 49, 77; decline of farm economy in, 13–14, 35, 41–42, 45; favored by federal programs, 50, 58–59, 66–67, 70, 97, 104, 107–10, 124, 129, 130, 179, 180–81, 260, 275; hospital admission rates in, 72; malaria and pellagra ignored in, 14; sixteen-state definition of, 3; social disorganization in, 42; and Southern Policy Committee, 105; and Southern Regional Education Board, 215, 222–28; state health spending in, 40, 58, 60, 67, 79, 109, 185–86, 203, 223–24, 228, 235, 277–78. *See also* Democratic Party; health reform; hospitals; liberalism; physicians; public

health; rural health; segregation, racial; Southern Conference for Human Welfare; Southern Governors' Conference; southernization of communicable disease; southern moderates; whites: southern and rural; war- and federally affected areas, federal aid to; *and individual cities and states*
South Carolina, 11, 78, 124–25; hospital segregation in, 73–74; maternity, midwifery, and birth control in, 33, 34, 60, 84, 93–95; mental institutions in, 191; mortality in, 15; school segregation in, 273, 276
Southern Conference for Human Welfare, 46, 61, 13, 106, 111, 120–21, 256
Southern Council on International Relations, 121
Southern Governors' Conference, 211, 212–13, 214, 222
southernization of communicable disease, 30–33, 39–44; venereal disease as prime example of, 63, 265
southern liberals. *See* liberalism
Southern Medical Association, 120
southern moderates, 2–3; silence of, on race, 3, 16, 110–12, 234–36; support of, for improving black health, 3, 16, 80, 90, 231–37
Southern Policy Committee, 105
Southern Regional Education Board, 215, 222–28
southern uplift. *See* equalization; *Report on the Economic Conditions of the South*
Southmayd, Henry, 165–66
Spalding, Hughes, 173
Sparkman, John, 70, 219
Spaulding, Charles C., 144, 209, 237
Squires, Carol, 94

St. Agnes Hospital (Raleigh), 192

Starr, Paul, 179

states' rights. *See under* health reform

statistics, morbidity and mortality: high rates of, among blacks, 18, 32, 54, 62–63, 77, 112, 265; improvement of, during mid-twentieth century, 49, 61, 65, 96, 99, 130, 260–61; underreporting of, among southern and rural blacks, 15–16, 40; and U.S. Death Registration Area, 10–11, 15, 40; used to oppose scientific racism and segregation, 16; used to support health reform, 4, 110–12; used to support scientific racism and segregation, 9, 11–12, 62–63, 143. *See also* health disparities; infant mortality; South

Stead, Eugene A., 219–20

Stevens, Rosemary, 205–6

Stewart, Tom, 216

Stiles, Charles Wardell, 13

St. Louis, Mo., 133–34, 172

Strickland, Stephen, 221

Stryker, Roy, 112

Sullivan, Patricia, 212

Summerville, James, 223

Sydenham Hospital (New York), 38

Sydenstricker, Edgar, 14

syphilis, 12, 13, 39, 42, 54, 58, 62–68, 87, 112, 130–34, 135, 265; rapid treatment centers for, 124, 129–34

Taft, Robert, 166, 254

Technical Committee on Medical Care, 103, 114

Temkin, Elizabeth, 128

Templeton, Charles, 187–88

Tennessee, 15, 18, 40, 130, 172, 226, 260

Texas, 40, 42, 130, 136, 191

Thomas, Elbert, 111, 213–14, 222, 224;

proposes federal aid to medical education bill, 217–19

Thomas, James Edward, 240

Thomasson, Melissa A., 180

trachoma, 40, 58

Truman, Harry S., 105, 115, 126, 166–67, 168–69, 254, 255; President's Commission on Civil Rights, 149, 230, 270, 276; President's Commission on the Health Needs of the Nation, 51, 145

Truman health plan, 3, 115, 148–49, 158, 255–56

tuberculosis, 11–12, 13, 39, 70, 135–36, 260

Tulane University, 33; medical school, 71

Tuskegee Institute, 19, 28, 30, 47, 65

Tuskegee Study of Untreated Syphilis in the Negro Male, 42, 64–65, 66, 67, 304n43

two-tiered public-private health system, 4, 116, 158, 278–79

typhoid fever, 13, 40, 41, 48

United Nations, 127

University of Alabama. *See* Medical College of Alabama

University of Arkansas Medical School, 70, 217, 238, 239

University of Cincinnati Medical School, 23

University of Florida, 186

University of Louisville Medical School, 239

University of North Carolina at Chapel Hill, 121, 143, 209, 229–30; North Carolina Memorial Hospital, 184, 194, 202; School of Public Health, 56, 79–80, 90, 195, 210, 230, 246–47, 262

—School of Medicine, 144, 184, 194, 195,

Whitaker, Paul, 145, 233–34, 235–36

White, Walter F., 113, 116; *The Fire in the Flint*, 27

whites: defense of segregation and white supremacy by, 2, 106, 120–21, 171, 211, 217, 230, 232–34, 237–38, 242–45, 246–47, 263, 266–67, 276–77; draft rejections among, 125–26, 143; southern and rural, 30–32, 34–35, 110–12, 129

Williams, Aubrey, 109, 270

Williams, R. C., 51, 113

Williamson, Joel, 4

Wilson County, N.C., 53, 54, 90–91, 160

women's health. *See* birth control; birth rates; Emergency Maternity and Infant Care; health professionals; maternal and infant health

Works Progress Administration (WPA), 48, 49, 68–70, 157

World Health Organization, 67, 135, 250, 262

World War II: as catalyst for health reform, 96–99, 126–28, 135–37, 183, 210; as cause of health professional shortage, 122–23, 136; health programs, 119–37; U.S. Army Cadet Nurse Corps, 67–68, 124–25; War Manpower Commission, 121. *See also* Emergency Maternity and Infant Care; Lanham Act; U.S. Senate Subcommittee on Wartime Health and Education; war- and federally affected areas, federal aid to

Wright, Louis T., 2, 26–29, 57, 138, 206, 208; Flexner compared with, 25, 28–29; as Harlem Hospital chief surgeon, 27, 78; as NAACP chair, 26–27, 113, 115–19, 169, 269–70; opposes black hospital in New York, 27; Rankin compared with, 28–29, 78

Wright, Richard, 170

Z. Smith Reynolds Foundation, 80

CPSIA information can be obtained at www.ICGtesting.com
Printed in the USA
LVOW061035201011

251140LV00005BA/2/P